Society in Early North Carolina:

A Documentary History

More than one visitor to North Carolina noted the importance of women's labor to the colony's economy. See page 1 for William Byrd's ascerbic comments on this topic. Illustrations from Tunis, *Frontier Living*, 59.

The Colonial Records of North Carolina
Special Series
Robert J. Cain, series editor

Society in Early North Carolina:

A Documentary History

Compiled and edited by
Alan D. Watson

Divison of Archives and History
North Carolina Department of Cultural Resources
Raleigh
2000

*The publication of this book has been assisted by the
North Carolina Society of the Cincinnati*

DEPARTMENT OF CULTURAL RESOURCES

BETTY RAY MCCAIN, *Secretary*
ELIZABETH F. BUFORD, *Deputy Secretary*

DIVISION OF ARCHIVES AND HISTORY

JEFFREY J. CROW, *Director*
DAVID J. OLSON, *Deputy Director*
JOE A. MOBLEY, *Historical Publications Administrator*

NORTH CAROLINA HISTORICAL COMMISSION

http://www.ah.dcr.state.nc.us/hp

Contents

Maps and Illustrations

Foreword

This book, *Society in Early North Carolina: A Documentary History*, is the inaugural volume in a "special series" appearing under the aegis of *The Colonial Records of North Carolina [Second Series]*. It is intended to be of interest to a wide range of readers, suitable for the classroom and indeed anyone curious about the lives of North Carolinians as recorded by the colony's citizens and visitors during the earliest years of its history.

As general editor of this series, I feel particularly fortunate that Dr. Alan Watson, professor of history at the University of North Carolina at Wilmington, has compiled and edited this first volume. There is no one better able to convey through the documents the complex texture of North Carolina society during this period. The careful and imaginative scholarship which he has brought to bear on a wide range of sources has set a high standard for succeeding publications in this series.

Robert J. Cain

Introduction

As part of a planned series of documentaries, *Society in Early North Carolina: A Documentary History* intends to illustrate by means of a variety of sources the essence of life in early North Carolina. Originating in the efforts of Walter Raleigh's colonists in the late Elizabethan era, present North Carolina became part of a formal English colony in 1629 upon a grant by King Charles I to Sir Robert Heath for an area called Carolana. In 1663 Charles II re-granted the colony under the name of Carolina to eight prominent Englishmen, the Lords Proprietors of Carolina. Subsequently the colony was divided in 1712 into North and South Carolina, and in 1729 was sold to George II, becoming a royal province. It retained that status until independence in 1776.

Although historians have intensely investigated many facets of colonial North Carolina, in the process producing numerous articles and monographs treating provincial society, a documentary history offers the benefit of revealing some of the source materials upon which the secondary works have been grounded. The opening chapter considers the peopling of North Carolina, the free and the indentured servants, focusing on the origins of the immigrants and their reasons for leaving Europe for America. At the same it looks at the natural elements confronting Carolinians, for the forces of nature greatly affected almost every aspect of life from the production of food to modes of dress and styles of architecture.

After establishing the presence of the people, the volume considers the character of Carolinians, their homes and furnishings, and family life. North Carolina evidenced a middle-class, "democratic" society, particularly as compared with neighboring Virginia and South Carolina, notwithstanding the inevitable extremes of wealth and poverty, all of which were reflected in their houses and possessions. Family life tended to revolve about marriage and child rearing, with the accouterments (or lack thereof) of courtship, the tribulations of widowhood for women, and the difficulties of orphanage for children. However, many Carolinians, married or not, failed to esteem the institution of marriage, posing the twin challenges to society of sexual immorality and illegitimate children.

Subsequent chapters look at salient aspects of life in early North Carolina-religion, education, recreation and entertainment, criminality, and health and mortality. Institutionalized religion, while resting lightly upon many Carolinians, offered immense emotional rewards for others, and North Carolina comprehended most of the prominent denominations in early America. Education in the form of schools was principally associated with the churches, though more broadly it encompassed the ability to appreciate the printed word in the form of books and newspapers, and the opportunity to send and receive materials via a postal system. Beyond written matter colonials enjoyed a variety of modes of entertainment-outdoor and indoor, public and private-many of which involved gambling. And gambling or, at least, illicit gambling, served as a reminder that Carolinians often flouted the law for which they might (or might not) suffer the consequences. And all those activities occurred within the confines of human mortality. Frequent accidents, ever-present maladies, and unavailable or undependable medical asistance rendered life tenuous.

Concluding the volume are chapters dealing with urbanization, travel, and taverns. Relatively few North Carolinians lived in towns, but urban areas were far more important than indicated by their number of residents because they served as centers of trade, politics, and culture. However, urban life presented unique difficulties for those living within the bounds of towns-street maintenance, fire control, and trash collection among others. Most of the early towns were located on or near water which offered the easiest means of travel in early America, but Carolinians necessarily developed a fairly intricate system of highway transportation by the time of the Revolution. Still, overland travel was arduous, expensive, and sometimes dangerous. Travelers found respite, such as it was, in taverns along the roads and in the towns. An important institution in early America which catered to travelers and local inhabitants, taverns offered food, drink, lodging, and an opportunity for social camaraderie in many forms that could be found nowhere else in early America.

The topics selected for inclusion in this volume represent a systematic attempt to examine the manifold facets of life in early North Carolina through a variety of documentary evidence. Still, the work does not claim to encompass all manner of living or all North Carolinians. It focuses on whites because additional volumes in this series propose to consider Native Americans and African Americans in colonial North Carolina. In selecting documents from the voluminous materials available for study, an effort was made to utilize a wide variety of sources to reflect the richness of the documentary evidence. Thus, the reader will find unpublished and published materials among which are public and private correspondence, journals, travel accounts, statutes, court proceeding, deeds, wills, inventories of estates, business accounts of merchants, physicians, and tavern keepers, church records, and newspapers. Individually and collectively these sources reveal the marvelous diversity of life among early North Carolinians.

Alan D. Watson
October 1, 2000

Character

Assessments of the Carolina character varied, but usually found women more admirable than men.

As for those of our own Country in *Carolina*, some of the Men are very laborious, and make great Improvements in their Way; but I dare hardly give 'em that Character in general. The easy Way of living in that plentiful Country, makes a great many Planters very negligent, which, were they otherwise, that Colony might now have been in a far better Condition than it is, (as to Trade, and other Advantages) which an universal Industry would have led them into.

The Women are the most industrious Sex in that Place, and, by their good Houswifry, make a great deal of Cloath of their own Cotton, Wool and Flax; some of them keeping their Families (though large) very decently apparel'd, both with Linnens and Woollens, so that they have no occasion to run into the Merchant's Debt, or lay their Money out on Stores for Cloathing [...] Both Sexes are generally spare of Body, and not Cholerick, nor easily cast down at Disappointments and Losses, seldom immoderately grieving at Misfortunes, unless for the Loss of their nearest Relations and Friends, which seems to make a more than ordinary Impression upon them. Many of the Women are very handy in Canoes, and will manage them with great Dexterity and Skill, which they become accustomed to in this watry Country. They are ready to help their Husbands in any servile Work, as Planting, when the Season of the Weather requires Expedition; Pride seldom banishing good Houswifry. The Girls are not bred up to the Wheel, and Sewing only; but the Dairy and Affairs of the House they are very well acquainted withal; so that you shall see them, whilst very young, manage their Business with a great deal of Conduct and Alacrity. The Children of both Sexes are very docile, and learn any thing with a great deal of Ease and Method; and those that have the Advantages of Education, write good Hands, and prove good Accountants, which is most coveted, and indeed most necessary in these Parts. The young Men are commonly of a bashful, sober Behaviour; few proving Prodigals, to consume what the Industry of their Parents has left them, but commonly improve it. [...]

Lawson, *A New Voyage to Carolina*, (1709), 90-91.

[1728] Surely there is no place in the World where the Inhabitants live with less Labour than in N Carolina. It approaches nearer to the

Description of Lubberland than any other, by the great felicity of the Climate, the easiness of raising Provisions, and the Slothfulness of the People.

Indian Corn is of so great increase, that a little Pains will Subsist a very large Family with Bread, and then they may have meat without any pains at all, by the Help of the Low Grounds, and the great Variety of Mast that grows on the High-land. The Men, for their Parts, just like the Indians, impose all the Work upon the poor Women. They make their Wives rise out of their Beds early in the Morning, at the same time that they lye and Snore, till the Sun has run one third of his course, and disperst all the unwholesome Damps. Then, after Stretching and Yawning for half an Hour, they light their Pipes, and, under the Protection of a cloud of Smoak, venture out into the open Air; tho', if it happens to be never so little cold, they quickly return Shivering into the Chimney corner. When the weather is mild, they stand leaning with both their arms upon the corn-field fence, and gravely consider whether they had best go and take a Small Heat at the Hough: but generally find reasons to put it off till another time.

Thus they loiter away their Lives, like Solomon's Sluggard, with their Arms across, and at the Winding up of the Year Scarcely have Bread to Eat.

To speak the Truth, tis a thorough Aversion to Labor that makes People file off to N Carolina, where Plenty and a Warm Sun confirm them in their Disposition to Laziness for their whole Lives[...]

I am sorry to say it, but Idleness is the general character of the men in the Southern Parts of this Colony as well as in North Carolina. The Air is so mild, and the Soil so fruitful, that very little Labour is requir'd to fill their Bellies, especially where the Woods afford such Plenty of Game. These Advantages discharge the Men from the Necessity of killing themselves with Work, and then for the other Article of Raiment, a very little of that will suffice in so temperate a Climate. But so much as is absolutely Necessary falls to the good women's Share to provide. They all Spin, weave and knit, whereby they make a good Shift to cloath the whole Family; and to their credit be it recorded, many of them do it very completely, and thereby reproach their Husband's Laziness in the most inoffensive way, that is to say, by discovering a better Spirit of Industry in themselves.

Byrd, *Histories of the Dividing Line*, 90, 92, 304, 306.

[March 1775]. But tho' I may say of this place [North Carolina] what I formerly did of the West India Islands, that nature holds out to them every thing that can contribute to conveniency, or tempt to luxury, yet the inhabitants resist both, and if they can raise as much corn and pork, as to subsist them in the most slovenly manner, they ask no more; and as a very small proportion of their time serves for that purpose, the rest is spent in sauntering thro' the woods with a gun or sitting under a rustick shade, drinking New England rum made into grog, the most shocking liquor you can imagine. By this manner of living, their blood is spoil'd and rendered thin beyond all proportion, so that it is constantly on the fret like bad small beer, and hence the constant slow fevers that wear down their constitutions, relax their nerves and infeeble the whole frame. Their appearance is in every respect the reverse of that which gives the idea of strength and vigor, and for which the British peasantry are so remarkable. They are tall and lean, with short waists and long limbs, sallow complexions and languid eyes, when not inflamed by spirits. Their feet are flat, their joints loose and their walk uneven. These I speak of are only the peasantry of this country, as hitherto I have seen nothing else, but I make no doubt when I come to see the better sort, they will be far from this description. For tho' there is a most disgusting equality, yet I hope to find an American Gentleman a very different creature from an American clown. [...]

The difference between the men and the women surprised me, but a sensible man, who has long resided here, in some degrees accounted for it. In the infancy of this province, said he, many families from Britain came over, and of these the wives and daughters were people of education. The mothers took the care of the girls, they were train'd up under them, and not only instructed in the family duties necessary to the sex, but in those accomplishments and genteel manners that are still so visible amongst them, and this descended from Mother to daughter. As the father found the labours of his boys necessary to him, he led them therefore to the woods, and taught the sturdy lad to glory in the stroke he could give with his Ax, in the trees he felled, and the deer he shot; to conjure the wolfe, the bear and the Alligator; and to guard his habitition from Indian inroads was most justly his pride, and he had reason to boast of it. But a few generations this way lost every art or science, which their fathers might have brought out, and tho' necessity no longer prescribed these severe occupations, custom has established it as still necessary for the men to spend their time abroad in the fields; and to be a good marksman is the highest ambition of the youth, while to those enervated by age or infirmity drinking grog remained a last consolation.

Andrews, *Journal of a Lady of Quality*, 153, 154-155.

∽ↄ⌒Გↄ~

Nonetheless, women as well as men could evidence a capricious nature.

North Carolina
Chowan ss.
At a Court begun Opened and held for the precinct aforesaid at the
Court house in Edenton on the Third Thursday in July anno Domi:
1737

Present The Worshipfull John Montgomery Esqs, Henry Bonner, Joseph Anderson, John Hodgson, Gentn Justices [...]

On a Complaint made to the Court against Jeremiah Vail Hannah Nugent Frans. Tool and William Bailey for striping themselves Naked and going in to the water together in the face of the Town which being duly proved the Court orders that Summons Issues to the Marshal to take the bodys of the said Jeremiah Vail Hannah Nugent Frances Tool and William Bailey so that they be and Appear before the Court at four of the Clock in the afternoon. Order issued. Then the Court adjourned till Three oClock in the afternoon. [...]

Pursuant to an order of this Court made in the forenoon the Marshall brought into Court the bodys of Jeremiah Vail Frans: Tool and William Bailey and on a full hearing of the Matter the Court orders that Jeremiah Vail Enter into Security for his good behavier and to Appear at the next Genl Court to be held for the province as aforesaid &ca and that William Bailey Likewise give Security for his good beheavor and to Appear at the next Genl: Court &ca and thereupon the said Wm Bailey Acknowledged himself Bound to Our Sovereign Lord the King in the Sum of Twenty pounds proclamation Money and Saml. Grafton and Thomas Maddin on his Securitys Acknowledged themselves bound Each in the Sum of Ten pound Like money With Condition that the said William Bailey be of Good beheavor till the next Genl: Court &ca. and their and there Appear to answer to the Complaint afrd: &ca. And that Francs. Tool be Carried to the publick Whiping post and there to receive Ten Lashes on her Bare Back well Laid on And Hannah Nugent Likewise be carried to the publick whiping post and receive Ten Lashes on her bare Back well Laid on. Order issued. [...]

Chowan County Court Minutes, July, 1737, State Archives.

Bertie County ss.
At a Ct. held for sd County on the second Friday in Novr. 1740
   Present: Benj. Hill Peter West Thos. Hansford Jno Edward Rowland William Esqrs &c. [...]
   Mrs. Preddam Informing this Court that John Hobbs Contrary to the Peace &cs. and in a Riatous manner Rode over a Boy on the Bridge before the Court house with a Jugg of Rum upon his head wch. was broke and split and on hearing the Evidences thereon upon Oath the same was proved It is thereupon Ordd. That the sd. John Hobbs be and he is hereby amerced the Sum of Eight Pounds Sixteen Shillings and Cost to be paid to the sd. Preddam and further that he the sd Hobbs give Security in the Sum of £10 pro: for his Good behavr: till the next Court and that he stand Comitted untill he perform the same.

Bertie County Court Minutes, November, 1740, State Archives.

My dear Nelly, [...]
   Seriously speaking, your Mamma bids me assure you, that she would certainly have wrote but for the lateness of the evening. She has however some reason to complain of your negligence and indolence in writing, and she hopes you will take a good deal of pains to bring your, volatility, at least some times, down to a reasonable standard. [...]

Higginbotham, *Papers of James Iredell*, 1:460-461.

North Carolina offered ample opportunity to obtain at least minimal subsistence, leading some to disclaim the presence of debtors, but the poor remained too evident.

[...] [1773] Here we see, that a man of small substance, if upon a precarious footing at home, can, at once, secure to himself a handsome, independent living, and do well for himself and posterity. The poorest man, if he can but work, procures, at once, plenty of subsistence, which grows yearly upon his hands, until, by gentle and agreeable labour, he arrives, at last, at a state of affluence and ease. None of either sex or profession need fear the want of employment, or an ample reward and encouragement in their different occupations and callings. [...]

Boyd, "Informations," 620-621.

[...] And what may well be look'd upon for as great a Miracle, this is a Place, where no Malefactors are found, deserving Death, or even a Prison for Debtors; there being no more than two Persons, that, as far as I have been able to learn, ever suffer'd as Criminals, although it has been a Settlement near sixty Years; [...]

Brickell, *Natural History*, 169.

An Act for the Relief for poor Debtors, as to the Imprisonment of their Persons.

I. Be it Enacted, by his Excellency the Governor, Council, and General Assembly of this Province, That if any Handicraft Tradesman, or any other Person whatsoever, shall be in Prison within this Province, on mesne Processes, or Execution for any debt, above Forty Shillings Proclamation money, and hath no visible Estate, Real or Personal, and shall make Oath, before the Court of the County where he is in Prison, or in the Vacation, before some two Justices of the Peace for that County, being both present together, the Creditor or Creditors at whose Suit he is confined being first personally summoned to appear at the same Time; That he hath not the Worth of Forty Shillings, Sterling Money, in any worldy Substance, either in Debts owing to him, or otherwise howsoever, over and besides his wearing apparel, working Tools, and Arms for Muster; and that he has not, at any Time since his Imprisonment, or before, directly, or indirectly, sold, assigned, or otherwise disposed of, or made over, in Trust for himself, or otherwise, any Part of his Real or Personal Estate, whereby to expect or have any Benefit or Profit to himself, or to defraud any of his Creditors to whom he is indebted; and if there be no person present than can prove the contrary, then such Person, by such Court or Justices, without Form or Trial, shall immediately be set at Liberty, and shall stand forever discharged of all such Debts so sued for, and all Costs of Suit: But in Case such Person shall afterwards be discovered to have sworn falsely, he shall be indicted for Perjury; and if convicted, shall lose both his Ears in the Pillory, and be liable to satisfy the Debt and Damages.

II. And be it further Enacted, That the Justices of the Peace, when the Proceedings are before them out of Court, shall put the same in writing, under their Hands, and return the same into the Court from whence the execution issued, there to be kept on Record, under the Penalty of Five Pounds Proclamation Money, for each Justice, for such his Omission or neglect; to be paid to the Person injured, by Order of the said Court.

III. And be it further Enacted, That if any Person, charged in Execution for any Sum in any Prison, within this Province, shall be minded to deliver up his Effects to his or her Creditors, it shall be lawful for such Prisoner to prefer a Petition to the Court from whence the Process issued setting forth the Cause of Imprisonment; and an exact Account of his or her Estate, and all Circumstances relating thereto; and on such Petition, the Court shall order the Prisoner to be brought, and the Creditors, at whose Suit he is charged, to be summoned; and on the Day of Appearance if any of the Creditors neglect to appear, on Proof made of the due Service of the Court's Order, the Court shall proceed to examine the Matter of the Petition in a Summary Way, and shall tender to such Person an Oath, to the Effect following:

I, A.B., do solemnly swear, in the Presence of Almighty God, That the Account by me delivered, with my Petition, into this Court, doth contain a full and true Account of my Real and Personal Estate, Debts, Credits, and Effects whatsoever, which I, or any in Trust for me, have, or at the Time of my said Petition had, or now can or then was, in any Respect, intituled to, either in Possession, Remainder, or Reversion, (Except my wearing Apparel for myself and Family, and the Tools or Instruments of my Trade and Arms for Muster,) and that I have not, at any Time since my Imprisonment, or before, directly or indirectly, sold, alienated, assigned, or otherwise disposed of, or made over, in Trust for myself, or otherwise, other than is mentioned in such Account, any Part of my Lands, Estate, Goods, Stocks, Money, Debts, or other Real or Personal Estate, whereby to have or expect any Benefit or Profit to myself, or to defraud any of my Creditors to whom I am indebted. So help me God.

IV. And be it further Enacted, That if such Person take such Oath, and the Creditor be satisfied with the Truth thereof, the Court may order the Effects contained in such Account, or so much as may be sufficient to satisfy the Debts and Fees due to the Gaoler, to be, by an Indorsement on the Back of the Petition, signed by the Prisoner, assigned to the Creditor or Creditors, or to one or more of them, in Trust for the rest; and by such an Assignment, the Estate and property of the Lands, Goods, Debts, and Effects, shall be vested in such Creditor or Creditors, in Trust, as aforesaid, and the Prisoner shall be discharged out of Custody, by Order of the Court, without Fee, and the Person or Persons to whom the Effects shall be assigned, paying the Fees to the Gaoler, shall divide the Effects, in Proportion to their Debts:

7

But if the Person or Persons at whose Suit the Prisoner is in Execution, shall desire Time to inform him, her, or themselves the Court shall remand the Prisoner, and direct him, and the Person or Persons dissatisfied, to appear, at a Day, in the next succeeding Court; and if at such Day the Creditor or Creditors make Default, or if he, she, or they, be unable to make Discovery of any Effects of the Prisoner omitted in his Petition, or to shew any Probability of his having being so sworn, the Court shall cause the Prisoner to be discharged, unless such Creditor or Creditors, on his being detained, agree, by Writing, to pay the Prisoner Ten Shillings, Proclamation Money, by the Week, to be paid Weekly, so long as he or she shall continue in Prison at his, her, or their Suit; and on Failure of Payment, the Prisoner shall, on Application made to the Court, be discharged by Order: And in case the Prisoner shall refuse to take the Oath, or shall be detected of Falsity therein, he shall be remanded.

V. And be it futher Enacted, That the Person of any Debtor so discharged shall, never after, be arrested for the same Debt; but the Judgment shall remain in Force, and Execution may be taken out against his Lands or Goods, (his wearing Apparel for himself and Family, Tools for his Trade, and Arms for Muster, excepted.)

VI. And be it further Enacted, That if any Person who shall take such Oath, shall, upon Indictment of Perjury, be convicted thereon, he shall suffer all Pains of wilful perjury, and shall be liable to be taken on a new Process; and shall, never after, have the Benefit of this Act.

VII. And be it further Enacted, That if the Effects assigned shall not extend to satisfy the whole Debts due to the Person or Persons at whose Suit such Prisoner was charged, and the Fees, there shall be an Abatement in Proportion; and the Gaoler shall come in, as a Creditor, for his Fees.

VIII. And be it further Enacted, That no Person, charged in Execution, shall be allowed to Petition by Virtue of this Act, unless such Prisoner do exhibit his Petition to the Court from whence the Execution issued, within Six Months after such Person shall be so charged in Execution.

IX. And be it further Enacted, That where by this Act an Oath is required, the solemn Affirmation of a Quaker shall be taken, in Lieu thereof; and every Person convicted of wilful and false affirming, shall suffer the like Penalties as for wilful and corrupt Perjury.

Laws, 1749, in Clark, *State Records,* 23:312-314.

North Carolina Craven County ss. In the Common Pleas Between Chas.
　　Smith Pet. and Richard Dew (alias Connor) Deft.

　　An Inventory of All and Singular the Good and Chattles of Richard
Dews (alias Connor) now in Custody of the Sheriff of the said County
for the Sum of Sixteen Pounds Proclamation Money given upon oath
before the Worshipful John Cletherell and Samuel Cornell Esqrs. two
of his Majesty's Justices of the Peace for the County aforesaid Persuant
to an Act of Assembly Pass'd in this Province for the Relief of Insolvent
Debtors Videlicet

One old Flock Bed	Value	0. 12. 6
One Blanket		0. 5. 0
One old Bason 4 Plates and 4 Pewter Spoons		0. 6. 8
One C[*illegible*]t Iron Pot and a pr. Pott Hooks		0. 5. 0
One old Spinning Wheel		0. 6. 0
7te. Wool		0. 7. 0
one Punch Bowl		0. 1. 4
2 flogg Matts		0. 1. 4
		2. 4. 10
1 Old Frying Pan		0. 1. 6
2 Knives and 2 forks		0. 0. 8
1 Old Pail		0. 1. 4
		2. 8. 4
To An Account against Isaac Austin		0. 10. 0
		Richd. Connor

[*Endorsed:*]
June 22th 1757 then Commuted
Richd Connor and the sute of Charles Smith.

> Inventory of Richard Dews (alias Connor), June 22, 1757, Craven
> County, Miscellaneous Records, Involvent Debtors, 1757-1837, State
> Archives.

　　To the Worshipfull the Justices of the Inferior Court of Craven
County
　　The Petition of John Pilchard Humbly sheweth
　　That your poor Petitioner is in the Prison of your County for an
Execution at the Suit of Wm. Brown for the Sum of Ten Pounds also
at the Suit John Smith for the Sum of Five Pounds Proclamation Money
and Costs And your Petitioner not having to the Value of Forty Shillings
Sterling in any Worldly Substance His wearing apparel working Tools,

and Arms for Muster Excepted therefore your Petitioner pray your Worships will cause Summons to Issue to the said Wm. Brown to shew Cause why your Petitioner shall not have the benefit of an Act of Assembly for the Relief of poor Debtors as to the Imprisonment of their Bodies and your Petitioner as in duty bound will pray.
December 14th 1770

John Pilchard

[*Endorsed:*]
John Pilchard Petition for the
Benefit of the Act of Assembly
for the relief of Insolvent Debtors
Summoned Wm. Brown

John G. Blount D. Sr.

> Petition of John Pilchard, December 14, 1770, Craven County, Miscellaneous Records, Insolvent Debtors, State Archives.

Whereas I am now confined in the public gaol of Edenton, on an execution at the suit of William Orrenton, for the sum of four pounds ten shillings, and not being possessed of any estate real or personal, and at this time in no capacity of making any payments to my creditors, and having a poor distressed wife and children who rely altogether on my labour for their daily bread: Do humbly and with reluctance give notice to my creditors, that I intend to take the aid of the act of Assembly which gives relief to poor, insolvent imprisoned debtors, that after having complied in all respects with the law, I shall apply to two Justices of the Peace of Chowan county, for relief and a certificate of discharge. Therefore I pray and request their attendance at the prison door in Edenton, on the sixteenth day of February next, to make objections against my discharge, if they have any; of which I humbly pray they will take notice.
Jan. 26 0 3

SAMUEL LATIMORE

The State Gazette of North-Carolina (Edenton), February 12, 1789.

In addition to the poor, the idle and dissolute remained a part of colonial society.

There are several other good Laws in this Province, and particularly, that no Vagabond, or inferiour Person is suffered to travel through the Country without a Pass from the Governor, or some of the Justices of the Peace, this is done to prevent Transports from *Europe* running away from their Masters.

Brickell, *Natural History*, 258.

An Act for the Restraint of Vagrants, and for making provision for the Poor and other Purposes.

I. Whereas divers idle and disorderly Persons, having no visible Estates or Employments, and who are able to work, frequently stroll from one County to another, neglecting to labor; and either failing altogether to list themselves as Taxables, or by their idle and disorderly Life, rendering themselves incapable of paying their Levies, when listed: For Remedy whereof.

II. Be it Enacted by the Governor, Council, and Assembly, and by the Authority of the same, That it shall not be lawful for any Inhabitants of this Government, to entertain, hire, or employ, in his or her House, above the space of Forty Eight Hours, any such Person or Persons whatsoever, being taxable, and removing from the Parish where he or she formerly resided, unless such Person shall first produce a Certificate, under the Hand of the Sheriff, or some Magistrate of the County from whence he or she came, that such Person paid Levy there for the preceding Year, or that he or she came into this Government since, or was a Servant at the Time of taking the last List of Taxables; and if any one shall entertain, hire, or employ, any such Person or Persons whatsoever, being taxable, not having such Certificate as aforesaid, he or she so offending, shall forfeit and pay Twenty Shillings, Proclamation Money, for every such offence, to the Informer; recoverable before any Justice of the Peace of the County where the offence shall be committed: And if any Taxable Person, not having such Certificate, shall offer himself, or seek to be employed, he shall be liable to the like Penalty of Twenty Shillings, Proclamation Money, to be recovered and applied as aforesaid.

III. And be it further Enacted, by the Authority aforesaid, That all able bodied Persons, not having wherewithal to maintain themselves, who shall be found loitering and neglecting to labour for reasonable Wages; all Persons who run from their Habitations, and have Wives and Children, without suitable Means for their Subsistence, whereby they are like to become burthensome to the Parish wherein they inhabit; and all other idle, vagrant, or dissolute Persons, wandering abroad, without betaking themselves to some lawful Employments, or honest Labour, or going about begging, shall be deemed Rogues and Vagabonds.

IV. And be it further Enacted, by the Authority aforesaid, That if any such Vagabonds shall be found in any County or Place, wandering, begging or misordering him or herself, it shall be lawful for any Justice of the Peace of that County, and he is hereby impowered and required, by warrant under his Hand, to cause such Vagabonds to be brought before him, and to examine and inform himself, as well by the Oath and Examination of the Person apprehended, as of any other Person or Persons which Oath or Oaths the Justice is hereby impowered to administer, and by any other Ways or Means he shall think proper, of the Condition and circumstances of the Person or Persons so apprehended; and if it shall appear that he or she is under the description of Vagabonds within this Act, the said Justice shall, by his Warrant, order and direct him or her to be conveyed and whipt, in the same Manner as Runaways are, from Constable to Constable, to the County wherein his Wife or Children do inhabit, or where he or she did last reside (as the Case shall be) and there delivered to a Justice of the Peace, who is hereby required to cause every such Vagabond to give sufficient Security for his or her good Behavior, and for betaking him or herself to some lawful Calling, or honest Labour; and if he or she fail so to do, then to commit him or her to the common Gaol of the County, there to remain until such security be given, or until the next Court; which Court is hereby impowered, if no Security be then offered, to bind such Vagabond to Service, on Wages for the Term of One Year; and such Wages, after deducting the Charges of the Prosecution, and necessary Cloathing, shall be applied towards supporting the Family of such Servant (if any) or otherwise paid to the Person so bound after his or her Time of Service is expired, in full of all other Recompence or Reward: But if any such Vagabond be of such evil Repute, that no Person will receive him or her into Service, in such Case the Court shall order him or her to receive Thirty Nine Lashes on his or her bare Back, well laid on, at the Public Whipping Post, and then to be discharged; and in both Cases every such Vagabond shall be afterwards liable to the like Prosecution and Punishment, for every offence of Vagrancy whereof he or she shall be guilty as aforesaid; and when any such Vagabond shall be brought before a Justice of the Peace and it shall not appear to the said Justice that he or she has acquired a legal settlement in any parish the said Justice is hereby required to cause such Vagabonds to give Security for his or her good Behavior, and for betaking him or herself to some honest Calling or Employment; and on Failure thereof, shall commit him or her to the Jail of the County, there to remain and be dealt with as is before herein directed.

Laws, 1755, in Clark, *State Records*, 23:435-436.

An Act concerning Idle and Dissolute Persons.

I. Whereas in several Parts of this Province there are Idle and Dissolute Persons, that frequently commit atrocious Crimes, such as stealing Horses, robbing Houses, and the like, to the great Injury of Honest and Industrious Inhabitants; and as such Persons are frequently Harboured, maintained and encouraged, by some House Keepers in this Province; For Remedy whereof,

II. Be it Enacted by the Governor, Council and Assembly, and by the Authority of the same, That from and after the passing of this Act, no Person or Persons, whatsoever shall Harbour or maintain in or about his or their house or Plantation, or knowingly suffer to reside on their Land, any loose or disorderly Person, who has not any Visible Way of Maintenance, or is of a Dishonest Character, under the Penalty of Twenty Pounds, Proclamation Money, for every such Offence; to be recovered by Action of Debt, in the Inferior Court of the County where the Offence is committed; one Half of which sum shall be paid to the Person informing against such Offender, and the other Half to be applied to the Contingent Charges of the County; and such Offender shall be further liable to be bound over to appear at the next Superior Court of the District where such Offence is Committed, there to abide the Determination of the said Court.

Laws, 1766, in Clark, *State Records*, 23:746-747.

North Carolina
Orange County Ss.
At an Inferior Court of Pleas and Quarter Sessions begun and held for the County of Orange at the Court house in CorbinTown on the Second Tuesday in June in Year of our Lord 1758.
Present his Majesties Justices to wit.
John Pryor Thomas Loyd Andrew Mitchell James Allison Esqrs [...]
Lawrence Thompson late Sherriff of Orange County Delivers up to Josias Dixon the Present Sheriff the following Prisoners now in Custody to wit Catherine Gordon, Committed on the Vagrant Act. [...]

On Examination of Catherine Gordon who was Committed on Suspicion of Sundry Misdemenors and in Evidence having appeared to prove the same, it is Ordered that she be Discharged on paying her fees, and that what Effects of hers that are in the Goalers Custody be sold for the same and that she Immidiately Depart this County.

Orange County Court Minutes, June 1758, State Archives.

❧❦

Nonetheless, some accumulated wealth, as evidenced by the large slaveholdings in Brunswick County in which slaves comprised almost 70 percent of the population at the time of the Revolution.

An Alphabetical List of Taxables in Saint Philips Parish Brunsk. County for 1772.

Names of Persons Returned	No. Chair Wheel	White Men	Negro Men	Negro Women	Negro Boys
A					
Ancrum John		1	9	11	
Allen Elinor		1	1		
Adderson Christopher		1			
Anderson John		1			
Allston Joseph			2	1	
Allen Drury		1	4	4	
B					
Bassett David		1			
Barrett William		1			
Boone Thomas		3			
Bearfield Miles		1	1		
Benton Moses		2			
Benton Job		1			
Barker Edward		1			
Bell James		2		2	
Bell John		2			
Baccott Samuel		1	2	3	
Bell James Junr.		2	1	1	

Bassford James		1	2		
Belloone Michael		1	4	3	
C					
Corbett James		1	1	1	
Cains Richard		1			
Conner Morris		1	1		
Caulkins Elias		1			
Cheeseborough John		1		1	
Cains John		1		1	
Clifton John		1			
Cains Christopher		1	1	3	
Cains William		1	3		
Carried Over		33	32	31	
Brought Over		33	32	31	
Cumbo Stephen		3			
Crandal Elijah		1			
Cumbo David		1			
Cheers John		1			
Caulkins William		1			
Cahoone Macajiah		1			
D					
Dry William	2	2	40	40	6
Davis William		2	10	6	1
Davis Jane				3	
Davis Thomas		1	16	18	2
Davis Roger	2	1	15	17	1
Daniell Robert		1	2	11	
Daniell Sarah			2	5	
Daniell Stephen		1	4	4	
Drew John		3			
Demont John		1			
Demont Charles		1			
E					
Eagles Richd. Estate			24	26	

Earle Joseph		2			
Eagan Elizabeth		1	4	6	
Ellis Robert		2	10	5	1
Etheridge John		1			
Etheridge Samuel		2		1	
Eagleson John		1	1	1	

F

Forristor John		1			
Frankum Joshua		1			
Fergus John	2	1	1	2	
Faulkner William		1			
Fowler Ann				2	

G

Gallaway William		1		2	
Gallaway Thomas		1	1		
Carried Forward	6	69	162	180	11
Brought up	6	69	162	180	11
Gibson Alexander		1	1		
Goldwin Ann			1	2	
Grange John	2	1	20	34	6
Godfrey William		1	1	1	
Gore William		1			
Grissett William		3	3	4	
Gause William		2	7	5	
Gause Nudham		2	3	2	
Gallaway John		1		2	
Generett John		1	1	1	

H

Hines Jonas		1			
Hines Daniell		1			
Hilliard Jessey		1			
Hawkins William		1			

Hilliard James		1		
Hewett Richard		1		
Holden Benjamin		2		
Hickman John		2		
Hall Thomas	2	1	10	10	2
Howes Robert	2	1	18	24	6
Hewitt Hezekiah		1		
Holmes Edmond		1	1	1
Hasell James		2	10	6
Hasell Susanah			3	2
Hart Abigal				1
Howard Jetus		1		
Hill William	2	1	1	4	1
Hewitt Elisha		1		
Hewitt Ebenezer Jur.		1		
Hewitt Joseph		2	2	
Hewitt Jacob		1		
Hewitt Philip		1		

I

Jacobs Zacheriah		1		
Carried Over	14	107	244	279	25
Brought Over	14	107	244	279	25

K

Keeter Charles		1		

L

Liles Benjamin		1		
Ludlam Jeremiah		1	1	1
Lay Enus		1		
Lay John		1		
Leonard Samuel		1		
Leonard Samuel Junr.		1		
Leonard Henry Junr.		1		
Leonard Henry		2		
Lewis Jacob		1		

Lord William	2	1	12	8	
Lockwood Joseph		1			
Ludlam Joshua		1			
M					
Mackay Arthur		1	1		
Moore George			7	1	
Munro Hugh		1		3	1
McIlhenny James		2			
Maclaine Bryant		1			
Marlow James		1			
Marlow John		1			
Mooney William		1			
Mills William		3			
Marion Isaac		1	5	6	
Marnan Thomas				7	
Mimms George		3			
Mimms David		1			
N					
Neale Samuel		1	6	7	
Neale Thomas		2	6	10	
Neale Margaret			1	2	
Nugent Edmond		1			
Carried Forwards	16	142	282	318	27
Brought up	16	142	282	318	27
O					
Ogden William		1			
P					
Potter Miles		2		1	
Potter Robert		1	1	1	
Phelps Jacob		1			
Pennington William		1		1	
Pryor Seth		1	1		

Q

Quince Richard	2	5	99	51	5
Quince Richard Jun.	2	1	23	23	
Quince Parker		1	2	9	2

R

Rogers John		1	1		
Roots John		1	1	1	
Rowan John	6	5	20	18	3
Russ Joseph		1			
Ris John		1			
Robbins Jethro		1			
Robbins Arthur		1			
Rogers Richard		1			
Rouse Thomas		1			
Robison John		1			

S

Simpson Willm. Jun.		1	1		
Simpson Willm. Sen.		3	4	4	
Smeeth David		1			
Savage Frances		1			
Swaine Rebecca		1	1	2	
Smith James		1			
Carried Over	26	178	436	429	37
Brought over	26	178	436	429	37
Swaine Arthur		1			
Swaine Jonathan		1	4	4	
Snow Robert	2	1	9	5	4
Skipper Clemonds		1			
Simmonds John		1	8	6	
Seller Elisha		1			
Sellers Martha		1			
Souls Silvenus		1			
Smith John		1			
Stevins Alexander		2			
Sellers Simon		1			

Smith Daniel		1			
Stone John		1			
Sellers James		1			
Sellers Joel		1			
Souls Joseph		1			
Simmonds Isaac		5	1		
Souls Gideon		1			
Sessions Thomas		1		1	
Stanton John		1		1	1
Stanaland Thomas		1			
Stanaland Samuel		1			
Stanaland John		1			
Sturgis Jonathan		1	1		
Swaine David		1			
Skipper Moses		1			
T					
Thomas John		1			
Todd Thomas		1	1		
Tyler John		1			
Tharp Samuel		3			
Carried Forward	28	215	460	446	42
Brought up	28	215	460	446	42
V					
Vernon Willm. Estate		2	9	13	1
Vines John		1			
W					
Williams Henry		1			
Waldron Isaac		1	8	8	1
Wells Robert		1	1	1	
White James		1			
Weaver Susanah			2	3	
Wilkinson John		2	3	1	
West Robert		1			
Ward John		1			

Williams Benedick		1			
West Arthur		1			
Wingate Edward		2	4	5	
Wingate John		1	3	5	
Woodside Robert		1			
West Merideth		1			
Willitts JoBuck		1	1		
Willitts Mary		1		1	
Willitts Samuel		1			
Waters Wm. Estate			5	3	
Waters Joseph Estate		1	13	11	1
Waters Samuel		1	17	18	1
Total	28	238	526	515	46
Moore Maurice					
Totaled Since	4	5	32	28	2
Whites	238				
Negro Men	526				
Negro Women	515				
Negro Boys	46				
In all	1325	Taxables			
Chair Wheels	28	in all			

A True Copy Examined by

Will. Lord Clk.

Brunswick County Tax List, 1772, G.A. 11.1, State Archives.

৶৻৶

In addition to agriculture and naval stores, the mercantile and legal professions offered avenues to riches, though lawyers in North Carolina were not always well regarded.

Mr. Cornell, a man of education, who has acquired in Trade a very considerable fortune from the lowest beginning, an adept in mercantile business, and of no knowledge or talent out of that line. He was brought into Council by Governor Tryon, who believed him well principled towards Government and who had found him useful by his money in some public exigencies, but detested in this place where he has made his fortune for his vanity and his griping and oppressive disposition.

> Governor Martin to the Earl of Dartmouth, April 6, 1774, in Saunders, *Colonial Records*, 9:973.

[...] another instance occurs in the person of Mr. Jno. W. Stanly, the husband of Mrs. Stanly already mentioned; this Man of whom the first knowledge I had, was, his being confined a prisoner in the Goal of Philadelphia for debt, upon his liberation removed to this Country, where by a Series of fortunate events in Trade during the War he acquired a great property, and has built a house in Newbern where he resides, that is truly elegant and convenient; at an expense of near 20,000 Dollars — He has a large Wharff and Distillery near his house; upon Neuse River side of the Town — and a fine plantation with sixty Slaves thereon. — [...]

> Rodman, *Journal of a Tour to North Carolina by William Attmore, 1787*, 16-17.

[...] For you may know, that the Lawyers, bad everywhere, (don't let the Doctor see this) but in Carolina worse than bad, having long abused the people in the most infamous manner, at length brought things to such a pass, that bond of £500. was taken for a single fee in trifling causes, and this bond put in suit and recovered before the business was done for which the fee was paid. [...]

> Richard Henry Lee to William Lee, June 19, 1771, in Powell, Huhta, and Farnham, *Regulators*, 482.

Wilmington March the 5th, 1757

Dear Sir,

[...] I However Made Shift to be present at the Tryale of two or three trifling Causes, But as the Evidance was plain they were left to the Jury without Summing up, So that I had no opportunity of hearing the Rethorical Talents of any of the Gentlemen of the Long Robe. The Attornies were Mr. Swann and Mr. Jones. Mr. Underhill was not Concerned in any of the Causes I was present at. I think I heard you Say You had never heard Mr. Jones Speak. He is a Gentlemen Bless'd with a Quick Perception and a Prompt Elocution. His Judgement and Knowledge of Law I Cannot pretend to Say anything of. I However observ'd He was Well Vers'd in that part Which is Call'd the Chicanerie and Quarks of the Law And His Practice in this as Well as the Method He takes of Confounding and Puzzaling His adversaries Witnesses I Cannot help Condemning. I am Sensible He has the Antiquity of Custom to plead in his behalf. But Still I think it a Base Ungenerous Unwarrantable Custom. It Can Never be urged it is the Business of his Office to Suppress insted of Investigate truth. Nor that He is under any obligations to His Clients to Practise Deceit or Patronize Delusion. No! I Entertain a More Honourable Idea of the Function that to beleive a Lawyer Oblig'd to maintain a Desperate Cause at all Events; What Love of Justice it discovers, to Attempt to Confuse an honest Witness With Interrogatories foreign to the purpose, till He is Bewilderd and Drawn into inadvertent Contradictions, I Cannot Conceive. To me it Appears Repugnant to Common Equity, Especially when those very Contradictions to which a Witness has been drove by Artfull Questions, are urgd as Arguments against his Veracity, in order to invalidate his Testimony. But I am far from Accusing Mr. Jones of this Practise it is however too much the Custom With some Attornies And I think Cannot lie too much discourag'd by Gentlemen who are desireous of Supporting the Credit of the Profession Which is Certainly a Necessary and Honourable and Would Never fail of Meeting with Respect was it not debased by persons unworthy of it Among which I Rank Underhill who I'm asham'd to Say was Drunk as a Beast for two Entire days, so as to be Incapable to Attend his Business at Court. By which the Interest of his Clients must undoubtedly have Sufferd; Certainly Such Behaviour Must tend to his Ruin.

> Peter DuBois to "Dear Sir" [Samuel Johnston], March 5, 1757, Hayes Papers.

Wealth often contributed to a penchant for lavish living and hospitality.

[...] Merchants in the town, and considerable planters in the country, are now beginning to have a taste for living, and some gay equipages may be seen; they are generous, well bred, and dress much; are polite, humane, and hospitable; and never tired of rendering strangers all the service in their power: nor is this mere pageantry and shew; their behaviour at home is consistent with their appearance abroad. Their houses are elegant, their tables always plentifully covered and their entertainment sumptous. They are fond of company, living very sociable and neighbourly, visiting one another often. [...]

Boyd, "Informations," 443.

Col. Dry['s] is justly called the house of universal hospitality— his table abounds with plenty—his servants excell in cookery—and his sensible lady exceeds (at least I think equals) Sister Q[uincy] in the pastry and nick-nack way.

Howe, "The Southern Journal of Josiah Quincy, Junior, 1773," 459.

Enclosed You have a Letter from M'Smith to whom I am much oblige for the Polite Usuage I mett with from the Gentlemen of Edenton in Generall and must acknowledge the Favour of your kind Recomendation to the Above Gentlemen the Hospitality of the Gentlemen of Carolina to Strangers is a thing not known in our more Northern Regions.[...]

Cha. Read to "Sir" [Joseph Hewes], June 27, 1775, Hayes Papers.

ಆಶಿ

A visitor from Massachusetts declared a decided preference for North Carolinians as compared to their wealthier neighbors to the south.

General Reflections and Remarks on North and South Carolina (as they rise).

The soils and climates of the Carolinas differ, but not so much as their inhabitants. Though little more than imaginary lines part these people, you no sooner enter the North province before you seem to see a surprizing change of men and things.

There is an affectation too prevalent in South Carolina of superiority over the Northern colonies, especially over poor North Carolina, which was much misrepresented to me, and might therefore cause a prejudice in their favour when I found things so different from the accounts received of them. But all prejudice apart.

The number of negroes and slaves are vastly less in North than South Carolina. Their staple commodity is not so valuable, being not in so great demand, as the rice, indigo, etc. of the South. Hence labor becomes more necessary, and he who has an interest of his own to serve is a laborer in the field. Husbandmen and agriculture increase in number and improvement. Industry is up in the woods, at tar, pitch, and turpentine in the fields plowing, planting, or clearing and fencing the land. Herds and flocks become more numerous, and they resemble not Pharoah's lean kine, so much as those of the Province I had just left. You see husbandmen, yeomen and white laborers scattered through the country, instead of herds of negroes and tawny slaves. Healthfull countenances and numerous families become more common as you advance North.

In Charlestown and so through the Southern province I saw much apparent hospitality, much of what is called good-breeding and politeness, and great barbarity. In Brunswick, Willmington, Newbern, Edenton, and so through the North province there is real hospitality, less of what is called politeness and good-breeding and less inhumanity.

Property is much more equally diffused in one province than the other, and this may account for some, if not all, the differences of character of the inhabitants.

Arts and sciences are certainly better understood, more relished, more attended to and better cultivated in the one province than the other. Men of genius, learning, and true wit, humour, and mirth are more numerous here than [in] the country I had just left; a country too, where the civilities I had received served to prejudice my judgment in its favour. [...]

[The] Carolinas [...] certainly vary much as to their general sentiments, opinions and judgments: they may well be considered as very opposite in character, and ' tis very apparent that no great friendship or esteem is entertained by one towards the other. [...]

Howe, "The Southern Journal of Josiah Quincy, Junior, 1773," 462-463.

ക്ടൂറ്റ്

On the whole, however, the state of North Carolina society failed to impress either contemporaries or later writers.

[...] [New Bern, January, 1783] The principal inhabitants present at that time were Mr. Ogden, Mr. Blount, Le Marquis de Bretigney (a French officer in the service of this state), Mr. Oram, Mr. Cooke, Mr. Sitgreaves, Mr. Ellis, Mr. Schilbeack, Mr. Goff, Monsieur Heró, Dr. McClure, Dr. Halling, Mr. Johnston, Monsieur Mayoli, etc. These came to call on me and honored me with the greatest hospitality, and this good treatment has continued throughout my residence here even though their ideas are generally not very liberal and the social system is still in its swaddling clothes.[...]

Miranda, *The New Democracy in America*, 5.

11. The first settlers in this county lived in a 'state of society' not far better than that of the Indians. If we may divide the stages of Society into the *savage*, the *barbarous* & *civilized*, we might place them in the second class. So late as 50 years ago there were only a few neighborhoods, on the water courses, that enjoyed the blessings of social life. [...]

Newsome, "Twelve North Carolina Counties in 1810-1811," 6:87-88.

Family

Marriage, a civil ceremony for which colonial governors experienced difficulty in collecting their fees, was deemed inevitable, and perhaps desirable, by most colonials.

An Act Concerning Marriages

I. For preventing clandestine and Unlawful Marriages, We pray that it may be Enacted, And be it Enacted, by his Excellency Gabriel Johnston, Esq., Governor, by and with the Advice and Consent of his Majesty's Council, and the General Assembly of this Province and it is hereby Enacted by the Authority of the same, That every Clergyman of the Church of England, or for want of such, any lawful Magistrate, within this Government, shall, and they are hereby directed, to join together in the Holy Estate of Matrimony, such Persons who may lawfully enter into such a Relation, and have complied with the Directions hereinafter contained.

Laws, 1741, in Clark, *State Records of North Carolina*, 23:158.

North Carolina'ss
By His Excelly WILLIAM TRYON Esqr.

A PROCLAMATION

Whereas by an Act of the General Assembly passed in the year 1741 — Intitled an Act concerning of Marriages, it is among things Enacted that all Marriage Licenses shall be Issued under certain Rules, & directions therein mentioned by the Clerk of the County wherein the Feme has her usual Residence and be signed & directed by the first Justices in the Commission of the peace for the County or by a Person Commissioned by the Governor for that Purpose, which power to a Justice for signing and directing of Marriage Licences has since been thought improper as having a Tendency to elude the payment of the Just and Legal fees to the Governor on Marriage Licenses [...]

In Order therefore to correct this mistake & to prevent such injurious practices to the Publick for the future.—I have thought fit by & with the Advice & Consent of His Majesty: Council to Issue this my Proclamation thereby Prohibiting and forbidding each and every Justice, & Clerk of any Inferior Court in this Province, hereafter to sign or direct (unless under my hand & seal) any Marriage License [...]

Powell, *Correspondence of William Tryon*, 2:16-17.

[...] I assure you, my dear Sir, that in this Country a young Man without the joys of a private Family leads [a] very dull, and I may add, a less improving Life. [...]

James Iredell to Francis Iredell, Sr., [October 22, 1772], in Higginbotham, *Papers of James Iredell*, 2 vols., 1:123.

Marriages here are of two varieties. The one, according to the church discipline, calls for three successive announcements of the banns. In the case of the other, which occurs with equal frequency, the procedure is in general as follows: The groom secures a certificate from the Superior Officer at Salisbury, comes riding along with his friends of both sexes, the bride riding by his side, to the pastor, of if none is available, to the Justice [of the Peace] where the ceremony is performed. He enters holding in his right hand his flask of rum, greets with a "good morning," drinks to the health of the one officiating, produces his certificate and then goes back to get his bride and the rest of the party. The questions directed to the groom are: whether he has stolen (that is, kidnapped) his bride,—which occurs frequently,—and whether the parents have given their consent. If one steals his bride and has a license from Salisbury the objections of the parents are of no avail. As a rule in this country the son, as soon as he has reached his twenty-first year, and the daughter as soon as she is eighteen years old, no longer stand under the control of their parents. In case of marriages, which, by the way, are often contracted very early in life, provision for the future need not be any great cause for worry. Whoever is willing to work can easily obtain a plantation and poor people generally are not to be seen here at all. [...]

Report of Rev. Mr. Roschen, 1789, in Boyd and Krummel, "German Tracts," 244.

∽❧

The prospect of marriage evoked different expectations of wives and husbands.

The DUTY *of a* WIFE.

FIRST, of her Lord, the Temper let her scan,
And lay thereon, of future Bliss, the Plan.
Whene'er his troubled Bosom heaves with Rage,
Try gentle Means the Tempest to assuage;

Or is some wayward Humours should appear,
To sooth, to overlook them, be her Care.
In Trifles if she mildly yields the Way,
With grateful Confidence her Love he'll pay;
To her will trust his Hopes, his Doubts, his Fears,
And frankly mingle all his Soul with hers.
The finest Form adorn'd with graceful Art,
Derives new Pow'r to captivate the Heart;
And if, before the Nymph became a Bride,
The various Ornaments of Dress she try'd;
Let her pursue the innocent Deceit,
And play, with double Diligence, the Cheat:
For tho' a Conquest is with ease obtain'd,
Once lost, alas! 'tis hard to be regain'd!
Therefore, if Dress assisted to allure,
Pursue it still, the Captive to secure.
With ev'ry Grace our Persons we should arm,
Nor lose, thro' Want of Ornament, a Charm:
Else languid soon the nuptial Flame will burn,
And the bright *Goddess* to mere *Woman* turn.
Yet be not Dress, tho' one, our only Care,
Eternal Charms, however soft and dear,
Cannot preserve the Ardour of Desire,
Unless the mental Virtues feed the Fire.
Good Sense will charm when *Beauty* is decay'd,
Good Sense, the blooming Sweet, that cannot fade.
But gains from Time an higher Strength to please,
And gives the Wife a Pow'r that ne'er can cease.
But then her Wit must never be display'd,
Where it the Husband's Province might invade:
[*torn*] *Mistress* to *remain*,
Nor poorly strive the *Mastership* t' obtain.
This would occasion Jars, intestine Strife,
Imbitter all the Sweets of nuptial Life!
Then let her not for Government contend,
But use this Policy to gain her End—
Make him *believe* he holds the Sov'reign Sway,
And she may *rule*, by seeming to *obey*.
No State can be replete entire with Joy,
Some Incidents will happen to annoy;
But she should never heighten the Distress,

Be it her Care to make the Crosses less:
Not spoil with discontented Frowns her Face,
Ill-Nature is an Enemy to Grace:
But fair *Good Humour* brightens all her Charms,
And even Misfortune's bitt'rest Rage disarms.

North Carolina Gazette (New Bern), July 14, 1775.

Choice of a HUSBAND, by a Gentlewoman of Prudence.

To meet with a man perfectly agreeable (though the person is least to be regarded) may be a gift of some difficulty, to a nice and discerning woman. His qualifications must be great to recommend him: But I shall offer some particulars, which, if observed, may contribute to a good choice, and are worthy of election, though seldom to be met with in one person. First; it is necessary that he be a man of virtue and morality, having a large share of natural sense and acquired knowledge, proceeding from a liberal education; that he be well read, and a man of conversation, so as to have a general knowledge of men and things; to be pretty much, if not entirely, master of his passions, but not without courage, though with discretion to use; naturally good humoured and loving, but not jealous, nor meanly submissive; one not a perfect stranger to vice, but has seen enough of it as to have a right notion of the folly and fatal tendency of it; he may be moderately addicted to all decent pleasures, and manly diversions; love his friend and bottle a little, but so as not to draw off his affection from his wife; to be a man of manners (though by no means foppish) enough to oblige and civilly treat persons of all tempers; not to be too profuse, but have conduct enough not to live beyond his circumstances, and application enough to his own business, to keep the world from imposing upon him.

Wilmington Centinel, and General Advertiser, June 25, 1788.

⤲⤳

Courtship found James Iredell wooing Hannah Johnston for over a year before seeking permission to marry from her brother, Samuel Johnston, in the absence of her deceased father.

[ca. April 1, 1772]

Madam,

I cannot, without doing the most painful violence to my Inclinations, any longer delay expressing the most tender and sincere Affection for you—Happy, inexpressibly happy shall I be, if the time rather than the subject of this Address, may appear exceptionable. It is not perhaps very becoming in a young Man with so scanty an Income as I have, to offer his Hand and Heart for a young Lady's Acceptance. I rely, Madam, upon your Goodness for an excuse of this Impropriety. My heart compelled me to a declaration as the only possible way of relieving it from the most anxious Inequitude; and I hope my Situation will not always be so discouraging as it now is. May I therefore presume to intreat your favorable Attention, and to hope you will consider me as a young Man, whose highest Wish it is to obtain, and whose constant Endeavour it shall be to deserve, your preferable Regard. Oh! could I but flatter myself with being possessed of it, I should then look forward with contented Satisfaction to some pleasing future day, which may be rendered auspicious by our Union; in which case, Madam, be assured, every thing you could expect from the most obliged, most grateful, and most happy of Men, you should certainly meet with from Your faithful and devoted Servant

Jas. Iredell

James Iredell to Hannah Johnston, [ca. April 1, 1772], in Higgin-botham, *Papers of James Iredell*, 1:94.

Edenton 7th April 1772

Dear Sir,

Ever since I have had the honour and happiness of your Acquaintance I have been particularly desirous to cultivate your Esteem, and to obtain your Approbation. I shall always be more or less happy in proportion as these are continued or with-held; and as I please myself with the assurance that this Circumstance will depend on my own Conduct, my utmost Endeavours shall be exerted to regulate it in the most prudent and cautious Manner.

The Solemnity of this Introduction will surprise you, Sir. The Occasion is important, and perhaps requires it. I fear to offend, and yet it becomes me to explain myself. A long and intimate Acquaintance with the many Excellencies of your Sister, Miss Hannah Johnston, has formed an Attachment that nothing but my Life can end. My Anxiety increased to a degree which made Suspence painful to me, and I have presumed to offer my Addresses to her. I am now inexpressibly happy in saying, my Anxiety is eased with the hope of Acceptance, and that all the uneasiness I feel is, lest my precipitate Declaration, in the present inadequate situation of my Circumstances, should incur your Displeasure. I know not whether I can be justified. I may however hope to extenuate my Conduct, by alleging an Ardour of Affection that gave me the most distressing Apprehensions. To your Goodness, Sir, I confide this Plea in favour of a young Man, who will endeavour by every Instance in his power to merit your Regard, and express his Gratitude to the dear Lady who has blessed him with the hope of being one day the happiest of Men.

As you will see Mr. Hewes in a day or two I need mention no other Particulars than that your Friends here are all well.

I have procured Alford Davis's affidavit, which is substantially such as you expected.

You will oblige me, Sir, by presenting my best Compliments to Mrs. Johnston, Doctor Cathcart, and Miss Peggy, and by being assured that I am, with the greatest Respect, Your most humble and obedient Servant.

Jas. Iredell

NB: A letter which accompanies this was brought by Capt. Rightson from Jamaica.

James Iredell to "Dear Sir" [Samuel Johnston], April 7, 1772, in Higginbotham, *Papers of James Iredell,* 1:96.

If uninterested, ladies were not expected to encourage their suitors.

It is thought Mr. Nelson's suit at Point Pleasant will end in matrimony—by his frequent stay there. For as Bevill (In Conscious Lover) says—'A denial is a favor every man may pretend to, and if a Lady would do honor to herself, she should never keep a gentlemen in suspense, if she knows she can't like him.'

As Miss _____ appears to be sweet, innocent young creature, I think she won't seem to encourage what she disapproves, and she is too sensible to trifle away his time without approbation. [...]

Elizabeth Catherine DeRosset to John Burgwin, August 25, 1775, in Battle, *Letters and Documents Relating to the Early History of the Lower Cape Fear,* 23.

However, some marriages were thrust upon young women.

[...] Heard in the Course of the Evening many discharges of Guns on acct. of Horniblow's being married to Nancy Rainbough—Was told she was averse to the Match, & forced to it by her Father & Mother.—Is it true? can such cruel Parents exist?—& too easy, too compliant Daughter with the desires of your Parents in a point they have no right to *command*.—But I hope it is not so.—I please myself with thinking I have reason to believe it is not. Otherwise her lot must be miserable.——The married State to Parties whose Minds are in unison with each other, & whose hearts are connected by the fondest Ties of Affections is the most blissful Situation The Mind of Man can conceive. [...]

This morning after Breakfast went up Town, [...] drank two congratulatory Glasses of Wine & Bitters with Horniblow,—received a kind invitation to dine with him to-morrow which I gladly accepted [...]

Then went to Horniblow's, where there were many Gents. to eat a Wedding Dinner with him. Not much like one tho', as there was no Bride at Table. [...]

> Diary of James Iredell, 1772, in Higginbotham, *Papers of James Iredell*, 1:183-185.

An Abstract of a Letter from a Gentleman in No Carolina to his friend in Maryland dated June the 7th 1762

DR. BETTY

A letter in these times of Bustle without News looses half its merit I cant give you the marches of a Broglio or the remarches of the Rus: These appertain to the Tragic Muse what I relate is Domestic; purely of the comic cast It will not only give action to your Philosophic vein, but to every Gelastic muscle of your Face—Our Old Silenus of the Envigorated age of Seventy Eight who still Damns this Province with his Baneful Influence grew stupidly Enamored with Miss Davis a Lovely Lady of sprightly fifteen of a good Family and some Fortune After much doting parade, Young Miss (for surely parents know best) is persuaded to be a Governor's Lady altho she loved and was beloved by Dear Eighteen Y—g M—r Q—n-ce The day is fixed the nuptial feast provided when Lo! a Discovery is made which surpasses in Villainy the Description of the most envenomed Satyrist It is much above my power I'll humbly therefore attempt the Tale in Common Homespun phrase The Catastrophe was truly Poetic Justice. When the Antedeluvian had agreed, the Old Fellow old in every human characteristic but sense and virtue sends for his Secretary a man of motly cast They form a conveyance of his whole Estate to his son (not even leaving a reversion of his Potatoe Lands near Carrick Fergus) which he enters into and Dispatches a Messenger with it to one of the Supr Court Judges Its proved *secundum Legem* How was this scheme marred! Some secret power blows the matter Some friendly Sylph protects the Lady The Deed's discovered Her friends warm with indignation send for the youth, the Pensive & Dejected Lover — relate the Injury, propose immediately to consummate the marriage Hymen attends Venus & Apollo add Ringlets and ten thousand Charms to adorn the Lovely pair Assist me some poet or assist me Dr Betty with your Fancy They are married! The Leecher waits, 10, 11, 12 past, the Day wakes, Accursed Jealousy takes place, his old Teeth of Enormous length that for many years despised to be clothed with Gums shake in his jaws with Rage He orders his horses to the chariot and feebly in his course would Emulate a Youthful passion he enters her parents house demands the Lady, is conducted into the apartment of Youth Love and Virtue Here I stop! for no pen can describe the Rage and Ridicule

Saunders, *Colonial Records of North Carolina*, 6:737-738.

❧⁊❦

Even though deceased husbands attempted to provide for their wives, single women remained dependent upon men for advice and support as did widow Penelope Dawson, who often called upon her cousin Samuel Johnston for assistance.

Imprs. I Give and Bequeath to my Loving Wife Elizabeth Barclift the use of one third part of the Plantation and Land whereon I now live during her natural Life, together with the use of the outward Room & upper Chamber of my house & also the use of the Lower Room of my Brick house; also I give to my wife the use and Labour of one negro man Called Tom and the use & Labour on one Negro woman Called joan During her natural life; also the use of my large Looking Glass, during her Natural Life; also the use of my desk during her Natural Life; also the use of one Chest; and the use of one Dozon of Chairs; also the use of one large Brass Kittle; also the use of one large iron Kittle, & the use of two iron Pots, she having her Choice; also the use of one yoke of Stears, with yoke, Ring and Staple, and two Ploughs; also the use of all the she Cattle in my Stock that runs on the Plantation whereon I now live; also the use of one Feather Bed & furniture, she having her choice;

also the use of one large black-Walnut Table, & the use of one 15 Bottle-Case; also one 3 Gallon jugg, & one Gallon Ditto; also the use of all my Pewter; also the use of one Black horse, also the use of Six Ewes & Lambs; also the use of 3 Iron Wedges; also the use of one falling ax, also the use of one hilling hoe & two weeding hoes and two Pr. Pot trammels & 2 Pr. Pot-hooks & Gridiron, & ho-cake-hoe; also the use of one Box iron & heaters, & one Tea Kittle, & one Sive and one Search; also two Buckets & two tubs; also one Pr. small Stilliards also one hand-mill being Cullen Stones; also Six Breeding Sows.

Will of John Barclift, in Grimes, comp., *Wills and Inventories*, 25.

Wednesday Morning

Dear Cousin

It gave me particular satisfaction to hear that you were all return'd in good health, may it long be continu'd dear Sir to you and yours, I hope to have the pleasure to hear particularly from you to day. Mr. Pearson upon the strength of hearing me say some time ago that I should like to put Billy to school on this side has engag'd him to Mr. Jacocks who has set up a school within a mile of his house and been very pressing to me to send him, I am very much oblig'd to him but told him I would by no means enter him for more than a quarter till I had seen you nor would I have done it for that had I expected you would have been up so soon. I have some time ago heard an extraordinary character of the man by Mr. Gray Mr. Johnson and several others who knew him, but would chuse to have Billy just where you thought best to put him as I desire to depend entirely on your judgment and friendship, I could not get off of sending him a quarter but shall engage him no farther and if the man will not take him on their terms will not send him at all Unless you should think it best he can now read and spell very well and shall desire he may be put to writing, I hope to have the pleasure to hear you are all well would have wrote to Mrs. Johnston but knew not of this oppertunity till just now, please to make my love and best wishes acceptable to her the girls and dear children and believe me dear Cousin your very affectionate

P. dawson

Penelope Dawson to "Dear Cousin" [Samuel Johnston], [ca. 1773], Hayes Papers.

Widows and women marrying for the first time might protect their property by means of premarriage contracts.

Articles of Agreement Indented made Concluded and Agreed upon the tenth day of February in the twenty sixth Year of the Reign of our Sovereign Lord George the Second King of Great Britain France and Ireland Defender of the Faith and so forth and in the year of our Lord on thousand Seven hundred and fifty three, Between Margaret Haynes Widow and relict of Roger Haynes late of New Hanover County and Province of North Carolina Deceased, of the one part and John Burgywn of Wilmington in the County and Province aforesaid merchant of the other part (that is to say)

In consideration of a Marriage by the Grace of God intented to be Shortly had and Solemnized between the Said John Burgwin of the one part and Margaret Haynes youngest Daughter of the Said Margaret Haynes Widow of the other part and of the sum of five pounds Proclamation money to him the said John Burgwin in hand paid before the Execution and Delivery of these presents by the said Margaret Haynes Widow, the receipt whereof he the said John Burgwin doth hereby acknowledge, He the Said John Burgwin doth for his Heirs Executors and Administrators and for every of them Covenant Promise and Grant to and with the said Margaret Haynes Widow her Executors and Administrators By these presents That he the Said John Burgwin Shall or will by Deed or Deeds Executed in his lifetime as soon as conveniently may be after the said marriage shall take effect well and sufficiently convey Settle and assure in Trust to the Said Margaret Haynes Widow all the Personal Estate belonging and coming to the Said Margaret his Intended Wife for and during the term of her Natural Life To and for her Seperate use benefit and behoof and do that the same shall not be subject to the Dissolution Debt Forfeitures engagements Incumbrances or Contracts of the Said John Burgwin her intended Husband, and after her Decease to the use of the Issue of the said intended Marriage, between them to be begotten to be divided among such Issue in equal portions share and share alike and in case there shall be no Issue or that such Issue shall Die before the age of twenty one years or Marriage that there and in that case the Trustee to whom the said Negroes and other Personal Estate aforesaid shall be so settled in trust as above mentioned shall convey the same to the Survivor of them the said John Burgwin and Margaret his wife and the Heirs Executors Administrators and Assigns of Such Surviving to the only proper use Benefit and Behoof of Such Service his or her Heirs Executors Adms.

and Assigns forever and the Said John Burgwin doth for himself his Heirs Executors Administrators and for every of them Convenant Promise and further Grant that the said John Burgwin will after the said Intended Marriage shall take affect as soon as the said Margaret his Intended Wife shall arrive at the age of twenty one Years and at any time after during the natural life of the said Margaret his intended Wife where required by the Said Margaret Haynes Widow or the said Margaret his intended Wife join with the Said Margaret his intended Wife in Signing Sealing and Executing all such Deed and Deeds as shall by the Said Margaret Haynes Widow or the said Margaret his intended Wife or their or either of their Council Learned in the Law be Devised Advised or Required for the suffisently conveying Settling and assuring all or any of the Lands lying on Prince Georges Creek belonging and coming to the Said Margaret his intended Wife as Coheir with her Sister Mary Haynes to her late Father Roger Haynes deceased to such Trustee or Trustees as the said Margaret Haynes widow or the said Margaret his intended wife shall nominate and appoint in Trust to and for the same uses Interests and purposes in the same manner the Personal Estate is above covenanted to be settled conveyed and assured during and excepting that the same Lands shall be settled to be divided between two of the Children of the Said Marriage at the most In Witness whereof the said parties first above named have hereunto respectively set their hands and Seals the Day and Year first above written.

Margaret Haynes (Seal)
John Burgwin (Seal)

Signed Sealed and Delivered in the presence of
Samuel Swann
Corns. Harnet

 The within articles of agreement were proved on the Oath of Samuel Swann Esquire of the Subscribing Witnesses thereto in due form of Law the 23 Day of September 1756 before,

Peter Henley C.J.

Let it be registered
Registered June 22 1757

> Articles of Agreement between Margaret Haynes and John Burgwyn, February 10, 1753, Deed Book D, 268-269, New Hanover County Deeds.

John Slingsby and I. McAllister In trust to James Murry

This Indenture made the eighteenth day of June in the thirteenth year of the reign of his Majesty King George the third in the year of our Lord one thousand seven hundred and seventy three by and between John Slingsby merchant of the first part. Isabella McAlister Widow Relict of the late Hector McAlister mariner deceased of the second part, and James Murray Esquire of the third part all of these parties residing at present in the town of Wilmington in the County of New Hanover and Province of North Carolina Witnesseth that whereas a marriage by Gods Grace between the said John Slingsby and Issabella McAllister is intended shortly to be solemnized and whereas it doth appear to the said parties equitable and reasonable that the Estate that was acquired by the said Hector McAllister should be set apart and appropriate to the use of his Widow and Children And Whereas the said Issabella McAllister stands seized in fee of part of part of a Lot of Land in Wilmington aforesaid having the tenement in which she dwells by virtue of a Deed from Robert and Mary Beard bearing date the third day of August in the year of our Lord one thousand seven hundred and Seventy two as by the said deed relation being thereunto had may more fully appear. The said Issabella McAllister in Contemplation of the said Marriage and for the reasons before suggested Hath by and with the consent and approbation of the said Slingsby given granted and conveyd and doth by these presents give grant and convey unto the said James Murray his heirs and Assigns all that piece of a Lot of Land before mentioned together with the houses and appurtenances thereof and thereon To have and to hold the Premises to the said James Murray his heirs and Assigns to and for the use and trust herein after mentioned that is to say in trust for the use and behoof of the said John Slingsby and Issabella his intended wife during their joint lives for the use and behoof of the said Issabella during her natural life if she shall survive the said John and for the use and behoof of the said John in case he shall survive the said Issabella until John McAlister son of the said Issabella shall attain the age of twenty one years and failing of the said John McAlister before he shall attain the age aforesaid then and in that case the said John Slingsby by surviving his said intended wife to have and enjoy the premises until Margaret McAlister daughter of the said Isabella shall attain the age of twenty one years it being the intent and meaning of the parties to these said Events that the use of the premises shall after the said Isabella's Death be vested in the said infant John McAllister on his attaining after Isabella's decease the age of twenty one years or at the determination of the said Isabella's life if that period shall happen after the said Jno. shall attain the said age and that in like manner the infant Margt. McAlister shall in case of the death of her brother John McAlister during his infancy succeed to and be invested in the fee of the premises and this trust shall then cease and determine And whereas the said Isabella McAlister is possessed of a Negroe girl named Celia of a Negroe woman named Peggy and her two Children named Ned and Jeany the said Isabella doth by consent of the said John Slingsby assign and deliver the said Negroes to the said James Murray his executors administrators and Assigns in trust for the use and purposes herein after mentioned that is to say the Negroe girl named Celia and her increase whatever that may be for the use of the said John Slingsby and the said Isabella and the survivor of them and the said Negroe Peggy her children Ned and Jeany and whatever other children she may or shall have to the said John Slingsby and his intended spouse Isabella until the said Margaret McAllister shall attain the age of twenty one years or arrive at the day of marriage then at the first of these terms the said Negroe Peggy and all her children then alive shall be deliverd to the said Margaret McAlister but in case of the death of the said Margaret before either of the said terms the said Negroe Peggy and her children shall remain to the use of the said John and Isabella and to the survivors of them and after the death of the said survivor shall be deliverd by the said Trustee or his assigns to the said Jno. McAlister provided nevertheless that it shall and may be lawfull for the said Trustee or his assigns with the consent of the said John Slingsby and Isabella or the survivor of them to sell and dispose of any of the said Negroes which they shall think proper to be sold and to put other of at least equal value in the room and for the same use of the sold and further the said John Slingsby and Isabella has intended wife promise covenant and agree to and with the said James Murray his heirs and Assigns that they the said John and Isabella shall and will when required, by the said James his heirs and assigns execute and deliver any other or further deed that shall be thought requisite or necessary for due execution of these articles according to the true intent and meaning thereof and the said James Murray for himself his heirs his Executors his administrators and assigns doth covenant agree and promise to and with the said John Slingsby And the said Isabella for herself and in behalf of her said Children Margaret and John McAlister that the trust hereby reposed shall be well and faithfully executed by him the said James his heirs or assigns In witness whereof the parties to these presents have hereunto set their Hands and Seals the day and year first above written.

Sealed and deliverd and the within named Negroe Celia for the whole Negroes delivered to the trustee in presence of
Margaret Murray
Jean Dubois

Ja. Murray (Seal)
Isabella McAlister (Seal)
John Slingsby (Seal)

The execution of the within deed by the within parties James Murray Isabella McAlister and John Slingsby were proved by the oath of Mrs. Jean Dubois one of the subscribing witnesses thereto. Let it be Recorded.

Sam. Ashe I.S.C.L.E.

Decr. 15th 1786

> Indenture between John Slingsby, Isabella McAlister, and James Murray, June 18, 1773, Deed Book H, 385-386, New Hanover County Deeds.

∽ঌ৯෯

Contracts, however, offered little protection against dissolute, abusive, and dangerous husbands.

[...] A mile farther up, on the same bank of the Cape Fear River, is the home and estate of the American General Howe. While he amuses himself in dissipation elsewhere, his unfortunate family lives here; the wife has the manner of a divorcée [...]

> Miranda, *The New Democracy in America*, 14.

Upon Mocon of Henry Overstreet by Tho. Jones his atty. setting forth that John Hurrell one of the Justices of the Court did lately Cause him the said Overstreet to be bound to a Large Sum to be of the peace towards Ann his wife for 12 Months with Bond not being returnd to this Court. It is ordered That the said Justice do return the said Bond to the next Court [...]

> Minutes of the Bertie County Court of Pleas and Quarter Sessions, November 1733, State Archives.

Mr. Joseph Hardy Coroner of this County moved the Court for Leave to sell the Personal Estate of John Jones who was Lately Executed for the Murder of his wife. Granted and ordered that the same be sold at Publick Vendue on the Third Thursday in August next at the Now Dwelling House of Benjamin Stone and make Return thereof to this Court at next.

> Minutes of the Bertie County Court of Pleas and Quarter Sessions, July 1758, State Archives.

⊶⊷

Although North Carolina had no general divorce law until the nineteenth century, unhappy couples separated, either by elopement, by mutual agreement, or, formally, by legislative enactment.

NOTICE is hereby given, to all persons whom it may concern, that my supposed wife, *Priscilla Hatcher*, by maiden name, and now goes by the name of *Priscilla Johnson*, as by a marriage name; the said unlawful woman has absented herself from her supposed husband's lawful commands—I the subscriber hereby forewarn all persons, under no pretence, to rely on me by the said above-mentioned woman. Contracts by accounts, deeds, notes, bonds, or orders, wrote or verbal, nor no contracts of conveyance whatever to come against me by the said woman.

MATTHEW JOHNSON.

Wilmington, Nov. 19.

> *Wilmington Centinel, and General Advertiser*, November 19, 1788.

To all to whom these Presents may come.

KNOW YE, that whereas I *Mary McGehe*, Wife of *Joseph McGehe*, of the County of *Bute*, in the Province of *North-Carolina*, being dissatisfied with my said Husband, and having eloped from his Bed for upwards of eight Months past, in which Time I have been gotten with Child by another Man, other than my said Husband, with which I acknowledge to be now pregnant, and being fully determined not to live with him more during my Life, nor at any Time hereafter to cohabit with him the said *Joseph McGehe*; and, in Consideration of the said *Joseph McGehe* delivering into my Possession, for my Use, one Hundred and Twenty Pounds Value in Effects, Part of his Estate, which I hereby acknowledge to have received, and am therewith fully satisfied, in full of the rateable Part of his Estate; and in Consequence said Estate being so delivered.

I do hereby covenant and agree with him the said *Joseph McGehe*, that I never will at any Time hereafter, directly or indirectly, presume to depend on him as my Husband; nor will I ever hereafter ask, demand, look to, or receive from him the said *Joseph*, any further Monies, Goods, Wares, Chattles or Estate, of any Kind whatsoever, but from this Day forward look on myself as divorced from him, and no longer his Wife, nor dependant on him in any Manner of Form whatsoever, for any further Livelihood or Sustenance of any Kind. And the said *Joseph*, on his Part, doth acknowledge and agree, that the said *Mary*, may and shall have the full Use and Occupation of the above-mentioned Effects, without any Hindrance or Molestation of any Kind by him, or any Person claiming by, from, or under him, but that she shall or may use, sell, and dispose of the said Effects as absolutely, to all Intents and Purposes, as she could or might do if she was his Wife, nor had never been married. And I do further agree, that I will never hereafter claim the said *Mary* as my Wife, but that she may from this Day forward be at large, and at Liberty to go to any Place or Part of the World she pleases, or any Choice, without Hinderance or Molestation. And further, the true Intent and Meaning of these Presents are, that we the said *Joseph* and *Mary*, have this Day most solemnly agreed before God and the World, to be no longer Man and Wife, but for ever hereafter be as if we had never been married, nor joined together as Man and Wife; but will live separate without Aid or Assistance of each other, from this Day forward to the End of our Lives. In Witness whereof, we have hereunto set our Hands and Seals, this 29th Day of *August*, 1769.

JOSEPH McGEHE
MARY McGEHE

Signed and acknowledged in the Presence of
ROBERT GOODLOE,
THOMAS JACKSON.

North-Carolina Gazette (New Bern), April 7, 1775.

Mr. Charlton presented the petition of Solomon Ewell complaining of the elopement of his Wife Lydia and her living in adultery with one Samuel Colten of Northampton County, and praying an Act may pass to dissolve the Marriage of the said Solomon and Lydia; and moved that a Committee be appointed to examine into the truth of the several allegations in the said petition contained, which was objected to; on which the motion was made and question put, if the said Committee be appointed or not and carried in the affirmative, and Mr Fanning, Mr

Charlton, Mr Dawson, Mr Bradford, and Mr Harris are appointed a Committee agreeable to the said motion; and that they have power to send for persons and papers, and report their proceedings thereon to the next Session of Assembly,

> Journal of the lower house of assembly, November 8, 1766, in Saunders, *Colonial Records*, 7:352.

ܗܘ܀

Marriage brought the expectation of children.

[...] The married women maintain a monastic seclusion and a submission to their husbands such as I have never seen; they dress with neatness and their entire lives are domestic. Once married, they separate themselves from all intimate friendships and devote themselves completely to the care of home and family. During the first year of marriage they play the role of lovers, the second year of breeders, and thereafter of housekeepers.[...]

> Miranda, *The New Democracy in America*, 5-6. Miranda made these observations in New Bern in June, 1783.

ܗܘ܀

Pregnancy, however, and the rigors of childbirth understandably found women apprehensive.

Mrs. Miller when at the Marsh settled with Miss McCulloch and Harry Montfort upon a Jaunt to Edenton and Perquimons they have been gone a fortnight I expect them home in a few days, she is now confirmed of her Pregnancy, which made a great deal of Alteration in her Spirits, before she went from here.

> Andrew Miller to "Dear Sir" [Thomas Burke], November 20, 1772, Thomas Burke Papers, Correspondence, State Archives.

[...] I Received your favor of the 10th Instant by Mr. Mainair Shall be glad to see you and Mrs. Burke here by the time you mention, When I hope Mrs. Miller will be in the Straw, and restored to her former Temper, which is what she Seldom has during the Months of Pregnancy.

Andrew Miller to "Dear Sir" [Thomas Burke], February 22, 1773, Thomas Burke Papers, Correspondence, State Archives.

❧❧

Such fears were not unfounded, for many women lost children and their own lives in childbirth or its complications.

JAMES MURRAY TO MRS. BENNET.

CAPE FEAR, MARCH 25th, 1758.

DEAR MADAM,—...The Waters continued on our low grounds part of July & August with little Intervals, and at going off in September the Vapours from the Swamps made the Inhabitants near the low Grounds very sickly. Hence Mrs Murray's and my Daughter Jeany's sickness begun. We went to the Sound near the Sea in October, & they recovered so fast that she was impatient to be home that I might be disengaged to look after my business; but no sooner came we home than she relapsed into her intermittent fevers, attended with Swellings. We went back to the Sound in Novr, but not with equal benefit....At length on the 17th of February Mrs Murray was deliverd of a Daughter in the 8th Month, and died on the 19th. The young child lived only a fortnight after her, and Jeany died on the 23d of this Month. I am

Your dutiful & Affecte Son

Tiffany, *Letters of James Murray*, 96.

It was particularly cruel of them, to use me so at this time, as in last novr it pleased Divine Providence to afflict me with the heavy loss of my most amiable wife, who died in childbed; the child also dying at the same time; I have just now no less than £21.9 s. to pay to Doctors bills, besides all other concomitants of that disastrous & melancholy occasion. And am left a poor distress'd widower, with a child, which was but a twelve month old, at my late Dear wife's decease.

Rev. John Macdowell to the Secretary of the SPG, April 16, 1761, in Saunders, *Colonial Records*, 6:553.

❧❧

The loss of wives left men like James Murray in the Lower Cape Fear and Samuel Johnston, Sr., in Onslow County, to cope with the burden

of raising surviving children, which no doubt hastened the advent of remarriage.

[...] I bring up my Girles, and am often olidged to be from home, To whose care shall I leave them in this heathenish place, no woman to look after them, must not John Mind them, I or they may be sick, who is to mind my affairs then [...]

Samuel Johnston, Sr., to "Dear Sam," April 6, 1755, Hayes Papers.

JAMES MURRAY TO DOROTHY MURRAY

CAPE FEAR, MARCH 21, 1758.

MY DEAR DOLLY,

Your Letter to your Mama of the 20th Feb came to my hand a few days since with the worked chair, both of which would have given her great pleasure, but she is gone to enjoy pleasures infinitely greater. This Loss, both you & I have Reason to thank God, will be well made up to you in an Aunt whose Affection has been always more like a Mamas than an aunt's; and as to the two younger Children, if they Survive, 't is probable I may get them tollerably well taken care of 'till you come up to be a Mother to them. If you answer my expectations, you may rest assured I shall be as good a father as you can desire. Such a one the Children of the best of Wives deserves, and shall glory in denying my self the enjoyments of a world I am shortly to leave in purpose that you may the better enjoy a world you are soon to come into. Have therefore no anxiety or Suspicion about my Conduct, but be careful of your own. [...]

JAMES MURRAY TO BARBARA CLARK.

CAPE FEAR, April 1st, 1758.

SISTER CLARK,—... thus it has pleased God in a very Short time to make a wide breach in my Family. May I learn from it to be more resign'd & to be faithful & Diligent in my part while I am left behind....

As to advice about your moving & the Children's Education & putting them to business, I am greatly at a Loss. Were it not for the uncertainty of the Times I should be glad to have you here with Tommy, since he inclines to be a planter. It will disappoint my Hopes to see him something of more importance than a meer Planter, but since it has pleased God to disable me to prosecute that Scheme as I intended and to reduce me to this Solitary Condition, his being here will be a present ease & help to me without, and your care will be no less necessary within doors, for I do not propose to take Dolly from her Aunt at Boston these two years. Jacky cannot be placed better than with his Uncle John to be brought up in his way, but his Education must be finished so as to make him fit for the business either there or thereabout if you come away. I have no Objections to James's being a Merchant, only let him be with one that is realy such and who is exact and regular in Method, and this on as easy Terms as may be. I suppose you'll bring Anny with you. I still think she ought to be bred under her Aunt at Boston, tho' I have heard nothing in approbation of what I formerly proposed about that either from you or them. If it should succeed, she must stay till Dolly comes away, that we may not be too burdensome.

Tiffany, *Letters of James Murray*, 96, 98-99.

&⁊&

Parents evidenced great affection for their children.

I am Sorry you took my last to you so much to heart, you Cant know the Bowels of one affectionate parent. Jno. has since cleard up that affair some and if it had been as I imagined I would have given way, I am apt to take things too Warmly at first. [...]

S[amuel] J[ohnston], [Sr.], to "Dear Sam" [Samuel Johnston, Jr.], June 2, 1755, Hayes Papers.

Yours of the 1st of Decr. last I received, the first paragraph made me uneasy, because I fancied it proceeded from insinuations of Mr. Rutherfords as if I was Angry with you, I never said so to him, tho Indeed I was not a litle, how long could that Continue with a fond father towards a beloved child, and indeed I have loved you since first I had you in my arms, with a fatherly affection, tho I have not been able to do so much for you as my inclinations led me to. [...]

Samuel Johnston [Sr.], to "Dear Sam," January 29, 1757, Hayes Papers.

Hillsborough Decr. 23d 1781

Dear Sir

Within a few weeks, perhaps days, I shall bid adieu to existence, to a life the latter stage of which has been marked with multiplied disapointments and exqusite misfortune. Nature is now almost exhausted by long and painful disease, and I should have little cause to regret its final period were it not to Seperate me from a child whose tender years and unformed mind demand the care of protection and of age and experience.

You have often seen my daughter Nancy and with pleasure have borne testimony to the strong resemblance of her features and appearance, to those of her deceased father. Pardon a Mother's fondness! That softness of manners and sweetness of disposition so conspicuous in her father, are not wanting in her and are an earnest for the most promising hopes.

She is the tender pledge of the mutual and sincere love to which she owed her birth, by which I attached myself to her dear father your intimate friend, General Nash called her his with all the warmth of paternal love and had he not been snatched so suddenly from the world I should not at this critical moment have sought protection for her from a family to which she can boast no connection but that of humanity and general benevolence. Yet she has still a stronger claim. Her father was your bosom friend. Where can I apply? To whom address my dying request? To you, Dear Sir, and to your worthy lady I implore permission to commit her.

She is young, but yet she may be useful in your family and in a great measure ease Mrs. Williams of the burthen of her domestick concerns, I have taught her industry by the habitual practice of it and inculcated upon her that upon this and upon the most rigid attention to a purity of character must depend her future happiness in life. My misfortune with one whose mind is enlarged as yours can never be imputed to her, and it will not restrain the offices of tenderness and friendship that the forms of the church did not give Sanction to the Union of her parents. Was it a Sin? My Sufferings have amply attoned for it and my death should wipe it away for ever. To her it can never be imputed. She surely is innocent as Heaven.

Farewell! The curtain will soon drop betwixt us for ever. Should it be the employment of departed Spirits to contemplate their connections left behind, It will minister to my joy to see my daughter sheltered under the guardian care of your worthy Lady and your self.

Again Adieu, May every blessing attend you and yours, May your lives be long and happy and their period without pain is the sincere prayer of your dying friend.

Ruthey Jackson

[*Addressed:*]

To The Honorable
John Williams Esqr.
Williamsboro'

> Ruthey Jackson to "Dear Sir" [John Williams], December 23, 1781,
> John Williams Papers, State Archives.

Mrs. Moore, Receiv'd us Very kindly, tho' Sorrowfully, being in Transports of Grief, for the Death of her Son, the news of which, had reach'd her, but Two days before our arrival, and the Sight of her Daughter and Little Granddaughter still Increased (if possible) her Distress, her Tender heart seem'd to be ready to burst, with Grief, not a Tear could she call to her relief, She mourned Excessively, Said all this worlds comforts were taken from her. She chose Death rather than Life, and refused To be comforted. Shee kept her chamber about a week, almost without Taking any of the necessary supports of Life but now She seems to be better composed, begins to walk about house and Take some notice of her Domesticl Affairs, which seem to Depend Very much upon her Superintendence: [...]

> John Whiting to Ezra Stiles, June 28, 1759, typescript, Frederick Nash
> Collection, State Archives.

ঔঙ্ঠ

Among the less fortunate children were the illegitimate.

Upon Petition of Susanna Bruton Setting forth etc. That she had had a Bastard by Wm. Drake who gave Suretys to observe the further Directions of this Court for the Maintainance of the said Child and having faild she has kept it 2 year and 3 Mo. and prays Relief etc.

It is thereupon Considered and ordered That the said Wm. Drake pay unto the said Susanna Bruton The Sum of Twenty five pounds and Cost als Execution   Issued Execution.

> Minutes of the Bertie County Court of Pleas and Quarter Sessions,
> August 1736, State Archives.

Upon Petition of Christna Rasberry shewing that She was Lately Delivd of a Bastard Child of which Nathl. Nichollas was the father that he has Entered into Bond to abide the order of this Court for the Maintance of the said Child and that he has as yet faild in Contribution any assistance towards Maintaining the said Child praying the Courts

Consideration [*illegible*] Who on Mature delibration Doth Order that the said Nathl. Nichollas pay to the said Christainna Rasberry or Order the sum of Six pounds for the first Month and [1]0/ per Month afterwards Inclusive from the 16th day of Nov. last for one whole year Suceding this Day.

Minutes of the Bertie County Court of Pleas and Quarter Sessions, May 1741, State Archives.

Robert Butler being brought regularly before the Court for being the father of a bastard Child begot by him on the body of Elizabeth Denby Ordered that he pay to the said Elizabeth Denby Eight pounds proclamation for the trouble and Expence she has already been at in raising the said Child Immediately down or give good Security for the same to be paid on sight of this Order, and also to give good Security for the payment of five pounds proclamation to the said Elizabeth for the said Childs Maintenance the Ensuing Year as also Security to Indemnify the parish According to Law, Whereupon Lodwick Alford his Security Came into Court and undertook to pay the money mentioned in the said Order and also to Indemnify the said parish Agreeable to the said Order.

Minutes of the Bute County Court of Pleas and Quarter Sessions, May 1772, State Archives.

ॐ

On occasion mothers resorted to infanticide to conceal their indiscretion.

Granville County sc.

The deposition of Samuel Henderson Esqr taken this 4th day of March 1746 before us James Paine John Martin and Gideon Macon Esqrs. etc. against Elizabeth Searcey who was taken and brought before us upon Suspicion of her having willfully murdered a Female Child born of the Body of the said Elizabeth this Deponant being first Sworn on the Holy Evangelists Saith that upon the Twelfth day of January last intimation was given to the Deponant that the said Elizabeth had been Delivered of a Bastard Child and had murdered it upon which this Deponant Sent a Constable, to take the said Elizabeth Sarcey into Custody which was done. That upon Examination the said Elizabeth

Confessed she had been Delivered of a Child which was born alive and that the Same had Perished for want of assistance, that the said Elizabeth went with this Deponant into the woods about half amile from her fathers House and Shewed the said Child to him which this Deponant found wrapped up in a Coat and Some Leaves by the side of a Logg Near the side of a Pond that there appeared no Symtoms of Violence upon any part of the said Child that the Navel String of the said Child was tied and the back part of the head of the said Child Seemed to have been stroaked with a hand That Edward Moors wife washed the said Child and told the said Deponant that the Navel String was tied well That the said Elizabeth Shewed this Deponant a forehead Cloath and a Long Stay for a Child as the women Present called them and the said Elizabeth told this Deponant that She had made'em the Saturday night before her Delivery which happened upon the day after, and further this Deponant Saith.

Saml. Henderson

Jas. Paine
Jno. Martin
Gideon Macon

> Deposition of Samuel Henderson, March 4, 1746, Granville County, Bastardy Bonds and Records, State Archives.

Att a Generall Court of Oyer and Terminer held for the said Province at the Generall Court house at Queen Ann's Creek in Chowan Precinct the 31st. March 1720 and Continued by Adjournment to the 2nd. day of Aprll. Following. Present Frederick Jones Esqr. Ch. Justice, Jno. Blount, Jno. Palin, Jams. Beazley, Thos. Pollock Esqr. Esqrs. Justices.

The Grand Jury are Impannelled and Sworn. Thos. Betterley Foreman, Thos. Rountree, Henry Clayton, Edwd. Wingate, Thos. Blitchendon, Jno. Jordan Jams. Williamson, Wm. Downing, Jno. Williams Thos. Jernegan, Isaac Hill, Jno. Worsland Lazs. Thomas Edwd. Howcott, Martin Frank, Samll. Pagett, Thos. Garrett Thos. Hoskins, Thos. Matthews, Robt. Lanier, Thos. Masters.

Upon the Return of the Grand Jury they Present the following Indictments.

<*Dominus Rex v. Colliar.*> To the Honorable Frederick Jones Esqr. Ch. Justice and to the rest of the Justices for holding the Generall Court of North Carolina.

The Jurors for our Sovereign Lord the King Present Magdalen <30> Collar alias Dictus Collard alias Colliar of the Precinct of Chowan in the County of Albemarle in the Province aforesaid with Malice Prepenced by force and Armes and against the Peace of our Sovereign Lord the King that now is she did Murder and privately bury and Conceal the Death of a Bastard Child which she brought forth and was Delivered of.

For that the said Magdalin Collar Alias Dictus Collard Alias Colliar on the four and twentyeth day of Novbr. 1719 at night was Privately Delivered of a Bastard Child born alive and the next morning being the five and twentieth day of Novr. aforesaid did bury the said Child by force and Armes etc. Against the Peace etc. and against the Royall Crown and Dignity and against the Laws and Statutes in Such behalf made and Provided etc.

Danll. Richardson pro Domino Rege.

Billa Vera
Thos. Betterley Foreman

<Plea.> To which Indictment the said Magdalin Colliar being Call'd Appear'd in Custody at the Barr and Pleaded Not Guilty. And for Tryall putt herself upon the Country. Which is referr'd till tomorrow morning.

Fryday Aprill the 1st. 1720. Mett according to Adjournment. Present as before.

Read the Indictment found by the Grand Jury Yesterday against Magdalin Colliar to which She had pleaded and being call'd Appear'd in Custody at the Barr. Then it was Commanded the Marshall that he should cause to Come Twelve etc. by whom etc. who neither etc. And there came Henry Speller, Henry Bonner, Patrick Maule, Thos. Luten, Junr. Thos. Paris, Fras. Branch, Wm. Bonnor, Wm. Haughton, Lewis Skinner, Wm. Havett Jno. Falconar and Thos. Yates who to Speak the truth of and upon the Premises Chosen Tryed and Sworn Say upon their Oaths.

<Verdict.> That she is Guilty of the Murder by which she Stands Indicted.

<Judgement.> Judgement to be hang'd.

Minutes of the General Court, April 2, 1720, in Price, *North Carolina Higher-Court Minutes, 1709-1723*, 212-213.

Surviving illegitimates and poor orphans awaited apprenticeship, in which case they might face masters who abused them or who sought to retain their services beyond their time of indenture.

[...] And that where such Estate shall be of so small value that no person will Educate or Maintain him or her for the Profits thereof, Such Orphan shall by direction of the Court be bound apprentice, every male to some Tradesman, Merchant, Mariner, or other person, approved by the Court, until he shall attain the Age of Twenty-one Years, and every Female to some Suitable Employment, till her Age of Eighteen Years, and the Master or Mistress of every Such Servant shall find and provide for him or her Diet, Cloaths, Lodging, and Accommodations fit and necessary, and shall Teach, or Cause him or her to be Taught, to read and write, and at the Expiration of his or her Apprenticeship shall pay every such Servant the like allowance as is by law Appointed for Servants by Indenture or Custom, and on refusal shall be compelled thereto in like manner; And if upon Complaint made to the County Court it shall appear that any such Apprentice is ill used, or not Taught the Trade, Profession, or Employment to which he or she was bound, it shall be lawful for such Court to remove and Bind him or her to such other person or persons as they shall think fit.

Laws, 1755, in Clark, *State Records*, 25:323.

Ordered by the Court That John Haiden a Bastard Child of Margaret Headen be bound to peter Hendley till he arrive at the Age of Twenty one, being 6 years old on the first June next to Learn the Trade of a Tinker and Pewterer, Said Master complying with the Act of Assembly.

Ordered by the Court That Bennet Headen a Bastard Child of Margaret Headen be bound to peter Henley 'till he arrive at the age of 21 Years being 4 Years old the first day of November last, said Master to learn him the Trade of a Tinker and Pewterer, and Complying with the Act of Assembly.

Ordered by the Court That Hannah Headen A Bastard Child of Margaret Headen be bound unto peter Hendley, until she arrive at the Age of 18 years, she being now about 8 Years old, about the first day of October last, said Master complying with the Act of Assembly. [...]

Minutes of the Rowan County Court of Pleas and Quarter Sessions, February 1775, State Archives.

Jacob Tayler brought in to Court an Infant Boy named James Beasley Son of Oxford Beasley and prayes to have him Bound unto himself on mature Consideration the Court agreed the said Infant should be bound unto the said Jacob Tayler till he be at the age of twenty one years and to teach the said Infant boy the art or mistery of a Cordwainer and Tanner and to learn him to Read the Bible in the English tongue and to write a Ledgable hand and, to find the Said apprentice Sufficient meat Drink washing and Lodging and to give his Said apprentice two Suites of apparel from top to toe at the Expiration of the said term. Ordr the Clark make out an Indenture for that purpose.

> Minutes of the Craven County Court of Pleas and Quarter Sessions, June 1741, State Archives.

[...] John Smith Apprentice to *John Murphy* Complained to this Court that his Master John Murphy misused him <*and hath not Taught or endeavoured to teach him his trade which he was Bound to Learn*> and Desired to be Discharged from said Murphy, the Court having taken the same into Consideration and Hearing their Aligations <*and Evidences on both Sides*> have thought fit to Discharge the said Apprentice from his said Master. [...]

> Minutes of the Craven County Court of Pleas and Quarter Sessions, February 1753, State Archives.

On Motion of Mr. Cumming ordered that Francis Butler be discharged from an Indenture of apprenticeship from Abel Miller the said Francis having shewn the Court by undoubted testimony that he is above the age of twenty one years it is likewise Ordered that the said Abell Miller do deliver imediately the said Francis Butler his Freedom due Court order issued [...]

> Minutes of the Chowan County Court of Pleas and Quarter Sessions, October 1763, State Archives.

᪣᪐᪣

Sufficiently wealthy orphans became wards of guardians. Depending upon the amount of their inheritance, some orphans enjoyed many advantages. At the same time some guardians were reluctant to release the assets of their wards when the children reached their age of legal majority.

III. And be it further Enacted by the Authority aforesaid, That the Superior Courts and Inferior Courts of Pleas and Quarter Sessions of this Province, within their respective Jurisdictions, have and shall have full power and authority, from time to time to take Cognizance of all matters concerning Orphans and their Estates, and to appoint Guardians in such Cases where to them it shall appear necessary [...]

V. And be it further Enacted by the Authority aforesaid, That when a Guardian shall be appointed to an Orphan by any Superior or Inferior Court Such Guardian shall at the next Court after his appointment exhibit an account upon oath of all the Estate of such Orphan which he or she shall have received into his or her hands or possession. And every Guardian heretofore or hereafter to be by any such Court appointed, shall annually exhibit his account and state of the profits and disbursements of the Estate of such Orphans upon Oath, and such Accounts so to be exhibited shall be entered by the Clerk in particular Books to be provided and kept for that purpose only, [...]

Laws, 1760, in Clark, *State Records*, 25:416, 417.

The Estate of Paulina Hall Orphan To John Thompson

		Dr.
1767		
Feby. 29 1 Cloak 27/ 10 yds. Linnen at 4/8		£3.13.08
2 yds. Linnen at 7/6 6 yds. Musline 7/6		3.
2 ¼ yds. Humtrums 12/6		1. 8.1 ½
1 paper Pins 10d. 1 Testament 1/8.		2. 6
2 yds. linnen at 3/6 1 oz. thread 1/8	. 8.8	
1 pr. Shoes	. 6. 3	8.19.2½
Feby. 4. 9 ½ yds. Cloth 3/1½	1. 3.1 ½	
3 ¾ yds. Musline 7/6	. 5. 7 ½	1. 8. 9
13. To Doctor Schulrer for Medcins and attendance		.13. 9
23. ½ yd. Musline 7/6		. 3. 9
1 ⅛ yds. Lawn 17/	1. 5. 4½	1.17.1½
March 2. 3 Handn. at 3/9		.11. 3
1 pr. Callo. Shoes	.12. 6	1. 3. 9
21. Cash paid Miss Geddy for making a Sack		.11. 3
April 8. 4 yds. Linnen at 3/4 3 ½ Yds. Check 3/4		1. 5.
May 10. 2 yds. Callies /fine/ 8/		.16.

21. 1 pr. Shoes   .10.
27. 1 paper Pins   . 1.
30. 1 pair Leather Shoes   . 7. 6
31. ½ yd. Gauze and 2 yds. Ribon   . 5. 6
2 ½ yds. Ribon 3/9. 1 pr. Gloves 3/11   . 7. 1
    Carried Over   £17.15.11
    Brought Over   £17.15.11
June 1. 1 yd. Check 3/4 1 Fawn 3/9   . 7. 1
23. 2 ¼ yds. Ribon 2/   . 4. 6
July 9. 1 Necklace 4/8 1 pr. Leather Shoes 7/6   .12. 2
23. 1 pr. Stays 22/ 2 yds. Ribon at 2/ 1 Box
15d.   1. 7. 3
Augt. 12. 1 yd. Linnen 3/9. 1 oz. thread 20d.
1 pr. Callo. Shoes 10/   .15. 5
18. 1 ½ yds. Holld. at 8/ 7 ¼ yds. Cloath
18/1d.   1.10. 1½
21. 1 ¼ yds. Gauze 7/   . 8. 9
2 Gauze Handrs. 6/4   .12. 8   1. 5. 5
24. Soling and healtoping 1 pair Shoes   . 2. 6
30. 2 Hanks Silk 1/   . 2.
Novr. 7. 1 pr. Garters 1/2 Hair Pins at 1/8
2 prs. Pins at 10d.   . 6.
Decr. 1. 11 ¼ yds. Cloth   1.12. 6
2. 1 pr Shoes 10/ 2 yds. Linnen at 3/   .16.
28. 3 yds. Ribon 20d.   . 5.
1 pair Shoes and 1 pair Gloves   .15. 6
2 pair Stockings at 8/4   .16. 8
1 Hair Pin 2/8 4 yds. Ribon at 4d.   . 4.
Paid Mr. Burgess for 1/4 years Schooling   .12. 6
    29. 6. 6½

1768 Jay. 1. To Ballance   19. 3.5½
Cr.   48.10.
By the Hire of one Negro named Napper   15. 0.0
By do. of one do. Named Dick   12.13.0
By do. of one do. Named Moll   8.10
By do. of one do. Named Dilot   4. 7
By do. of one do. Named Iris   8.   48.10. 0
Edgcombe County ss. January Court 1768
    Exhibited on Oath and Ordered to be Recorded.
        Test. Jas. Hassell

<50> Dr. The Estate of Paulina Hall in Ac:t with John and Peter
    Thompson For

1768. January 15. 2 yards fine Muslin 10/	1. .	
1 Egrit 4/8. 3 ½ yds. Ribon 20d.	.10. 6	
Expence's setling the Acct. of Guardianship	1. 8. 8	
23. 1 Rugg for Moll	12. 6	
		2.19. 2
1 doz. Needles	. . 5	12.11
February 1. 4 yds. fine Durants 5/4		1. 1. 4
1 yd. Shalloon 4/. 1 pr. Tape 1/8	. 5. 8	
8 hanks of Silk 1/	. 8.	
		1.15
16 nm Pins 1 doz. needles 3 hanks silk		. 4. 4
March 8. 4 yd. of Holland at 6/3 10 yds.		
Do. at 5/4	3.18. 4	
1 ounce of fine thread 1 yd. Camborck	1.10. 4	
1 pr. Sizars 1/3 1 pr. Gloves 4/8	. 5.11	
2 yds. Hollond 9/4d.	.18. 9	
		6.13. 4
18. 12 yds. Strip'd Lutstring 12/6	7.10.	
2 ps. Chints	3.12. 6	
1 yd. Linen 4/8. 1 yd. Ditto 3/4	. 8.	
1 yd. fine durants. 5/4 1 pr. tape 3/	. 8. 4	
30 yds. ferriting 13/1 4 hanks Silk 4/	.17. 1	
Paid Molly Cary for Makin Sundry Cloths	.15. 8	
		13.11. 7
May 13. 2 pr. fine thread hoes	.18. 8	
1 onz. thread 2/6 ¾ yd. Linen 3/4	. 5.	
1 pr. Callo. Shoes 10/. Cash pd. for Sundrys 10/	1.	
		2. 3. 8
June 1. ½ yd. Cos. Hollond 1 pr. Gloves 3/	4. 8	
1 pr. Callo. Shoes 10/. nm Pins 16d.	.11. 4	
nm ditto 1/. 1 combe 1/	. 2.	
1 Sattin hatt 18/9 2 thimbles 10d.	.19. 7	
1 hand of Silk 1/. 2 yds. Ribon 20d.	. 4. 4	
1 yd. Ribon	. 1. 8	
		2. 3. 7
July 6. 1 pr. Mitts 3/12 2 yds. Ribon	. 7. 12	
1 onz. of thread	. 2. 8	
		. 9.9½
11 yds. Ribon	.16.10½	

2 pr. Sizars	. 3. 1	
8 yds. Ribon	. 8. 4	
		1. 8. 3½
16. 1 pr. Shoes 10/. 1 pr. Gloves 4/81/4	.14. 8¼	.14. 8¼
20. 1 Bible 5/. 1 Spelling Book 2/	. 7.	
nm pins 1/3 Cash pd. for Sundrys 2/6	. 3. 9	
		.10. 9
Septr. 17. ½ yd. linen 2/6 1 Trunk 10/	.12. 6	
nm pins. 1 hank silk	. 2. 3	
		.14. 9
Carried Over [...]		£34. 2. 3¼
		Cr.

1768. Januy. 1. By Ballance due at last		
Settlement	19. 4. 2½	
with Interest from this date till the 1st of		
Jary. 1769	1. 3. ½	
1769. Janry. 1. By Thos. HazHall for 1		
years hire of Dick	16. 5.	
By Jos. Long for 1 years hire of Napper	15.	
By John Millikin for 1 years hire of Iris and		
Vilot	8.17	
By Messrs. Young Miller and Co. for 1 years		
hire of Moll	10.	
		70. 9. 3
		£70. 9. 3
Debt Brought Over		£34. 2. 3¼
1768. Sepr. 22. 1 pr. fine Worsted Hose	11. 3	
1 yd. Linen 3/4 ½ yd. Do. 1/3	. 4. 7	
1 onz. fine thread 2/6. 1 ps. tape 1/1	. 3. 6	
2 hanks silk 1/	. 2.	
1 ps. Chints	6.17. 6	
		7.18.10
Octobr. 3. 1 nm Pins 2/1 1 yd. ferret 6d. 2 yds	.	
Silk gause at 7/6	.17. 7	
1 ps. tape 1/7. 1 pr. gloves 3/9 4 ½ yds.		
Ribon 6/7	.11.11	
paid for makeing a Gown	. 9. 6	
	1.19.	
14. 1 Capucheen 50/ ½ yd. Persian 1 silk		
lace	2.13. 9	
1 pr. fine hose 11/3 nm pins 1/. 1 pr. shoes		

10/   1. 2. 3
pd. for making a Sack 18/9 1 yd. Book
Muslin 25/   2. 3. 9
1 yd. Ribon 1/8. 1 pr. Sizars 1/8. 2 yd.
Callman 1/8   . 5.

         6. 4. 9
20. To Dor. Fredrick Schuger   2.17.4½
Novr. 16. 2 ½ yds. Cotton at 3/4 4 yds. ozns.
at 15d. for Negroe Girl   .13. 4
1 onz. thread 2/6 nm Pins 1/3. 1 hank silk 1/   . 4. 9
2 ¼ yds. Hollond 6/8. ½ yd. Linen   .16. 6
1 ½ yd. Muslin 6/8. 4 yds ferreting 4d   .11. 4

        2. 5.11

Demr. 23. 1 Scarlt. Cardinal 66/. 9 ½ yds.
    Camblet 3/   4.14. 6
1 pr. Gloves 4/. fine thread 6/8   .10. 8
1 yd. linen 3/5. 1 yd. Hollond. 7/6 nm pins
2/6   .13. 5
1 pr. Shoes 10/. 1 yd. Ribon 1/8. lapwire 5/   .16. 8
6 doz. Needles   . 2. 8

        6.17.11
        62. 6. 1¾
To Ballance Carried Over   8. 3. 2¾
        £70. 9. 3

<51> Dr. The Estate of Paulina Hall in Acct. with John and Peter
    Thompson
1769.
Feby. 14. 1 Pick tooth case 1 thimble 8d. 4 yds.
ferrt. 1 hank silk.   3.
½ yd. linen 1/6 5 doz. Needles 2/1 1 onz.
    thread   . 3. 8
10 ¼ yds. hollond at 7/4. 2 ¼ yds. ditto
8/4   4.13.11
12 yd. strpd. Holld. 4/2 2 yd. linen 3/4   2.16. 8
Cash pd. for Sundrys   .18. 4

        8.15. 7

March 5. 1 Silk lace. nm pins 2/. ½ yd.
Pirsian 2/   . 4.
2 ⅛ yd. Lawn 22/. 1 ¾ yds. Muslin 8/6   3.12.7½

        3.16.7½

April 7. 2 pr. Cotton hose 16/1 pr. Callo.

Shoes 10/. 2 ½ yds. Ribon		1.10. 8
23. nm pins 1/. Cash 25/	1. 6	
May 19. 4 yds. Ribon 2/6 Cash 9/2	.11. 8	
James Hall for Sundrys at Tarborough	1.15	
June 26. 1 Necklace 6/3 2 ½ yds. Ribon 5/	.11. 3	
1 pr. gloves 3/4 hanks silk 10d.	. 6. 8	
2 Necklaces 1/8. 1 onz. thread 2/	. 3. 8	
1 pr. Shoes 10/. 1 pr. gloves 4/8. Cash 5/4	1.	
July 12. 1 pr. Kid Gloves	.6	
27. 1 pr. Garters 1/. 10 yds. hollond 5/4	2.14. 4	
2 yd. hollond. 9/4 ¼ yd. Cambrick 16/8	1. 2. 7	
1 pr. gloves	. 3. 9	
		10. 1. 2
		24.4.0½

Ballance due to P. Hall	31. 1. 5
John Thompson <...>	£55. 5. 5½
By Ballance brought from the other side	8. 3. 2½
with Intrest from the 1st of Jany. 1769 to	
1st of Jany. 1770	. 9. 9¼
1770. Jany. 1. By Jas. Long for 1 years	
hire of Napper	15.
By Christopher Dudly for 1 year hire of Dick	15.12. 6
By Young Miller and Co. for 1 years hire of Moll	10. .
By Martin Smith for 1 years hire of Vilot	6.
	55. 5. 5½

Febry. Court 1771
Edgecombe County ss. The above acct.
was Exhibited on Oath ordred. to be Registred
Test. Jas. Hassll [...]

£55.5.5.½

Estate of Paulina Hall, 1767; 1768; 1769, in Edgecombe County, Guardians' Accounts, 1764-1778, pp. 28b, 29; pp. 50a, 50b; p. 51a, State Archives.

<64> Dr. Jeremiah Hilliard orphan of Jacob Hilliard		
1772. To 1 pr. Shoes	5	4
To 5 yds. Doulas	12	2½
To 2 ½ yds. Irish linen 4/8	11	8
To 1 quire of paper 1/8 and a paper Ink pow-	2	6½
der 10d. ½		

To 1 pr. Shoes 5/4 and 1 pr. Stockins 4/4		9	8
To 1 Slate 2/. and a Quire paper 1/8		3	8
To 1 Rackoon hatt 26/8. and 1 pr. Shoes 5/4		1	12
To 1 Qur. paper 1/8. and 1 penknife 1/		2	8
To 7 yards Striped linen 3/		1	1
To 2 3/8 yds. Checks 3/4		7	11
To making 1 Jacket 3/4. and to 1 yd. Salloon 3/4		6	8
To money paid for ten months Board	3	6	8
To money paid for ten months Schooling	1	2	2½
To money paid for making of Leather Breches		5	4
To my Trouble with his Estate for one year 1773.	15	9	6½
Jary: 1. The whole Ballance due to the said Orphan [...]	680	1	4
£	695	10	10½

1772.

To 1 pr. Shoes 5 1/4 and 4 yds. ozen. 4/5.		9	9
To 1 Saddle and bridle	2	13	4
To 1 Saddle Cloth 3/8. and 1 pen knife 2/		5	6
To 1 pr. Rushe Drill Britches		6	
To 1 pr. Knee buckels 1/4. and 1 pr. thread hoes		6	8
To 2 ¾ yds. Brown holland at 2/8		7	4
To making a Jacket and find thread		4	
To some Cambrick for a Stock		1	8
To 1 pr. Shoes 6/. and a quire of paper		7	8
To 10 yds. Dowlas at 2/4	1	3	4
To 1 fine hatt		12	
To 4 ½ yds. Garman Large 9/4		2	2
To 3 yds. Shalloon 3/8		11	
To 2 Sticks of twist 1/8. and 1 onz. of thread 10d.		2	6
To 3 hanks silk 3/. and 14 large buttons 1/8		4	6
To 19 Small buttons 1/4. and ¾ yd. Cuerans 2/		3	4
To 2 ½ yds. Dowlas at 3/4		8	4

To 1 Silk Hank.		7	4
To money paid for making a Suit of Cloths		16	6
To my trouble with his Estate one Year		5	
	16	13	3
1774.			
Jary 1. To the whole Ballance due to the said Orphan	43	1	2
£	559	14	5

<70.> Dr. Jeremiah Hilliard orphan of Jacob Hilliard decd. in Acct. with Elisha Battle Guardian

1774.

To 1 Dutch Blanket for a Negro		13	4
To 1 pr. Shoes 6/8. and 1 pr. buckels 2/		8	8
To 2 ¾ yds. Chex 7/4. and 1 Snuff box 8d.		8	
To makeing a Shurt and finding thread		2	4
To 1 ½ yds Coo. Holland at 3/4		5	
To makeing a Jacket and finding thread		2	10
To money pd. for a quarter of a Years going to Singing School		5	
To 2 yds. Chex 3/4		6	8
To 1 yd. Striped linnen 2/. and 1 Checkt. hankers 1/4		3	4
To a pr. of Ozinbrigs trousers		4	8
To pr. Shoebuckels 2/2 and 1 pen knife 10d.		3	
To 2 qr. paper 1/8		3	4
To 1 ¾ yds. forrest Cloth 13/4	1	3	4
To 1 doz. mettle buttons 1/. and 1 Stick of twist 8d.		1	8
To 1 onz. thread 8d. and 1 hank Silk 8d.		1	4
To 1 ¼ yds. Shalloon 4/		5	
To 1 ½ yds. Dowlas 2/5		3	8
To 1 pr. worsted hose 5/ and 1 qr. paper 1/8		6	8
To 8 Ells Chex at 3/8	1	9	4
To money pd. for 9 Months Schooling	1	4	6
To his board for the above said time	3		
To makeing a Jacket		4	8
To 1 pr. Shoes 6/8. and 1 pr. mittens 1/8		8	4

To pd. William Horn for 1 Day Shewing lines of Land		2	
To 3 ¼ yds. mild Dissil at 12/	1	19	
To ½ yd. Shalloon 1/10. and 20 large buttons		4	1
To 1 onz. thread 10d. 1 Stick twist 10d.		1	8
To 1 Years leavy for a Negro		14	4
To my Trouble with his Estate	6		
	20	15	9
1775. January. to the whole Ballance due to the said Orphan	801	15	1
£	822	10	10
			Cr.
<71.>1774. By the whole principle of his Estate in bonds	743	1	2
By the Interest of the above said principal one years	44	11	3
By the Rent of three plantations for one yeare	18	18	
By the hire of a Negro man one year	16		
£	822	10	5

Error Excepted per Elisha Battle Guardian
Edgcombe County sc. January Court 1775.
    Exhibited on Oath and ordered to be Recorded.

                Test. Edward Hall C.C.C.

      Estate of Jeremiah Hilliard, 1772; 1773; 1774, in Edgecombe County, Guardians' Accounts, 1764-1778, p. 64, 68, 70-71, State Archives.

[...] Present Thos Weekes John Harvey, William Wyatt Esqrs.
    The Petition of Jonathan Jessup read and granted and Ordered that Robert Evans formerly Guardian to the said Jonathan pay and deliver to him all the Estate he hath in his Hands of the said Jonathan he having arived to the Age of twenty one years Issued fees Due

      Minutes of the Perquimans County Court of Pleas and Quarter Sessions, April 1755, State Archives.

Upper. New Bern Academy was founded as an Anglican institution in 1764 and continued into the next century to be one of the outstanding schools in the state. See pages 288-294. Photograph from the files of the North Carolina Division of Archives and History, Raleigh. *Lower.* Apprenticeship in a craft or trade was an important part of the education system of North Carolina and the other colonies. See pages 52-53. The illustration depicts articles of apprenticeship being drawn up by a clerk. From Tunis, *Colonial Living,* 14.

The short-lived (1662-65) settlement on the Cape Fear christened "Charles Towne" by its founders is indicated on this map of 1738 as "Old Town." Throughout its early history, North Carolina had no urban centers to rival those of its neighboring colonies. See pages 179-206. Wimble Map from the files of the Division of Archives and History.

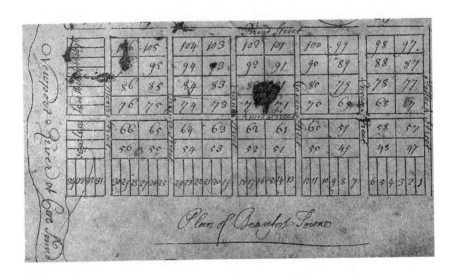

Upper. This rough sketch of Wilmington in 1774 was made by the postal official Hugh Finlay, who was less than enraptured with Wilmington and its environs. See page 221. *Lower.* Plan depicting lots in the town of Beaufort, chartered in 1723. Photographs from the files of the Division of Archives and History.

Taverns were abundant in North Carolina. This one at Old Salem survives from the colonial era. See pages 89-104. Photographs from the files of the Division of Archives and History.

Immigration

The beauty of North Carolina greatly impressed the Europeans, as evidenced by the reaction of Giavanni da Verazzano in 1524, the first to sight and leave a written description of the region in modern times. Echoing such sentiments was Ralph Lane, governor of Sir Walter Raleigh's first colony on Roanoke Island.

The shore is all covered with small sand, and so ascendeth upwards for the space of 15 feet, rising in the form of little hills about 50 paces broad. And sailing forwards, we found certain small rivers and arms of the sea, that fall down by certain creeks, washing the shore on both sides as the coast lieth. And beyond this we saw the open country rising in height above the sandy shores with many fair fields and plains, full of mighty great woods, some very thick, and some thin, replenished with divers sorts of trees, as pleasant and delectable to behold, as is possible to imagine. And your Majesty may not think that these are like the woods of Hercynia or the wild deserts of Tartary, and the northern coasts full of fruitless trees: but they are full of palm trees, bay trees, and high cypress trees, and many other sorts of trees unknown in Europe, which yield most sweet savors far from the shore, the property whereof we could not learn for the cause aforesaid, and not for any difficulty to pass through the woods, seeing that they are not so thick but that a man may pass through them.

Corbitt, *Explorations, Descriptions, and Attempted Settlements of Carolina*, 141-142.

In the meane while you shall vnderstand that since sir Richard Greenuils departure from vs, as also before, we haue discouered the maine to bee the goodliest soile vnder the cope of heauen, so abounding with sweete trees, that bring such sundry rich and most pleasant gummes, grapes of such greatnes, yet wild, as France, Spaine nor Italy hath no greater, so many sortes of Apothecarie drugs, such seuerall kindes of flaxe, and one kind like silke, the same gathered of a grasse, as common there as grasse is here. [...]

Ralph Lane to Richard Hakluyt the Elder and Master H___ of the Middle Temple, September 3, 1585, Quinn, *The Roanoke Voyages*, 1:207.

⊰⊱

Although John Lawson, the surveyor who platted New Bern, wrote rapturously about the prospects of North Carolina early in the eighteenth century, he apparently misused the Swiss and German Palatines brought by Baron Christoph von Graffenried in 1710 to settle the town.

When we consider the Latitude and convenient Situation of *Carolina*, had we no farther Confirmation thereof, our Reason would inform us, that such a Place lay fairly to be a delicious Country, being placed in that Girdle of the World which affords Wine, Oil, Fruit, Grain, and Silk, with other rich Commodities, besides a sweet Air, moderate Climate, and fertile Soil; these are the Blessings (under Heaven's Protection) that spin out the Thread of Life to its utmost Extent, and crown our Days with the Sweets of Health and Plenty, which, when join'd with Content, renders the Possessors the happiest Race of Men upon Earth.

The Inhabitants of *Carolina*, thro' the Richness of the Soil, live an easy and pleasant Life. The Land being of several sorts of Compost, some stiff, others light, some marl, others rich black Mould; here barren of Pine, but affording Pitch, Tar, and Masts; there vastly rich, especially on the Freshes of the Rivers, one part bearing great Timbers, others being Savanna's or natural Meads, where no Trees grow for several Miles, adorn'd by Nature with a pleasant Verdure, and beautiful Flowers, frequent in no other Places, yielding abundance of Herbage for Cattle, Sheep, and Horse. The Country in general affords pleasant Seats, the Land (except in some few Places) being dry and high Banks, parcell'd out into most convenient Necks, (by the Creeks) easy to be fenced in for securing their Stocks to more strict Boundaries, whereby, with a small trouble for fencing, almost every Man may enjoy, to himself, an entire Plantation, or rather Park. These, with the other Benefits of Plenty of Fish, Wild-Fowl, Venison, and the other Conveniencies which this Summer-Country naturally furnishes, has induc'd a great many Families to leave the more Northerly Platations, and sit down under one of the mildest Governments in the World; in a Country that, with moderate Industry, will afford all the Necessaries of Life. [...]

Lastly, As to the Climate, it is very healthful; our Summer is not so hot as in other places to the Eastward in the same Latitude; neither are we ever visited by Earthquakes, as many places in *Italy* and other Summer-Countries are. Our Northerly Winds, in Summer, cool the Air, and free us from pestilential Fevers, which *Spain*, *Barbary*, and the neighbouring Countries in *Europe*, *&c* are visited withal. Our Sky is generally serene and clear, and the Air very thin, in comparison of many Parts of *Europe*, where Consumptions and Catarrhs reign amongst the Inhabitants. The Winter has several Fitts of sharp Weather, especially when the Wind is at N. W. which always clears the Sky, though never so thick before. However, such Weather is very agreeable to *European* Bodies, and makes them healthy. The N. E. Winds blowing in Winter, bring with them thick Weather, and, in the Spring, sometimes, blight the Fruits; but they very seldom endure long, being blown away by Westerly Winds, and then all becomes fair and clear again. Our Spring, in *Carolina*, is very beautiful, and the most pleasant Weather a Country can enjoy. The Fall is accompanied with cool Mornings, which come in towards the latter end of *August*, and so continue (most commonly) very moderate Weather till about *Christmas*; then Winter comes on apace. Tho' these Seasons are very piercing, yet the Cold is of no continuance. Perhaps, you will have cold Weather for three or four days at a time; then pleasant warm Weather follows, such as you have in *England*, about the latter ends of *April* or beginning of *May*. [...]

Lawson, *A New Voyage to Carolina*, 86-87, 93-94.

At this very time there came over 10,000 souls from Germany to England, all under the name of Palatines, but among them were many Switzers and people brought together from other provinces of Germany. This caused the royal court as well as private individuals much concern and also unspeakable costs, so that they were embarrassed because of these people, and therefore there soon went out an edict by which it was allowed to many persons to take some of these people and care for them, and a good share of them had been sent into the three kingdoms, but partly because of their laziness, partly because of the jealousy of the poor subjects of the country, they did not do so well as it was supposed they would, and so they had begun to send a considerable number of these people to America and the Queen had had great sums distributed for that purpose.

At this juncture different persons of high and of middle rank, to whom my undertaking was known, advised me not to lose so favorable an opportunity; and at the same time gave me good hopes that, if I wished to take a considerable number of these people, the Queen would not only grant me the money for their passage, but in addition, would give me a good contribution for them. These hopes were realized and the sum reached almost 4,000£ sterling. Besides this, the Queen had granted to the royal council land upon the Potomac River, as much as we immediately needed, and moreover had given strong recommendations to the governor of Virginia. All this with the advantageous promises of the proprietors of Carolina gave to the undertaking a good appearance, and there was as much hope for a fortunate outcome as the beginning seemed good and prosperous.

To provide for and send this colony I took indescribable pains, 1. I tried to choose for this project healthy, industrious people and among them those of all sorts of trades necessary for this undertaking. 2. A supply of all kinds of necessary tools and things. 3. As also sufficient and good food. 4. Good ships and sailors, also certain over- and under-directors for this people, to keep every thing in good order. 5. In order that no negligence or lack of knowledge should be attributed to us, I have begun nothing without the knowledge, advice, and instruction of the royal committee. 6. Upon the ships, as afterwards upon the land, the over-directors were three of the most prominent persons from Carolina itself, who had already lived there many years and were acquainted with everything in those parts. These were the Chief Judge or Justice of the Peace, the Chief or General Surveyor, and the Receiver General, who were on business in London at this very time and were appointed by the royal committee, as well as by the Lords Proprietors, to have a close, faithful, and good watch over these people. The under-directors were composed of more than twelve of the most orderly and honorable men among the people—according to appearances.

So then, after everything had been adjusted, concluded, and ratified, by the royal committee as well as by the Lords Proprietors for me and the people, yet even before the departure, I begged the royal committee to be pleased to send some of their members, who were experienced in travel by ship, to examine whether everything was arranged as it should be, and to talk with the captain; this they did and the report was given in the committee. The day before the departure I went, with the pastor who remained in London after the company had gone to America, to Gravesend; to which place, because I was waiting for the little colony coming on from Berne, as well as for some of my associates, I could not go with them. I took my leave of them with a necessary exhortation, and then, when the German minister, Mr. Caesar, had given the people a fine sermon, commending them to the protection of the Most High, I let them sail away, yet not without taking precaution on account of the dangerous war times, for I then obtained this favor from the chief admiral, Count Pembroke, that he ordered Vice Admiral Norris to accompany our people or ship with his squadron out upon the broad sea or towards Portugal. This took place in the winter—in January—and then, because of the rough winds and storms, this ship was so driven about that it did not arrive in Virginia until after thirteen weeks. This, along with the salt food to which the people were not accustomed, and the fact that they were so closely confined, contributed very much to the sickness and death of many upon the sea. Others could not restrain their desires when they came to land, drank too much fresh water and overloaded themselves with raw fruit, so that they died of fever, and this colony therefore had half died off before it was well settled. N. B. The one ship which was filled with the best goods and on which those in best circumstances were traveling, had the misfortune, at the mouth of the James River, in sight of an English man-of-war, which however lay at anchor, to be attacked by a bold French privateer and plundered. This is the first misfortune.

After the surviving colony had regained health in Virginia where they were received very kindly, they betook themselves about twenty English miles towards Carolina, all of which, along with the goods cost a great deal. And now when they came into the county of Albemarle to the home of one Colonel Pollock upon the river called Chowan, a member of the council and one of the wealthiest in North Carolina, he provided these people, (but for money or the worth of it) with ships, so that they were conducted through the Sound into the County of Bath upon the River Neuse, with provision for only the most urgent necessity; and there the Surveyor General settled them on a point of land between the Neuse and the Trent River. This place called Chattoka is where the city of New Bern was afterwards founded.

Here begins the second fatality or misfortune. This surveyor general L_____ by name, who should have located the people immediately upon their allotted land and the plantations assigned to them, claimed that, in order to save time to enable them to clear their land, he had placed them on the south side of this point of land along the Trent River, in the very hottest and most unhealthy portion, instead of toward the north, on the Neuse River, where they could have been better placed and in a more healthy locality. But he did it for his own advantage, because this was his own land, in order that it might be cleared by these people for his benefit. But since he sold that same land and ours—and dear enough—yes wrongfully, (for he had no right to it), and moreover, since it was inhabited by Indians, (although he sold it to us for unencumbered land) the poor people had to live in great distress until fall, when I came. From lack of sufficient provisions they were soon compelled to give their clothes and whatever they possessed to the neighboring settlers for food. The misery and wretchedness were almost indescribable, for, on my arrival, I saw that almost all were sick, yes, even in extremity, and the well were all very feeble. In what a labyrinth and danger I then found myself, even my life not safe, the good Lord knows.

Todd, *Christoph von Graffenried's Account of the Founding of New Bern,* 224-226.

❧❧❧

Despite the early tribulations, immigration continued apace. James Murray offered several reasons that induced him to leave England for the Lower Cape Fear.

London 13 May 1735.

...The small encouragement that I have to stay here and not so much as the prospect of doing better has determined me to accept of the first good opportunity to push my fortune in any other part of the world; which I told a particular friend of mine here....He has since had Letters from the Governor of North Carolina (with whom he is very intimate) acquainting him of the growing State of that province and of his intention to remove his court to part of it where there is a fine navigable river lying in a convenient place of trade call'd Cape Fare River. There I intend to go some time in August next. I am not able in the compass of a letter to give you all the reasons for such a choice, but for your satisfaction shall give you a few of the most material.

1. It is a climate as healthy as England.

2. It is cheaper living there than anywhere in Scotland.

3. Land which may now be bought there for 1s. or 18d. per acre will in all probability double the value every year, the place growing daily more populous as the Land Lower down in that River has already done. This determines me to go so soon as August, that I may be there and purchase about one thousand acres before it is known that the Governor intends to remove thither.

4. I am sure of the Governor's interest to support me.

5. My own fortune is sufficient both to buy a handsome plantation and carry on as large a trade as I have occasion for; the profits of which I may expect will at least defray the charges of settling me the first two years and afterwards lay up £200 sterling pr. An.

6. The place by its situation is entirely out of the power of a foreign enemy, which is no small advantage in these uncertain times.

7. I have the advantage of two faithful correspondents, Gentn. of Substance and Experience, one in England and another in the West

Indies, who are willing to join Interests with me so far as our little trade requires it....

James Murray to Andrew Bennet, in Tiffany, *Letters of James Murray*, 17-19.

❖❖❖

At mid-eighteenth century many immigrants, most notably Scotch-Irish and Germans, arrived overland from northern colonies as well as from abroad, according to royal Governor Gabriel Johnston, President of the Council Matthew Rowan, and Governor Arthur Dobbs.

[...] Inhabitants flock in here daily, most from Pensilvania and other parts of America, who are overstocked with people and some directly from Europe, they commonly seat themselves towards the west and have got near the mountains. [...]

Gabriel Johnston to the Board of Trade, February 15, 1750/1, Saunders, *Colonial Records*, 4:1073.

In the year 1746 I was up in the Country that is now Anson, Orange and Rowan Countys, there was not then above one hundred fighting men there is now at least three thousand for the most part Irish Protestants and Germans and dayley increasing. [...]

Matt. Rowan to "My Lords" [Board of Trade], June 28, 1753, Saunders, *Colonial Records*, 5:24.

There are at present 75 families on my Lands. [...] They are a Colony from Ireland removed from Pensylvania, of what we call Scotch Irish Presbyterians who with others in the neighbouring Tracts had settled together in order to have a teacher of their own opinion and choice; Besides these there are 22 families of Germans or Swiss, who are all an industrious people, [...]

Arthur Dobbs to the Board of Trade, August 24, 1755, Saunders, *Colonial Records*, 5:355-356.

For NORTH-CAROLINA in America,

THE SHIP DOBBS GALLEY, Capt. James Leslie, Burthen 200 Tons, a prime Sailor, being well mann'd and Victalled, and properly fitted with every Thing commodious for Passengers of every Degree, and will be ready to sail from CARRICKFERGUS about the First Day July next at farthest.

Whoever has a Mind to go as Passenger, Redemptioner, or Servant, may apply to Samuel Smith Merchant in Belfast, Robert Willson Merchant in Larne, or to the Captain on board his Ship at Carrickfergus, where they will know the Terms, and meet with good Encouragement.

The Belfast Newsletter, May 20, 1755.

❧❧❧

The number increased during the French and Indian War, as attested by the Rev. James Maury of Virginia in 1756.

Not to mention the repeated Acts of Hostility and Violence, committed on our Fellow-subjects, in the remoter Parts of this Colony, by those bloody Instruments of french Policy, the Indians; nor the great Extent of country, on both Sides the Alleganies, now almost totally depopulated by them; which are Facts long since notorious to all: I beg Leave to inform You, that such Numbers of People have lately transplanted themselves hence into the more southerly Governments, as must appear almost incredible to any, except such, as have had an Opportunity of knowing it, either from their own Observation, or the credible Information of others, or both. From the waters of Potomac, James and Roanoke Rivers on the eastern Side of the above-mentioned Ridge of Mountains, nay from the same Side of the blue Ridge, hundreds of Families have, within these few Months past, removed, deserted their Habitations, & conveyed themselves & their most valuable Movables into other Governments. By Bedford Court-house in one week, 'tis said, &, I believe, truly said, near 300 Persons, Inhabitants of this Colony, past, on their way to Carolina. And I have it from good Authors, that no later in Autumn than October, 5000 more had crossed James River, only at one Ferry, that at Goochland Court-house, journeying towards the same place: &, doubtless, great Numbers have past that way since. And altho' these had not all been settled in Virginia, yet a large Proportion of them had. From all the upper Counties, even those on this Side of the blue Hills, great Numbers are daily following, & others preparing to follow in the Spring. Scarce do I know a Neighbourhood, but what has lost some Families, & expects quickly to lose more. And, what aggravates the Misfortune, is, that many of these are, not the Idler & the Vagrant, Pests of Society, whom 'tis ever salutary to a Body politic to purge off, but the honest & industrious, Men of Worth & Property, whom 'tis an Evil, at any Time, to a Community to lose, but is most eminently so to our own, in the present critical Juncture. [...]

"Letter of Rev. James Maury to Philip Ludwell, on the Defence of the Frontiers of Virginia, 1756," 293.

∽৫৯৶

Encouraged by "Scotus Americanus," Scots continued to enter North Carolina in great numbers, according to reports of the Commissioners of the Customs in Scotland.

[1773] Migrations to America from many parts of Britain, particularly to the province of North Carolina, from the Highlands and isles of Scotland, have, of late, become very frequent and numerous, and are likely to continue so. [...]

And now, is there any wonder, if, under their present [11] discouraging circumstances, and considering the dark and gloomy prospects they have before them at home, that the Highlanders should seek for refuge in some happier land, on some more hospitable shore, where freedom reigns, and where, unmolested by Egyptian taskmasters, they may reap the produce of their own labour and industry. For this purpose, where can they better betake themselves than to the large continent of America, to that part of it especially, to which some of their countrymen went sometime ago, where their posterity still live well and independently, and to which, of late, numbers have gone, who shew no inclination to return; but, on the contrary, send the most favourable accounts to their friends and acquaintance in the Highlands, and the most pressing invitations for them to follow after them across the Atlantic. Here they still belong to the British empire, and are happy under the benign influence of its administration. Here, at ease, they may enjoy all those civil blessings which the noblest constitution under heaven was intended to communicate to all ranks belonging to it, and to make these blessi[n]gs permanent and sure. [...]

Boyd, "Informations," *North Carolina Tracts*, 435.

Report of the Examination of the Emigrants from the Counties of
    Caithness and Sutherland on board the Ship Bachelor of Leith
    bound to Wilmington in North Carolina.

William Gordon saith that he is aged sixty and upwards, by Trade
a Farmer, married, hath six children, who Emigrate with him, with the
Wives and Children of his two sons John & Alexander Gordon.
Resided last at Wymore in the Parish of Clyne in the County of
Sutherland, upon Lands belonging to William Baillie of Rosehall. That
having two sons already settled in Carolina, who wrote him encouraging
him to come there, and finding the Rents of Lands raised in so much
that a Possession for which his Grandfather paid only Eight Merks Scots
he himself at last paid Sixty, he was induced to emigrate for the greater
benefit of his children being himself an Old Man and lame so that it
was indifferent to him in what Country he died. That his Circumstances
were greatly reduced not only by the rise of Rents but by the loss of
Cattle, particularly in the severe Winter 1771. That the lands on which
he lived have often changed Masters, and that the Rents have been
raised on every Change; and when Mr. Baillie bought them they were
farmed with the rest of his purchase to one Tacksman at a very high
Rent, who must also have his profits out of them. All these things
concurring induced him to leave his own country in hopes that his
Children would earn their Bread more comfortably elsewhere. That one
of his sons is a Weaver and another a Shoe Maker, and he hopes they
may get bread for themselves and be a help to support him.

William McKay, aged Thirty, by Trade a Farmer, married, hath three
children from Eight to two years Old, besides one dead since he left his
own country, resided last at _____ in the Parish of Farr in the County
of Strathnaver upon the Estate of the Countess of Sutherland. Intends
to go to Wilmington in North Carolina, because his stock being small,
Crops failing, and bread excessively dear, and the price of Cattle low,
he found he could not have bread for his Family at home, and was
encouraged to emigrate by the Accounts received from his Countrymen
who had gone to America before him, assuring him that he might
procure a Comfortable Subsistence in that country. That the land he
possessed was a Wadset of the Family of Sutherland to Mr. Charles
Gordon of Skelpick, lying in the height of the country of Strathnaver,
the Rents were not raised.

Wm. Sutherland, aged Forty, a Farmer, married, hath five children
from 19 to 9 years old, lived last at Strathalidale in the Parish of Rea, in
the County of Caithness, upon the Estate of the late Colonel McKay of
Bighouse; Intends to go to North Carolina; left his own country because

the Rents were raised, as Soldiers returning upon the peace with a little money had offered higher Rents; and longer Fines or Grassums, besides the Services were oppressive in the highest degree. That from his Farm which paid 60 Merks Scots, he was obliged to find two Horses and two Servants from the middle of July to the end of Harvest solely at his own Expence, besides plowing, Cutting Turf, making middings, mixing Dung and leading it out in Seed time, and besides cutting, winning, leading and stacking 10 Fathoms of Peats yearly, all done without so much as a bit of bread or a drink to his Servants.

John Catanoch, aged Fifty Years, by Trade a Farmer, married, hath 4 Children from 19 to 7 years old; resided last at Chabster in the Parish of Rae, in the County of Caithness, upon the Estate of Mr. Alexr. Nicolson, Minister at Thurso, Intends to go to Wilmington North Carolina; left his own Country because crops failed, Bread became dear, the Rents of his Possession were raised from Two to Five Pounds Sterling, besides his Pasture or Common Grounds were taken up by placing new Tennants thereon, especially the grounds adjacent to his Farm, which were the only grounds on which his Cattle pastured. That this method of parking and placing Tenants on the pasture Grounds rendered his Farm useless, his Cattle died for want of Grass, and his own Corn Farm was unfit to support his Family, after paying the Extravagant Tack duty. That beside the rise of Rents and Scarcity of bread, the Landlord exacted arbitrary and oppressive Services, such as obliging the Declarant to labour up his ground, cart, win, lead and stack his Peats, Mow, win and lead his Hay, and cut his Corn and lead it in the yard which took up about 30 or 40 days of his servants and Horses each year, without the least Acknowledgement for it, and without Victuals, save the men that mowed the Hay who got their Dinner only. That he was induced to Emigrate by Advices received from his Friends in America, that Provisions are extremely plenty & cheap, and the price of labour very high, so that People who are temperate and laborious have every Chance of bettering their circumstances- Adds that the price of Bread in the Country he hath left is greatly Enhanced by distilling, that being for so long a time so scarce and dear, and the price of Cattle at the same time reduced full one half while the Rents of lands have been raised nearly in the same proportion, all the small Farms must inevitably be ruined.

Eliz: McDonald, Aged 29, unmarried, servant to James Duncan in Mointle in the Parish of Farr in the County of Sutherland, Intends to go to Wilmington in North Carolina; left her own country because several of her Friends having gone to Carolina before her, had assured her that she would get much better service and greater Encouragement in Carolina than in her own Country.

Donald McDonald, Aged 29 years, by Trade a Farmer and Taylor, married, hath One Child six years Old. Resided last at Chapter in the Parish of Rae in the County of Caithness upon the Estate of Mr. Alexr. Nicolson Minister at Thurso, intends to go to Carolina; left his own Country for the reasons assigned by John Catanoch, as he resided in the same Town and was subjected to the same Hardships with the other. Complains as he doth of the advanced price of Corn, owing in a great measure to the consumption of it in Distilling.

John McBeath Aged 37, by Trade a Farmer and Shoe maker, Married, hath 5 children from 13 years to 9 months old. Resided last in Mault in the Parish of Kildonnan in the County of Sutherland, upon the Estate of Sutherland. Intends to go to Wilmington in North Carolina; left his own country because Crops failed, he lost his Cattle, the Rent of his Possession was raised, and bread had been long dear; he could get no Employment at home, whereby he could support himself and Family, being unable to buy Bread at the prices the Factors on the Estate of Sutherland & neighboring Estates exacted from him. That he was Encouraged to emigrate by the Accounts received from his own and his Wife's Friends already in America, assuring him that he would procure comfortable subsistence in that country for his Wife and Children, and that the price of labour was very high. He also assigns for the Cause of Bread being dear in his Country that it is owing to the great quantities of Corn consumed in brewing Risquebah.

James Duncan, Aged twenty seven years, by Trade a Farmer, married, hath two Children, one five years the other 9 Months old. Resided last at Mondle in the Parish of Farr in the Shire of Sutherland, upon the Estate of Sutherland, Intends to go to Wilmington in North Carolina; left his own Country because Crops failed him for several years, and among the last years of his labouring he scarce reaped any Crop; Bread became dear and the price of Cattle so much reduced that One Cows price could only buy a Boll of Meal. That the People on the Estate of Sutherland were often supplied with meal from Caithness, but the Farmers there had of late stopt the sale of their Meal, because it rendered them a much greater Profit by Distilling. That he could find no Employment at home whereby he could support his Family. That he was very promising Prospects by the Advices from his Friends in Carolina, as they have bettered their circumstances greatly since they went there by their labours. Lands being cheap and good Provisions plenty, and the price of Labour very encouraging.

Hector Mcdonald, Aged 75, Married, a Farmer, hath three sons who emigrate with him, John Alexander & George from 27 to 22 years old, also two Grand Children Hector Campbell aged 16, and Alexr. Campbell aged 12, who go to their Mother already in Carolina. Resided last at Langwall in the Parish of Rogart in the County of Sutherland, upon the Estate of Sutherland. Intends to go to North Carolina, Left his own Country because the Rents of his possession had been raised from One pound seven shillings to Four pounds, while the price of the Cattle raised upon it fell more than One half, and not being in a Corn Country the price of Bread was so far advanced, that a Cow formerly worth from 50 sh. to £3 - could only purchase a Boll of Meal. He suffered much by the death of Cattle, and still more by oppressive Services exacted by the factor, being obliged to work with his People & Cattle for 40 days and more Each year, without a bit of Bread. That falling into reduced Circumstances he was assured by some of his children already in America that his Family might subsist more comfortably there, and in all events they can scarce be worse. Ascribes the excessive price of corn to the consumption of it in distilling.

William McDonald, Aged 71, by Trade a Farmer married hath 3 children from 7 to 5 years Old, who emigrate with him. Resided last at little Savall in the Parish of Lairg in the county of Sutherland, upon the Estate of Hugh Monro of Achanny. Intends to go to Wilmington in North Carolina; left his own Country because Crops failed, Bread became dear, the Rents of his possession were raised, but no so high as the Lands belonging to the neighboring Heritors, by which and the excessive price of Meal, the lowness of the price of Cattle, and still further by a Cautionary by which he lost 30 £ Sterling, his Circumstances were much straightened, so that he could no longer support his Family at Home, tho' Mr. Monro used him with great humanity. That his Friends already in Carolina, have given him assurance of bettering his condition, as the price of labour is high and Provisions very cheap. Ascribes the high price of Corn to the Consumption of it in Distilling.

Newsome, "Records of Emigrants," 130-133.

Many of the Scots and other immigrants arrived as indentured servants. Most came voluntarily, including the redemptioners; others, involuntarily, as convicts sold into service.

An Act Concerning Servants & Slaves.

I. Be It Enacted by his Excellency the Pallatine & the Rest of the True & Absolute Lords Proprs. of Carolina by & with the Advice & Consent of this Present General Assembly now met at Little River for the No. East part of the said Province.

II. And It Is Hereby Enacted that all Christian Servants Imported or to be Imported into this Government above Sixteen Years of Age without Indentures shall serve Five Years. And all under the Age of Sixteen Years at the time of their Importation shall serve till they be Two & Twenty Years of Age. And the Age of such Servant or Servants to be adjudged by the Precinct Court where the Master or Mistress of such servant resides. Provided the Master or Mistress of such servant do carry him or her to the said Court within Six Months after their Importation. Otherwise such Servant or Servants shall serve no longer than those of Sixteen years are above appointed to serve by virtue of this Act.

III. And Be It Further Enacted by the Authority afors'd that every Christian Servant whether so by Importation or by Contract made in this Government that shall, at any time or times absent him or herself from his or her Master or Mistress' service without his or her License first had shall make satisfaction by serving after the time by Custom or Indenture or Contract for serving is expired, double the time of Service lost or neglected by such time or times of Absence & also such longer time as the Court shall see fit to adjudge in consideration of any further Charge or Damages accrueing to the Master or Mistress by such time or times of Absence as aforesaid.

IV. And Be It Further Enacted that if any Christian Servant shall lay violent hands on his or her Master or Mistress or Overseer, upon proof thereof made, shall for every offence suffer such corporal punishment as the Court shall think fit to adjudge. And as an Incouragement for Christian servants to perform their service with Fidelity & cheerfulness.

V. Be It Further Enacted that every Master or Mistress shall provide for their servants so Imported or Indented Competent Dyet, Clothing & Lodging. And shall not exceed the Bounds of moderation in correcting them beyond their Demerits. And that it shall & may be lawfull for any Servant having just Cause of Complaint to repair to the next Magistrate who is hereby impowered, required & directed to bind over such Master or Mistress to Appear & answer the Complaint the next precinct Court and there to stand to & abide by such Orders &

Judgment as the Court shall think fitt to pass thereon. And if the Magistrate shall see just cause he shall also take further security that he or she shall not in the mean time abuse such servant. And as a Further Encouragement for the faithful discharge of the such Imported or Indented Servants' services.

VI. Be It Enacted that every Christian Servant shall be allowed by their Master or Mistress at the expiration of his or her time of service Three Barrells of Indyan Corn & two new Suits of Apparrell of the Value of Five pounds at least or in lieu of one suit of Apparrell a good well-fixed Gun, if he be a Manservant. [...]

XII. And Be It Further Enacted that if any Woman Servant shall be gotten with Child in this Country & bring it forth in the time of her Servitude she shall serve Two Years to her Master or Owner for her Offence over & above what punishment she shall be & is Lyable unto for her Fornication.

XIII. Provided always that Women Servants comeing into this Country with Child shall not fall under the Penalty of this Act. And in case a Woman servant shall in the time of her servitude be delivered of a child begotten by her Master then instead of the two years servitude to her Master she shall be sold by the Church Wardens of the Precinct or parish where the fault is committed for two years after her time by Indenture or Custome is fullfilled. And the Money arising by the said sale shall be disposed of by the Vestry for the use of the Parish.

XIV. And Be It Further Enacted by the Authority afors'd that where any White woman whether Bond or Free shall have a Bastard child by a Negro, Mulatto or Indyan over & above the Two years service to her Master or Owner she shall immediately upon the Expiration of her time to her present Master or Owner pay down to the Church Wardens of the Parish wherein such shall be born for the use of the said Parish the sum of Six pounds Current Money of this Province or be by them sold for two years to the use aforesaid.

XV. And Be It Further Enacted that in the case last aforementioned the Church Wardens aforesaid are hereby Impowered to bind out the said children to be servants untill they arrive at & be of the full age of Thirty One Years. And if any Proffits shall accrue or may be made by the Binding out of such Children the same shall be accounted for by the Church Wardens to the Vestry or applied for & toward the use of the Parish.

Laws, 1715, in Clark, *State Records*, 23:62-63, 64-65.

[...] [1773] A friend of mine, a few years ago, carried over passengers to Cape Fear; among these there were many poor people unable to pay for their passage, who therefore went as redemptioners; that is, if in 40 days after landing, they could not find money among their friends or acquaintance, or by some shift of their own, to pay for their passage, [28] they were then bound to serve for 3 years after landing; there was none of them but relieved themselves before the time; many of them having no friend or acquaintance in the place, got people there to take them by the hand, and pay for their passage, and soon fixed them in such a manner, as that they had plenty to live on. [...]

Boyd, "Informations," *North Carolina Tracts*, 447.

Thomas Jardon and Elinor his Wife servants formerly belonged to Samuel Henney for the space of Seven years being Convicts and by the said Samuel sold them to Edward Cusick his Heirs and Assigns they the said Thomas and Elinor came into Open Court and Acknowledged themselves Servants from the Sixth Day of June Last past and from the of Seven years to be fully Compleated and Erided.

Minutes of the Rowan County Court of Pleas and Quarter Sessions, July 1756, State Archives.

⋅⊱⧉⊰⋅

Although protected by contracts, many servants complained of mis-treatment. County justices of the peace dismissed some pleas, chastised masters in other cases, and, in extreme instances of abuse, removed servants from the care of their masters.

Whereas Mary Coogan a Servant Maid of Rd. Lovets came into Court and Complaining says that her Mistress and Master has very much abused herby Beating want of Cloathing and otherwise without just provocation. The Court taking the same into Consideration and or hearing the Allegations of both parties and viewing the Servant as to the Beating do find that She has not been imoderately Corrected. The said Mary Coogan, therefore, Ordered to repair home to her said Masters Service.

Minutes of the Craven County Court of Pleas and Quarter Sessions, December 1746, State Archives.

Whereas Mable Ryley Exhibited a Complaint against her master Mr. Ed. Howard Concerning Rigirous abuce Comitted by the said Howard on the body of the said Mable, Ordered the said that the said Howard do not Correct the said Mable for any Triviall Offences but for such offences as the said Mable as shall be Deemed Cullpable by the next Majestrate, Mr. Howard pays fees.

> Minutes of the Onslow County Court of Pleas and Quarter Sessions, January 1735/36, State Archives.

John McGlawling a Servant man comes into Court and Complains that his Master Thomas Jornagan ill uses him. Ordered that Mr. Rhodes take Care of him and hire him out till next Court and Buy a Shirt etc. and that his master be Summoned to next Court to answer the Complaint. Wm. Stafford and Andrew Fullwood to be Summoned. [...]

On hearing the Several Evidences in the Complaint of John MaGlothlin against him Master Thos. Journagan the Court are Unanimous of Opinion his Master has usd him Extreamly Ill. And Orderd that be sold according to Law.

> Minutes of the Onslow County Court of Pleas and Quarter Sessions, July, October 1768, State Archives.

❧❧

Rivalling the number of complaints by servants of mistreatment was the frequency with which masters contended that female servants during their servitude bore illegitimate children, the penalty for which was lengthening their time of indenture.

On Motion of Alexr. Martin Esqr. Orderd that

Carlotte Dearmond a White Woman servant the property of Major John Dunn being brought in to Open Court and Charged upon Oath of having two Bastard Children during her Servitude the One a White Child and the Other a Mulatto, it is Adjudged by the Court According to the Act of Assembly in Such Case made and provided that the said Charlotte dearmond after the Expiration of the Term of her said Service by her Inditement shall Serve her Master or his Assigns One Whole year for the Offence of having a White Bastard Child as aforesaid and it is further adjudged that After the Expiration of the said Term of One Year She the said Charlotte Dearmond Shall be Sold According to Law to Serve Two Whole Years Longer for the Offence of Having the Mulatto bastard Child as aforesaid.

And it is further Orderd by the Court that the said Molatto Bastard Child being a Female by the name of Jenney be Bound to Major John Dunn till She Arive to the Age of Thirty One years [...]

On Motion of Alexr. Martin Esqr.

Ordered by the Court that Charlotte Dearmond a White Woman Servant the property of Mr. James Karr Being brought Into Open Court and Charged of Having Two Bastard Children During her Servitude, and it is adjudged by the Court that She the Said Charlotte Dearmond Agreable to Act of Assembly Do Serve One Year for Each Child Over and above the Time of her former Servitude [...]

Ordered by the Court that Charlotte D'Armond Continue in the Service of Manassah Lamb in quality of a Servant one year Longer than prescribed by a former Indenture and Order of Court dated the first Tuesday in May in the year of our Lord 1772 for having brought forth a Bastard Child since the date of her Said Indenture and Order of Court Agreeable to an Act of Assembly in that case made and Provided.

Minutes of the Rowan County Court of Pleas and Quarter Sessions, February 1769; May 1772; May 1774, State Archives.

'◈'

Mistreatment, prolonged servitude, and simply the desire for freedom prompted many servants to run away. If apprehended, the justices of the peace according to law compensated masters for the lost time and expenses by extending the period of indenture.

March 29.

North-Carolina, Chowan County,

RUN away from the subscriber, on the 29th of *February* last, an indented servant man named *John Bunkley*. He is a well set fellow, of a middle stature, about 30 years of age, of a dark and sun burnt complexion, and has lost his left leg below his knee, which is supplied with a wooden one. He had on when he went away, a dark brown kersey coat, a pair of blue frize breeches, an oznabrigs shirt, a felt hat, a yarn stocking, a country made shoe, and a green cloth boot. Whoever apprehends the said runaway, and delivers him to me, or secures him in gaol, so that I get him again, shall receive a reward of three pounds *Virginia* money.

LUKE SUMNER.

Virginia Gazette (Williamsburg), April 14, 1768.

August 22d 1773.

THREE POUNDS REWARD.

RUN *away from the subscriber September 8th, 1773, an Indented Servant Girl named* MARY KELLY *lately from Ireland, but says she has lived 14 years in London; is about* 18 *or* 20 *years of age, five feet six or eight inches high, stoops in her walking, fair complection and redish hair; had on when she went away a little round man's hat, green peticoat and black stuff shoes; took with her, two striped blew and white cotton, and one calico with red flowers, short gowns, and 6 yards of dark coloured calico not made up. Whoever takes up the said run-away servant, and secures her in any of his Majesty's Goals so that she may be had again, shall be intitled to the above reward, and if brought home all reasonable charges paid by me.*

GEORGE BARNES,

at the sign of the Harp and Crown in Wilmington.
September 13, 1773.

Cape Fear Mercury (Wilmington), September 23, 1773.

John Marshal complaind against John Henecy his Servant for running away absenting himself fourteen days and putting his said Master to the expence of Twenty eight pounds to have him taken up and for a Gun Value £15 which said Henecy carried away of his Masters and Sold and prayed the Court to order Satisfaction by Service or otherwise as they should think proper. Ordered that the said Jno. Henecy shall serve four Weeks over and above the time mencioned in his Indenture for the fourteen Days absence pursuant to an Act of Assembly of this Province and at the Expiration of the said four Weeks he shall pay to the said Jno. Marshal forty three pounds Currency or Serve him Eighty Six days over and above the said four weeks. [...]

Minutes of the New Hanover County Court of Pleas and Quarter Sessions, June 1739, State Archives.

Servants who fulfilled their contracts still on occasion had to sue for their freedom and freedom dues.

And now at this Day Robert Warran appeared and Delivered the Indenture which by order of this Court Yesterday he was Ordered to do to the Clk. of this Court who produced the same to this Court Whereupon the said Hannah Skinner by John Hodgson her Attorney pray'd that she may be allowed her Freedom dues from the said Robt. Warren in whose Service she was at the Expiration of her Indenture. It is thereupon Considered and Ordered that the said Robert Warren do pay to the said Hannah Skinner Two New Suites of Apparell or in Lieu thereof Five Pounds and Three Barrels of Indian Corn and that he pay Cost als Execution the said Hannah received 5£ for satisfaction for the two Suites of Apparell. [...]

> Minutes of the Bertie County Court of Pleas and Quarter Sessions, August 1733, State Archives.

Ordered by the Court that Samuel Knox furnish Owen Duff his late Servent with the following Articles (Viz.) one Coat, waistcoast, one pair of Breeches one pair Leggins of Common County Cloth, one felt Hatt, two Oznabrig Shirts one pair Shoes-or in Lieu thereof the sum of six Pounds Proclamation to purchase the Articles aforesaid.

> Minutes of the Mecklenburg County Court of Pleas and Quarter Sessions, July 1775, State Archives.

⋘⋙

Despite the pleasant prospects offered by North Carolina to free and servants alike, nature wreaked havoc with the inhabitants. Heat and drought took their toll; excessive rains produced freshets, swollen rivers that swept all in their paths; destructive hurricanes, including that which caused so much damage in New Bern and its environs in 1769, ravaged the colony.

The Weather for sometime past has been so extreamly hot that severall labouring persons both black and white have died in the field as well here as in Virga. and it is thought the specific drought for this month past will be very hurtfull to the planters in their Crops.

> Samuel Johnston to Thomas Barker, August 20, 1766, Hayes Papers.

[...] [May, 1775]. The heat daily increases, as do the Musquetoes, the bugs and the ticks. The curtains of our beds are now supplied by

Musquetoes' nets. Fanny has got a neat or rather elegant dressing room, the settees of which are canopied over with green gauze, and on these we lie panting for breath and air, dressed in a single muslin petticoat and short gown. Here I know your delicacy will be shocked, and I hear you ask, if our young man bear us company in this sequestrate apartment. Oh yes, my friend, he does, but he is too much oppressed himself to observe us. This serock [sirocco] has the same effect here as Briden tells us it has in Sicily; it has ruined all vivacity, as my pen shows you, and renders us languid in thought, word and deed.

Andrews, *Journal of a Lady of Quality*, 182-183.

About a fortnight agoe we were greatly alarmed with an amazing quantity of Trees and Rubbish coming out of the mouth of Roanoke the wind being about South west the whole Bay and Sound opposite to Edenton were soon covered with loggs fence Rails Scantling and parts of broken houses with Corn Stalks and a variety of other Trash so that it was with difficulty boats could pass our Apprehensions of the cause were soon confirmed to be too well grounded by an Account of the most terrible Inundation in Roanoke River exceeding anything in the Memory of the oldest man in the Country, The Damage that the Inhabitants have sustained is incredible every thing in the Marshes and low grounds is lost, the Inhabitants will be greatly distressed not only for this years bread but the next for all their old Corn was damaged and the Crop on the ground intirely destroyed and many fields covered with Sand so as to render them useless for ever tho it was not too late for planting yet the fences were so much destroyed that it will not be easy to repair them time enough to make half a Crop of Corn there is an entire end to the Crop of Wheat and there will be very little Tobacco from the loss of Plants. [...]

Samuel Johnston to Thomas Barker, June 10, 1771, Hayes Papers.

[...] The Effects of the Storm which happened in the Night of the 7 Instant, is so fatal to Newbern that I cannot omit giving Your Excellency the best Account I can of it. Beginning with Mr. John Smith whose Store full of Goods was undermined with the washing of the Waves and tumbled down and broke to Pieces and scattered along Shore. The Cellars of the House where he lived being well stored with Wine, Rum, Sugar &c.; were undermined and destroyed and all it contained either stove to Pieces or floated away by the Violence of the

Wind and Current. He saved himself and Family by cutting through in the Garret to Mr. Cornells House which they entered but soon were obliged to leave, carrying along with them Mr. Cornells Children and the Nurse by which means they were saved for the Floor of the House very soon after fell in and with the Furniture washed away. Mr. Smiths two Sloops are also lost one stove to Pieces at the Wharf, the other drove up near the Edifice so high that She never will be got off—it is supposed his losses cannot amount to less than three thousand Pounds. Mr. Cornells Cellar under his dwelling house was undermined, and the Wall destroyed. The Piazza all thrown down and carried away. Out of the Cellar floated away and stove together near two hundred hogheads of Molasses, Eighty hogsheads of Rum and several Pipes of Wine, besides many other Articles of Value, some of the Wine, Rum and Molasses have been since found. Two Store Houses that stood on his Wharf well filled with very valuable Goods, beat down and carried away together with the Wharf. The Goods all lost and destroyed. His Brig drove over the large Marsh to the South Westward of the Town quite into the Woods and is entirely lost. Also two large Sloops belonging to Strangers drove up and lost near the Brig. Mr. Cornells ready Money store kept by Partridge at the Corner opposite Mr. Ellis's destroyed with all the Goods and Money, and the Store Keeper so bruised that it is thought he cannot live. All the houses on the left hand side of the Street from the Corner up as far as Mr. Cogdells washed down and floated away. Two Women Mrs. Johnston & Mrs. Pape [Pope?] with their two Children and two Negro's were drowned or killed by the ruins of these Building—no other Life lost that we know of as yet. Mr. Ellis's Wharf and Store Houses with the Goods in them washed away and entirely lost. The Cellar of his Store opposite the Front of his dwelling House undermined and the Rum, Wine &c: &c: washed out and stove to Pieces. Those Buildings of Mr. Clitheralls where Mr. Neale lived and kept the Public Ferry and those long Houses of Mr. Wiltons next adjoining are entirely destroyed, not one Store left upon another. The part of the Mill House next the Water beat down, and the Works destroyed almost irrepairable. Docter Haslens Tan House, Stores and Yard entirely ruined and destroyed and the Chimneys of his dwelling house fallen on the Roof but luckily did it no damage. His Garden is quite torn up and ruined. Mr. Davis's House a mere Wreck, his Printing Office broke to Pieces, his Papers destroyed and Types buried in the Sands. His Desk Stove and what Money he had with all his private Papers entirely lost. The pailing where Your Excellency lives when in Newbern blown down and the Front of the Lott up to the Gates washed away. [It] will take much Time and Trouble to secure it from the Influence of any common brisk Easterly Wind. Mr. Coors Store with the Store House on the Wharf next to his, thrown down and carried away, with all the Goods they contained. Colo. Leeches Tan House with thirteen other little houses situated about it and belonging to Him are entirely destroyed. Many other People have lost all they had in the World, among these is the unfortunate Mr. Setgreaves who with a large Family of small Children has not now a second Shirt to his Back.

The Edifice has received no Damage that I know of if any it must be very inconsiderable for though I have seen Mr. Hawks he never has mentioned any thing of the Kind to Me.

Newbern is really now a Spectacle, Her Streets full of the Tops of Houses, Timber, Shingles, Dry Goods, Barrels & Hogshead, empty most of them, Rubbish &c &c: in so much that You can hardly pass along. A few Days ago so flourishing and thriving—it shows the Instability of all Sublunary Things.

Thus I thought it my Duty Sir, to give Your Excellency the best Account I could of an Event so fatal to a place which has always had Your Protection and Encouragement & which I hope will still merit a continuance of the Favors it has received from Your Excellency.

Mr. Cornells losses from a moderate Computation cannot amount to less than four or five Thousand Pounds.

Thomas Clifford Howe

Thomas Clifford Howe to William Tryon, September 10, 1769, Powell, *Correspondence of William Tryon*, 2:362-363.

৶৹৻৩

As a result, from the earliest days of settlement in the Albemarle region, North Carolinians endured the tribulations of nature.

An acompt how I have Imployed my Selfe & Servants in the Setlinge of a plantation for the Right honorble My Lord the Earle of Craven my Lord Berkeley Sr George Carteret Sr Peter Colleton in Albemarle in the province of Carolina, with what Stormes or haricanes hath happened Since my being their as Followeth./ Wee arived in Albemarle the 23d of ffebr 1664/5 & went to Colleton Island acording to Instructions where I found a 20 foot dwelling howse a 10 foot hogg howse & apsell of wild hoggs butt Nothing towards a plantation soe that I was to make a plantation out of the wilderness wee cleered what ground we could on powells pointe & plant it with corne which produced litle by reason that wee were all Sick all the Sumer that wee could nott tend it & the Servants Soe weake the fall & Spring that they could doe little worke

1666

We cleered fenced & planted what ground we could wee built a hogg howse of 80 foot Long & 20 broad with nessesarie partitions on powells pointe & gott the hoggs theire which I received that trived very well at first butt by the Last of October I had los neere a third pt of them Nottwithstanding I Kept a man to look after them & corne to give them this yeare wee have made aboute 150 bars of Corne-.

1667

We planted what corne & tob: wee could & made what preparations was nessesarie for to make Oile August ye 27th heere happened a great storme or reather haricane that destroyed both corne & tob: blew downe the roof of the great hogg howse that I had built the yeare before caried away the frame & boards of two howses soe that I was forced to bee at the charges of getting of other timber this yeare wee have made about 30 bar of Oile butt could nott gett fright for it that yeare soe yt their was great Lakages.

1668

Wee cleered more grownd and repaired or fences planted both corne & tobacco butt Such a great Drough happened for about 3 month yt burnt up all the tob. & stented the corne that it produced little ye 30th: July the raignes begone & continued untill the Later End of August soe yt the great abundance of raignes did as much hurt as the drough had before we made 5 hods of tob & about 80 bars of of Oile-

1669

Wee repaired or fences planted both corne & tob: which was very hopfull the 2d of August wee howsed a bout a hod of tob ye 18 ditto a violent haricane as bad as the former Only did nott last soe Long destroyed what tob was out broke & spoiled most of the corne this yeare wee have made 1 hode of tobackoe and aboutt 52 barrels of Oile/.

1670

Wee planted both Corne & tob: proportionable to the Number of Servants that I had left the 6th of August wee had a violent haricane that Lasted 24 howers broke downe timber trees blew downe howses destroyed both corne tob: soe that it was Lick to bee a famine amongst us corne was sold in virginia for 3£ sterling a barell & with us at 250£ of & tob: it blew downe to the ground the hogg howse & a howse on the South side of the Inlette wher was aboutt 30 barells broke & spoiled & caried away a small howse On the North Pt of the Inlette where was 4 tunes of corke redy trimed for to putt in On aboutt ye begininge of Septembr we had an other storme but nott altogether soe violent as the former this yeare Very few whales came On Shoare wee made aboutt 38 bar's of Oile-[...]

> Peter Carteret's Account of the years 1666-1673 in Albemarle, December 3, 1674, Powell, *Ye Countie of Albemarle in Carolina*, 61-63.

✥✥✥

Still, immigrants flocked to North Carolina, and not surprisingly according Samuel Johnston, though some of the settlers gave North Carolina a less than desirable reputation.

You mention the Spirit of Emigration which of late years has prevailed so universally in most parts of the Island having reached your part of the County it is no wonder people who are only desirous of acquiring a Subsistance should flock to a Country where the mere Necessaries of life are so easily acquired a Country capable of feeding more than ten times the number of Inhabitants which at present inhabit it tho those who aspire of the Luxuries of Life find as great or greater difficulties as in any Country or Greater notwithstanding the vast numbers that have come abroad there has not one landed within two hundred miles of this place, it would be greatly for the Advantage of individuals in this part of the Country if they could get honest industrious Farmers to Cultivate their Lands, instead of Wretches, who have no other Motive to the discharge of their duty than the fear of p[*illegible*].[...]

> Samuel Johnston to Robert Cathcart, November 28, 1774, Hayes Papers. Johnston is writing from Edenton.

[...] [April 5, 1765]. by Computation, there is in this province from 25 to 30 thousand white taxables, or men from the age of 16 to 60—whom are musterd 4 times a year as militia; there but very few if any rich people. their fortunes Consist generally in lands, which are for the most part uncultivated, and Consequently of no advantage or value for the present, but the Inhabitants augment fast. this province is the azilum of the Convicts that have served their time in virginia and maryland. when at liberty they all (or great part) Come to this part where they are not Known and setle here. it is a fine Country for poor people, but not for the rich.

"Journal of a French Traveler," 738.

The inhabitants of North Carolina are of two kinds. Some have been born in the country, and they bear the climate well, but are lazy and do not compare with our northern colonists. Others have moved here from the northern colonies or from England, Scotland, or Ireland, etc. Many of the first comers were brought by poverty, for they were too poor to buy land in Pennsylvania or Jersey, and yet wished to have land of their own; from these the Colony receives no harm. Others, however, were refugees from debt, or had deserted wives and children, or had fled to escape punishment for evil deeds, and thought that here no one would find them, and they could go on in impunity. Whole bands of horse thieves have moved here, and constantly show their skill in this neighborhood; this has given North Carolina a very bad name in the adjoining Provinces. [...]

Spangenburg Diary, 1752, Fries, *Records of the Moravians*, 1:40-41.

Taverns

Lodging along the highways and in towns might be found in the colonial tavern, also called an ordinary and public house of entertainment, licenses for which were granted by the county courts.

An Act for Regulating Ordinaries and Houses of Entertainments; and for other Purposes.

I. Whereas the Laws at present in Force, have been found ineffectual for the Due Regulation of Ordinaries, and Restraint of Tippling Houses.

II. Be it Enacted, by the Governor, Council, and Assembly, and by the Authority of the same, That all Persons hereafter retailing Liquors, shall sell the same by sealed Measures, according to the Directions of an Act of Assembly, intituled, An Act for regulating Weights and Measures; Provided, that it shall and may be lawful for Ordinary Keepers, licensed agreeable to the Directions of this Act, to sell liquor in Bottles, Bowls or Mugs, so as they sell for no more than the Quantity the said Vessels contain.

III. And be it further Enacted, by the Authority aforesaid, That no Person not having a License for keeping an Ordinary, shall sell or retail Liquors in smaller quantities than is by this Act permitted, under the Penalty of Five Pounds, Proclamation Money; one Half to the Governor or Commander in Chief for the Time being and the other Half to the Informer.

IV. And be it further Enacted, by the Authority aforesaid, That any Person by applying to the Court of the County in which such Person dwells, and Praying a License to keep an Ordinary, may, at the Direction of Such Court, be ordered to have a License for the purpose aforesaid; unless it shall appear to the said Court that the Person so applying is a Person of Gross Immorality, of such Poor circumstances, and slender Credit, that they think it will not be possible for him or her to comply with the intention of this Act, or usually suffers excessive or unlawful gaming in his or her House; [...]

VI. And be it further Enacted by the Authority aforesaid, That if any Ordinary Keeper shall sell to any Person, in his or her House, immoderate quantities of strong Liquors, whereby such Person may be intoxicated on the Lord's Day; or entertain Servants and Slaves Against the Will of their Masters or Mistresses; or common Sailors, against the Direction of the Masters of Vessels to which they belong; every Ordinary keeper so offending, shall and may, by Order of Two Justices, before whom such offence shall be proved, be, from thenceforth, suspended and disabled from keeping an Ordinary, as if he or she had never obtained a Licence for that Purpose. [...]

IX. And be it further Enacted, by the Authority aforesaid, That the Justices of each County, annually, at the next County Court after the First Day of May, shall rate the Prices of Liquors, Diet, Lodging, Fodder, Corn, Provender, and Pasturage, to be taken by Ordinary Keepers; and every Ordinary Keeper shall, within One Month after the Rates shall be set by the County Court where his or her License shall be granted, obtain of the Clerk a fair Copy of such Rates; for which the Clerk may take and receive Two Shillings and Six Pence, Proclamation Money, and no more; which Copy shall be openly set up in the common entertaining Room of such Ordinary, and there kept till the Rates are again altered; and every Ordinary Keeper failing herein shall forfeit Five Pounds Proclamation Money [...]

Laws, 1758, in Clark, *State Records,* 23:492-493.

Wm. Robertson Presented a Petition Shewing he is an Inhabitant of Beaufort Town Praying this Court will grant him a Licence at his now Dwelling House ordered the Clk. Issue Licence Accordingly sd Robertson giving bond according to Law.

Robert Gaskins Presented a Petition Shewing he is an Inhabitant of Portsmouth Town Praying this Court will Grant him Licence at his now Dwelling House Ordered the Clk. Issue Licence Accordingly said Gaskins Giving Bond according to Law.

Minutes of the Carteret County Court Minutes of Pleas and Quarter Sessions, May 1764, State Archives.

ൟൟ

Tavern keepers sought locations, such as proximity to courthouses, that might attract large numbers of patrons.

The Petition of Evan Skinner read in these Words Videlicet. Praying the Court to permitt him to Errect and Build a Sufficient house of Entertainment on the lott and half of Ground laid out for Publick Buildings on Perquimans River on Phelps Point which was Accordingly Granted by the Court that he have Liberty to Build as aforesaid Issued, fees pd.

Minutes of the Perquimans County Court of Pleas and Quarter Sessions, January 1753, State Archives.

Ralph Outlaw Exhibited in to Court his Petition Praying leave to Build a House of Entertainment upon the Land Appurtaining to the Court House Ordered that he have leave to do so on the following Conditions part of the said Ralph Outlaw do and will Build a good and Sufficient House not less then thirty eight or forty feet in Length and Eighteen in Bredth which house shall be of a proportionable Highth to its Dimentions in Length and Bredth with at least one Good Brick Chimney the said House to be Built on the ground Appurtaining to the Goal on the south End of the said Goal with a Passage at least Ten feet in width through it opposite to the Door of the said Goal and the said Ralph Outlaw to Inclose the said Goal with strong Post Rails and Poles not less then Tenn Feet High all which shall be Compleated in Twelve months after Date [...]

Minutes of the Bertie County Court of Pleas and Quarter Sessions, August 1763, State Archives.

∾৯৶৵

Although the majority of tavern keepers were men, many women took up the business as described by William Attmore when he stayed in Tarboro in 1787.

We rode about 10 Miles, to the house of Wm. Tuton and were informed there, that he was gone to Tarborough and was not expected home for several days, this determined me to accompany Mr. Jones to that place, we accordingly rode on five Miles further and about night fall arrived at the house of Mrs. Cobb, and ancient woman, who keeps a petty Ordinary—We concluded to stay here all night, not being sure of obtaining a lodging in Tarborough if we went there, as we had heard that every house was crowded, the Assembly being then met at that place. Mrs. Cobbs' house consisted of two Apartments, one was the sitting Room, the floor was of Clay or dirt, and there was one Bed in the Room—The other Apartment was floored with Boards and contained four good Beds, two on each side of the Room.—*Mrs. Cobb;* is a Woman between 83 and 84 years of Age, as she told me; she was born in the Isle of Wight County, Virginia, she retains her faculties and is as brisk and lively as most Women of 30 years of Age—She waits on Travellers herself and even goes to the Stable and takes care of their Horses herself. This not from necessity, having assistance enough if she chooses it; but seems to plume herself on her activity, and attention to her Guests and to their Horses—This Woman has near 50 descendants Children,

Grandchildren, and Great Grandchildren—We complained on entering the House that the Fire was almost out, she went and brought a load of Wood, threw it on, and with a pleasant air said "There it will be a fire when it burns"—alluding I suppose to the Story of the Fox that made the Ice smoke—We were furnished with a very indifferent supper; but our Horses being well taken care of in regard to food and each one being fastened by himself in a cover'd log Pen, we getting clean and good beds for ourselves were not uneasy.—[. . .]

> Rodman, *Journal of Tour to North Carolina by William Attmore, 1787*, 32-33.

❧

Not all abided by the law.

Upon Complaint being made that Valentine Wade one of his Majestys Justices of the Peace for the County of Carteret and who keeps a Tavern in the Town of Portsmouth in said County, Permits suffers and encourages disorderly persons, to dance and play at cards and dice in his house upon the Lords Day and upon reading the Affidavit of Joseph Ryall and another Affidavit of said Joseph Ryall and John Bragg

It is Ordered that the said Valentine Wade appear before his Excellency the Governour in Council on Tuesday the 20th day of Novr. next at Wilmington to Shew cause why he should not be Struck out of the Commission of the Peace for the said County

> Meeting of the Council, September 1, 1759, Cain, *Records of the Executive Council, 1755-1775*, 64.

It appearing to this Court that Mrs. Lettia Blackmore, and Mrs. Elizabeth Saunders are guilty of keeping disordly houses, and harbouring and detaining Common Sailors, to the great Injury of the Merchants and Masters of Vessells trading to the river of Cape Fiar. Order'd that their Licences be taken from them, and that if they permit for the future any Sailors or other disordly person or persons to tipple any Liquors in either of their houses, the Kings Attorney will directed to prosecute them, according to the Acts of the General Assembly in that case made and proved And that the Clerk give them Notice hereof.

> Minutes of the New Hanover County Court of Pleas and Quarter Sessions, April 1768, State Archives.

⤜⤛

Tavern keeping sometimes served as a springboard for advancement.

In a little emigration to Osborn Jefferies's, esq. on the banks of Tar-River, my horse falling lame, obliged us to call and make some stay at an ordinary, inn, or tavern, at Bute county courthouse, kept by one Jethroe Sumner, where we found an excellent dinner as well as an agreeable facetious host.

[This inn-keeper has distinguished himself in the course of the late war, being the general Sumner, of the American army, who has been so active in the Carolinas.

He is a man of a person lusty, and rather handsome, with an easy and genteel address: his marriage with a young woman of a good family, with whom he received a handsome fortune; his being a captain of provincials last war; but above all his violent principles, and keeping an inn at the courthouse (which is scarcely thought a mean occupation here), singular as the latter circumstance may appear, contributed more to his appointment and promotion in the American army, than any other merit.

For it is a fact, that more than one third of their general officers have been inn-keepers, and have been chiefly indebted to that circumstance for such rank.

Because by that public, but inferior station, their principles and persons became more generally known; and by the mixture and variety of company they conversed with, in the way of their business, their ideas and their ambitious views were more excited and extended than the generality of the honest and respectable planters, who remained in peace at their homes.]

Smyth, *A Tour of the United States of America*, 1:113-115.

⤜⤛

By law the county courts established taverns' rates for food, drink, lodging, and provender, though tavern keepers often successfully appealed for higher rates.

August Term 1774
Tavern Rates for Rowan County

	£	
To every Gallon West India rum	16	
To Ditto...New England	10.	8
To ditto...Brandy and Whiskey	10.	
Beer with 4 Bushills Malt and proportionable quantity of Hops to the Barrill per Quart		6
Peach Brandy or Whiskey made into Cordial per jill		.4
Sheaf Oats by the Sheaf 5 inches Diameter		.4
Sheaf fodder by the Sheaf well Cured and well bound 7 Inches Diameter		.4
Beer with 5 Bushills 3 Months old per Quart		.8
A Quart Toddy made of West India rum with loaf Sugar	1	4
A pint Sling made of the Same	1	4
Ditto of New England	1	
Ditto of Brandy or Whiskey	1	
Maderia or Vidonia Wine per Gallon	16	
Sanger with loaf Sugar per Quart	1	4
Stabling each horse 24 hours with plenty of Hay or Fodder and if of Common woods hay		8
If English Grass such as Timothy or Clover	1	
Corn or Oats per Quart		2
Breakfast or Supper with hott meat and Small beer drink		8
Ditto with Coffee	1	
Dinner with a Sufficient Dish of Wholsome well dressed and well served up meat	1	
Good pasture for a horse per night		8
Lodging per night good bed and Clean Sheets		4
Boiled Cyder per Quart		8
Cyder Royal per Quart	1	4
Draught Cyder per Quart		8
Clarrett per Bottle	7	6
Punch per Qt. wth. Orange or lime Juice	2	

And so in proportion for larger or smaller Quantity's [. . .]

Minutes of the Rowan County Court of Pleas and Quarter Sessions, August 1774, State Archives.

Read the Petition of Wm. Robertson and George Bell Shewing that The Tavern Rates in Some things is Too Little, the Court Taken the Same into Considiration and Granted the Same as Follows videlicet

Brackfast	£	0 .1. 0
Dinner		0 .1. 4
West India Rum per jill		0. 0. 6
New England Rum pr. jill		0. 0. 4
Norward cider pr. Quart.		0. 0. 4
North Carolina Do. per Quart [shall same] To be [Crab Cider]		0 .0. 6

> Minutes of the Carteret County Court of Pleas and Quarter Sessions, December 1766, State Archives.

∿❧❧

Accounts kept by tavern keepers revealed an even greater variety of drink as well as recreational activities and even banking operations.

1723.	Dr.	
May. Jacob Brooks	1	0
2. To beer	2	0
5. To Rum	1	6
7. To pay in Club	3	6
8. To beer	1	6
10. To beer	1	0
12. To rum and beer	2	6
13. To Egg punch	3	0
14. To sleep	1	3
To beer	1	0
15. To rum	1	6
17. To beer and rum	2	6
18. To beer	2	0
To rum	1	6
22. To sleep	1	3
25. To sleep	5	0
26.To sleep	2	6
To beer	1	0
27. To sleep	1	3
28. To Rum		9
To beer	1	0
29.To Rum		9
To Diat	1	3

	£	s	d
To sleep		2	6
To Do.		2	6
31. To sleep		2	6
To Diat		1	3
To sleep		1	3
To Diat		1	3
June 1. To 2 Diats		2	6
To beer		1	0
To 2 Diats		2	6
3. To sleep		2	6
To 2 Diats		2	6
4. To 2 Diats		2	6
5. To beer and sleep		2	3
To Rum			9
7. To milk punch		1	6
10. To Rum and beer		2	6
16. To Diat and punch		3	9
To Diat and beer		2	3
To sleep		1	3
17. To rum and beer		2	6
18. To pay in Club		2	10
19. To sleep and beer		3	3
20. To rum and beer		1	6
To sleep		5	0
22. To rum		1	6
23. To a weeks Diat		10	0
To beer		1	0
To pay in Club		2	4
£	5	8	2

[*Endorsed:*]
Jacob Brooks account

Recorded £1.14. 6

Errors Excepted
per James Palin

Jacob Brooks Account with James Palin, 1723, Chowan County, Miscellaneous Records, Personal Accounts, 1700-1789, State Archives.

Peter Young		Dr	
1740.			
To the Ballance of an old Acct.	1	15	
8ber. 2d. To 1 Bowle of Punch with Briggs		5	
12th. To 2 Do. with Willkins		10	
19th. To 1 Gill of Rum and 1 Bowle of Punch		7	
23d. To 3 Bowles of Punch wth Rowsom		15	
24th. To 3 Gills of Rum		6	
To 1 Quarter of Pork		12	6
1742.			
8ber. 22. To 3 Bowles of Punch		15	
To 3 Gills of Rum		6	
To 1 Bowle of Punch with Robinson		5	
23d. To 1 Gill of Rum		2	
24th. To 1 Bowle of Punch with Rogers		5	
9ber. 1. To 1 Gill of Rum and 1 Bowle of Punch		7	6
3d. To 1 Bowle of Punch with Clark		5	
To 1 Shoal		12	6
8th To 1 Bowle of Punch wth Liles		5	
To 72 lb. weight of Beef	3	12	
9th. To 2 muggs of flip		10	
To 5 Gills of Bitters		2	6
To Bills Paid him	13		
To 1 Gill of Rum		2	
10th. To 2 Gills of Rum		4	
13th. To 1 Mugg of Punch		5	
22d. To Supper and 1 Mugg of Punch		10	
23d. To 1 Gill of Rum		2	
26th. To 1 Gill of Rum		2	
28th. To 1 Mugg of Flip		5	
To 1 Gill of Rum		2	
Decbr. 13th. To 1 Bowle of Punch		5	
14th. To 4 Do.	1		
15th. To 1 Do. with Collins		5	
22d. To 6 Do.	1	10	
Janry. To 1 Do.		5	

	£			
To Club with Standing			5	
To 1 Gill of Rum			2	
14th. To 1 Mugg of Flip and Breakfast			10	
19th. To 1 Mugg of Flip			5	
20th. To money			12	6
To 1 Mugg of Flip			5	
Febry 1st. To 1 Do.			5	
Carried up	£	31	19	6
Brought up		31	19	6
Febry. 1st. To Club with Jesse			4	
2d. To Sundrys		1	2	6
March 6th. To 2 Bowles of Punch			10	
7th. To 1 Do. with Liles			5	
15th. To 1 Mugg of flip			5	
20th. To Club in Wine			15	
21st. To 2 muggs of flip			10	
To money Answered Luke		1		
1743.				
April 5th. To 1 Bowle of Punch			5	
To 1 Gill of Rum			2	
24th. To 1 Bowle of Punch			5	
25th. To 1 Gill of Rum			2	
May 3d. To [*blank*]			7	6
8th. To 1 Gill of Rum			2	
30th. To 1 Bowle of Punch			5	
July 3d. To 1 Do.			5	
4th. To 1 Do.			5	
11th. To 1 Gill of Rum			2	
To 1 Bowle of Punch			5	
12th. To 1 Do. with Frasier			5	
Augst. 4th. To ½ a Gallon of Cyder			4	
5th. To 1 Mugg of Cyder			2	
6th. To 2 Do.			4	
7th. To 2 Do.			4	
8th. To 1 Do.			2	
9th. To 3 Do.			6	
29th. To 1 Bowle of Punch			7	6
Sep:er. 3d. To 2 Do.			10	
12th. To 1 Gill of Rum			2	
16. To 1 Bowle of Punch			5	
Octo. 14. To 1 Gill of Rum			2	

		£		
25th. To 1 Do.			2	
Novbr. 3d. To 2 Bowles of Punch			10	
5th. To 4 Bowles of Do. with Butler	1			
To 1 Do. by yr. Self			5	
6th. To 1 Gill of Rum and Cyder			4	6
To 1 Bowle of Punch			5	
13th To 1 Do.			5	
22d. To Dinner and Club			10	
24th To Lodging 1 Gill Rum and Punch			9	6
£		44	15	

This 4th day october 1744 Came up Samuell Gregoy personly before Me and maid oath on the hole avengelles that the above account is just and true.

Witness   J. Butler JP

Peter Young Account with ?, 1740, Chowan County, Personal Accounts, State Archives.

Dr Smith Warff in Acct. Current with Jno. Vaun	£	s.	d.
1757.			
Sept. 5. To an Acct. Settled of Ballance Due		7	5
1758.			
May 13th. To proclamation Lent		5	
26. To 1 Nip of Porter			8
June 1st. To Do.			8
3d. To 1 Bowl of Porter at ShuffleBoard		1	4
8th. To proclamation Lent	1	10	
17. To Do.		5	
26. To a full Rum 4d. 1 Bowl of Porter 1s. 4d.		1	8
To Club to Porter with Parson Hall		1	8
27. To 1 Nip Porter			8
28. To Do.			8
29. To Proclamation Lent		8	
July 1st. To 2 gills of Rum 8d. Nip Porter 8d. Proclamation Lent 3s/		4	4
8th. To 1 Nip Porter			8
12. To a Pale 1s/6d Nip of Porter 8d/		2	2
19. To 2 Cordials			8
22d. To 1 Nip of Porter			8

31st. To proclamation Lent		15	
1st. To Cr. Gave Mr. Stevenson	1	5	
Augt. 10. To 1 Bowl of Porter		1	4
11. To ½ Gallon Rum		2	8
To 1 Pair of Compasses		1	
12. To a Bowl of Porter		1	4
14. To 4 lb. of Choalk at 2d.			8
18. To 5 Nips of Porter at Shuffle Board		3	4
19. To 2 Cordials			8
28. To Proclamation paid James Bond		15	6
as per Order			
Sept. 2d. To Do. to Daniel Yates		9	
4th. To 1 Bowl of Porter		1	4
9. To 1 Mint Dram			8
13. To 1 Bowl of Porter with Gibson Do.		2	8
with Yeomans			
22d. To 1 jill Rum 4d a Nip of Porter 8d		1	
Octobr. 2d. To 500 of 10d Nails 6s/ 500 of		9	4
6d at 3/4			
To 2 Cordials			8
30. To Proclamation paid in part of the		10	
the Schoolhouse			
31st. To Do. Lent £2.0. 1 Nip of Porter	2		8
8d/			
Novr. 7th. To gill of Rum			4
20. To 2 Nips Porter 1s/4d Victuals		2	8
Pro Negros 16d			
21st. To 1 Bushell of Salt		6	
To 1 Cordial			4
22d. To 1 Dram 8d 1/2 Bowls of Porter		2	8
2s/			
23. To 1 Dram			4
24th. To Do.			4
25. To 1 Nip of Porter 8d 1 Bowl of Do.		2	
1s/4d			
26. To 1 Dram			4
30. To Do.			4
1758.		s	d
Decr. 2d. To Sundries Brought forward	£11	8	7
To 1 Dram 4d 3 Nips of Porter at		2	4

Description		s	d
Shuffleboard 2/			
To 2 Nips of Do. with Alen p. Warburton		1	4
6th. To 1 Nip of Porter at Cards			8
8. To 1 Dram			4
11. To Do.			4
21st. To a Bowl of Porter with Jones		1	4
30th. To 1 Dram 4d Mint Dram 1s/		1	
1759. To 1 Nip of Porter			8
Janry. 2d. To 1 Do.			8
8th. To Mint Dram			8
Mar. 9th. To 1 Nip of Porter			8
To 1 Bowl of Porter sent to Rosses		1	4
10. To Proclamation Lent to Buy fish		1	4
May 26. To 1 Long Dram			8
June 22d. To 1 Small Bowl of Porter		1	
26th. To 1 Bowl of do.		2	
July 12. To Do. with Willm. Jones		1	4
21st. To Club to Do. with Do. 1s/4d small Bowl Porter 1s/		2	4
23d. To 1 Small Bowl of Porter		1	
Augt. 3. To 1 Long Dram			8
6th. To 1 small Bowl Porter 1s/ Club to Do 8d		1	8
7. To ½ Bottle of Beer		1	
8. To a Bowl of Porter		1	4
9. To 1 Dram			4
Sept. 6. To 1 Bottle of Wine		5	8
10. To 1 pt. of Do.		2	6
1760.			
April 1st. To 2 Small Bowls of Porter		2	
Octobr. 18th. To proclamation pd. Wm. Badham Pr. Order of Court	3		
	£16	4	9
Contra			Cr
By 42 foot of Gutters at 3d ½		12	3
By 3000 Bricks at 20s. Per	3		
By fixing Up 5 Small Shelves		4	
By Moving a Small Store from one yard to the Other		15	
By 22 Lights of sashes at 8d		14	8

By Building a Piase at the Schoolhouse	1	15	
By 3 bills	2	14	
Ballance Due to J. V.	6	9	10
Errors Excepted	£16	4	9
per Jno. Vaun			

[*Endorsed*:]
John Vaun vs. Smith Waffe Acct.

Account to bring
to Chowan County

Smith Waffe Account with Jno. Vaun, 1757-1759, Chowan County, Personal Accounts, State Archives.

∽⟨∘⟩∽

Recognizing the value of taverns to travelers, the General Assembly in 1741 mandated two such establishments for the newly-created town of Johnston, and in 1767 required operators of longer ferries throughout the colony to maintain ordinaries.

X. And be it further Enacted, by the Authority aforesaid, That for the Encouragement of the said Town, after there shall be Two good Public Houses, fit for the accommodation of Travellers, and good Boats provided, viz, one on each side of the said River, for transporting of Travellers, and their Horses, the said Houses and Boats to be approved of by the Justices of the Court of the said County, when the greater Number of the Justices are in Court, that then the Court of the said County, and all General Musters, shall be held in the said Town, and all other the Public Business of the said County shall be transacted in the said Town, and in no other Place or Places whatsoever.

Laws, 1741, in Clark, *State Records*, 23:171.

XV. And be it further Enacted by the Authority aforesaid, That from and after the Passing this Act, all Keepers of Public Ferries or Bridges within this Province, where the Ferriage or Bridge Toll is above Four Pence, Proclamation Money, for a Man and Horse, shall be obliged to furnish all Travellers with Entertainment at Tavern Rates, and shall take out License for that Purpose; and if any Keeper of any such Public Ferry or Bridge shall refuse or neglect to furnish such Entertainment, or to take out such License such Ferry or Bridge Keeper shall forfeit and pay for each Offence the Sum of Ten Pounds, Proclamation Money, to any Person who shall sue for the same.

Laws, 1766 [1767], in Clark, *State Records*, 23:728.

⊰⊱

Taverns may sometimes have offered more than food, drink, and lodging to their patrons.

[...] [1725] <*Marston v. Havett. Case.*> Elizabeth Marston Widow of Edenton in Chowan precinct Tavernkeeper comes by Thomas Swann her Attorney to prosecute William Havett and Mary his Wife late of the precinct aforesaid in custody of the Marshall etc. in a plea of the Case for Scandalous Words Spoken by the said Mary of the plaintiffe. To witt that the Said Elizabeth (the said plaintiffe meaning) is a common Bawd and keeps a Common Bawdy house and that her two daughters are the young whores by which she carrys on her trade of whoring with her customers that use her house (the house of the plaintiffe meaning) and afterwards these following words Videlicet That she the said Elizabeth (the plaintiffe meaning) is an Old Whore and keeps a common bawdy house (the house of the plaintiffe meaning) and She (the plaintiffe meaning) kept two of her daughters for whores with intent to entertaine and draw Lewd and wicked people to her house (the house of the plaintiffe meaning) being a publick house of entertainment and that Six men hath been taken in bed with her daughters in one night in her house etc. [. . .]

Marston v. Havet, in Cain, *North Carolina Higher-Court Minutes, 1724-1730*, 128.

[...] [1729] <*Marston v. Trotter*> [...] And now here at this day (Videlicet etc.) Came the aforesayd Elizabeth having filed her Declaration in these words Videlicet Elizabeth Marston Tavernkeeper of in the Town of Edenton in the precinct of Chowan Widow Complaines of James Trotter of the Same Town and precinct Taylor in custody of the Marshall of a plea of Trespass on the Case [...] Yet the aforesayd James Trotter not being ignorant of the premises but envying the happy Estate and Condition of the sayd Elizabeth and malitiously intending not only to deprive her the Sayd Elizabeth of her good name fame Credit Estimation and repute aforesayd and to bring her the Sayd Eliza. in the hate and evill opinion of all her Customers Neighbours and other worthy persons of this Government But also innocently to cause her to be brought into danger of Great fines and forfeitures and Corporall punishment did on the Sixth day of July last past at Edenton in the precinct of Chowan and within the Jurisdiction of this Court These false feigned Scandalous and opprobious Words following in the presence of divers of her Neighbours and Customers who then frequented her House and other worthy persons of this Government then and there being present and hearing Openly and publickly and with a loud Voyce the sayd James did Speak Declare and publish to the Sayd Elizabeth Videlicet You (meaning the sayd plaintiff) are an Old Bawd and are a Bawd to Your own Daughters And that You (meaning the Sayd plaintiff) putt two of Your own daughters to Bed with two Men in Virginia and received a pistole of the Sayd Men for So doing [. . .]

> Marston v. Trotter, in Cain, *North Carolina Higher-Court Minutes, 1724-1730*, 554-555.

⤝⤞

In addition to taverns, at least one coffee house opened for the benefit of gentlemen and businessmen.

WILMINGTON, (N. Carolina) Sept. 5.

A Coffee-House, is this Day opened at the Printing Office in Wilmington, for the Accomodation of such Gentlemen as are pleased to make Use thereof. Letters and Messages sent there, will be taken Care of, by the Proprietor of the same.

> *North-Carolina Magazine*; or, *Universal Intelligencer* (New Bern), September 21, 1764.

Criminality and Law Enforcement

Criminal activity reflected the tension, frustation, and desperation within colonial society.

The Jurors for Our Sovereign Lord the King on their Oath do present that Mary Cotton late of Bath Town in the County of Bath in the province of North Carolina aforesaid Spinster on the twentieth day of November in the Year of Our Lord One thousand Seven hundred and twenty three and in the tenth Year of the reign of Our Sovereign Lord King George by force and Armes etc. at Bath Town aforesaid One certain white Cotton and linnen sheet of the value of ten shillings belonging to Roger Kenyon of Bath Town aforesaid did then and there take and feloniously carry away and afterwards Videlicet on the twenty seventh day of the said Month of November at Bath Town aforesaid one other white Cotton and Linen sheet of the goods and chattells of the said Roger Kenyon and of the value of ten shillings and two linen shirts One Window Curtain and a Chest of drawers Cloth of white homespun damask all of the value of forty shillings she the said Mary then and there feloniously took and carryed away. And afterwards Videlicet on the twentieth day of December following One three pounds Bill one of the publick Bills of Credit of this Province belonging to the said Roger Kenyon she the aforesaid Mary at Bath Town aforesaid then and there being did feloniously take Steal and carry away and afterwards Videlicet on the twenty fifth day of the said Month of December at Bath Town aforesaid One five pounds Bill one of the publick Bills of Credit of this Province to the aforesaid Roger Kenyon belonging then and there being she the said Mary did take Steal and carry away Contrary to the peace of Our said Lord the King that now is his Crown and dignity etc.

Cain, *North Carolina Higher-Court Minutes, 1724-1730*, 27.

ONE HUNDRED POUNDS REWARD.
WHEREAS on Friday the 3d Instant, two Men came to my House, who lodged there that Night, and eat Breakfast next Morning; when they gave me a Thirty Shilling Bill to change, in Order to pay their Reckoning. I accordingly went into a Room adjoining to change it when they rushed in upon me, presenting their Rifles at me, and ordered me to deliver up my Keys; and upon my telling them I had not the Keys, they made my Negro Wench bring them a Hammer, and compelled me

to break open the Chest, when they took thereout 375 l. Proc. They then proceeded to another Chest, made me unlock it, and plundered it of near the like Sum. They likewise took with them a light-coloured Great Coat, a Pair of Leather Breeches, a Pair of Leather Bags, &c.

One of the above Men is about six Feet high, between 25 and 30 Years old, of a sandy Complexion, sandy red Beard; and has a down Look; had on a snuff coloured Surtout Coat, with a Piece off the left Skirt, a blue Jacket, and black Breeches, and rode a large blaze Face Sorrel Stallion, about 15 Hands high, all four Feet white, and was lame with travelling. The other is about five Feet seven Inches high, between 28 and 30 Years old, has curled Locks, full mouthed, talks very pertly, and a lame in his right Knee and Leg; had on a pale blue Surtout Coat, Leather Breeches, a half-worn small brim'd Hat, Leggins the same as the Surtout, and a Silver Spur; and took with him a black roan Horse, (the Property of the Subscriber) near 14 Hands high, about 7 Years old, one of his Feet white to the Footlocks, has a Roman Nose, full of grey Hairs, pretty lively, a natural Trotter, and branded on the near Buttock I.W.

Whoever apprehends the above Persons, and secures them and the Money, shall receive the above Reward, or in Proportion to the Money they shall find with them.

JOHN FOY.

Craven County, February 6, 1775.

North Carolina Gazette (New Bern), April 7, 1775.

Ordered by the Court that James Cole and William Whitlock be committed to the public Goal for the District of Salisbury on suspicion of having knowingly passed Counterfeit Money of this province until discharged by due course of Law [...]

Minutes of the Rowan County Court of Pleas and Quarter Sessions, May 1774, State Archives.

[July, 1702]. The Jurors for our Soveraign Lady the Queen Present upon their Oaths that Susannah Evans of the precinct of Coratuck in the County of Albemarle in the aforesaid Province Not having the fear of God before her Eyes but being led by the Instigation of the Devill did on or about the twenty Fifth day of July last past the body of Deborah Bourchier being then in the peace of our Soveraigne Lady the Queen Devilishly and malitiously bewitch and by assistance of the

Devill afflict with Mortall paines the body of the said Deborah Bourchier whereby the said Deborah departed this life and alsoe did diabolically and Malitiously bewitch Severall other of her Majesties Liege Subjects against the peace of our Said Soveraigne Lady the Queen and against the forme of the Statute in that Case made and provided etc.

Price, *North Carolina Higher-Court Records, 1702-1708,* 70.

[November, 1695]. North Carolina To the Honorable Generall Court
The Jurors for our Soveraigne Lord the King humbly presents that Geo. Scarbrough of the precinct of Pascotanck planter the fift day of October last past not haveing the fear of God before his eyes but being seduced by the Instigation of the Divell of his Malice forethought with force and armes in and upon James Sanderling the younger on the plantation wheron Mr. Jno. Jenings liveth in the precinct aforesaid in the peace of god therebeing an assault did make and with one Gun of the value of twenty shillings which the said Geo. Scarbrough held in both his hands the said Gun being loaded with one leaden Bullet and severall leaden shott the said James Sanderling in the hinder part of his left thigh and lower part of his belly did shoot and severall mortall wounds to him the said James Sanderlin in his said left thigh and lower part of his belly did give one Wherof that is to say in the hinder part of his left thigh was nine Inches deep of which mortall Wounds the said James Sanderling in the precinct aforesaid from the said fift day of October untill in or about the seventeenth day of the same moneth did languish upon or about which seventeenth day of October the said James Sanderlin of the mortall Wounds aforesaid died and soe the Jurors aforesaid say that the aforesaid George Scarbrough in maner and forme aforesaid of his malice forethought the said James Sanderling Wilfully and feloniously did Kill and murder against the Peace of our Soveraigne Lord the King and contrary to the forme of the statute in that case provided. [...]

Parker, *North Carolina Higher-Court Records, 1670-1696,* 221-222.

Law enforcement centered upon justices of the peace in the respective counties, who collectively comprised the county court, both a judicial and adminstrative body. Appointed by the governor, the justices or

magistrates convened quarterly in the county courthouses, and proved jealous of their dignity and authority.

A New Commission of the Peace and Dedd. Potestation from his Excellency Arthur Dobbs Esqr. Governor etc. was Produced and Read Directed to James Hasell, John Swann, John Dawson, Lewis DeRossett, John Rieusett, Edward Brice Dobbs, Richard Spaight, Charles Berry and Maurice Moore Esqrs. Members of his Majestys Council, And to John Brown, John Hill John Campbell, Robt. West Junr. Cullen Pollock, Thomas Pugh, John Baker, Henry Hill, John Brickell, Edward Rasor, Henry Hunter, William Gray, Joseph Jordan, Robert Sumner Lillington Lockhart, Peter West, Thomas Slatter, and James Moore Esqrs. appointing them Justices of the Peace for the County of Bertie in the Province of North Carolina. At the same time John Hill, Thomas Pugh, Joseph Jordan and William Gray appeared in the Court House And the said John Hill Administered the Oaths by Law appointed for the Quallification of Publick officers to Thomas Pugh, William Gray and Joseph Jordan who at the same time Read and Subscribed the Test. And then the said John Hill Administred to the said Thomas Pugh, William Gray and Joseph Jordan the Oath of a Justice of the Peace after which the said John Hill was duly Quallifyed as a Justice of the Peace for the County aforsaid by having the Several Oaths Administered to him by William Gray Esqr. and by Reading and Subscribing the Test and also taking the oath of office. And after Which Quallifycations the said John Hill, Thomas Pugh, William Gray and Joseph Jordan took their seats on the Bench And Ordered the Sheriff to open the Court which was Accordingly Done. [...]

> Minutes of the Bertie County Court of Pleas and Quarter Sessions, October 1760, State Archives.

An Act, for settling the Precinct Courts and Courthouses

I. Whereas through the great Taxes and Charges this Government hath laboured under, by Means of the late Indian War, there has been no Care taken by preceding Assemblies to settle the several Precinct Courts to any fixed or Certain Place, but have always hitherto been kept and held at private Houses, where they have been, and are liable to be removed, at the Pleasure of the person or persons owning such Houses, to the great Annoyance of the Magistrates and People: For the Prevention of which for the Future;

II. Be it Enacted, by his Excellency the Pallatine, and the rest of the true and absolute Lords Proprietors of the Province of Carolina, by and with the Advice and Consent of the rest of the Members of this present General Assembly, now met at Edenton, at Queen Anne's Creek, in Chown Precinct for the North East part of the said Province, and it is hereby Enacted, by the Authority of the same, That from and after the Ratification of this Act, the Justices of the Peace that are now appointed for and in every respective Precinct in this Government, or shall hereafter be appointed within the Time limited in this Act for Building the Precinct Court-houses, or the greatest part of them, are hereby required and impowered to purchase the quantity of One Acre of Land, in such Place or Places of their several Precincts, as in and by this Act is hereby nominated and appointed, for erecting the said Court-houses on.

III. And for the better enabling the said Justices, or the greatest part of them, to purchase said Lands, and build the said Court houses: Be it Enacted, by the authority aforsaid, That the said Justices, or the greatest Part of them, shall have full power and Authority to raise Money, by a Poll Tax on the several Inhabitants of their respective Precincts, for the Purchasing such lands and building the said Court-houses thereon, not exceeding the sum of five Shillings per Poll per Annum; which said Tax or Levy shall be paid to them the said Justices, or whom they, or the greatest part of them, shall appoint to receive the same, by each and every person respectively, in the same Manner and Form as they do their Public Levy, and under the same Fines and Forfeitures. [...]

Laws, 1722, in Clark, *State Records*, 23:100-101.

William Bryan, Theophilus Hunter, John Gyles Thomas, Jopha. Horton and Joseph Lane Esqrs. are appointed a Cometee to lay out Ground for a Court house on Hintons Quarter Provided they find a Convinient place Otherways make a Report next Court, And to Contract for the Building a Court House Prison and Stocks, the Courthous to be 30 foot in Length and 20 foot Wide, and twelve foot Pitch between the Joints to be Covered with Pine Heart Shingles, The Frame all Sawd Boarded with Fether Edgd Boards sawd Cills 12 In by Ten and Plates 12 by 4 Postes 8 by 4 and Studs 4 by 3 Rafters 4 by 3. To lay the floors above and below Inch and quarter from the Saw, Justices Seat to be three foot and a half from the Floor with handreals and Banisters, Lawiers Barr Banisterd and Clarkes Table and Seats, [Furins] for the

Jurys, Stairs to the Jury Room, Two Doors and five Windows below and Two Windows above To be Set a foot from the Ground, [...]

> Minutes of the Johnston County Court of Pleas and Quarter Sessions, April 1759, State Archives.

It is this day Order'd. That whatEver Persons Shall [*illegible*] respect aboute an Officer of this Court during the Time of the Court Sitting, he Shall be Liable to Answer for the Same, immediately before the Justices then Sitting [...]

Samuel Hallowell appear'd to his Recognizance for the Abuse he gave Nicho. RoutLedge Esqr. in the Month of August Last, and whereas the Said Hallowell (in open Court) acknowledg'd himself very Sorry for the Offence and promised that he would not be guilty of the Like any more, Mr. RoutLedge forgave him, and thereupon, this worshipful Court thought fit to Discharge him from the Said Recognizance. [...]

> Minutes of the Craven County Court of Pleas and Quarter Sessions, September 1738, State Archives.

❧❧❧

By law justices acted individually or in pairs to adjudicate a variety of matters when the county court was not in session—the "magistrate's court"—but their decisions could be appealed to the county court.

An Act for the Tryal of Small & Mean Causes.

I. Whereas the Charges in the Genl. Precinct Courts of this Governmt. in many Actions of small value do very often surmount the demand of the Pltfs. to the very great damage of the Partys.

II. Be It Enacted by His Excellency the Pallatine & the Rest of the True & Absolute Lords Props. of the Province of Carolina by & with the Advice & Consent of the rest of the Members of this Genl. Assembly now met at Little River for the No. East part of the said province.

III. And It is Hereby Enacted by the Authority of the same that any two or more Justices of Peace, whereof one shall be of the Quorum, are hereby Impowered by their warrant under their hands & Seal directed to some one of the constables, in all actions of debt or other Demands whatsoever for any sum or matter to the value of Forty Shillings or under (which Actions are Hereby made Issuable, Tryable &

Determinable only before two justices of the Peace, whereof one shall be of the Quorum as afors'd, and in no Court of Pleas or Judicature whatsoever) cause to be apprehended & brought before them any person or persons which have & do refuse or neglect to pay any Creditor complaining of his or their debt or debts or demands afors'd with all witnesses which are required by either Pltf. Or Deft. for the better Proof Clearing & Opening the Actions afors'd & after both Partys with witnesses if any be required before them are come to Examine, Hear, Trye, Adjudge & finally Determine all Complaint & Action of Debts or Demands as afors'd before them brot. And the said Justices are hereby Impowered in case Witnesses or other Reasonable or sufficient Proof are not & cannot be produced to prove any debt Matter or thing which shall or may be brought before them as afors'd to take the Party or Partys Oath or Oaths complaining touching all matters that shall be in dispute which Oaths shall be first proposed or given to the Dft. or Dfts. & upon his or their refusal to take an Oath & answering to such questions as shall be demanded by the s'd Justices relating to the s'd cause then the Justices shall have power to examine the Pltf. or Pltfs. on his or their Oaths & Adjudge & Determine all matters afors'd according to Justice & Equity: And after Determination, Execution upon the Goods & Chattels of the Dft. to the full value of the debt due & the Costs and Charges hereafter in this Act provided to be paid to cause to be Levied & for want of Goods & Chattels the Bodys of the Deft. or Defts. to the common gaol to Committ until he or they shall pay his or their debts as afors'd according to the practice of the Court of Pleas. [...]

Laws, 1715, in Clark, *State Records*, 23:27-28.

Dec. 1 [1766]. There was trouble in our Tavern this morning. A young man refused to pay all he owed, and attacked Br. Schille, angrily placing a loaded gun twice against his breast, and hurting his own thumb badly in trying to cock it. Br. Schille pushed the gun aside, and others disarmed the fellow, who struck them in the face, so that the blood flowed freely. Br. Loesch tried him, and sent him bound to the prison in Salisbury, under guard of Joseph Müller and Ziegler. [...]

Fries, *Records of the Moravians*, 1:337.

[...] Geo. Mears Esqr. James Henesey, James Rogers and John Henesey having been warranted and Judgment pass'd against them by

Alexander Duncan Esqr. for not attending to give their vote at the last Election for Vestry men appeal'd to this Court from sd. Judgment and having Shew'd Sufficient cause upon Oath, was Excus'd and the aforesaid Judgment revers'd.

> Minutes of the New Hanover County Court of Pleas and Quarter Sessions, September 1764, State Archives.

❧❦

The county sheriff, who was nominated by the justices and appointed by the governor, constituted the principal law enforcement officer in the county. Sheriffs appointed deputies, subject to the approval of the county court, but deputies may have enjoyed less respect than the principal officer. The county coroner substituted for the sheriff when the latter was unavailable.

Present His Majestys Justices, to wit Aguila Sugg, Edward Moore, Duncan Lamon, William Haywood, Sherwood Haywood, Henry Irwin, Patrick McDowall, Jesse Hare

This being the Court appointed by Act of Assembly for the Recommendation to his Excellency the Governor of Gentlemen properly qualified to be appointed and to act as Sheriff of this County for the ensuing Year The Majestrates abovementioned voted in the following Order for the following Persons, to wit,

	Voted for
Edward Moore	Sherwood Haywood, Duncan Lamon, Jesse Hare
Aguila Sugg	Sherwood Haywood, Duncan Lamon, Jesse Hare
Duncan Lamon	Sherwood Haywood, Duncan Lamon, Jesse Hare
William Haywood	Sherwood Haywood, Duncan Lamon, Jesse Hare
Sherwood Haywood	Sherwood Haywood, Duncan Lamon, Jesse Hare
Henry Irwin	Sherwood Haywood, William Haywood, Aguila Sugg
Patrick McDowall	Sherwood Haywood, William Haywood, Aguila Sugg
Jesse Hare	Sherwood Haywood, William Haywood, Aguila Sugg

So that	had
Sherwood Haywood	8 Votes
Duncan Lamon	5 Votes
Jesse Hare	5 Votes
William Haywood	3 Votes
Aguila Sugg	3 Votes

> Minutes of the Edgecombe County Court of Pleas and Quarter Sessions, May 1770, State Archives.

This day came into Open Court James McCay and prodused a Commission from his Exelincy William Tryon thereby Constituting and Appointing him the Said James McCay High Sheriff of Rowan County dated the 18th day of June 1771 and ofered for Security, Henry Sloan Thomas McCartney, David Smith William Lynn, and Hugh Jinkins which was Approovd of by the Court and the Said James McCay Appeard and Accordingly and Quallifyed in Open Court According to Law and Subscribed the Test. etc. [...]

> Minutes of the Rowan County Court, August 1771, State Archives.

John Council Bryan produced a Commission from William Bryan Esqr. Sheriff appointing him Deputy Sheriff of Craven County, which was Read, and then upon the Qualifyed by taking the Oaths by Law Appointed for the Qualification of Public Officers [...]

Ordered that William Tisdale be fined Forty Shillings Proclamation Money for his Contempt in Refusing to Obey the Summons of John Council Bryan Deputy Sheriff this day to Serve as a Juror, and Ordered that the Sheriff Levy the Same on his Goods and Chattles unless he shew Cause for such failure and Contempt to the Next Court.

> Minutes of the Craven County Court of Pleas and Quarter Sessions, September 1771, State Archives.

Mr. Joseph Hardy Coroner of this County moved the Court for Leave to sell the Personal Estate of John Jones who was Lately Executed for the Murder of his wife. Granted and ordered that the same be sold at Publick Vendue on the Third Thursday in August next at the Now Dwelling House of Benjamin Stone and make Return thereof to this Court at next.   Dr [...]

Minutes of the Bertie County Court of Pleas and Quarter Sessions, July 1758, State Archives.

◈

Assisting the county court and sheriffs were constables, appointed for one-year terms by the magistrates. It was a demanding and occasionally perilous position. By law constables could turn to the public when they needed aid, but support was not always forthcoming. Even former constables, having themselves been rebuffed during the course of their duty, sometimes showed little respect for the constabulary.

This Court Appints William Robertson, on Hunting Quarters Constable from Hogg Island to the Oyster Creeks and order that he appear before Edward Fuller Esqr. and Quallifie.

Likewise Robert Gaskell Constable from Portsmouth to Thompsons Hammocks.

Likewise Thos. Hampton Constable from the Oyshter Creeks to the Lee Side of North River inCluding Harkers Island and the Banks from Topsail Inlett to Capelookout Bay.

Likewise Charles Gutry Constable from North River to Core Creek. [...]

Minutes of the Carteret County Court of Pleas and Quarter Sessions, June 1765, State Archives.

Jan. 15 [1770]. This afternoon there was an unpleasant occurrence in our Tavern. A man, Sam Moore, came in, and met Joseph Phelps, who is a Constable. Moore was angry, knowing that Phelps had a Warrant against him and wanted to arrest him, and although Phelps told him that he did not have the Warrant with him Moore cocked his gun and shot at Phelps, the ball passing through his clothing, though it fortunately did not hit him. Br. Jacob Bonn had Moore arrested, and having heard the case he ordered him bound and taken to jail at Salisbury by Constable Phelps and three other men. [...]

Fries, *Records of the Moravians*, 1:410.

On Motion of Mr. Stokes on Behalf of John Burroughs Constable of The Town of NewBern Alledging that William Barnes being Present on Board the Brigantine [*blank*] himself Master and Charged by said Constable to Aid and Assist him in the Execution of his office which said Barnes Neglected to do whereby the Said Burroughs was much beat and ill treated, The Facts Alledged appeared to be true on the Oath of said Burroughs.

Ordered said Barnes be fin'd £10 Ni si for such his Contempt And that Summons Issue to said Barnes to Shew Cause etc. [...]

Ordered that Goddard Debruhl be fined Forty Shillings Ni Si for his Contempt in Refusing to Obey the Summons or Order of John Burroughs Constable in not Aiding and Assisting him in the Execution of his office and that he have Notice. [...]

> Minutes of the Craven County Court, June 1769; September 1771, State Archives.

James Barnes a Sworn Constable made return of a Search Warrant Issued by Mr. Justice Edwards on Complaint of Capt. Benjamin Hill that he had severall Neet Cattle strayed awayed from him And accordingly the said Barnes together with the said Hill went to the plantation of Saml. Cotton where there was Two Steers which the said Hill Claimed as his proper Steers And One Joseph Cotten Brother to the said Saml. interposing, Swore and Violently threatd to Shoot and Destroy the said Barnes if he should Dare to come within the said Samuels fenced Grounds, and the said Joseph being arrested in the Kings Name to appear before Mr. Edwards refused to Obey the Authority or appear before Mr. Edwards or any other Justice. All which Doings being in great Contempt of the Authority and Laws of this Province and against the Peace And the Court taking the same into Consideracion Doth thereon Ordered That the said Joseph Cotten be amerced for his said Contempt in refusing to Obey the Officer the Summ of £10 and Cost And the Marshall Is hereby ordered to Estreat the same And it is further Ordered that the Marshall do take the said Cotten into Custody untill he shall give Secuty before some Magistrate in the Sum of £50 Ster to be of his good behaviour etc. [...]

Whereas Saml. Cotton Const. hath this day made Complaint to this Ct. that James Barnes, of this precinct on Monday last resisted him with Force and Arms in Executing a Warrant from John Edwards Gent. one of his Majestys Justices for this precinct concerning a Negro Claimd by James Thompson in the possession of the said James Barnes and that he resqued the said Negro from him and beat and abused him in the Execution of his Office. Ordered that the Marshall do forthwith take the said James Barnes in Custody and bring him before this Court Tomorrow by Twelve of th' Clock and that there are sufficient assistance for apprehending the said Barnes to answer the said Complaint. [...]

Minutes of the Bertie County Court of Pleas and Quarter Sessions, August 1732, May 1736, State Archives.

∽⑥✍

Provincial law required each county to construct a jail or prison, which one county attempted to make more secure by means of a stockade. A pillory, stocks, and whipping post usually accompanied the jail. At the behest of the county courts, sheriffs obtained shackles to secure prisoners.

An Act to impower the Justices of Currituck County to build a Prison, Pillory, and Stocks, in the said County, on the Lot whereon the Court House now stands, for the Use of the County.

I. Whereas the Prison in the County of Currituck is in great Decay, and in so ruinous a Condition, that the Prisoners cannot be held or detained therein; Therefore,

II. Be it Enacted, by the Governor, Council and Assembly, and by the Authority of the same, That Joshua Campbell, John Woodhouse, and William Mackey, are hereby appointed Commissioners; and they or the Majority of them, shall and may, and they are hereby required, within Six Months after the Passing of this Act, to agree and contract with Workmen for the Building and erecting a New Prison, Pillory, and Stocks, in and for the Use of the Country aforesaid. [...]

Laws, 1766, in Clark, *State Records*, 23:747.

This Court takeing into Consideration the Great Necessity and want of a prison in Beaufort Town for the Good and benifit of the Proclamation Did Agree and bargain with Mr. Daniel Resse of Beaufort Town to Build a prison on the Lot Number Seven in Beaufort Town and to be of the following Dementions viz. The Length to be Twenty Feet the Width Fifteen Feet The Walls of the prison to be Saw'd Loggs not less then Foure Inches Thick and Duftails at the Corners The Floors above and below to be layd with planck not less than foure Inches Thick also a partition to be in the Middle of said prison with a Doore and lock to it Also one strong Double Door on the out Side not less than three Inches thick with good Strong Iron Hinges and a Substantial Lock fiting for such a Doore Two Front Windows Two feet High and Eighteen

Inches Wide with proper Iron Grates to the Same The pitch or Distance between Floors and Doors within Side to be not less than Seven Feet. The Roof to be Covered with good pine Shingles well [parted]. The whole Worke to be done and performed Workman like for Such a Building and to be Compleaded in Foure Moneth time from this day being December the 10th 1736 And this Court promise to See the Said Danl. Ress pay'd for the performance of Said Worke as also the Sum of One Hundred Thirty Five pounds this Court hath Appointed Mr. James Salter Mr. Tho. Dudley and Capt. Ward to be Commissioners to See that Said Worke performed Also there is to be a good Strong Substantial pair of Stocks to be made by the Said Dan. Rees into the Afforsaid Bargain Further this Court hath Ordered the Marshall to Levey five Shillings per pole from every Tytheable in this precinct in Order to Defray the Afforesaid Said Sum of 135 pounds and that the Marshall have Ten per Cent for Collecting Said Money and pay Such Money be Collected to one or More of the Said afforesaid Commissioner in Order to be pay'd to the Said Workman as he goe on with the assortd Worke.

Then this Court Adjourned till tomorrow Morning Nine of the Clock.

The Court Met according to Adjournment.

> Minutes of the Carteret County Court of Pleas and Quarter Sessions, December 1736, State Archives.

Ordered that Thomas Hart and Francis Nash Employ Workmen to sett up Stockaids round the Prison the Stocks to be ten feet above Ground and the whole to be done in the Safest manner as shall appear to the Discretion of the said Hart and Nash and that they bring in their Charge of the same to the next Court.

> Minutes of the Orange County Court of Pleas and Quarter Sessions, November 1763, State Archives.

Ordered that the Sheriff Provide Handcuffs and Fetters for the Felons and Other things necessary for the Securing of Felons that are or hereafter maybe Committed to the Publick Goal of this Province in New Bern.

> Minutes of the Craven County Court of Pleas and Quarter Sessions, August 1752, State Archives.

◈◈◈

Sheriffs routinely complained of the inadequacy of the jails in order to absolve themselves from the responsibility for jailbreaks. Jailers could not always ensure the incarceration of prisoners. Rapid deterioration of the structures, isolated locations, vandalism, and prisoners determined to abscond, sometimes with external assistance, meant that prisons often failed to serve their intended purpose.

[...] Personally Edmd. Son Edward Smithwick and Made Oath that the Gaol of the said County of Tyril is Insufficient to Detain Prisoners and Further maketh Oath that Several having been Lately Committed by Process as well from the Superior Courts as Inferior Court has made their Escape out of the said Goal he the said Sheriff doth therefore Enter this his protest.

> Minutes of the Tyrrell County Court of Pleas and Quarter Sessions, February 1770, State Archives.

Ordered that the Sheriff Immediately procure some person as Goaler to reside in the Goalers House Built for that purpose in order to prevent escapes which of late have too often happen'd on that Account and that he be Served with a Copy of this Order

> Minutes of the New Hanover County Court of Pleas and Quarter Sessions, September 1764, State Archives.

Whereas Redmans old Field on Tyancoca the Place appointed by Act of Assembly for holding the Court for this County is very inconvenient for those whose Business is to attend Court Genl. Musters and other public duties and from Exparience it is found that a Goal cannot be built there at so as to confine the Criminals and others put therein that either they are let out by assistance from without the Goal or burnt down by Idle disorderly People who are frequently in the Part of the County where the Court is held as the place is very thinly inhabited and for as much as there has been no Tax laid on the Inhabitants to build a Court house for this County. It is therefore Ord'red that the Clerk do certifie to the next General Assembly that it is the Unanimous decision of this Court that an Act of Assembly do pass for building a Courthouse Prison and Stocks for the Use of this County in the Town of Tarborough wherein those who are obliged to attend Public duties may be accomodated and Criminals who shall be comitted secured so as to meet With the Punishment inflicted on such by Law.

Minutes of the Edgecombe County Court of Pleas and Quarter Sessions, April 1763, State Archives.

Arthur Benning, Esq., High Sheriff, informed the Court that the County Jail "had been set on fire and greatly impair'd, and thereby render'd insufficient for the detention of Felons," which he protested.

Minutes of the New Hanover County Court, October 1772, State Archives.

The Examination of Elizabeth Scamp who was Commiped (sic) on Suspicion of Aiding and Assisting in Breaking the Goal of the said County of Orange and thereby forwarding the Escape of John and James Scamp who pleads not Guilty:

Andrew Mitchell Esqr. who being sworn on the Holy Evangelist of Almighty God, do say that he heard Elizabeth Scamp say, that the Tools with which John and James Scamp Broke the Prison of Orange County belonged to James Espay, and that she the said Elizabeth did take the tools back to the said ESPEYS Shop and left them there, and further that the said ESPEY had Received a piece of Bearskin Cloth of about 3 ½ or 3 ¾ Yards for the use of the said Tools, and for Drink to make the Guard Drunk or words to that Effect.

Robert Reed who being duly sworn on the Holy Evangelists &c. do say, that in the Night on the twenty Sixth of May Last past, before John and James Scamp broke out or made their Escape out of the Goal of the County of Orange, he this Deponant did see a Certain Elizabeth Scamp at the Back side of the Goal and Immediately after he did see a hole under the Prison where he found two Case Knives and a small Trowell. and having asked the said Elizabeth about diging the Hole, or breaking the Goal, she Answered that she was trying or Indeavouring to help her Husband out of Prison or words to that Effect.

Minutes of the Orange County Court, June 1758, State Archives.

Given the flimsiness of jails, or their absence, and the need for labor in early America, lawbreakers were usually subjected to fines or some form of corporal punishment rather than prolonged confinement.

<*Dominus Rex v. Tho. Grey*> William Little Esqr. Attorney General comes to prosecute the Bill of Indictment found by the Grand Jury against Thomas Gray for Felony in these Words Videlicet North Carolina sc. To the Honorable Christopher Gale Esqr. Chief Justice and the rest of the Justices of the General Court at a Session begun and held at Edenton On the last Tuesday in October One thousand Seven hundred and twenty Six <*Indictment.*> The Jurors for Our Sovereign Lord the King on their Oath do present that Thomas Gray of perquimons precinct Labourer not having the fear of God before his eyes but moved by the instigation of the Devil Videlicet in the precinct aforesayd on or about the tenth day of Aprill One thousand seven hundred and twenty Six by force and Armes did fraudulently and feloniously Steale take and carry away from Thomas Speight Esqr. of the sayd precinct half a Side of Leather and a quantity of Sheeps Wooll and a parcell of Nayles Some Cottons and Some blew linen all of the value of twenty Shillings Sterling against the peace of Our Lord the King that now is his Crown and dignity etc. <*Plea.*> Upon which Indictment the Sayd Thomas Grey was Arraigned and upon his Arraignment pleaded not guilty and for Tryall thereof putt himself upon God and the Country Whereupon the Marshall was commnded to cause to come twelve etc. and there came Mr. John Woodhouse John Charlton George Turnedge Joseph Stockley Richd. Willson Thomas Hoskins Francis Branch William Halsey Edward Moore Joshua Turner John Relf and Ralph Bozeman <*Verdict.*> who being impanell'd and sworne Say Wee of the Jury do find the prisoner at the Barr guilty of goods Stolen to the value of ten pence Sign'd John Woodhouse Foreman.

Then the Sayd Thomas Gray being asked if he had any thing to say why Sentence Should not pass against him as the Law in that Case hath provided and he offering nothing in avoydance thereof <*Sentence.*> Therefore It is Consider'd and Adjudg'd that he be carried to the publick Whipping post and that he there receive thirty lashes on his bare back And that he give Security for his good behaviour for twelve months and a day himself in the sum of fifty pounds Sterling and his Suretys in the Sum of twenty five pounds Sterling each and that he remaine in custody untill he performe the same <*Recognizance.*> [...]

Cain, *North Carolina Higher-Court Minutes, 1724-1730,* 323.

<Dominus Rex v. Stanton.> William Little Esqr. Attorney General comes to prosecute the Bill of Indictment found by the Grand Jury against Elijah Stanton for Burglary and Felony which was read in these Words Videlicet North Carolina sc. To Christopher Gale Esqr. Cheif Justice and the rest of the Justices for holding the General Court of Sessions begun and held at Edenton the last Tuesday in July One thousand Seven hundred and twenty Seven The Jurors for Our Sovereign Lord the King On their Oath do present that Elijah Stanton of the precinct of perquimons in the Sayd province planter not having the fear of God before his Eyes but being moved and instigated by the Devill in the precinct of perquimons aforesayd on the Sixteenth day of June One thousand Seven hundred and twenty Seven in the night of the Same day by force and armes the Mansion or dwelling house of Thomas Weeks of and in sayd precinct planter feloniously and burglariously did break into and enter and thence feloniously and Burglariously did take and carry away eight pounds five shillings publick Bills of Credit of this province and between two and three Gallons of Hogs lard or Fatt two Middle peices of Bacon and eighteen Yards of Cloth being the moneys or Bills and proper goods and Chattells of the sayd Thomas Weeks against the peace of Our Lord the King that now is his Crown and dignity etc. Upon which Indictment he was arraigned and upon his Arraignment he pleaded (Not Guilty) and for Tryall thereof putt himself Upon the Country Whereupon the Marshall was commanded to cause to come twelve etc. and there came Capt. William Downing William Charlton Capt. John Span Mathew Casewell John Lewis John Falconar William Charlton Junior Thomas Williams John Relfe Ralph Bozman Francis Branch and Joseph Hudson who being impanell'd and Sworne on their Oath do Say Wee of the Jury do find the prisoner Guilty of Felony to the value of thirty shillings Sign'd Wm. Downing Foreman. And then the Sayd Elijah Stanton being called and brought to the Barr and being ask'd if he any thing had to Say why Sentence of Death should not pass against him pray'd the Benefit of the Act of parliament made in the twelfth Year of Queen Anne wherein the Clergy is allow'd if the goods are not found to be of the value of forty shillings Wherefore It is consider'd Sentenc'd and adjudg'd that he be burn't in the hand with the Letter T also that he give Security for his good behaviour for twelve Months and one day himself in the Sum of fifty Pounds and two Suretys in twenty five pounds each And then be discharg'd paying fees.

Cain, *North Carolina Higher-Court Minutes, 1724-1730*, 423-424.

[...] [July, 1702].The Jurors for our Sovereigne Lady the Queen Do Present That Tho. Dereham Gentleman of the County of Bath have not the feare of God before his Eyes but being Led away by the Instigation of the Devill Did feloniously and of mallice prepensd att Severall times with Sevrall Weapons But more perticularly to Witt on or about the tenth day of Sept. Last past in the County of Bath aforsaid against the Peace of our Late Sovereigne Lord the King Did with force and Armes Assault the Body of Wm. Hudson then being in the Peace of god and the Lord the King and him the Said Wm. Hudson Did then and there with a Certain Weapon Comonly Called or Known by the Name of a Catt of Nine tayles Feloniously and malitiously Strike beat Wound and Kill That the aforsaid Wm. Hudson Afterwards to Witt on or about the 20th Day of Sept. Last past in the Countey of Bath aforsaid then and there by reason of the aforsaid Mortall Strokes and Wounds Did Depart this Life against the Peace etc. Who being areigned Pleads not Guilty and Casts himself upon god and the Countrey and Richd. Plater Esqr. Attorney Generall Likewise And the Marshall is Comanded that he Cause to Come twelve good and Lawfull men of the Vicinage and who etc. By whome etc. And there Came Mr. Fra. Foster Benj. Tull: Saml. Paine: Wm. Armor: Deniss McLendon: Jams Oats Jenkin Williams: Fra. Beasly: Abraham Warren: Jno. West Wm. Gascins: Jno. Bird And being Sworn Upon the Holy Evangelist to give true Verdict in the Premists Upon the Holy Evangelist Say

Wee find him Guilty of Man Slaughter And the said Dearham humbly Prays that Sentens may be suspended till to morrow. [...]

Thomas Dereham haveing yesterday been Convicted [of] Manslaughter and Savd by his Book and Sentens Suspended

Ordered that the Said Thomas Dereham be Burnt in [*torn*] Brawne of the Left thumb with a hott Iron haveing the Letter M And Pay all Costs that Doth acrue.

And upon the Humble Petition of the Said Tho. Dereham [*torn*] Court in Clemency Doth Repreive the Said Sentence Untill [*torn*] Majesties Pleasure therein be farther known.

Price, *North Carolina Higher-Court Records, 1702-1708*, 33-34.

<*Dominus Rex v. Sol. Smith.*> Wm. Little Esqr. Attorney General comes to prosecute the Bill of Indictment against Soloman Smith in these Words Videlicet North Carolina Sc. To Christophr. Gale Esqr. Cheif Justice and the rest of the Justices for holding the General Court at Edenton the last Tuesday of this Instant March 1729. The Jurors for

Our Sovereign Lord the King on their Oath do present that Soloman Smith late of Bertie precinct Labourer in the precinct aforesayd not having the fear of God before his Eyes but being moved and Seduced by the instigation of the Devil on or about the first day of November last past in the Evening of the Same day at Bertie precinct in the province aforesayd by force and Armes in and upon One William Coyne in the peace of God and Our Sayd Lord the King then and there being an Assault did make And the sayd Soloman Smith with a Knife of the value of three pence in his hand then and there drawn had and held feloniously and voluntarily the aforesayd William Coyne at Bertie precinct in the province aforesayd did Stabb and wound the Sayd William not having any Weapon then drawn nor having then there first Struck the Sayd Soloman and to the Sayd William Coyne at Bertie precinct in the province aforesayd feloniously and of his Malice forethought with the aforesayd knife One mortall wound in and upon his left breast did give about One inch and half long and about five inches in depth with which mortall wound the Sayd William Coyne instantly dyed and So the Jurors aforesayd upon their Oath do Say that the aforesayd Solomon Smith on the day and year aforesayd in Bertie precinct in the province aforesayd in manner and form aforesayd killed and murder'd the Sayd William Coyne against the peace of Our Sayd Lord the King his Crown and dignity etc. and against the Statute in that Case made and provided Upon which Indictment the Sayd Solomon Smith was arraign'd and upon his Arraignment pleaded Not Guilty and for Tryall thereof putt himself upon God and the Country And William Little Esqr. Attorney General on the behalf of Our Sayd Lord the King likewise Whereupon the Marshall was commanded to cause to come twelve etc. and there came Francis Pugh William Bryan John Earley James Smith John Champion John Howell Robt. Jefferys John Dunning John Blackman James Bate Jacob privett and Wm. Charlton Junior who being impannell'd and Sworne on their Oath do Say Wee Jurors do find the prisoner Solomon Smith Guilty Sign'd Francis Pugh Foreman Then the Sayd Solomon Smith being ask't if he had any thing to Say why Sentence Should not pass against him as the Law in that Case hath provided And he offering nothing in Avoydance thereof It is Therefore Consider'd Sentenced and by the Court here adjudg'd that the Sayd Solomon Smith Shall returne to the place from whence he came and from thence to the place of Execution there to be hang'd by the Neck till his Body is dead.

Cain, *North Carolina Higher-Court Minutes, 1724-1730*, 569-570.

[April, 1702]. The Juriors for our Sovereigne Lord the king Do present That Abraham Hobbs of the Precinct of Pequimons not haveing the feare of god before his Eyes did on or about the 18 or 19th of day of November Last past in the precinct of Pequimons feloniously with force and arms Kill and beare away one hogg of the Value of Eighteen shillings properly belonging to the Honorable President Contrary to the pease of our sovereigne Lord the king his Crowne and Dignity and against the statutes in that Case made and provided. And the said Abraham Hobbs being Areigned Pleads not Guilty and Casts himself upon god and the Countrey and Rich. Plater Esqr. Attorney Generall who prosecutes on his Majesties behalf Likewise And the Marshall for the tryall thereof hath Empaneled Mr. Jno. Blount Mr. Wm. Long Mr. Brian Fitzpatrick Mr. Rich. Davenport Mr. Jno. Foster: Mr. Robt. Fendell Mr. Saml. Parsons Mr. Tho. Boyd: Mr. Argill Symonds <149> Mr. Wm. Simpson: Mr. Wm. Barrow: Mr. Nich. Tylor who allso Came and to give a true Verdict in the premisses being sworne upon the Holy Evangelist say he is guilty and he humbly praying Transportation Ordered that he be Banisht out of the Government for Ever.

Price, *North Carolina Higher-Court Records, 1702-1708,* 11.

∞᧚᧓

Because corporal punishment sometimes included the cropping of ears, people who lost those extremities in other ways made a public record of the occurrence at the county court in order to distinguish them, if necessary, from criminals.

Read the following taken from the Cumberland County Court Minute Docket for April 1760:

Malcolm Blue of the Province and County aforesaid came into Court and brought in his son Neill Blue, a boy about seven years old, who had in last July a piece of his ear bit off with a dog. Sd Malcolm Blue father to the sd boy mead oath that he saw the bit which the dog tore out of the sd boy's ear lying in his yard but did not see him bite him as he was not then immediately upon the spot and that there is not any person that can prove that the dog bit him, there not being anybody then on their plantation but his own family—which is ordered to be recorded.

Corbitt, "Historical Notes," 369.

John Marr Came into Court and produced John Patterson a Witness to prove how and in what mannor he lost his Ear, who made Oath that after a Battle between Said Marr and one Wagstaff Cannady, He the sd. Patterson found a piece of his Marrs Ear on the Ground (towit) the Right Ear.

Minutes of the Wake County Court of Pleas and Quarter Sessions, March 1773, State Archives.

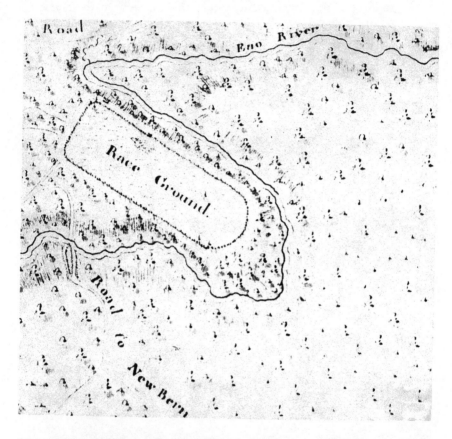

The racecourse at Hillsborough, as rendered in the Sauthier map of 1768. Horse racing was a popular amusement throughout the colonies. Photograph from the files of the North Carolina Division of Archives and History.

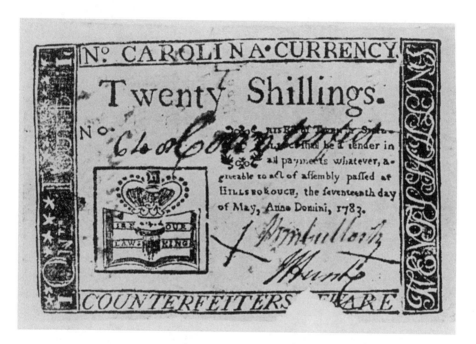

Counterfeiting was a capital offense during the colonial era. The admonition ironically emblazoned on this counterfeit currency note of 1783 warned of the fate that in fact befell three unfortunates at New Bern in 1752. See page 267. Photograph from the files of the Division of Archives and History.

Fighting, often accompanied by eye-gouging, was virtually a form of recreation in early North Carolina. Children's games were usually less violent. Illustrations from Tunis, *Frontier Living*, 45, 149.

1732

Mr. Ross to Abra. Blacha ... Dr.

<table>
<thead>
<tr><th></th><th></th><th>£</th><th>s</th><th>d</th></tr>
</thead>
<tbody>
<tr><td>Mar. 25</td><td>A dose of Specifick Pills for yr wife ———</td><td>0</td><td>7</td><td>6</td></tr>
<tr><td></td><td>A purging Bolus ———</td><td>0</td><td>10</td><td>0</td></tr>
<tr><td>28</td><td>Ditto ———</td><td>0</td><td>10</td><td>0</td></tr>
<tr><td></td><td>The Pills repeated ———</td><td>0</td><td>7</td><td>6</td></tr>
<tr><td>April 6</td><td>Three Blister plaisters to yr Arm ———</td><td>0</td><td>15</td><td>0</td></tr>
<tr><td></td><td>Melilot plaisters No. Six ———</td><td>0</td><td>9</td><td>6</td></tr>
<tr><td>14</td><td>Six papers of Specifick powders ———</td><td>1</td><td>10</td><td>0</td></tr>
<tr><td>29</td><td>Ditto ———</td><td>1</td><td>10</td><td>0</td></tr>
<tr><td></td><td>A bottle of Lotion for yr Arm ———</td><td>0</td><td>10</td><td>0</td></tr>
<tr><td>May 2</td><td>A compound Gargle ℥x for yr self ———</td><td>0</td><td>12</td><td>6</td></tr>
<tr><td>9</td><td>A dose of Specifick Pills ———</td><td>0</td><td>7</td><td>6</td></tr>
<tr><td></td><td>A purging powder ———</td><td>0</td><td>10</td><td>0</td></tr>
<tr><td>12</td><td>Bleeding ———</td><td>0</td><td>10</td><td>0</td></tr>
<tr><td></td><td>The Gargle repeated ———</td><td>0</td><td>12</td><td>6</td></tr>
<tr><td></td><td>The purging Powder as before ———</td><td>0</td><td>10</td><td>0</td></tr>
<tr><td>13</td><td>The Lotion again for yr Wife ———</td><td>0</td><td>10</td><td>0</td></tr>
<tr><td>14</td><td>The purging Powder rep. yr self ———</td><td>0</td><td>10</td><td>0</td></tr>
<tr><td>16</td><td>Ditto ———</td><td>0</td><td>10</td><td>0</td></tr>
<tr><td>31</td><td>The Lotion as before for yr Wife ———</td><td>0</td><td>10</td><td>0</td></tr>
<tr><td></td><td>for severall visits & attendance ———</td><td>9</td><td>0</td><td>0</td></tr>
<tr><td></td><td>for salivating yr wife & medicines &c. ———</td><td>20</td><td>0</td><td>0</td></tr>
</tbody>
</table>

pounds was pd to the nurse. £ 44 — 10 — 0

Errors excepted ꝑ Abr. Blacha

Medical treatment could be costly, as attested by this physician's account from 1732. See pages 165-166. But lotions, potions, powders, purges, bleedings, salivations, and other means of treatment often proved ineffectual and necessitated the services of a carpenter rather than a physician. Illustration from Tunis, *Colonial Living*, 91.

Water transport was more reliable and widespread than that by land, and the ferry constituted an important part of that system. Bridges were a vital element in land travel. See pages 208-209. Illustrations from Tunis, *Colonial Living*, 121.

Homes and Possessions

Homes varied widely depending upon the wealth of the owner. Most were wood, log or frame, though a few were brick, including in New Bern the most imposing structure in the colony, the Palace, a combination of governor's residence and statehouse.

Their Houses are built after two different Ways; *viz.* the most substantial Planters generally use Brick; and Lime, which is made of Oyster-shells, for there are no Stones to be found proper for that purpose, but near the Mountains; the meaner Sort erect with Timber, the outside with Clap-Boards, the Roofs of both Sorts of Houses are made with Shingles, and they generally have Sash Windows, and affect large and decent Rooms with good Closets, as they do a most beautiful Prospect by some noble River or Creek.

Brickell, *Natural History*, 37.

Most of the Houses in this Part of the Country are Log-houses, covered with Pine or Cypress Shingles, 3 feet long, and one broad. They are hung upon Laths with Peggs, and their doors too turn upon Wooden Hinges, and have wooden Locks to Secure them, so that the Building is finisht without Nails or other Iron-Work. They also set up their Pales without any Nails at all, and indeed more Securely than those that are nail'd. There are 3 Rails mortised into the Posts, the lowest of which serves as a Sill with a Groove in the Middle, big enough to receive the End of the Pales: the middle Part of the Pale rests against the Inside of the Next Rail, and the Top of it is brought forward to the outside of the uppermost. Such Wreathing of the Pales in and out makes them stand firm, and much harder to unfix than when nail'd in the Ordinary way. [...] Their Vanity generally lies not so much in having a handsome Dining-Room, as a Handsome House of Office: in this Kind of Structure they are really extravagant. [...]

Byrd, *Histories of the Dividing Line*, 94, 96. The Virginia, William Byrd, was writing in March, 1729, about the countryside in the vicinity of Edenton. A "house of office" was a privy.

The Common peoples houses here are in generall tarrd all over to preserve them instead of Painting & all have Wooden Chimneys which I admire do not catch fire oftener than they do.[...]

"William Logan's Journal of a Journey to Georgia, 1745," 9. Logan made these observations while travelling through Perquimans County.

[Russelborough, Brunswick, July 26, 1765]. As you are acquainted with Mrs. Tryons Neatness you will not wonder that we have been pestered with scouring of Chambers White Washing of Ceilings, Plaisterers Work, and Painting the House inside and out. Such is the Sickness and indolence of the Workmen in this Hot Climate that I shall not I am persuaded get rid of these nuisances this month. This House which has so many assistances is of an oblong Square Built of Wood. It measures on the out Side Faces forty five feet by thirty five feet, and is Divided into two Stores, exclusive of the Cellars the Parlour Floor is about five feet above the Surface of the Earth. Each Story has four Rooms and three light Closets. The Parlour below & the drawing Room are 20 x 15 feet each; Ceilings low. There is a Piaza Runs Round the House both Stories of ten feet Wide with a Ballustrade of four feet high, which is a great Security for my little girl. There is a good Stable and Coach Houses and some other Out Houses. [...]

Powell, *Correspondence of William Tryon*, 1:138.

[...] Mr. Roger More hearing we were come, was so kind as to send fresh horses for us to come up to his house, which we did, and were kindly received by him; he being the chief gentleman in all Cape Fear. His house is built of brick, and exceeding pleasantly situated about two miles from the town, and about half a mile from the river; though there is a creek comes close up to the door, between two beautiful meadows about three miles length. He has a prospect of the town of Brunswick, and of another beautiful brick house, a building about half a mile from him, belonging to Eleazer Allen, Esq., late speaker to the Commons House of Assembly, in the province of South Carolina. [...]

A New Voyage to Georgia, 2:55.

[June, 1783]. The population of this city is composed of five hundred families of all classes. The houses are middling and small as a rule, but comfortable and clean; almost all are made of wood. The church and the assembly house are of brick and are suitable to the town. The finest building of all and one which really deserves the attention of an educated traveler is the so-called "Palace," built eighteen years ago by an able English architect, Mr. Hawks, who came from England with Governor Tryon for this purpose and still remains in the city. I have conversed with him very particularly, and he possesses an admirable character. The building is entirely of brick, and its construction is in the pure English styling; the ornaments are very simple and placed with much taste and intelligence. In the great audience, or assembly room, there is the decoration of a marble fireplace of good taste, wrought in England; one infers from an inscription over the interior door of the portico that this fireplace is a gift from Sir William Draper, who was here on his return from the expedition to Manila in 1763, visiting his friend Tryon. The building is situated on the banks of the river Trent in a somewhat elevated spot, which gives it the command of a prospectus of more than twelve miles over the river Neuse and makes its location quite pleasing.

Miranda, *The New Democracy in America*, 6-7.

Inclosed You will receive a Sketch of the Fences You desired both the Chief Justices and my own, but I am not certain that I have mechanical phrases enough to convey to You a distinct and clear explanation of them however I will try, In the first place then the Chief Justices is shewn by that part of the Sketch marked A. for this is all the same Figure, beneath the Chinese Work it is planked with plain Boards horisontally directed to the Bottom without either a Bricked Wall at the Bottom or Railes instead of the planks as is represented by the figure of the Gate, which Rails my whole Fence is done with as well as the Gate, My Fence has also a double Figure represented by the whole Sketch and in each panel there are three parts, Two of one sort Viz. show distinguished by the Letter A. and one of the other distinguished by B. and in the panel adjoining there is two of B and one of A. The Brick Wall shews 12 Inches above the Ground, The next part is 22 Inches and the Chinese Work 16 Inches with the three Rails of 4 Inches each makes the Fence 5 Feet two Inches high. The pieces that compose the chinese work are Five eighths of an Inch Thick and an Inch and Three quarters Broad the Rails, or if You will Pales are an Inch and Quarter Square and are mortised into the lower and middle Rail. The ports are five Inches Square and the panel from the inside to inside of the ports is seven Feet two Inches. The Gates (double) are Six Feet six Inches Wide, three Feet each Gate with a piece of three Inches fixed to the Gate ports to hang the Gates to the Gate ports are Fourteen Inches Square, Seven Feet high above

Ground with a Ball of Twenty Inches high on the Top. This is all of my own the Judges differs in several respects. His is a single Gate the proportions of which I dont exactly remember, his is much less expensive but I confess I think not near so elegant and if You propose making one at all You may assure Yourself that the difference of the expence is abundantly compensated by the additional Beauty and elegance of the Werk therefore don't at a principle of Frugality prompt You to spoil a pice of Work which only becomes valuable by its neet, light Airy and elegant look.

> I[saac] Edwards to "Dear Sir" [John Williams], July 20, 1773, John Williams Papers.

∽🙥🙥∾

Homes, outbuildings, and yards contained the myriad possessions of the colonials. Inventories of estates reflected the contents of colonial households, which in turn bespoke of the affluence of the colonials.

INVENTORY of the Estate of Seth Pilkington Deceased taken by Michl. Coutanche Feb. 27th 1754.[...]

In the Kitchen
2 old Ladles 1 peck
2 Plows 1 Garden Pot
1 Cullender 4 Pewter Dishes
4 Tubs 1 frying Pan
5 Iron Potts 1 Ketle
1 Large Brass Ketle
1 Brass Scillet
1 Grid Iron 1 Spit
4 pot tramells
2 hooks 5 pr pot hooks
1 pair hand Irons
1 pair Tongs
1 Wooling Wheel
3 washing Tubbs
3 washing Tubbs
4 Water pails
2 pair old wool Cards
1 Smal funnell
1 flesh fork & —

1 Brass Scimmer
1 Kitchen table
out of Doors
1 Plough 1 large pitch ketle
4 Bay boats bars
1 Bay boat
2 Canoos 1 flat
1 Large boat anchor
1 pair hand Screws
1 Grindstone 1 hhd Lime
1 flax Brake
in the Barn
about 40 lb Corn
27 bus Pees 4 bus small
1 lb & ⅔ of fine salt
about 6 bus Coarse Salt
11 old hhd 11 old bb
about 12 bus beens
in the house
2 Silver Salts 2 Silver Spoons

1 Silver Pepper Box
2 Glass Canns 6 Wine Glasses
1 China Jack 2 Decanters
2 Delph Punch Bowls
1 Black Pitcher
2 Glas Viniger Cruits
1 Glass tankard 6 beakers
6 China Chocolate bowls
6—1 tea Pot
Silver tongs & 6 teaspoons
1 pr hand Irons
1 fire Shovel & tongs
1 Clock 1 Great Chair
6 flagg Chairs 1 Elbow Dito
4 Blak walnut framed Chairs
&c.
1 maple table
1 Black Walnut Do 1 Oak Desk
1 Broken looking glass
2 pr money scales in the Desk
1 pr shot mouls 1 pr Knipers
1 Shoe hammer 1 Pr Marking
Irons
1 pr bullet Moulds 1 brass Cock
1 pr Shoe Pincers 1 pr Spoon
Moulds
5 awls & 2 Gimbletts
1 Seringe 1 hoan 2 Rasors
1 Rasor strap about 500 Needls
horse flems 1 fountain pen
2 Sticks hair 11 Doz shirt butt
2 pr Sleave butts 3 mend Books
2 Smal files 1 pr Compasses
2 Westband Buckely
2 Doz butts 2 pen Knives
2 pr Specticals 1 burning Glass
2 Inck glasses 1 Gunter Scale
12 feet Rule 1 pr thumb screws
1 botel Batemens Drops
1 pr nail Cutters Some Rats been
about 3 Doz fish hooks

1 glass Ink stand
1 Sand Box 1 Sliding Rule
2 Saw Setts 1 Pockett Book
1 Pr Silver Shoe buckeles
1 Silver Watch
2 Lancetts 1 pr Silver Knee buckles
14 Silver Jackett butts
1 Silver Neck buckle
13 Silver Small buttons
1 piece of Silver watch chain
1 Smal pad lock 1 Silver Knee buck
1 Green Silk Purse
10 ¼ pisterins
1 pr Smal Scales
1 pr bellows in Back Room
1 Smal White Table
1 Black walnut Do
1 Warming pan
1 Close Stool 3 old Chairs
1 Large Bed & furniture
1 Smal Bed & Dito
1 Chest Drawers 1 looking
glass Smal
1 pr hand Irons
1 pr Shovel & tongs
1 black tea Pot 1 black Jack
1 earthen bowl 3 Glasses
1 pint mugh 1 Pitcher
1 tea pot 1 tea Chest
1 Canister 3 Doz round botells
1 Case with 28 botels
½ gal pot 6 lb Soap
6 fayall Basketts
2 Box Irons & heaters 1 Stan
½ gl Peuter Pot 1 Chest
1 Cotton Mill 3 pr Snuffers
4 brass Candle Sticks
2 Guns 2 hammers
2 Spinning Wheels
3½ Doz tin Candle Moulds

1 Case & 12 botels
1 tin Candle Box
1 hatchett 1 Coffee pot
1 pickle Pot 2 tea Ketles
1 Grater 1 Copper Sauce pan
1 Cannister 2 Shoe brushes
1 Doz Case Knives 1 D forks
4 pr shoes
1 new Suit Broad Cloth
5 flanell Jacketts
3 Coats
3 bever hatts
1 Read Jackett & britches
1 gray Jacket
1 morning gown
9 pr Stockings
3 pair gloves
1 pair Lather bridches
8 white shirts
2 check Dito
1 par Garters
3 neckleths
4 doz & 8 plates
7 Dishes
1 Gl Bason
3 ½ Gal Dito
3 3 pint Do
2 2 quart Do
1 Doz milk pans
1 Doz Chairs at Bath town
1 Great Coat D.
⅓ of 3 New Cables D
⅓ of 3 Anchors Do
5 Volumes Doctr. Scots Sermons
1 Map North America
the Compleat Surveyor 1 Vol
Laws of Virginia 1 D
The Athenian Oracle 1
Beveridge thoughts on Crist Life
A Geographical Dictionary 1
Bishop Hoadlys Sermons 1

John Hill Arithmetick 1
16 Sermons by Durham 1
new Calender
feast & fast of the Church
Etimological Dictionary 1
Cores Exposition
Merchants Magazine 1
Wells Geography 1
Popes Essay on Man
Practice Piety
Stanupe on Salvation
Smal Book of Rates
2 Psalm Books
Henrey's Sermons
New Atlantis 1
testement
Etinuler's Practice of Phisick
Decimal Arithmetick
2 old Epitome 1 old grammar
Geography of Children
familiar Letters
Margl of Argyle Instr to his son
Doctr Hammon works 2 Vol
Introdn to the Lord Supper
Marriner Compass
Instruction for the Indians
1 Large Common Prayer
3 Small Common Prayer Books
1 Large Bible 2 Small Dito
4 Ledgers A B C D & Sundry
Day Books
3 Canes 1 Gauging Rod
about 5 m New Engld Bricks
6 Dry hides 1 Calf Skin
1 horse Bell 2 ox Belles
2 wheel Barrows 18 plant axes

12 hoes 2 pr Iron Wedges
2 Grubing hoes 3 Carts
1 pair of Oxen
6 Cows & Calves
4 Cows not Calves
22 young Catle to 3 years old
4 horses & 1 mare
29 Sheep & 7 Lambs
10 Breeding Sows & 9 Pigs
20 Shoats 1 Large Iron Pot
16 new Oak Barels 2 hand mills
1 Conner table up Stairs
6 Chairs flag bottoms
1 Trunck ½ minute glass
5 Bed & furniture
1 trunk 1 pair tongs
1 Small looking Glass
2 Chest 3 Sifters
5 pair Cards 4 Bowls
1 Suit Curtains 6 old barils & Cags
1 buckett 1 pr Lather Bags
3 bags 6 Bowls
4 pint mugs 6 half pints D
a Small persell wool Cotton & flax
yarn & Cotten Spun a Small
quantity

Cows
Steers
Steers
2 Plows
1 P Cartwheels 1 horse
2 mares & Colts
1 ax 1 hoe
at Plantation up the River
Cows & Calves
Steers
Hogs
Tar at the Landing
163 bb on floyd Creek not filled
1 Large Tar Kill running off
2 Smaller to runn off

3 Chamber pots 1 Small Box
Wind Glass
1 Cedar Desk 8 pair Sheets
1 pr Blanketts 2 bed quilts
1 Rugg 4 Diaper Table Cloths
4 Linnen Table Cloths 6 Towells D
6 Diaper Napkins
6 pr thread Stockings
Negroe Men
Jupiter, Lankeshire, Catto
Darby, Cudgo, old Tom
young Tom, Jack, Pomp,
Fortune, George, Dublin,
Noridge
Negro Boys
Mustifer, Cain, York, London,
Bristol,
Wenches
Africa, Grace, Jenny Florra old
Betty,
Girls
Jenny, Pheby, Hannah,
White Boys
4 prantices
at Plantation Warynunty
7 Cows & Calves

yett unknown

yett unknown

& about 200 bbSett up for Tar
2 Iron Potts at Tar Kill
Notes of Hand

Willm Ballard for	£4. 5. 0 Proc.
John Porters for	12. 6. 9 Sterling
James Event for	0.10. 0 Vir cur
Abram Tyler	6. 0.0
Griffin Floyd for 28bb	***
John Campbell	1.17.6 Vir
Charles Pringle	3.16.6 Vir
John Knowis Ball	2. 1.6 Proc
MICHL. COUTANCHE Exectr	
WINIFRED PILKINGTON	

Inventory of Seth Pilkington, Grimes, *North Carolina Wills and Inventories*, 526-529.

The Enventory of John Calloways Estate Desease Retund by me Hopkin wilder administrator

To 1 bed
To 1 wheel
To 1 pot
To 1 pan
To 1 Chest
To 1 Table
To 1 skillet
To 2 Dishes
To 4 knives and 2 forks
To 2 Chares
To 1 trunk
To 2 Cows and 1 hearlen
To 4 head of Sheep
To 60 head of hoggs
To 1 hors
To 1 ox
To 1 hog
To 1 Plow ho
To 2 qeurts bottls
To 1 m[*illegible*]fter

To 1 tole and pole
To 1 met table
To 1 mel bag
To 1 Lining wilat
To 1 Ink vial
Sworn to in Open Court
June 15. 1763.

Wm. Cray
Clerk of Court

Inventory of John Calloway, Onslow County, Estates Records, 1735-1914, State Archives.

Clothes constituted particularly valuable possessions. Tailors and cobblers found a ready market for their services. Colonials, however, may not have laundered their garments carefully.

<*Mary Gainers Inventory.*> An Inveterry of the Estate of Mary Gainer Deceas'd.

One young Horse, fifteen head of Cattle, and Seventeen head of hogs, and Six puter Dishes, and five puter plates; and one puter Bason, and three puter Spoons, and one Beaker, and a parsel of Shoemaking tools, and Curvying Knife, and one fleshing Knife, and one Crass Shimmer, and one feather Bed and furniture, and two Chests and one Box, and one Iron pot, and one frying pan, and Eleven Gowns and Habbits, and five polly Coats, and five Shifts and a persal of Caps and handkerchiefs and Aprons, and two hats, and one sheepe, and two Baskets, and two bottles, and one piller, and one small Bible and Eight yds. of Cloath, and two pare of Stockins, and one pare of Shoes, and two pare of Gloves, and three quarters yd. Linnen, and half yd. Muslin, and two pounds ten Shillings Cash Virgina money, and one Iron Spitt, and one Chear, and one Case Knife and fork.

Wm.   <*his   mark*>
Gainer Executor

Edgecombe County. ss February Court 1752
The above Inventory was Exhibited into Court on Oath etc.
Test.

Benjn. Wynns Clerk
Court

Inventory of Mary Gainor, February Court, 1752/53, Edgecombe County, Inventories, Accounts, and Sales of Estates, 1748-1753, State Archives.

Wee the Subcribers being Duly Sworn to a praise and sett a Value upon the Goods and Chattles of James ambrose Deceasd and is as Follows

	£	s	d
Four Cows Two yearlings and Two Calves at £	9.	0.	0
one mair and one year old Colt	4.	0.	0
Nine sows and 42 pigs and Two year old Barrows at	10.	4.	0
Two White holland Shirts at	2.	8.	0
Two pair of Leather Briches at	2.	0.	0
One Cloath Coat and one Cloth pr. of Briches at	4.	0.	0
One Rackoon hat at	1.	10.	0
three course Shirts at	0.	12.	0
one Broad Cloth West at	2.	05.	0
one homespun West one old Bair Skin West at	0.	18.	0
three pair of stockins one old homespun West at	0.	15.	0
one pair of Indian Boats at	0.	4.	0
one Voolen at	0.	10.	0
one hand saw at	0.	6.	[torn]
one froe at		[torn]	
145 lb. of Tobacco at	1.	1.	8
one sadle and bridle at	0.	14.	0
one Barrill and a half of Corn	0.	15.	0
one Gun at	1.	5.	0
one Cutlas one Cotouch Box at	0.	3.	0
one set of Shoemakers Tools at	1.	0.	4
one pair of sadle Bags at	3.	8.	0
one pair of Shues at	0.	5.	0
one Chest one small Trunk at	0.	13.	0
one horse Bell at	0.	4.	0
one small Gimblet at	0.	0.	4
one hive of Beas at	0.	2.	0
one Ink Glass one pocket Book at	0.	3.	0
one pair of silver Sleave Buttons at	0.	6.	0

one pair of Brass Buckles at	0. 2. 0	
one pair of thread Stockins and pair of Garters at	0. 9. 4	
one pair of Cotton Do. and garters Do. at	0. 8. 0	
one Bible, at	0. 6. 0	
Eight Shillings proclamation money	0. 8. 0	
To Two Sides of Leather at	0.16.4	
	£48. 4.0	

Apraised This 17th Day of may 1762 by

> Thos. Johnston
> Joseph <*his mark*>
> Beryman

Inventory of James Ambrose, May 17, 1762, Onslow County, Estates Records, State Archives.

George Brownrigg Esqr. To Wm. Askins

Dr.

1760 Augst. 2d	To Making Breeches and Jacket for boy	6	
Septr. 10d	To do. per A Vescoat for Jones	10	
	To 3 yds. Oznabrigs at 18	4	6
	To 1½ Doz. Small Buttons at 12	1	6
	To Twist and Thread	2	4
Decembr. 14th	To Making a Vescoat for boy	6	
	To do. and Breeches	11	
	To Sundrey Trimmings	6	8
1761	To Mending a pr. Breeches	4	
Janry. the 21.	To 1 Pr. Breches for the boy	14	4
Febry. 20.	To making a Coat for do.	8	
	To Twist	1	
March the 10	To Making a Vescoat for the Pilott	10	
	To Mending 1 pr. Breeches	1	4
May the 16	To Making a Coat Vescoat of 2 Pair of Breeches	1 15	
	To Making of 4 Pr. of Draw's at 2/.	8	
	To Tape	2	
June 7th	To Mending a Great Coat for Capt. Jones	1	
	To Making a Vescoat and 1 pr. Breeches	9	
	To Proc. Answerd pr. Nicholl. Collins	9	

		£	s	d
Augst. 4	To yr. Assumption for Thos. Bell	3	7	
12	To Making a Vescoat for a Sailor		10	
Sepr. 6	To do.		10	
	To 2 do. and 2 Pr. Breeches	1		
	To Making 1 Vescoat		10	
11	To do. 2 do.		18	
28	To Seeting a pr. Breeches		4	
Octobr. 1d	To making 2 Shirts for Sailors		4	
Novbr. 2	To Making 2 Vescoats and 1 Pr. Breeches for Negroes		11	
12	To making 1 Pr. Draws		2	8
Decemb. 19	To Proc. Answer for Thos. Bell		12	8
	To do. for the Corker	1	10	
	To Making 2 Vescoats and 1 Pr. Breeches for Negroes		13	
	Carried over £	18	0	
1761	Brought Over			
	To Sundries £	18		
Decembr. 29	To yr. Assumption for Clark Pike	1	12	8
	To Balance of Edward Bells Accts.	1	5	
	£	20	17	8

Errors Excepted per Wm. Askins.

George Brownrigg to William Askins, 1760-1761, Chowan County, Miscellaneous Records, Personal Accounts, 1700-1789, State Archives.

Caleb Gardner to Daniel Marshall
Dr. done for Work

		£	S	D
1756 Aug. 21.	To 2 pair of Womans Pumps	0	6	4
Sep.	1 pair of Mens Do.		3	7
	To 1 pair of silk Shoes and white Rands		5	4
	To 1 pair of red cloth Shoes		4	4
	To 1 pair of Crown Cloth Do.		4	4
	To 2 pair Womans Pumps		6	4
	To 2 pair black strif Shoes		8	11
Octbr.	To 1 pair Pumps for Mr. Ross		3	2
	To 1 pair for Mrs. Vaun of Cloth Shoes		4	4
	To 1 pair Woman's Pumps		3	2

		£	s	d
	To 2 pair Pumps for Mr. Duckingfeild		6	4
	To 1 pair of Do. for Mr. Orms		3	2
	To 2 pair of Shoes heal'd		0	8
Novr.	To a amail pillean making	0	1	4
	To a pair Saddle Bags mending		1	
	To a Bout mending		1	4
	To 1 pair Womans Shoes		3	2
	To 1 pair Womans Do.		3	2
	To a pair of Goloshoes		5	4
Decemr.	To 2 pair Womans Pumps		6	4
24	To 1 pair Shoes		3	2
1757. Januy.	To 1 pair of Goloshoes		5	
31	To 2 pair Single Channels		8	
feby.	To 1 pair of Pumps solded		1	
	£	4	18	4

Caleb Gardner to Daniel Marshall, 1756-1757, Chowan County, Miscellaneous Records, Personal Accounts, State Archives.

[…] [July, 1775]. They are the worst washers of linen I ever saw, and tho' it be the country of indigo they never use blue, nor allow the sun to look at them. All the cloaths coarse and fine, bed and table linen, lawns, cambricks and muslins, chints, checks, all are promiscuously thrown into a copper with a quantity of water and a large piece of soap. This is set a boiling, while a Negro wench turns them over with a stick. This operation over, they are taken out, squeezed and thrown on the Pales to dry. They use no calender; they are however much better smoothed than washed. Mrs. Miller offered to teach them the British method of treating linens, which she understands extremely well, as, to do her justice, she does every thing that belongs to her station, and might be of great use to them. But Mrs. Schaw was affronted at the offer. She showed them however by bleaching those of Miss Rutherfurd, my brothers and mine, how different a little labour made them appear, and indeed the power of the sun was extremely apparent in the immediate recovery of some bed and table-linen, that had been so ruined by sea water, that I thought them irrecoverably lost. […]

Andrews, *Journal of a Lady of Quality*, 204.

Within the home colonials enjoyed a diversity of food and drink, though some, of course, possessed a greater abundance than others.

Their Diet consists chiefly of Beef, Mutton, Pork, Venison in Abundance, Wild and Tame Fowl, Fish of several delicate Sorts; Roots, Fruit, several kinds of Sallads, good Bread, Butter, Milk, Cheese, Rice, *Indian* Corn, both which they concoct like a *Hasty-Pudding*: But as I shall treat more particularly of the Productions of the Country in the succeeding Pages, I shall now proceed to their *Liquors*.

The *Liquors* that are in common in *Carolina* at present, and chiefly made use of, are, Rum, Brandy, Mault Drink; these they import. The following are made in Country, *viz.* Cyder, Persimon-Beer, made of the Fruit of that Tree, Ceder-Beer, made of Ceder-Berries; they also make Beer of the green Stalks of *Indian-Corn*, which they bruise and boyle: They likewise make Beer of Mollosses, or common Treacle, in the following manner, they take a Gallon of Mollosses, a Peck of Wheaten Bran, a Pound of Hops, and a Barrel of Fountain Water, all which they boile together, and work up with Yest, as we do our Malt Liquors; this is their common Small-Beer, and seems to me to be the pleasantest Drink, I ever tasted, either in the *Indies* or *Europe*, and I am satisfied more wholsom. This is made stronger in proportion, as People fancy.

It is necessary to observe that though there is plenty of Barly and Oats in this Province, yet there is no Malt Drink made, notwithstanding all kind of Malt Liquors bear a good Price, nor have any of the Planters ever yet attempted it.

Chocolate, Teas, and *Coffee,* are as common in *Carolina* as with us in *Ireland,* particularly the last, which of late Years they have industriously raised, and is now very cheap: These are sober Liquors, and take off the better Sort from Drinking what are hot and spirituous, who are not so addicted to Rum and Brandy as the inferior Sort, *Caslena* or *Yaupan,* an *Indian Tea,* which grows here in Abundance is indifferently used by Planers and *Indians.*

Brickell, *Natural History,* 38-39.

[…][Russelborough, Brunswick, July 26, 1765]. I shall & must build a good Kitchen, which I can do for forty Pounds Sterling of 30 f x 40 f—The garden has nothing to Boast of except Fruit Trees. Peaches, Nectrs Figgs and Plumbs are in perfection and of good Sorts. I cut a

Musk Melon this week which weighed 17½ Pounds. Apples grow extremely well here I have tasted excellent Cyder the Produce of this Province. Most if not all kinds of garden greens and Pot herbs grow luxuriant with us. We are in want of nothing but Industry & skill, to bring every Vegetable to a greater perfection in this Province. Indian corn, Rice, and American Beans (Species of the Kidney Bean) are the grain that is Cultivated within a hundred and fifty Miles of the Sea Board. [...]

Powell, *Correspondence of William Tryon,* 1:138-139.

[...] The agriculture one sees in the vicinity amounts to little and consists mainly of corn, potatoes, and fruit trees, which form an extensive orchard. [...] With apples, pears, and peaches, they make excellent cider and brandy.

Miranda, *The New Democracy in America,* 8. The author was visiting the plantation of a Mr. Green, twelve miles from New Bern, in June, 1783.

[December, 1783]. At Edenton we were for the first time regaled with the domestic tea universally known and beloved in North Carolina. This is made from the leaves of the *Ilex Cassine L.,* a tolerably high and beautiful tree or shrub, which growing abundantly in this sandy country is very ornamental with its evergreen leaves and red berries; more to the north and even farther inland it is rare. It is here generally called Japan, but has this name in common with the South-Sea tea-tree (*Cassine Peragua L.*), which likewise grows on the Carolina coast, and is also greatly esteemed for tea. The people here have a very high opinion of the good qualities of the Japan; they not only make use of it for breakfast instead of the common Bohea, but in almost every kind of sickness as well. Near to the coast, where the drinking-water is not altogether pure, it is pretty generally the custom to boil the water with these leaves. Such an infusion is not unpleasant, if it is properly managed. There are those who in a slovenly manner chop up the fresh leaves, the twigs, the wood, and the bark all together; but this gives the water a repulsive taste. More careful housekeepers have the leaves, which may be gathered at any season of the year, culled out in a cleanly way, and dried in an iron kettle over a slow fire; they pound them a little in a mortar, so as to keep them the better in glass bottles, but before putting them up they let them evaporate a while in the air. Prepared thus, the taste betters by keeping, and not seldom a pound fetches one to one and a half Spanish dollars. [...]

Schoepf, *Travels in the Confederation*, 2:113-114.

[...]stop'd at one Fishers, after riding about 20 miles, to get our Dinners & bate our Horses, but were vilely entertained, having nothing but Potato Bread mixed with Indian Corn & rank Irish Butter, & as unmannerly cross a Land Lady as ever I met with. [...] Mounted again & in 15 miles further distance came to—Stoakley's, where we stoped to Bait, could get nothing for our horses here neither, but Blades. Had a couple of Chickens boiled for Dinner but the Woman, tho' she told us we might have anything for dinner we pleased, had nothing in the house, not even Bread of any kind, nor had had, as she said, for several days, living entirely on Potatoes; such is the fare of the Common people in these parts.

"William Logan's Journal of a Journey to Georgia," 10-11, 13. The author made these observations in October, 1745, somewhere between Bath and Wilmington.

These people are the most wretchedly ignorant of any I ever met with. They could not tell me the name of the place, county, or parish they resided in, nor any other place in the adjacent country; neither could they furnish me with any directions, by which I might again discover and ascertain the right way. [...]

With much persuasion, I procured one of these lumps of mortality to accompany me as a guide to this Mr. Tyers's. [...]

His house was the seat of plenty and plainness, mirth and good-humour, and genuine hospitality without ostentation; but entirely out of the way from all public roads.

Here I found a large table loaded with fat roasted turkies, geese, and ducks, boiled fowls, large hams, hung-beef, barbicued pig, etc. enough for five-and twenty men.

Smyth, *A Tour in the United States of America*, 1:104-105. The locals described by Smyth lived west of the Chowan River in the present counties of Northampton and Hertford. Their reticence possibly had less to do with ignorance of their location than with a dislike for their interrogator.

Colonials were far from self-sufficient, resorting to mercantile stores not only for clothing, food, and drink, but for a variety of other items.

What are called shops in England, are known here by the appellation of stores, and supply the inhabitants with every individual article necessary in life, such as linens, woollens, silks, paper, books, iron, cutlery, hats, stockings, shoes, wines, spirits, sugars, &c. and even jewelry; for which in return they receive tobacco, skins, furs, cotton, butter, flour, &c. in considerable quantities at a time, being obliged to give a year's credit.

By this it appears, that there is but little specie in circulation; indeed there is no great occasion for it; for a planter raises his own meats, beef, and bacon, his own corn and bread, his drink, cyder, and brandy, his fruit, apples, peaches &c. and great part of his cloathing, which is cotton.

He has no market to repair to but the nearest store; which chiefly supplies him with finery, besides the useful and necessary articles for agriculture, and what little clothing his slaves require, for which he pays his crop of tobacco, or whatever else may be his staple produce, and is always twelve months in arrear.

Smyth, *A Tour in the United States of America*, 1:99-100.

JUST IMPORTED, From LONDON and LIVERPOOL,
A neat ASSORTMENT *of* European *and* India GOODS, *suitable for the Season, and are now selling at* Three *for* One *from the* Sterling Cost, *for Cash, or Produce in Hand, by the Subscriber, at his Store, formerly kept by Messrs.* Knight *and* Green, *in* NEWBERN;
CALLICO and cotton chints,
Printed linens,
7-8 *&* yd. wide *Irish* do.
3 4, 7 8, & yard wide cotten and linen check, Apron wide do.
Striped hollands,
English, Scotch, and *Russian* oznabrigs,
Dutch blankets,
Spotted rugs,
Negro cloths and baizes,
Flannel and lincey,
   White and brown *Irish* sheeting,
Dowlas and prince's linens,
Diaper and huckaback,

Brass and iron candlesticks,
Hard soap,
Flat irons,
Cotton cards,
Bedbunts and ticking,
London pewter,
Coffee and tea,
Loaf and powder sugar,
Mustard, pepper and nutmegs, &c.
West India and *Philadelphia* rum and molasses
Frying pans and bar iron
FF powder and shot,
Writing paper and ink powder,
Pins and needles,
Superfine broad cloths,
Mens and womens white silk-stockings,
Mens turned ribb'd do.
Masquerade do,
Men and womens thread and worsted do.
Silk and worsted breeches patterns,
Womens black and colour'd silk mits,
Silk, cambrick, and check linen handkerchiefs,
Ear rings and necklaces,
Cyprus and figur'd gauzes,
Pompoons and patchboxes,
Black satten hats,
Gauze caps,
Silk and cotten laces,
Cambricks and lawns,
Callimancoes and durants,
Shalloons and tammies,
Fine jeans and fustians,
Barragan and dimmeties,
Scotch and colour'd thread
Shoe and knee buckles, of the newest fashion,
Tobacco and snuff-boxes,
Knives, scissars and raizors,
Sleeve buttons,
White and striped tapes,
Coat and waistcoat buttons,
    Gartering, Buckram,

Stay tapes, &c. &c.

N.B. Any one that will please to favour me with their Custom or Orders, may be certain of being served on the most reasonable Terms, as I am certain my Goods are as cheap laid in as any in *America*, and will give the Top of the Market for Deer skins, Bees-wax, Myrtle-wax, Furs, Tallow, Feathers, Pitch, Tar, or any Country Produce that will suit.

JOHN TOMLINSON.

North Carolina Magazine; or, *Universal Intelligencer* (New Bern), January 18, 1765.

Mr. William Wooton To John Wright

	Dr.
	£ S D
1758. Augst. 1st. To Proclamation Money lent you	0. 9. 8
9. To 2 Candlesticks at 1/8	0. 3. 4
17. To 1 Boys Hatt	0. 3. 4
23. To 10 lb. of Beef	0. 1. 8
Sepr. 17th. To 1 Ink Stand	0. 1. 8
To 3 ½ Yards Irish Linnen at 6/.	1. 1. 0
Octor. 18th. To 1 Scane of Silk	0. 1. 4
To 1 ½ Dozen of Buttons at 1/0	0. 1. 6
To 1 pr. of hand Bellows	0. 6. 8
Decemr. 15th. To 1 Yard of Oznabrigs	0. 2. 4
1759 Jany. 16th. To 3 lb. of Shott and 1 lb. of Powder	0. 6. 2
April 13th. To 1 Hoe	0. 4. 0
May 8th. To 4 yards of Holland at 6/.	1. 4. 0
To 5 lb. of Sugar at 12 d.	0. 5. 0
To 3 ½ yards of Check Linnen at 3/.	0.10. 6
To 1 ½ Dozen Scarlett Buttons at ¼	0. 2. 0
To 2 yards of Check Linnen at 3/	0. 6. 0
To ½ yard of Buckram	0. 2. 0
1760. To Cash on Account of Abram. Banks	0. 3. 0
To Cash lent you to Buy Syder	0. 5. 0
Feby. 1st. To 4 Dozen of Needles at 4d.	0. 1. 4
24. To 1 Boys Hatt	0. 2. 4
To 1 Snuff box	0. 1. 8
To 1 Lawn Handkerchief	0. 4. 0
To 1 quart of Rum	0. 3. 8
To 2 Dozen of Needles at 4d.	0. 0. 8
March 3d. To 1 ½ Gallon of Rum at 12/	0.18. 0

4. To Cash lent	0. 5. 4
5. To 1 Bottle of Snuff	0. 2. 8
To 2 ¾ yards black Drugged at 5/4	0.14. 8
To ½ Gallon of Rum at 12/	0. 6. 0
9. To 1 Card of Sleeve Buttons	0. 1. 4
22. To ½ Gallon of Rum at 12/	0. 6. 0
29. To 4 Yards of Shalloon at 4/4	0.17. 4
April 20th. To 12 Almanacks at 8d.	0. 8. 0
June 7th. To ½ lb. of Tea at 12/6	0. 6. 3
July 12th. To 1 Yard broad Cloth	1.10. 0
To 1 Yard blue Shalloon	0. 4. 4
To 1 ½ Dozen Jackett buttons at 2/	0. 3. 0
To 1 Stick mohair	0. 1. 0
To 5 ½ Yards White Linnen at 1/8	0. 9. 2
To 2 Yards black Drugged at 5/4	0.10. 8
To 2 Dozen Jackett buttons at 2/	0. 4. 0
To 1 Stick mohair	0. 1. 8
	£13.19.11
By Cr.	5.11. 0
Balance due	£ 8. 8.11
Errors Excepted per [*illegible*]	

Mr. Willm. Wooton's Acct.	Cr.
1758.	£ S. D.
By makeing Willm. Gibb's Coat	0.16. 0
By making me a Coat and pr. Breeches	1. 1. 4
By Cash	1. 5. 0
1760. By making a blue Coat and Breeches	1. 3. 0
By making 2 Loose Coats	0.16. 0
By making a Coat for Carney	0. 8. 0
June 7th. By Bills	0. 1. 8
	£ 5.11. 0

William Wooten to John Wright, 1758, Hyde County, Miscellaneous Records, Personal Accounts, 1735-1952, State Archives.

Edenton 8th Augt. 1772.
Mr. Luke Taylor
Borrower of Millen and Morris

2 lb. Shott at 6d.	1

October	15th	1 Gallon rum		6	8	
	30th	1 Gallon do.		6	8	
	31.	1 Blue Rugg	2			2. 13. 4
Novemr.	1.	8½ yds. Russia Dreel 3/2	1	6	11	
	13th	1 Gallon Rum		6	8	
	25th	1 Ladys Hatt 19/, 1 Sett pinchback Buckles 4/	1	3		2. 16. 7
Decemr.	15th	4¼ yds. Humums 14/.	2	19	6	
		4 yds. white Ribbon 8 ½ yd. Silk gauze 3/4		11	4	
		1 Necklace 4/, 1 pair Womans thd. Stockings 8/3		12	3	
		1 Lawn Handkerchief 6/, 1 Oz. white thd. 1/8		7	8	
		9 yds. Demothy 3/	1	7		
	17th	2 yds. Clear Lawn 9/		18		
		1 yd. Sheeting 3/, 1 pair Womans Shoes 10/		13		
	19th	2 Gallons rum 6/8		13	4	
	22d	1¼ yd. Oznabrigs 16d.		1	8	
		1 Gallon Rum 6/8, 1 Gall. Melasses 3/4		10		
		2 Bushels fine Salt 6/8, 2 Boys Hatts 4/8		11	4	
1773.	31st	1 Gallon Rum 6/8, 1 Gall. Melasses 3/4		10		9. 15. 1
Febry.	6th.	5 ½ yds. Irish Linen 3/6		19	3	
		1 Gallon rum		6	8	
	24th	1 lb. Bohea Tea		8		1. 13. 11
March	10th	2 ⅛ yds. Irish Linen 5/8		12	½	
		2¼ yds. ditto 3/2.		7	1½	
		1 Gallon rum 6/8, 1 Gall. Melasses 3/4		10		
	23d	1 Gallon do.		6	8	1. 15. 10
		Carried over			£	18. 15. 9
1773.		Brought over				18. 15. 9
April	1st	1 Gallon rum		6	8	
	10th	1 Loaf 11½ lb. Sugar 1/6.		19	2	
		1 Curry Comb		2		
		1 Bushel Salt 3/, 1 Gallon Melasses 3/4		6	4	1. 14. 2

May	26th	1 pair Womans Shoes 9/6,		13		
		1 pair do. Gloves 3/6				
		7 yds. printed Linen 6/.	2	2		
		1 Silk gauze Handkerchief		8	8	
		6/, 1 yd. Linen 2/8				
		18 yds. Coat binding 3/, 1		4		
		hank Silk 1/				
		4 yds. Oznaburghs 16d.		5	4	
	27th	1 Gallon Rum		6	8	3. 19. 8
June	7th	1 Gallon ditto		6	8	
	22d.	2 Gallons ditto 6/8		13	4	1.
July	26th	1 Fan 2/6, 2 yds. white		5	6	
		Ribbon 3/				
	27th	1 Gallon rum		6	8	
	30th	3 yds. Sheeting 3/4		10		
		1½ yd. Shaloon 7/, ½ yd.		8	4	1. 10. 6
		Buckram 1/4				
Augt	24th	1 pair Womans Shoes	1	11	6	
		9/6, 6 lb. Sugar 5/				
		1½ yds. Bedlyke for		5	3	
		Boots 3/6				
		3 yds. tape do. 2d.		6		1. . 3
October	2d.	4 lb. Sugar 9d				3.
Novemr.	5th	1 Gallon rum		6	8	
	27th	1 Gallon do.		6	8	13. 4
Decemr.	22d.	1 Bushell Salt 3/,		3		
	24th	1 Gallon rum		6	8	9. 8
					£	29. 6. 4
Amount due Quintin Miller per Account						9. 4. 9
		Carried over Total			£	38. 11. 1
1773.		Brought over			£	38. 11. 1
				Cr.		
Decemr.	22d	By 1393 lb. Pork at 22/6	15	13	6	
	31.	By 708 lb. do.	7	19	3	23. 12. 9
		Total Ballance			£	14. 18. 4

Edenton 22d June 1774. The above Account proven before me according to Law.

Joseph Hewes

<marked out> Please pay the above Ballance of Fourteen pounds Eighteen Shillings and four pence proclamation to Mr. Charles Haughton Value received of him.

Millen and Morris

<marked out> To Messrs. Jno. Wilkins and Jno. Taylor
<marked out> Executors on the Estate of Luke Taylor

Amount of Quintin Millen's Account	£9. 4. 9
Balance of Millen and Morris Do.	5. 13. 7
Total Balance as above	£14.18. 4

[*Endorsed:*]
Account
Mr. Luke Taylor To Millen and Morris
1772.

Luke Taylor to Millen and Morris, [1772]-1773, Chowan County, Miscellaneous Records, Personal Accounts, State Archives.

John Harris of Sherwood Dr. To Robert Reid and Co.
1769.

Date	Description			£		
Octr. 1	To Balance due this Date			£ 74	5	8¼
16th.	To ½ lb. Powder	1	6			
	1 ½ lead.		10¼		2	4¼
Novr. 7.	To 1 Boys Hatt				2	
Decr. 1.	To 1 quart rum				2	4
26.	To 1 lb. powder	3				
1770.	4 lb. Lead	2	4		5	4
Janry. 5.	To John Hudspeth			12		
10.	To 1 lb. Gunpowder	1	6			
	1 quart Bottle	1				
	March pd. Samuel Medlock	3			5	6
29.	To 1 pad Lock				2	10
Feby. 23.	To ½ Gallon rum vc	vc			4	
June 14.	To 1 quart rum £2.					
	1 Silk Handkerchief 6. 4	8	4			
23.	To 2 ¾ yards Checks	7	6½			
30.	To 5 quarts rum £7. 6					
	6 lb. Sugar 4.6					
	1 Handkerchief 2					
	2 ⅛ yd. Linen 11.8¼ 1	5	8¼			

		£	s	d	£	s	d
Augt. 9.	To 1 lb. Shott £ 5						
	1 pr. Buckles 1. 6		1	11			
Sept. 10	To Merchant pd. Hays £ 10						
	1 pr. Cairds 3. 4		13	4			
22.	To 1 quart rum		1	6			
Decr. 8.	To 2 lb. Sugar		1	4			
21.	To 5 pr. Sleeve Buttons £ 10						
	1 Gallon rum £ 5		5	10			
	£	3	5	5¾	£ 87	10	1
					VC Procklamation		
1771.	Amount Brought forward £3		5	5¾	£ 87	10	1
Apl. 27.	To 1 Crupper £ 1. 8						
	Merchand pd. Negroe [Sam] 3		4	8			
July 9.	To ½ lb. powder		1				
Augt. 15	To Balance in Callemance £. 1. 7 ½						
	¼ yd. Checks 7 ½						
	1 oz. thread 6						
	2 yard ribbon 2. 5						
	2½ yds. Oznaburgs 2. 2¼						
	1 pr. paddlestraps 10		8	5 ¼			
Sepr. 22.	To Colonel Fanning				1	10	
Novr. 15.	To 1 pr. Nanges		1	6			
Decr. 2.	To William Alston	7	10				
Ma. 3.	To 1 Tinpan			7½			
March 16.	To James Reavis	1	4	4½			
Sepr. 4.	To 100 2d Naills £. 1. 3						
	500 10 Ditto 5		6	3			
	£	13	2	4			
	33 ⅓ per Cent for Procklamation	4	7	5¼	17	11	9¼
1769	Contra Credit Procklamation £				106	11	10¼
Octr. 11.	By John Tatums Bond £ 70						
1770.							
Janry. 20.	By Cash 12						
1771							
June 28.	By Colonel Fanning 6	£88					

150

Balance due Robt. Reid and Co   £ |18 |11 |10¼

May 12th 1773. Robert Reid made oath that the above Balance of Eighteen pounds Eleven shillings and ten pence farthing proclamation Money is Justly due him and Co. from the deceast John Harris.

Reuben Searcy

[*Endorsed*:]

Account

John Harris To Robert Reid and Co.

1772

John Harris to R. Reid and Co. Acct.

> John Harris to Robert Reid & Co., 1769-1771, Granville County, Miscellaneous Records, Personal and Merchants' Accounts, State Archives.

Miss Catherine Hunter To Thos. and Blake B. Wiggins

Dr.   Virga. money

1772.

Date	Item	£	s	d
March 22d.	To 8 ⅝ yds. Linen at 7/	£3	0	4 ½
	1 yd. ditto		3	3
	1 oz. Nuns Thread		1	2
	2 Thimbles 4d., 1 Bunch Tape at 20d.		2	
	4 ¼ yds. Dewrance at 2/8		11	4
	1 hankerchief silk 12d., 2 ½ yds. Binden 3d		1	3
May 20th.	1 ⅜ yds. Linen at 4/		5	6
	1 ¾ yds. ditto at 3/		5	3
June 9th.	1 doz. neadles 4d., 1 Ladys fann 12/		12	4
	½ yds. Chinch at 65/	3	5	
	6 yds. Oznabrigs at 11d.		5	6
	2 yds. Silk Gawze 5/4, 1 Necklas 7d./		17	8
ditto 19th.	6 ¼ yds. Checked Hollen at 2/6		15	7½
	4 ½ yds. Linen at 2/8		12	
	5 scanes Thread 10d., 1 paper pins 9d.		1	7
	1 Lwooking Glass at		2	8

July 10th.	6 yds. Linen at 4/	1	4	
	Thread and Neadles at		1	9½
Augt. 6th.	½ yds. Callinanes 14d., 1¼ yds. Ribband 18½		2	8½
	Tape and feariden, 2/1, 1 hank silk 7d.		2	8½
	1 yd. Linen 3/10, 6 seanes Thread 12d.		4	10
Septmr. 15th.	2 yds. Ribband 2/6, ⅝ yds. Silk Gauze 2/8		5	2
Octor. 8th.	¼ yds. Cambrick at 10/		2	6
	17 yds. Duck at 3/, ½ paper pins 4d./		3	4½
Novmr. 13d.	1 N. [Earc] per Negroe		6	
	¾ yd. Oznabrigs 9d., 1 handkerchief at 3/3		4	
	2 ½ yds. Linen at 2/6		6	3
	1 yd. Ribband, 15d.		1	3
	1 Cloth Cardernal at 32/6	1	12	6
	4 ½ yds. Cottens per Negroes at 2/4		10	6
Decmr. 21st.	3 ½ yds. Oznabrigs per Ditto at 11d.		3	2
	1 pr. yarn Stockings		2	6
	1 yd. Ribband		1	
	1 sealskin Trunk at 25/	1	5	
	Carried Over	£18	1	9½
1773.	Brought Over	£18	1	9½
Janury. 13th.	½ yd. Callico at ¾		1	8
ditto 22d.	4 yds. Linen at 2/		8	
	3 ½ yds. Cotten Cloth at 2/		7	
	⅜ yd. Callico at 4/		1	6
	¾ yd. Linen 2/6, 1 oz. Thread Thread 1/3		3	9
	ditto 29th. 1 paper pins			7½
Febury. 28th.	8 ⅝ yds. Linen at 2/6	1	1	6¾
	6 yds. Ribband 4d., 4 scanes Thread 2d.		2	8
March 18d.	1 pr. shoe buckels 18d., 4 ½ yds. Riband at 15		2	9
	2 yds. Cambrick at 17/6	1	15	
	1 ¼ yds. Musling at 9/6		11	10½
	1 sattan Quilt at 80/	4		

Date	Item	£	s	d
	1 pr. silk Hoes at 25/	1	5	
ditto 30th.	6 ½ yds. striped Hollen at 2/6		16	3
	1 ⅛ yd. Linen at 2/2		2	6
	½ yds. Chinch at 72/6	3	12	6
Apr. 13d.	1 ¼ yd. Linen at 3/9		4	8
May 24d.	7 yds. Oznabrigs per Negroes at 11		6	5
	6 ¾ yds. Linen at 2/6		16	7½
July 6th.	1 pr. Callimanes Shoes at		8	3
	1 Wriden Whip 3/9 ½ yd. Riband 7d.		4	4
	3 Necklasies, 2/ 1 paper pins 9d.		2	9
ditto 12th.	1 satten Bonnett and 1 ½ yd. Ribband 20d.		15	6
	1 pr. Silver Shoe buckels at		15	6
ditto 16th.	1 Looking Glass		2	8
	2 yds. Ribband 22d. 1 oz. Thread 16d.		3	2
	1 pr. Thread Hoes at		4	6
Augt. 17th.	To Cash pd. Doct. peel		5	6
	2 ½ yds. Ribband-3/9, 1 pr. Garters 42d.		4	12
	1 snuf Box 12. 1 hankerchief silk at 9d.		1	9
	1 ⅛ yd. Linen at 2/10		3	2
	1 pr. Ribband at		12	
	1 Comb and Case at		1	
Septmr. 7th.	⅝ yd. Lawn at 17/		10	7½
	1 paper pins-9d. Neadles 42d.		1	1½
	¼ yd. Thread yarne 6/		1	9
	Carried forrod	£38	19	10¼
1773.	Brought fourrd, £38	19	10¼	
Octor. 4th.	2 Cambrick Handkerchief at 6/3		12	6
	1 Checked ditto 2/6, 1¼ yds. Riband 1/3		3	9
ditto 28th.	1 paper pins 6d., 1 oz. Thread at 1/3		1	9
Novmr. 6th.	3½ yds. Linen at 4/8		16	4
	¼ yd. Cambrick 18d. 3 scanes Thread 6d		2	
ditto 8th.	9 yds. Ribband at 19d.		14	3
ditto 22d.	5¾ yds. Cottens per Negroes at 2/8		15	4

		£	s	d
	3½ yds. Oznabrigs 3/6, 4 yds. Roles at 10d.		6	10
	1 pr. Womans Worsted Hoes at		4	3
	1 stock Lock, 2/6, 1 felt Hatt 3/		5	6
	1 m. 10d. Nails, 9/6, 150 20d. nails 1¾		11	6
ditto 25th.	½ yds. Calico at 27/6	1	7	6
	1 yd. Linen 2/, 1 oz. Thread at 2/3		4	3
	1 pr. Worsted Hoes at		7	
Decmr. 1st.	½ yds. Chinch at 7 2/6	3	12	6
	1 Gross Handkerchiefs at		4	6
ditto 13th.	5¾ yds. Ribband at 18d.		8	6
	1 pen knife 20d. 1 Bunch Tape at 15d.		2	11
ditto 21st.	1 silk Lace 12d., 1 pen knife at 8d.		1	8
	6 yds. Linen at 2/4		14	
	1 Checked Handkerchief, 2/, 1 ½ yd. Riband 18d.		3	6
	1½ yds. Silk Gauze at 3/9		4	8¼
	1¼ yds. flannel at 3/		3	9
ditto 27th.	1 Stripd Blanket for Negroe at		12	6
1774.	To Cash pd. for weaven		4	
Janury. 4th.	1 Rug for Negroes at		16	3
ditto 15th.	1¼ yds. Ribband 1/9, 1 paper Pins at 9d.		2	6
	2¼ yds. Linen at 3/		6	9
	1 yd. Dowlas 2/2, 1 Thimble at 4d.		2	6
ditto 20th.	To Cash pd. for spinning		7	6
	1 Bunch Nonsopruty at		1	3
ditto 31st.	1 pr. Cullard Gloves at		2	4
Febury. 5th.	1 ¼ yds. Linen and Two scanes Thread		3	0½
	1 Teapot salt and Cruet		2	4½
	1 pocket Book 9/ and Cash 2/		17	
	Carried Over	£55	6	7½
1774.	Brought Over	£55	6	7½
Febury. 9th.	⅝ yds. Musling at 7/		4	4½
	8 yds. Cap Lace at 2/		16	
	2 yds. Ditto at ¾		6	8
ditto 17th.	1 yd. Linen and Three Thread Laces		4	11
	¼ yd. Cambrick at 13/4		3	4

	1 Tumbler Glass at		1	
March 10th.	3 yds. Silk Gauze at 4/6		13	6
	1 yd. Callico 4/6 1 hankerchief silk, 9d.		5	3
	1¼ yd. Ribband, 18d. silk Gauze and pins 2/		3	6
	1 pr. Gloves at 3/		3	
ditto 16d.	1 snaffle Bridle at		4	6
ditto 19d.	1 black Satten Hatt at		13	4
	8 yds. Callico at 5/	2	0	0
Aprl. 4d.	1 Ink stand, 12d. and paper at 6d.		1	6
ditto 6d.	¾ yd. silk Gauze at 4/6		3	4½
	1 sugar Bowl 12d. ¾ yd. Ribband at 12d.		2	
	3 Necklasces at		11	
ditto 22d.	3 Thread Laces 6d., 1 Grater 12d.		1	6
	Virgina. Currency	£62	5	4½
	Exchange 33⅓ for Procklamation	£83	0	6

[*Endorsed:*]
Hunter to Wiggens Acct.

Catherine Hunter to Thomas and Blake B. Wiggins, 1772-1774, Bertie County, Miscellaneous Records, Individual Accounts, State Archives.

Health and Mortality

North Carolinians suffered from various maladies.

The Diseases that are most common in *Carolina* are, *Agues*, or intermittent *Fevers, Cachexia, Diarrhœa, Dysenteria,* the *Clap* and *French Pox,* the *Yaws, Chollicks, Cholera-Morbus, Convulsions, Hooping-Cough, Cutaneous Disorders,* such as *Tetters, Ring-worms, Rashes, prickley-Heats,* and the *Itch*.

The *Agues* or *intermittent Fevers,* do generally admit of the same method of Cure as with us in *Ireland,* so that it would be needless to repeat it here, which almost every old Woman pretends to have an infalible Cure for.

The *Cachexy,* or ill habit of Body, is a very common Distemper in these Parts; 'tis very stubborn in its Nature, and tedious and difficult to be cured. In this disorder, the Face is very pale and discolor'd, and the Body big and swoln; this Distemper is principally owing to their eating great quantities of Fruit that this Country produces, and to a sedentary way of living, and their eating Clay and Dirt, which the Children, both Whites and Blacks, and some of the old People are very subject to; by which means the whole Humours of the Body are corrupted and vitiated to that degree (through surfeits and ill digestion) that they will hardly admit of a Cure. Steel'd Wines, and other Preparations of filing and rust of Iron, strong Purgers, and Exercises, are the only Methods to perfect the Cure of this Distemper.

The *Cholera-Morbus,* is a vehement Perturbation of the whole Body and Bowels, from a deprav'd Motion of the Ventricle and Guts, whereby bilious, sharp, or corrupt Humours, are plentifully and violently discharged upwards and downwards. This disorder is happily carried off by giving proper Doses of the *Ipecauacana,* that grows plentifully in *Carolina,* which I have already made mention of.

The *Cramp* or *Convulsions,* is a Motion whereby the Muscles or Membranes are contracted and remitted, without the Will. This Disorder is common in these Parts, and especially amongst the *Negroes* or *Blacks,* whereof many die, either for want, or before Medicines can be administer'd; it admits of the same method of Cure as with us in *Europe*.

The *White* and *Bloody-Flux* are common Distempers in *Carolina,* and so are the *Clap* and *French Pox;* these are cured after the same manner as with us.

The *Yaws,* are a Disorder not well known in *Europe,* but very common and familiar here; it is like the *Lues venerea,* having most of the Symptoms that attend the Pox, such as Nocturnal Pains, Botches, foul

Erruptions, and Ulcers in several parts of the Body, and is acquired after the same manner as the *Pox* is, *viz.* by Copulation, *&c.* but is never attended with a *Gonorrhœa* in the beginning. This Distemper was brought hither by the *Negroes* from *Guinea*, where it is a common Distemper amongst them, and is communicated to several of the *Europeans* or Christians, by their cohabiting with the Blacks, by which means it is hereditary in many Families in *Carolina*, and by it some have lost their Palates and Noses.

This Distemper, though of a venereal kind, is seldom cured by Mercurials, as I have often experienced, for I have known some undergo the Course of three Salvations to no purpose, the virulency still continuing as bad as ever: Wherefore I judge it not amiss to set forth the most effectual method for curing it, which I have often experienc'd, and never without good success (during my residence in those parts) though the Distemper was of ever so violent a nature, or long continuance; it is as follows:

Take four Ounces of the Bark of the Spanish Oak, *two Ounces of the middle Bark of the* Pine Tree, *two Ounces of the Root of the* Sumack, *that bears the Berries, of these Ingredients make a strong Decoction, whereof let the Patient drink a full Pint milk-warm and half a Pint cold, this gives a strong Vomit, by which abundance of filthy Matter is discharged,* This is what is to be done the first Day. *Then let the Patient drink half a Pint three times a Day,* viz. *in the Morning, at one o'Clock in the Afternoon, and at Night, for six Weeks; and if there be any outward Sores, wash them clean five or six times a-Day with part of the same Decoction, 'till they are all healed up, and the Patient becomes well.*

The Patient must abstain from all sorts of flesh Meat, and Strong Liquors during the said Course, his principal Diet must be Broth, Gruel, Penæda, and the like. They may boil the above quantity of Ingredients four times, if more, it will be too weak; this Method effectually cures the *Yaws* in the said time, and the Patient becomes as strong and healthy as ever. I have here given the true method of the Cure of this Distemper, it being little known in *Europe*.

The *Cholick,* or *Dry Belly-ach,* is another common Distemper in this Country, and is often attended with such violent Convulsions, that frequently the Limbs are so contracted (and especially the Hands) that for want of Care and good Advice, they have continued so all their life time; though I have known some of them die in these Fits, which are attended with such a violent constipation of the Bowels, that they cannot void any thing either upwards or downwards. Strong Vomits, Purges, Clysters, and Oyntments, for the contracted Limbs, are the most effectual Methods to carry off this Disorder.

Rashes and *Prikley-heat*, are common Disorders here; in the extremity of the hot Weather, which suddenly comes after cold, they are attended with extream Itchings all over the Body, especially the Legs, which if scratched immediately, inflame, and become inveterate Sores and Ulcers; to prevent which, Spirit of Wine and Camphir or any other Spirit, is of excellent use, by applying it to the Parts.

Tetters and *Ring-worms*, are common in this Province, and are easily cur'd by several Plants in this Country, and especially by the Juice of the Sheep-Sorrel, by applying it to the Part infected.

The *Hooping-Cough*, at my arrival in *Carolina*, was an universal Disorder amongst young and old, whereof several *Negroes* died. It continued in this Province for seven or eight Months successively, beginning in *September*, and ending in *June*; after Bleeding and Vomiting, I found the *Jesuite Bark* to be of excellent use in this disorder. I was assured by many in *Carolina*, that they never knew this Distemper in these Parts before that time.

The Children are much afflicted with the *Worms*, which is owing to their eating vast quantities of Fruit, this excess sometimes occasions Fevers amongst them, yet they are cured after the same manner as with us, likewise with many Plants growing here. [...]

Brickell, *Natural History*, 46-50.

⋘⋙

Many of the illnesses were unknown, but often along the coast malaria, or the ague and fever, was the culprit. The western area of the colony appeared healthier.

May 5. On Friday last Capt. *Cowdry* arriv'd here in 12 days from Bath County of *North-Carolina*, and informs us that it is exceeding sickly there, especially in the North-Country, where, 'twas judg'd above half the Inhabitants were dead; that whole Families were carry'd off thereby, the Distemper begins with a violent pain in the Eye, and the Sick continue but about 20 or 30 Hours before they die. [...]

South-Carolina Gazette (Charles Town), June 28, 1735.

Eden House Septr. 16th [1771]

Dear Cousin

I have not till now had an oppertunity of thanking you for your two last kind favours or should not have so long deferr'd Expressing my obligation to you for them and am much obligd to you also for the sugar which we were in great want off. It gave me more concern than I can express to hear of your being so much indisposd and the rest of the family, particularly dear little Pen who I hop'd would have escap'd this Season, I had the satisfaction of hearing from Mr. Blair by way of Dukinfield that you were all better, if I had been at home I should have sent over on purpose to have known, but my Mrs. Pearson sent their Canoe on Sunday for me I have been retain'd ever since by the weather till this morning, Molly and Betty have had two slight fits of the ague and fever since I left home and to day about 3 OClock were both taken and have now then past nine very high fever and do nothing but groan and complain terribly of a violent pain in their heads, they are very ill which obliges me to send in the morning very early for something for them or if not an alteration for the better before then for the doctor to come over, Billy has never been well since I see you tho' never very ill till to day, I take the oppertunity of enquiring how you all are as I am very anxious to know, hope you are all quite recoverd and that I may expect the pleasure of seeing you and yours as soon as the court is over, please to present my Love to Mrs. Johnston and all the family and beleive me ever my dear Cousin yr. oblig'd and affectionate

Penl. Dawson

Penelope Dawson to "Dear Cousin" [Samuel Johnston], September 16, [1771], Hayes Papers.

[...] It is generally said and believed that Carolina is unhealthy, having many kinds of disease. There is however a great difference between the eastern and western parts. The low land near the sea is unhealthy, owing to the absense of good springs, and to the sluggish streams, whose outlets to the sea are choked by sand-banks, so that there is much foul, stagnant water, especially in summer. But no one should say that the land toward the mountains is unhealthy, for it has fresh air and fresh water, and when one studies the matter it appears that the illnesses of the people there result from their irregular living, now with an abundance of food, now in want, and doing little of the work to which they were previously accustomed.

Fries, *Records of the Moravians*, 1:105.

Newcomers often underwent a "seasoning process" by which they contracted the diseases incident to the climate, usually malaria.

[...] As to Health Mrs Tryon and the little girl have enjoyed a very happy share of it. As to Myself I cannot say so much, having been sharply disciplined with a Billeous disorder in my Stomach and Eruptions of the Rash kind, on my Legs, this I got over the latter end of April last. About a Month since I had a return tho' not so Violent, a Strong Emetic was administered which handled me very Severely, however it effected the cure, and I have Supported the heats very well since. The Thermometer (made by Adams) was in June in a Cool passage at 88°-0' at the highest, and this Month it has been from 79 to 87°-0'. The day after my last letter of June to Ld H the glass in twenty hours sunk from 87°-0' to 71°-30'. Which great change caused much Sickness in in [*sic*] the Province. If I was to Muster my family I should not be able to return many fit for Duty. The Lad we took from Norfolk, a sailor I have made my groom and a little French boy I got here, is all the Male Servants, well, Le Blanc, Cuisinier; & Turner, the Farmer, have both fevers and are taking the bark. Georges Senses just returned with some favorable Symptoms and lastly the girl we took from my Farm has been so ill that she has done an hours work these two months. I sent her last week to a Plantation on the Sea Side, for a change of Scene, and air, She is getting better. These are inconveniences I am told every newcomer must experience in this Colony they term it a seasoning. [...]

William Tryon to Sewallis Shirley, July 26, 1765, Powell, *Correspondence of William Tryon*, 1:140-141.

In the low and marshy parts of the country, the inhabitants, particularly new-comers, are apt to fall into those diseases incident to a moist climate, especially in July and August, when the weather is hottest, and the air becomes stagnant; and, in September, when the weather changes, and the rains fall heavy; then, I say, they are subject to agues, fluxes, and intermitting fevers; but these do not prove mortal; and, in general, it is allowed, that the inhabitants are not affected by any particular distemper, except such as proceed from intemperance, and a neglect of themselves upon their first arrival. [...]

Boyd, "Informations," *North Carolina Tracts*, 438.

Finding myself rather indisposed, I stopped at a house on the banks of a watercourse named Napareed's Creek, and was compelled to remain there all night.

In the morning I became much worse, and soon found myself seized with a most severe sickness, here called a *Seasoning* (to the country and climate.) It was a violent bilious fever, and soon reduced me to the verge of death.

There was nothing to be procured in this place fit for a sick person, not even a nurse. Nature and a good constitution were my only physicians and medicines.

I lay for ten days quite delirious and helpless, and it was five weeks before I was out of danger; but even then, so extremely weak and low, that I was scarcely able to walk across the room.

My strength returned so very slowly, that I was obliged to make a long residence in this solitary place, [...]

Smyth, *A Tour of the United States of America*, 1:130-131.

❧❦❧

Some sought relief by going to more temperate climates in the northern colonies.

[...] set out for New York and towards the end of July arrived in Boston where I got rid in a few days of what afflicted me most to wit a very sharp pain in the pit of my stomach—About the middle of August it was extremely hot in the City and I had some slight fits of intermitting fever which brought the bleeding of the nose upon me, and being told that Rode Island was healthy I went thither and in ten days was perfectly recovered, after I had been there five weeks and proposed to return by way of Philadelphia I unluckily sprained my back by trying to save myself from a fall out of a chair [...]

Rev. James Moir to the Secretary, October 13, 1766, Saunders, *Colonial Records*, 7:265.

❧❦❧

Epidemic diseases, including smallpox, occasionally appeared, despite efforts by the government to prevent their intrusion.

An Act to prevent malignant and infectious Distempers being spread by Shipping importing distempered Persons into this Province; and other Purposes.

Whereas, there is no Provision made by any Law of this Province to compell Vessels arriving from Foreign Ports with the Plague, Small-Pox or other infectious distempers on Board (except such as may arrive at Port Brunswick), to perform Quarantine, altho' the other Parts of this Province are liable to be infected thereby, unless timely prevented:

I. Be it therefore Enacted by the Governor, Council and Assembly, and by the Authority of the same, That from and after the passing of this Act the Master of every Vessel coming in at Occacok Inlet, before he proceeds with his said Vessel to any other Port of this Province, shall go on shore at Fort Granville and there make Oath, before the Commander of the said Fort for the Time being (who is hereby authorized and impowered to administer the said Oath to such Master or Masters), whether or not he hath any contagious Distemper on Board such his Vessel, under the Penalty of Fifty Pounds, Proclamation Money; and the Pilots attending the said Bar or Inlet are hereby commanded and required not to proceed with any Vessel further than the Swatch until such Master of Vessel shall go on shore at Fort Granville and declare, upon Oath, before such Commander for the Time being of the said Fort, whether there be any contagious Distemper on board his Vessel, and until a Permission be given by the Commander of the said Fort for that Purpose, under the like Penalty of Fifty Pounds, Proclamation Money; for which Oath and Permission the Commander of the said Fort for the Time being shall and may have and receive from the Commander of such Vessel the sum of Five Shillings, Proclamation Money.

II. And be it further Enacted by the Authority aforesaid, That if it shall happen that any such Vessel shall have contagious Distemper on Board, the Commander of the Fort shall order such Vessel to lie opposite to such Fort, or such other Place as he may think proper, until further Orders shall be given by the Governor or Commander in Chief for the Time being, who is hereby authorized and impowered to give such Direction for the said Vessel and her Crew's performing Quarentine as he shall think necessary; and if any Master of a Vessel so ordered to perform Quarentine shall not obey such Order, such Master shall forfeit the sum of Five Hundred Pounds, Proclamation Money, One Half to be applied towards the Contingent Charges of the Government and the other Moiety to the Informer.

III. And be it further Enacted, That if any Person, Mariner or Passenger, on board such Vessel ordered to perform Quarentine, shall presume to desert or come on shore from the said Vessel, without Licence from the Commander in Chief for the Time being, until she hath fully performed such Quarentine, such Person shall forfeit and pay Fifty Pounds, Proclamation Money; And if any Person or Persons not belonging to such Vessel shall presume to go on board such Vessel before she hath fully performed Quarentine, such Person shall be compelled to stay on board during the whole Time, under the like Penalty of Fifty Pounds.

Laws, 1755, in Clark, *State Records*, 25:328.

Saturday 6 [February, 1773]

This morning going up Town to prepare for my Journey, expecting Bob every minute, I called to speak to Mr. Pearson at Robert Blair's— Found there many Gentlemen assembled, and had the melancholy intelligence that the Disorder suspected to be the Small Pox was certainly it. [...] We had a good deal of conversation about the Disorder in Town—I see no other alternative for my near and dear Friends but either to go to Mount Galant with Mrs. Dawson, or to be inoculated— The former will be killing, deprivation of their company to me,—the other may produce dreadful consequences—But as I should abhor my self, did I think of my own situation when theirs is in so much danger, I heartily wish the former scheme may be adopted — tho' at their return they may be still in danger—God grant a happy termination of this evil—I fear it will be a most unhappy one— [...]

Higginbotham, *Papers of James Iredell*, 1:216-217.

Ordered that John Ingles be Allowed the Sum of Fifteen pounds for Nursing and Attendance with Burying etc. Edward Barton a person who was put under his Care with the Small pox, And that he have an Order for the same Out of the County Tax.

Minutes of the Craven County Court of Pleas and Quarter Sessions, June 1774, State Archives.

∽ↂↂ∾

Physicians, whose qualifications varied widely, sometimes recognized their inadequacy, but usually treated their patients with a variety of medicines as circumstances allowed. Compensation was slow and might be subject to arbitration.

[...] Poor John Dawson mr. Gray writes me still continues ill, I should have seen him long before this, had I not been prevented by one of the most obstinat and troublesom Coughs I ever had attended with a small fever and pain in my right side yesterday was the first Day I ventured without the door my pain is not yet gone my Cough is Prett well and Meg and I are much upon the recovery, as soon as I can with safty I intend to visit mr. Dawson, not that I had pretend to be of any Service as a Doctor I find my intellect so much decayed to pretend to any thing that way especially in so nice a case as his, had I been below I should have advised their stating his case and sending it to Doctor Segary at Williamsburg, who from his Learning and Long and extensive practice must be much more capable than any this way to order what Diet, and medacenes mr Dawson ought to have however agreeable such a proposal would be so the Gentlemen who attend mr. Dawson I cannot Judge,

Will Cathcart to D[ea]r Sir, February 27, 1770, Hayes Papers.

1732.	Mr. Ross to Abra. Blackall	Dr.
		£ S D
Mar. 25.	A doze of Specifick Pills for yr. wife	0. 7. 6
	A purging Bolus	0.10. 0
28.	Ditto	0.10. 0
	The Pills repeated	0. 7. 6
April 6.	Three Blister plaisters to the Arm	0.15. 0
	Melilot plaisters No. Six	0. 7. 6
15.	Six papers of Specifick powders	1 .10. 0
29.	Ditto	1 .10. 0
	A bottle of Lotion for the Arm	0.10. 0
May 2.	A compound Gargle [oz]x for yr. Self	0.12. 6
9.	A doze of Specifick Pills	0. 7. 6
	A purging powder	0 10. 0
12.	Bleeding	0 .10. 0
	The Gargle repeated	0 .12. 6
	The purging Powder as before	0.10. 0
13.	The Lotion again for yr. Wife	0 .10. 0
14.	The purging Powder repeated yr. Self	0 .10. 0
16.	Ditto	0 .10. 0
31.	The Lotion as before for yr. Wife	0 .10. 0
	for Severall visitts and attendance	3. 0. 0
	for Salivating yr. Wife and whereof ten	30. 0. 0

pounds was pd. to the nurses.   £44.10 .0

Errors excepted per Abr. Blackall

November the 21. 1732
Recd. in part of the within Acct. the Sum of eight pounds bills per Abraham Blackall.

December the 6th. 1732
Recd. by a note Endorsed in part of the within Acct. ten pounds bills per

Abraham Blackall

44.10.0
19
£ 26.10.0 Ballance

[*Endorsed*:]
Blackhall at Ross
acct 26.10.0 due etc.

Mr. Ross to Abra. Blackall, 1732, Chowan County, Personal Accounts, 1700-1789, State Archives.

1742.	Mr. Peter Fresneau Dr. to Abra. Blackall	
Septr. 18.	To a vomiting dose	0 .15. 0
21.	To do.	0 .19. 0
22.	To two papers of Antefebrifuge powders	1. 0. 0
24.	To Six papers do.	3 .0. 0
28.	To Six do.	3. 0. 0
27.	To Six do.	3 .0. 0
29.	To Six do.	3. 0. 0
O[c]tr. 2.	To 1 vial of peruvn. drops	1 .0. 0
4.	To do.	1 .0 .0
7.	To do.	1 .0. 0
Jan. 15.	To nine doses of flor'. Sulph. at 2/6	1. 2. 6
1742/3.	To visits, attendance and curing an Ulcer on yr. Leg	10 0. 0
		£28.12. 6
	By 2 pounds of Bohea Tea at 3/10	7 .0. 0
	By 2 pound of chocolate at 35 S.	3.10. 0

Ballance due 18.02. 6

Mr. Peter Trudeau [Fresneau?] to Dr. Abra. Blackall, 1742, Chowan County, Personal Accounts, 1700-1789, State Archives.

1755.	Mr. James Campbell to J. Craven	Dr.
		£. S. D.
Augt. 4th.	To a Vial of a oz. Opthalonier	0. 2. 0
Octr. 18th.	To a Corroberating Electuary	0. 6. 8
21	To a Catharatic Electuary	0. 8. 0
	To Pill prop.	0. 4. 0
29	To a Vial of Corroberating Drops	0. 5. 0
Novr. 5th.	To a Balsamic Electuary	0. 6. 0
11.	To Do. repeated	0. 6. 0
14.	To Purging Pills	0. 2. 0
17.	To a Corroberating Electuary	0. 6. 8
25.	To a Box of Restringnt. Pills	0. 7. 6
Decr. 6.	To a Vial of Corroberative Balsam	0. 4. 8
13.	To a Box of Corroberative Restringnts.	1. 1. 4
1756.		
Feby 3d.	To a Vial of Balsamic Drops	0. 4. 8
25.	To a Box of Pill Corrob.	0. 7. 6
March 8th.	To a Vial of Balsamic Drops	0. 4. 8
	To short Paid for 3 Doses Purging Pills	0. 1. 0
15.	To £ the Corroberative Pills repeated	0.10. 8
Apl. 1.	To a Box of Pill Restringt.	0. 5. 4
	To 4 times Bleeding	0. 5. 4
Novr. 25th.	To Gutt Salure for Daugr.	0. 4. 0
29.	To Bleeding	0. 1. 4
	To Sundry Medicines	6. 4. 4
	for your friend Deliverd	3. 2. 8
	to you	9. 7. 0
1756.	Dr. Mr. James Campbell His Acct. Current	
	with J. Craven	Cr.
		£ S D
	To Sundrys As per Acct. Proclamation	9. 7. 0
		2. 9. 6
		6.12. 6
	By Proclamation	0.15. 0
	By Greaves Board for 3 weeks	1. 4. 0
	By Writing and 4 Sheets of Paper	.10.

> Mr. James Campbell to J. Craven, 1755, Chowan County, Personal Accounts, State Archives.

I HAVE just opened a large assortment of fresh imported medicines, among which there is a greater quantity of almost all the following articles, than I could consume in my own practice, in many years, therefore would be glad to supply others, at the lowest terms with whatever they may want, of Peruvian bark, camphire, sweet mercury, opium, rheubarb, jallap, I-pecacuanha, aloes, myrrh, gummastick, magnesia, Spanish flies, Venice treacle, borax, saltpetre, volatile salt of hartihorn, do. of salamoniac, camamile flower, brimstone, and flowers of sulphur, etc.

ALEX. GASTON.

Newbern, May 22

> *North Carolina Gazette* (New Bern), May 22, 1778.

[Edenton, December, 1783]. We lived in the same house with a doctor who, like many country-doctors in America, had all his medicines exposed in the window; his store was very restricted, little besides tartar-emetick, flowers of antimony, tartar, saltpetre, Peruvian bark, and a few other mixtures of sorts. He complained of slow and small pay. As yet there are no medical regulations in America, and if any one thinks his doctor's charge too high it is the custom to submit the matter to some neighboring practicioner, or to several of them, who allow or reduce the amount according to the circumstances or the degree of friendship or spite they have for their colleague. But if injustice is done, the charge can be very easily made good by an affidavit.

> Schoepf, *Travels in the Confederation*, 2:116.

⊷⦵⊷

Death occurred all too suddenly in the colony, and the introspective James Iredell reflected upon that eventuality at the demise of George Blair of Edenton.

The Death of George Blair

[1772?]

Let the Melancholy Train of my Thoughts have vent. Let me unburthen, as to a kind of second self, the great Grief which overwhelms my Heart. Let me regret for others, ill-deserving such Affliction, if it was to be uncompensated, the loss of a Husband and a Father—a Man who not only held those Ties by Nature, but by the tenderest affection, and most anxious solicitude for the welfare of those who were so connected with him. Let me endeavour to conceive *their* distress, the afflicting misery of *their* situation, bereaved at once, and of a sudden of a dear, how dear a Friend! and of a most tender Guardian. From the thought, though but for a moment, of Distress like this, I can the more readily pass to consider the condition of those amiable Friends who sympathize in their affliction, and feel for their own loss but as for a secondary one. How amiable, but how unhappy, a sight was it for me to see the dear Miss Johnstons—bursting from their affectionate Hearts a continual succession of tears and sighs—the tender effusions of Grief for themselves, their sister, and their young Relations. Admirable Girls! lovely Women! May your lives be happy as you deserve. You cannot wish them happier. Mrs. Dawson will have a complicated share of distress to struggle with. When the sympathetic Goodness of her Heart has time to subside into reflection, how cruel will be the remembrance, how cutting the Thought, that she has once passed in her own person a scene like that which Mrs. Blair suffers.

For two such Women to have occasion for Grief like theirs, would be (would it not be?) an unprovidential allotment, was this world to terminate our Existence. No! an hereafter will reconcile all. Then the best will be the most happy. Upon that future state to which we are all hastening, must our Thoughts direct themselves. Nothing is more uncertain than a life here, nothing more transitory than the Enjoyment of it. One day happy in conversing with a Friend, in all appearance promising to live many years; another viewing him on the bed of sickness; a third on a *death-bed*. Gracious God! This is Affliction in the extreme. Yet thou ordainest it, and we submit. Thou canst not, thou dost not, forbid the tear of sorrow, or the heart of grief. Otherwise it would not be that the best People have usually the most sensibility. Humanity requires, and religion does not forbid, that we should mourn for the loss of valuable Friends. This even adds an increased motive to be virtuous and good—to direct our steps according to thy precepts. To reflect, and to feel, how fleeting are all our joys here, and how liable we are at all times, even when we think ourselves most secure, to be deprived of the comforts and blessing of life, must (it is the only consolation left) lead us to consider, that soon, perhaps very soon, we may pass the verge of this world, and enter (if we be not wanting to ourselves) into immortal happiness in another. We are too apt to think, our Stay here momentous to our Welfare. There cannot be a more mistaken notion, as every day's Experience testifies. Here one sorrow quickly succeeds another, and the happiest days are not without alloy. Yet even these would have less, did we possess a philosophic indifference for the shadowy advantages of this World, and look forward, with the Confidence of a good Conscience, to the blissful prospects of another. Young as I am, I have seen much affliction, have been witness to much unhappiness, and in some, a personal, an immediate sufferer —in all I trust (I should despise myself if I was not) a distressed sympathizer. I have passed through a School of Misery, which I cannot, however, now regret for myself, as it has given my Mind a turn of sobriety and reflection. May I daily endeavor to improve its disposition, and cultivate it with virtuous resolutions, and may I be enabled to carry these Resolutions into practice, and by an uniform Intention of doing my Duty, make the Tenor of my Conduct here, deserving of Happiness.

Higgenbotham, *Papers of James Iredell*, 1:98-100.

Edenton was located in the notoriously unhealthy Albemarle region, whose inhabitants became somewhat fatalistic about their future.

[...] [December, 1783]. In addition to the usual bilious and intermittent fevers, there prevailed last fall a bad form of quinsy, which carried off many people in these parts. In so small a place as Edenton there were 9 bodies to be buried in one day. The people here are too much given to a belief that there is no way of avoiding frequent sickness, and consequently they take little trouble to be rid of their plagues, regarding it as matter of fact that no physician can cure their 'fever and ague.' They try a few doses of quinquina, and if this does not help they give themselves up to the fever, hoping that with the approach of winter they will grow sound. [...]

Schoepf, *Travels in the Confederation*, 2:115-116.

By law the county coroner held inquests to determine the cause of death in suspicious or unknown circumstances.

No. Carolina Granville County ss.

Inquisition Indented taken *at* the Cross Roads leading from Taylors ferry to Howel Lewis's and from Nutbush to Graves's in the County aforesaid the Seventh day of July, in the year of our Lord one thousand Seven hundred and Sixty five. before one Samuel Henderson a Coroner of the said County. upon the View of the body of John Allin late of the said County then and there lying dead and upon the Oaths of John Williams, William Graves, William Yancey, Michael Williamson, James Williams, John Pettigrew, Lovett Gales, James Henderson James Hunt, Jonathan Knight, John Trevilian, Samuel Henderson Junr. James Waldrup Good and lawfull men of the parish of Granville in the said County of Granville who being Charged and Sworn to Enquire how and in what Manner the said John Allin by his death Came upon their Oaths do Say that on the Sixth day of July in the year and at the place aforesaid the said Allin Was Riding along the Road on a Black Mare and was by the said Mare Violently dash'd against a tree, and being thereby Mortally wounded did in a Short time Expire of the wound aforesaid In testimony whereof as well I the said Coroner as the Jurors aforesaid to this Inquisition have Severally put our Seals the day Year and place first above Mentioned.

Michl. *<his mark>* Williamson (Seal), James Williams (Seal), John Pettigrew (Seal), Lovitt *<his mark>* Gales (Seal), Jamese hendeson (Seal), James Hunt (Seal), Jona. Knight (Seal), John Trevilian (Seal), James hendeson (Seal), James Waldrop (Seal), Saml. Henderson (Seal), John Williams SD (Seal), William Graves (Seal), William Yancey (Seal)

One parcill of Joyners Toolls in Posission of John Weatherspoon

	£ s d
Acct. Against James Criswell for	21. 3. 3
Acct. Against John Howard for	4. 9. 6
with Some Other Accts. Deliverd to	
Saml. Henderson Coroner	

[*Endorsed:*]
Allen Jakes Jr.
Inquest on the
Body of John Allen

Granville County, Coroners Inquests, July 7, 1765, State Archives.

No. Carolina Granville County ss.

Inquisition. Indented taken at David Mitchels Near Sties Road. in the County aforesaid the Sixteenth day of June in the year of our Lord Christ one Thousand Seven hundred and Sixty Seven before me Samuel Henderson a Coroner of the said County upon View of the body of Dennis Driscol Taylor, of the said County then and there lying dead, and upon the Oath of Joseph Williams, Harris Gillam, John Mitchel, Daniel Williams John Williams Senr. David Mitchel Thomas Critcher Evan Ragland Isham Harris John Gillam Samuel Jestor Joseph Bishop, Leonard Sims William Gillam, John Vanlandingham and John Bird, good and lawful men of the County aforesaid who being Charg'd and Sworn to Enquire how, and in what manner the said Dennis Driscol by his death Came upon their Oaths do Say that on or about the fourteenth day of this Instant June, and at the place aforesaid the said Daniel Driscol did die by the means of heat of Weather and the said Driscols Voluntarily, drinking two large a Quantity of Spirituous Liquors. In Testimony whereof I the said Coroner as well as the Jurors aforesaid hath hereunto Set our hands and Seals the day and year aforesaid

Saml. Henderson Coroner (Seal), Joseph Williams (Seal), Harris Gillum (Seal), John mitchel (Seal), Daniel Williams (Seal), John Williams (Seal), David Mitchel (Seal), Thomas Critcher (Seal), Evan Ragland (Seal), Isham Harris (Seal), John Gilliam (Seal), Saml. Jester (Seal), Joseph Bishop (Seal), Lennard Sims (Seal), William Gilliam (Seal), John Vanlandingham (Seal), John Bird (Seal)

Granville County, Coroners Inquests, June 16, 1767, State Archives.

No. Carolina Granville County ss.

The Inquisition Indented taken at a Schoolhouse in the County aforesaid the 21 day of Septembr. in the year of our Lord one thousand Seven hundred and Sixty Eight before one Samuel Henderson Coroner of the aforesaid County upon View of the body of Thomas Springfield late of the said County then and there lying dead and upon the Oaths of John Williams Senr. Solomon Langston Christopher Harris John Morris John Tuder John White Robt. Allison Carter Hudspeth Giles Hudspeth Malachy Reavis Wm. Roberts Wm. Parker Isham Coddell good and lawful men of the aforesaid County who being Charged and

Sworn to Enquire how and in what manner the said Thos. Springfield by his death came upon their Oaths do say that on the 20th day of Septr. in the year and at the place aforesaid the said Springfield did hang himself and thereby was guilty of his own death.

John Williams (Seal), Solomon Lanston (Seal), Christopr. Harris (Seal), John <*his mark*> Morris (Seal), John Tudor (Seal), John White (Seal), Robert Allison (Seal), Carter <*his mark*> Hudspeth (Seal), Giles <*his mark*> Hudspeth (Seal), Malachy <*his mark*> Reavis (Seal), William Roberts (Seal), William parham (Seal), Sam. Caudle (Seal), Saml. Henderson (Seal)

Granville County ss. Novr. Ct. 1768. Then was this Inquisition Returnd into Court by Samuel Henderson Coroner, and on Motion Ordered to be Recorded.
Test. Saml. Benton C.C.

> Granville County, Coroners Inquests, September 21, 1768, State Archives.

❧❧❧

At the death of Governor Arthur Dobbs in 1765, no Anglican clergyman was available to perform the service. Nonetheless, the governor's passing was observed with suitable ceremony.

[...] I reached Wilmington the 30th of March and to my surprize found they had buried the Governor and for want of a Clergy, the Funeral Service was performed by a Majestrate of Peace. [...]

> Powell, *Correspondence of William Tryon*, 1:138.

April 3. On Thursday, the 28th of March, died, at his Seat near Brunswick, His Excellency ARTHUR DOBBS, Esq; Captain General and Governor in Chief in and over this Province.

His Excellency's Remains were interred on Friday Evening, in the new Church of Brunswick, with all the Respect and Decorum which the Situation and Circumstances of the Place would permit: Many of his real Friends accompanied him to the Grave, with sorrowful Hearts. Minute Guns were fired from Fort Johnston, from his Majesty's Ships lying in the River, and from a temporary Battery at Wilmington; and every other Military Honour paid to the Memory of that great and good Man.

Pennsylvania Gazette, May 9, 1765.

ఆఖచ్ఖ

Funerals were often well attended but not necessarily decorous affairs.

[Northeast Cape Fear River, March or April, 1775]. Mr Rutherfurd had my two brothers and some other Gentlemen with him, and every thing prepared to lay her in the grave in a manner suitable to her fortune, and the obligations he had to her friendship. Every body of fashion both from the town and round the country were invited, but the Solemnity was greatly hurt by a set of Volunteers, who, I thought, must have fallen from the moon; above a hundred of whom (of both sexes) arrived in canoes, just as the clergyman was going to begin the service, and made such a noise, it was hardly to be heard. A hogshead of rum and broth and vast quantities of pork, beef and corn-bread were set forth for the entertainment of these gentry. But as they observed the tables already covered for the guests, after the funeral, they took care to be first back from it, and before any one got to the hall, were placed at the tables, and those that had not room to sit carried off the dishes to another room, so that an elegant entertainment that had been provided went for nothing. At last they got into their canoes, and I saw them row thro' the creeks, and suppose they have little spots of ground up the woods, which afford them corn and pork, and that on such occasions they flock down like crows to a carrion.

Andrews, *Journal of Lady of Quality*, 171.

[...] [Washington]. In the afternoon went with Doctor Loomis & others to the funeral of John Bonner, about a Mile in the Country; when we arrived at the house, we found it crowded with a mixt Company of Men and Women, sitting & standing round the Corpse, which was nailed up in a Coffin and cever'd with a Sheet, Parson Blount was standing with a Tea Table before him, to hold his Books, and an Arm Chair for him to sit down if he chose it — He went thro' a long service from the Liturgy of the Church of England Prayers, Creeds, Psalms, &c. and afterwards preach'd a very excellent Funeral Sermon; and instead of a fulsome eulogium on the deceased, he very pathetically exhorted his hearers to consider the shortness of life, the certainty of

Death & the necessity of a preparation for the World to come.— I staid till Sermon was over, when being very cold, I came away —[...]

Rodman, *Journal of a Tour to North Carolina by William Attmore, 1787*, 25.

"Funerals take place in the following manner: If the church is too far removed the dead are buried at their home, occasionally also at the home of a good neighbor where then gradually a sort of a churchyard is formed. If, however, as is usually the case, they are brought to the church, (to a regular cemetery) the coffin is at first placed before the front door of the house. At the foot of the corpse stands the preacher, and around the coffin on all sides, the congregation. No invitations to a funeral are sent out. Everybody considers it his duty to come, and indeed on horseback. Then the pastor has a song, or at least a few verses, sung, after which he gives a short address of about eight to ten minutes. Meanwhile the lid of the coffin is removed and the women crowd around uttering a pitiful wail. Then the pastor orders the coffin to be closed and placed in a wagon while the people mount their horses. Thus after refreshments of bread and rum at the house of the deceased the procession moves to the church. Upon arriving at the church the pastor commands a halt, the corpse is let down from the wagon, a few verses are sung, the coffin is again opened, and while singing the crowd marches by twos to the grave. After the body has been lowered a silent prayer is offered and the grave is filled during the singing of a song. Then still continuing their chant they betake themselves to the church where the funeral sermon is given from the pulpit." [...]

Report of Rev. Mr. Roschen, 1789, in Boyd and Krummel, "German Tracts," 243-244.

❧❧

Funerals might occasion considerable expense, leading Cornelius Harnett during the straitened times of the American Revolution in 1781 to ask for a simple ceremony.

Rubin Proctor To Elisha Whitfield	Dr.
Octob. the 4th 1762. To Proclamation money	£ 15.
To 6 Bushels of Indian Corne at 2/8	15.
To 1 Qut. of brandy at 2/	2.
To 5 Gallons of Cyder at 8d.	3. 4
To 1 Winding Sheet	1. 2. 6

To 1 Qut. of Brandy	2.
To 3 pounds of Suggar	3.
To paid Mr. Howard for Reading	2 .8
To plank and nails for a Coffin	4.
To paid Edward Collins for making a Coffin	6 .8
To Goeing To Jordan Thomas' and sundrie other Places in Scotland neck with Expence in going	15
To my Charge for Attend him in his sickness	1.10
To my Charge for feading his horse and Takeing Care of him about a month	[torn]
To paid the Cryer for selling his Estate	2.
To paid for Letters of Administration	2. 10
	£9. 3 .[torn]

Errors Excepted per Elisha Whitfield
sworn to

[*Endorsed:*]
Whitfield
vs
Procter Acct.

Rubin Proctor to Elisha Whitfield, October 4, 1762, Bertie County, Individual Accounts, State Archives.

[New Bern, November 25, 1787]. It is the custom here With some, if they can afford it, when a burial happens in their families, to give the Minister and bearers white scarffs and Bands the Scarff is composed of about 3 yards & a half of white linen and hangs from the right shoulder & is gathered in a knot below the left Arm, with a Rose and Ribbands, also white; from the knot the two ends or tags hang down; the Band for the Hat is of white linen also, about 1 1/2 yards or sometimes that quantity will make two Bands if split down the middle — This is tied round the Crown of the Hat & the two ends streaming down —

The Sunday after the Funeral, the bearers assemble somewhere, with these decorations to their persons and go in a body into Church, where the Minister dress'd in the like manner receives at the door.

This custom I had the opportunity to observe today, there having been a funeral last Week, the bearers assembled at the Tavern where I stay, opposite the Church, in order to go into Church together. The Linen is of a convenient quantity to make a shirt after ceremonies are over.

Rodman, *Journal of a Tour to North Carolina by William Attmore, 1787,*
18-19.

I, Cornelius Harnett having executed the within written Will think
it not improper to add that as I have ever considered expensive Funerals
as ostentatious Folly, it is my earnest Request (and from my present
Circumstances now doubly necessary) that I may be buried with the
utmost Frugality.

Cornl. Harnett

Will of Cornelius Harnett, April 8, 1781, Will Book AB, 485, Office
of the Clerk of Superior Court, New Hanover County Courthouse,
Wilmington, N.C.

Towns

Important as they were as commercial and social centers, North Carolina towns, including perhaps the largest, Wilmington, paled in comparison to the urban areas of Europe, at least to European travelers.

However, the generality of the towns are so inconsiderable, that in England they would scarcely acquire the appellation of villages. [...]

Wilmington has no appearance of ever having been the capital of a province, being nothing better than a village, containing near about two hundred houses, a few of which however are pretty good and handsome.

Smyth, *A Tour of the United States*, 1:98, 2:87.

❧❧

In chartering towns, the North Carolina legislature mandated a commission form of government, either self-perpetuating or elective, but Governor Arthur Dobbs (1754-1765) introduced the municipal corporation, or borough, which was common in England and in some of the northern colonies.

An Act for the better settling, regulating, and improving the Town of Beaufort, in the County of Carteret; and for annexing Ocacock Island to the said County.

I. Whereas the Laws hitherto made for regulating the Town of Beaufort, have been found Inconvenient; For Remedy whereof,

II. Be it Enacted by the Governor, Council and Assembly, and by the Authority of the same, That from and after the passing of this Act, William Thompson, William Cole, William Robinson, Joseph Bell, Jun., and John Easton, Gentlemen, shall be, and are hereby appointed Commissioners of the said Town; And in Case of their or any of them, dying, removing, or refusing to Qualify as such, it shall and may be lawful for the remaining Part, or a Majority of them by and with the Consent and Approbation of the County Court, to nominate and appoint another, in the Room of such dying or removing, or refusing to qualify: [...]

Laws, 1770, in Clark, *State Records*, 23:805.

NEWBERN, July 13.

The 1st of this Instant, being the Day on which the Election of a Mayor for the Borough of Newbern is annually held, the Mayor, Recorder, Alderman, and Common Council, met at the Courthouse in Newbern, to proceed to the said Election; when THOMAS HASLIN, Esq.; was unanimously chosen MAYOR for the said Borough for the ensuing Year; who, after having taken the Oaths of Government, and those appointed for his Qualification, was placed in the Chair by SAMUEL CORNELL, Esq.; the late Mayor, who resigned his Mayoralty. An elegant Dinner was provided by the Mayor, for the CORPORATION, where all the Gentlemen in Town were invited.

The North Carolina Magazine, or *Universal Intelligencer* (New Bern), July 13, 1764.

[January 15, 1760] GEORGE the Second by the Grace of God of Great Britain France and Ireland King Defender of the Faith and so forth To all and singular our faithful subjects Greetings. WHEREAS a commodious Place for Trade and Navigation Situate on the East side of Cape Fear River Containing about four hundred acres of Land by Act of Assembly of our Province of North Carolina hath been appointed and laid out for a Town called by the name of Wilmington a Plan whereof remains in the Secretary's Office of our said Province And divers of our loving Subjects have seated themselves & families upon the same And the said Town is likely to Increase greatly in the Number of Inhabitants and Buildings if duly encouraged KNOW Ye that we being willing to encourage all our good and faithful Subjects as well at present residing and Inhabiting as who shall or may here after reside or Inhabit within the said Town of our Royal Grace good will certain Knowledge and mere Motion with the advice of our Council of our said Province, HAVE constituted and erected And by these our letters Patent Do constitute and erect the said Town of Wilmington a Borough by the name of Wilmington, and for us our Heirs and successors Do by these presents grant to the Inhabitants of the said Borough that the said Borough shall be a Borough Incorporate, consisting of a Mayor, one Person learned in the Law for bearing the Office of Recorder of the said Borough and Eleven Aldermen, [...]

Lennon and Kellum, *Wilmington Town Book,* January 15, 1760, 127.

An Act for regulating Proceedings in the Court held for the Borough of Wilmington.

I. Whereas his present Majesty, by his Royal Charter, bearing Date the Fifth Day of March, in the Year of our Lord 1763, hath been graciously pleased to constitute the Town of Wilmington, with the Precincts and Liberties thereof a Borough, by the Name of the Borough of Wilmington; and among other privileges, hath impowered the Mayor, Recorder and Aldermen, of the said Borough, and their Successors forever, or any Three of them, whereof the Mayor or Recorder to be One, to hold a Court within the said Borough every Two Months with Power to hear and determine all Suits, Matters and Things, brought before them, where the cause of Action between Persons resident in the said Borough, and transient Persons not residing in the Province, shall arise within the said Borough, or the liberties thereof; and where the Debt or Damages shall not exceed Twenty Pounds Proclamation Money, and holding said Courts Regularly, will tend greatly to promote the Trade and Commerce of the said Borough:

Laws, 1764, in Clark, *State Records*, 23:654.

❧☙

Not only were they small, but towns appeared tardily. Bath Town, North Carolina's first, was chartered in 1705/6, a half century after the permanent settlement of the colony, and remained little more than a village throughout the colonial era.

An Act for Appointing a Town in the County of Bath and for Securing the Publick Library belonging to St. Thomas's Parish in Pamptecough.

I. Whereas at the request of Mr. John Lardson, Mr. Joel Martin and others a certain Tract of Land purchased by themselves lying in the Old Town Creek in Pampticoe & containing by estimation Sixty Acres be the same more or less being part of a larger Tract then belonging to one David Perkins but now in the tenure & Possession and of right belonging to Col. Thomas Cary & divided from thence by a Headline of Marked Trees from the Old Town Creek to Mr. Barrow's line, now also the right & Possession of the said Cary, was Incorporated & made a Township by an Act of the General Assembly made and Ratified at the House of Capt. John Hecklefield the 8th day of March, 1705, With divers privileges & immunities therein granted which said land was therein & thereby Invested in the same John Dawson, Joel Martin & Nicholas Daw to and for the uses afors'd.

II. And Whereas Damage may accrue to the further Settlement & Increase of the said Town for want of Trustees to dispose of Lotts & a Better Regulation of the Methods to be observed in settling the same. To promote therefore as much as may be the Settlement, Growth & Increase we pray that it may be Enacted.

III. And Be It Enacted by His Excellency the Pallatine & the rest of the True & Absolute Lords Props. of Carolina by & with the Advice & Consent of this present General Assembly now met at Little River for the No. East part of the said Province & by the Authority of the same that the said land be & it is hereby henceforward Invested in Mr. John Porter, Mr. Joel Martin, Mr. Thomas Harding & Capt. John Drinkwater or any two of them to & for the use afors'd & declared confirmed & incorporated into a Township by the name of Bath Town with all priviledges & Immunities hereafter Exprest forever Pursuant to which it is hereby Enacted that convenient places & proportions of Lands be laid out & preserved for a Church, A Town-House a Market Place & that the rest of the Land which is not already laid out be forthwith laid out into lotts of halfe an Acre each with convenient streets & Passages by the said Trustees or any Two of them.

Laws, 1715, in Clark, *State Records*, 23:73.

Bath Town, is the Second considerable Town in this Province, and is most delightfully seated on a Creek on the Northside of *Pamticoe* River, with the same beautiful Advantages of the former: It's Navigation is much better, being the most considerable and commodious for Trade in this Province, except *Cape Fear*.

Brickell, *Natural History*, 8.

৵৵৵

Chartered in 1720, Edenton evoked vastly different reactions among visitors.

An Act for Enlarging and Encouragement of the Town called Edenton, in Chowan precinct.

Whereas, Thom's Peterson, late of Chowan Precinct, Esq'r., dyed seized in his Demesen as of Fee a certain Tract of Land or plantation lying in the Fork of Queen Ann's Creek, in Chowan precinct, containing two hundred and Seventy Acres, be the same more or less adjoining to the Lands of the Town now called Edenton, which Lands on the

Decease of the Said Thom's did descend unto Ann, the Daughter of the Said Thomas; And, whereas, Johanna, the Mother of the said Ann, upon her humble petition to the General Biennial Assembly held for the Year 1715, obtained an Act of Assembly intitled an Act of impowering Johanna Peterson, Widow of Thom's Peterson, late of Albemarle County, Esq'r., to make Saile of certain Lands belonging to the said Tho's Peterson for Ann, Daughter of the said Tho's Peterson, to whom the Lands do Descend, Thereby impowering the said Johanna to make Sale of the Said Lands for the Benefit and Advantage of her said Daughter, and her better Advancement, and the Said Lands remaining as yet unsold and lying very convenient to be added to Edenton for the Enlargement of the said Town; and the said Johanna referring the Valuation thereof to the Assembly,

I. Be it Enacted by his Excellency, the Palatine, and the rest of the true and absolute Lords Proprietors of the Province of Carolina, by and with the Advice and Consent of the rest of the Members of the General Assembly, now met at Edenton, at Queen Anne's Creek, in Chowan Precinct, for the North-East Part of the said Province, and it is hereby Enacted, that the Lands already laid out for the Said Town called Edenton, together with the aforesaid Tract of Land, two hundred and Seventy Acres lately belonging to the Said Tho's Peterson adjoining to the said Town, be henceforward invested in Christopher Gale, Jn'o. Lovick and Edward Mosely, Esq'rs., and Nicholas Crisp, to and for the Uses aforesaid, And declared confirmed and incorporated into a Township by the name of Edenton, with all privileges hereafter expressed for ever,

Laws, 1722, in Clark, *State Records*, 25:175-176.

[1728] Within 3 or 4 Miles of Edenton, the Soil appears to be a little more fertile, tho' it is much cut with Slashes, which seem all to have a tendency towards the Dismal.

This Town is Situate on the North side of Albemarle Sound, which is there about 5 miles over. A Dirty Slash runs all along the Back of it, which in the Summer is a foul annoyance, and furnishes abundance of that Carolina plague, musquetas. They may be 40 or 50 Houses, most of them Small, and built without Expense. A Citizen here is counted Extravagant, if he has Ambition enough to aspire to a Brick-chimney. Justice herself is but indifferently Lodged, the Court-House having much the Air of a Common Tobacco-House. I believe this is the only Metropolis in the Christian or Mahometan World, where there is neither

Church, Chappel, Mosque, Synagogue, or any other Place of Publick Worship of any Sect or Religion whatsoever.

Byrd, *Histories of the Dividing Line*, 96.

The next thing to be considered, is the Towns and their beautiful Situation. And first, *Edentown* is the largest, consisting of about Sixty Houses, and has been the Seat of the Governors for many Years, and is pleasantly seated on a Creek on the North-side of *Roanocke* River; where you have a delightful Prospect of the said River.

Brickell, *Natural History*, 8.

⋖⋗

Erected in 1739/40, Wilmington contained more than fifty houses in 1754, some of which were quite impressive, but its merchants and shopkeepers failed to offer a leisured social set.

An Act, for Erecting the Village called Newton, in New Hanover County, into a Town and Township, by the Name of Wilmington, and Regulating and ascertaining the Bounds thereof. [...]

I. Whereas several Merchants, Tradesmen, Artificers, and other Persons of good Substance, have settled themselves at a Village Called Newton, lying on the East Branch of Cape Fear river; and Whereas the said village by reason of its convenient situation at the meeting of the Two Great Branches of Cape Fear River, and likewise, by Reason of the Depth of Water, is capable of receiving Vessels of considerable Burthen, Safely in its Roads beyond any other part of the River, and the secure and easy Access from all Parts of the diffrent Branches of the said River, is, upon all those and many other Accounts, more proper for being erected into a Town or Township, than any other part of the said River.

II. Be it Therefore Enacted by his Excellency Gabriel Johnston, Esq., Governor, by and with the Advice and consent of his Majesty's Council, and General Assembly of this Province, and it is hereby Enacted, by the Authority of the same, That the Village heretofore called Newton, lying on the East side of the North East Branch of Cape Fear River, in New Hanover County shall, from and after the passing of this Act, be a Town and Township, and the said Village is hereby established a Town and Township, by the Name of Wilmington, [...]

Laws, 1739, in Clark, *State Records*, 23:133.

[1755] It was Unanimously agreed to lay a Tax on all Houses pursuant to a Law passed the 19th Febry. 1754, to purchase a Water Engine or Engines, Bucketts, &c. When the Commissioners proceeded to Value Every House in the Said Town, and laid a Tax on the Owners according to the following Valuation after the rate of One per Ct. and order'd that an Advertisement be Immediately Set up requiring the Several persons therein Taxed to pay the same to Mr. Arthur Mabson within two months from this date—

John Maultsby's Houses valued		£150	Taxed	£1.10.	Paid
Thomas Nunns	Do.	50	Do.	.10	Paid
Joseph Mott	Do.	15	Do.	. 3	Paid
Gabriel Wayne	Do.	25	Do.	. 5	Paid
Magnus Cowan	Do.	50	Do.	.10.	Paid
Frederick Gregg	Do.	225	Do.	2. 5	Paid
John McKenzie	Do.	285	Do.	2.17	Paid
David Lindsay	Do.	100	Do.	1. 0	Paid
Hugh Murray	Do.	5	Do.	. 1	
John Rutherfurd	Do.	225	Do.	2. 5	Paid
John Morris	Do.	250	Do.	2.10	Paid
Doctor Saml. Green	Do.	275	Do.	2.15	pd. all
Arthur Mabson	Do.	512.10	Do.	5. 2. 6	pd.
Ann Wright	Do.	225	Do.	2. 5	pd.
William Faris	Do.	150	Do.	1.10	Paid
Alice Marsden	Do.	337.10	Do.	3. 7. 6	pd.
James Arlow	Do.	150	Do.	1.10	pd.
George Moore	Do.	200	Do.	2. 0	Paid
John DuBois	Do.	375	Do.	3.15	Paid
William Veale	Do.	60	Do.	.12.	Paid
Thomas Finney	Do.	175	Do.	1.15	
Thomas Cuningham	Do.	37.10	Do.	. 7. 6	Paid
John Cook	Do.	50	Do.	.10.	pd.
John Walkers	Do.	75	Do.	.15.	Paid
Annabella McVicar	Do.	20	Do.	. 4	Paid
John Smith	Do.	25	Do.	. 5.	Paid
John Lyon	Do.	200	Do.	2. 0	Paid
Ann Cowan	Do.	50	Do.	.10	Paid
Caleb Mason	Do.	150	Do.	1.10	pd.
Joshua Grainger	Do.	2.10	Do.	. 0. 6	pd.
Charles Harrison	Do.	75	Do.	.15.	Paid
Richd. Hellier	Do.	50	Do.	.10.	pd.

John Walker, Taylr.	Do.	5	Do.	. 1.	Paid
Hugh Purdie	Do.	125	Do.	1. 5	Paid
Benjn. Wheatley	Do.	75	Do.	.15.	Paid
Alexr. Mackay	Do.	75	Do.	.15.	Paid
Alexr. McKeithein	Do.	100	Do.	1. 0	
David David	Do.	50	Do.	.10.	Paid
Thomas James	Do.	100	Do.	1. 0	Paid
Joshua Toomer	Do.	25	Do.	. 5.	pd.
Mary Porrington	Do.	37.10	Do.	. 7. 6	pd.
Lewis DeRosset	Do.	150	Do.	1.10	pd.
Ann Player	Do.	37.10	Do.	. 7. 6	pd.
Rose Long	Do.	5	Do.	. 1.	Paid
John Campbell	Do.	50.	Do.	.10.	
David Brown	Do.	100	Do.	1. 0	Paid
Wm. Dry	Do.	150	Do.	1.10	Paid
Doctor Armand DeRosset	Do.	25	Do.	. 5.	Paid
Thos. Newton	Do.	25	Do.	. 5.	Paid
Margaret White	Do.	100	Do.	1. 0	Paid
Daniel Dunbibin	Do.	100	Do.	1. 0	Paid
John Sampson	Do.	150	Do.	1.10	Paid
Corns. Harnett	Do.	225	Do.	2. 5	Paid
Moses DeRosset	Do.	150	Do.	1.10	Paid
Alexr. Blythe	Do.	5	Do.	. 1.	pd.
James Campbell	Do.	187.10	Do.	1.17.6	Paid
Ann Walker	Do.	25	Do.	. 5.	Paid
James Murray	Do.	15	Do.	. 3.	Paid

Lennon and Kellum, *Wilmington Town Book*, 77-78.

I Have not yet had time to Take a minute Survey of this Town; But from what I Have Yet Seen, it has greatly the preferrence in my Esteem to New Bern. I Confess the Spot on which its Built is not So Level nor of So good a Soil But the Regularity of the Streets are Equal to those of Philadelpa. And the Buildings in General very Good. Many Of Brick, two and three Stores High with double Piazas which make a good appearance. But I Cannot yet find a Social Co., who will Drink Claret and Smoke Tobacco till four in the morning. I Hope However to Make some proselytes soon, [...]

Peter DuBois to "My Dear Johnston," February 8, 1757, Hayes Papers.

Some one hundred miles north of Wilmington along the Cape Fear River appeared Cross Creek, settled approximately 1760, and Campbellton, chartered in 1762. The two merged as Campbellton in 1778, and became Fayetteville in 1783.

An Act for establishing a town on the lands of John and William Russell, Minors, sons of John Russell, deceased, on the West side of the North-West branch of Cape Fear River, near the Mouth of Cross Creek, by the Name of Campbelton, and other purposes.

I. Whereas, the establishing a town on the lands of John and William Russell, minors, sons of John Russell, deceased, on the west side of the north-west branch of Cape Fear river, near the mouth of Cross Creek, will greatly encourage honest and able traders to reside therein; by means whereof, the trade of the counties of Anson and Rowan which at present centers in Charlestown, South Carolina, to the great prejudice of this Province, will be drawn down to the said town; And whereas, the erecting a town on the said lands will be of great benefit and advantage to the said minors, in as much as the lands adjoining thereto will become of much greater value; therefore,

II. Be it Enacted by the Governor, Council and Assembly and by the Authority of the same, That the Honorable John Sampson, Esq., Cornelius Harnett, Maurice Moor, Hugh Waddle, William Dry, Hector McNeile, Walter Gibson, Alexander McAlister, Richard Lyon, William Bartram, and John Wilcocks, Esquires, are hereby appointed commissioners and are vested with full power and authority to lay off one hundred acres of land, part of a tract of six hundred and forty acres, belonging to John and William Russell, minors, sons of John Russell, deceased, situate on the west side of the North-West branch of Cape Fear River, below the mouth of Cross Creek, for a town by the name of Campbelton; and the said Commissioners, or the majority of them are hereby directed and impowered, to lay out the said one hundred acres of land, as soon as conveniently may be, after the passing of this act into lots of half an acre each, with convenient streets, and a square for public buildings.

Laws, 1762, in Clark, *State Records*, 25:470.

[December, 1777]. Crossed Rock-fish, a large branch of the North West, near its mouth or confluence, and at evening arrived at Cross-Creeks, another very considerable branch of the river, flowing in through its West banks. This creek gave name to a fine inland trading town, on some heights or swelling hills, from whence the creek descends precipitately, then gently meanders near a mile, through lower level lands, to its confluence with the river, affording most convenient mill-seats; these prospects induced active, enterprising men to avail themselves of such advantages pointed out to them by nature; they built mills, which drew people to the place, and these observing eligible situations for other profitable improvements, bought lots and erected tenements, where they exercised mechanic arts, as smiths, wheelwrights, carpenters, coopers, tanners, etc. And at length merchants were encouraged to adventure and settle: in short, within eight or ten years, from a grist-mill, saw-mill, smith-shop and a tavern, arose a flourishing commercial town, the seat of government of the county of Cumberland. The leading men of the county, seeing plainly the superior advantages of this situation, on the banks of a famous navigable river, petitioned the Assembly for a charter to empower them to purchase a district, sufficient for founding a large town; which being granted, they immediately proceeded to mark out its precincts, and named the new city Cambelton, a compliment to _____ Cambel, Esq., a gentleman of merit, and a citizen of the county. When I was here about twenty years ago, this town was marking out its bounds, and there were then about twenty habitations; and now there are above a thousand houses, many wealthy merchants, and respectable public buildings, a vast resort of inhabitants and travellers, [...]

Bartram, *Travels Through North and South Carolina, Georgia, East and West Florida*, 475-476.

◈◈◈

Established in 1760, Tarboro remained small, though it managed to host a session of the General Assembly in 1787 and President George Washington on his Southern Tour in 1791.

An Act for establishing a town on the land of Joseph Howell, on Tar river.

I. Whereas, it hath been represented to this Assembly, that the land of Joseph Howell, lying on the South side of Tar river, in Edgecomb county, is a healthy, pleasant situation, well watered and commodious for trade and commerce: And James Moir, Lawrence Tool, Aquilla Sugg, Elisha Battle, and Benjamin Hart, have contracted with the said Joseph Howell, for the purchase of one hundred and fifty acres of the said land, and have accepted and taken a deed of feoffment for the aforesaid one hundred and fifty acres from the said Joseph Howell and caused the same to be laid off in lots and streets, and also a part thereof for a common for the use of the said town and have sold a great number of the said lots of half an acre each to sundry persons, who are desirous that a town shall be established for promoting the trade and navigation of the said river:

II. Be it therefore Enacted, by the Governor, Council, and Assembly, and by the authority of the same, That the said one hundred and fifty acres of land so laid off by the trustees or commissioners as aforesaid, be, and the same is hereby constituted and erected, and established a town and shall be called by the name of Tarboro.

Laws, 1760, in Clark, *State Records*, 25:451-452.

[December 20, 1787]. TARBOROUGH, is the County Town of Edgecombe County; it is situated on the Southeast side of Tar River, at this place about eighty yards over, the Town contains about twenty Families, and for the size of it has a considerable Trade, [...]

We found upon our arrival at Tarborough the place much crowded; the Legislature being sitting for the dispatch of business—The size of the Town appear'd so inadequate to the comfortable accomodation of a Legislature composed of about 120 Commons or Delegates and about 60 Senators, together with the people attending the Sessions in business or going there on motives of pleasure that you will not easily believe that it was possible to provide for them, Yet provided for they were, and they said themselves, very comfortably; One old Countryman said that he had cause to be satisfied that he lived there much better than at home.—

Rodman, *Journal of a Tour to North Carolina by William Attmore, 1787,* 34, 36-37.

[April 18, 1791]. Monday 18th. Set out by Six oclock—dined at a small house kept by one Slaughter 22 Miles from Hallifax and lodged at Tarborough 14 Miles further.

This place is less than Hallifax, but more lively and thriving; it is situated on Tar River which goes into Pamplico Sound and is crossed at the Town by means of a bridge a great height from the Water and notwithstanding the freshes rise sometimes nearly to the arch. Corn, Porke and some Tar are the exports from it. We were recd. at this place by as good a salute as could be given with one piece of artillery.

Jackson and Twohig, *Diaries of George Washington,* 6:114.

ஃ⸘

**First chartered as Childsburg in 1759, Hillsborough was a thriving
village soon after its name changed in 1766.**

An Act for establishing a town on the land formerly granted to William
    Churton, gentleman, lying on the north side of the river Enoe, in
    the County of Orange.

    I. Whereas, it hath been represented to the Assembly by petition,
that in the year of our Lord one thousand seven hundred and fifty-four,
four hundred acres were granted to William Churton, which was
afterwards laid off by him into a town and common, and that part of
the said four hundred acres hath been likewise laid out into lots of one
acre each on some of which good habitable houses hath been erected;
and that by reason of the healthfulness of the said place and the
convenient situation thereof, for inland trade, the same might soon
become considerable if it was erected into a town by lawful authority,
to which the said William Churton who is now seized in fee, of the
greatest part of the said four hundred acres and those who claim by
conveyance under him, having consented:

    II. Be it therefore Enacted, by the Governor, Council, and Assembly
and by the Authority of the Same, that the said four hundred acres of
land be, and the same is hereby constituted, erected, and established a
town, and town common, and shall be called by the name of Childsburg.

Laws, 1759, in Clark, *State Records,* 25:402.

An Act to amend an Act, intitled, An Act for establishing a town on the
    land formerly granted to William Churton, gentleman, lying on the
    North side of the Eno river in the County of Orange.

    I. Whereas, the erecting and establishing a town in the county of
Orange has been found serviceable, in promoting inland trade and
commerce in the western part of this Province; and whereas, the Act of
Assembly passed at New Bern in the year of our Lord one thousand
seven hundred and fifty-seven, for establishing the same, is found to
stand in need of many alterations and amendments;

    II. Be it therefore Enacted, by the Governor, Council, and Assem-
bly, and by the Authority of the same, That the four hundred acres of
land, by said Act constituted, erected, and established a town, and town

common, by the name of Childsburg, shall from and after the passing of this Act, be known and called by the name of Hillsborough.

Laws, 1766, in Clark, *State Records*, 25:500.

In 1764 my father purchased a farm and removed his family near to Hillsborough, which was the metropolis of the county, where the courts were held and all the public business was done. It was a small village, which contained thirty or forty inhabitants, with two or three small stores and two or three ordinary taverns, but it was an improving village. Several Scotch merchants were soon after induced to establish stores that contained a good assortment of European merchandise, which changed the state of things for the better. A church, court-house and jail were built, but there was no parson or physician.

"The Autobiography of Col. William Few," 344.

◦◦◦

Established by law in 1768, Charlotte hardly betokened its future size when visited by William Moultrie in 1772.

An Act for establishing a Town in Mecklenburg County.

I. Whereas it hath been represented to this Assembly that Three Hundred and Sixty Acres of Land was granted to John Frohock, Abraham Alexander, and Thomas Polk, as Commissioners, in Trust for the County aforesaid, for erecting a Court House, Prison and Stocks, for the Use of said County; which said Three Hundred and Sixty Acres of Land was afterwards by them laid off into a Town and Common; and that Part of the said Three Hundred and Sixty Acres of Land hath likewise been laid out into Lots, of Half an acre each, on some of which good habitable Houses have been erected; and that by Reason of the Healthiness of the Place aforesaid, and convenient Situation thereof for Trade, the same might soon become considerable, if it was erected into a Town by Lawful Authority, to which the said Frohock, Abraham Alexander, and Thomas Polk, Commissioners aforesaid, who are now seized in Fee of the said Three Hundred and Sixty Acres, and those who claim under them, having consented.

II. Be it therefore Enacted, by the Governor, Council, and Assembly, and by the Authority of the same, That the said Three Hundred and Sixty Acres of Land, so laid off by the Commissioners or Trustees as aforesaid, be, and the same is hereby constituted, erected, and established, a Town and Town Common, and shall be called by the Name of Charlotte.

Laws, 1768, in Clark, *State Records,* 23:722.

[1772]. Sunday halted from business; some of us took a ride to Charlotte Town in Meclinburgh [Mecklenburg] County. The Town has a tolerable Court house of wood about 80 by 40 feet, and a Goal [*sic*], a store, a Tavern, and several other houses say 5 or 6, but very ordinary built of logs. [...]

"Journal of William Moultrie," 553.

⊰⊱

Townspeople, often unable to produce sufficient foodstuffs, depended upon their municipal markets, which were regulated for the benefit of the public.

An ACT, for Establishing Markets in the Borough of Newbern, *and for regulating the same.*

WHEREAS divers Inconveniencies do daily happen, as well to the Inhabitants of the said Borough, as to the Country People who bring Provisions to sell therein, for want of a settled known Place for the vending and buying thereof; in as much as they who bring Provisions to the said Town, are generally obliged to hawk the same about in order to look for a Purchaser, whilst many of the said Inhabitants are distressed for want thereof: And whereas his Majesty GEORGE II, of happy Memory, late King of *Great Britain,* and so forth, did, by his Royal CHARTER of Incorporation, bearing Date the Thirty First Day of *May,* in the Thirty Third Year of his Reign, amongst other Things, grant unto the Mayor, Recorder, Alderman, and Common Council of the said Borough, full Power and Authority to hold Two Markets Weekly within the said Borough, *viz.* on every *Wednesday* and every *Saturday.*

Therefore, in Pursuance and Execution of the said Power, and for remedying the Inconveniences aforesaid, to the End that all the Inhabitants of the said Borough, Poor as well as Rich, may be the better accommodated and supplied with Provisions, by knowing where to resort for the purchasing thereof; and also for accommodating the Country People with a proper and convenient Place for vending such Articles of Provision as they shall respectively bring to the said Town; *It is Ordained and Established, by the Mayor, Recorder, Alderman and commons in this Common Council assembled, and by the Authority of the same,* That the open Space or Floor under the Court-house in *Newbern* aforesaid, and the open Ground round about the same, be, and the same is hereby Established, made and appointed, to be the Market Place of the said Borough, for the vending and selling of Cattle, Goods Wares and Merchandizes, and all Manner of fresh Provisions, of Beef, Mutton, Lamb, Veal, Swines Flesh, Venison, Poultry, Corn, Meal, Flour, Butter, Eggs, and Garden Wares.

And it is Ordained, That on the Feast of St. *Michael* the Archangel next, being the Twenty Ninth Day of this Instant *September,* and on every *Wednesday* and *Saturday* afterwards, it shall and may be lawful to and for all Butchers, Poulterers, Country Planters, and others, to bring to the said Market, all Manner of Cattle, Goods Wares and Merchandises, and there sell and utter the same; and also to hang up, or put to open Shew or Sale, his or their Beef, Mutton, Lamb, Veal, Swines Flesh, Venison, Poultry, Corn, Meal, Flour, Butter, Eggs, and Garden Wares, from Sun rise until Ten of the Clock in the Forenoon, and on *Saturdays* between the First of *May* and First Day of *October,* from the Hour of Four of the Clock until the Hour of Ten of the Clock in the Afternoon.

And for remedying the Inconveniences that do and may arise from the vending corrupt, unfound, and adulterate Provisions, which is a Nusance of the most dangerous Nature, and hurtful to the Health of his Majesty's Subjects, by Persons hawking the same about in the Out skirts, and other Parts of the said Borough, whereby they evade the Inspection of the Chief Magistrate, whose Duty it is, as far as in him lies, to prevent and prohibit the same from being sold, or imposed upon his Majesty's Subjects: And also, for the better Encouraging of Country Planters and others to bring in and furnish the said Markets with wholesome Provisions on the Days aforesaid, and that they may have the greater Certainty of selling and disposing of the same; *It is Ordained, by the Authority aforesaid* That from and after the said Twenty Ninth Day of *September,* no Person or Persons whatsoever shall hawk about, or expose to Sale, any Provisions on any other Day or Place except such Part as shall remain unsold after the Hour of Ten of the Clock on the Market-days aforesaid; under the Penalty of Five Shillings Proclamation Money; to be levied by Distress and Sale of the Offenders Goods, and applied for the Public Use and Benefit of the said Corporation.

And it is likewise Ordained, (in Regard the Markets are principally intended for the Benefit of House keepers who buy for their own private Use.) That the Retailers or Traders of this Borough who buy Corn, Meal, Butter, and Eggs, to sell again, shall not enter into the said Market to buy from the Country People to carry the same to their Houses or Shops, until after the Hour of Nine of the Clock on the respective Days, to the End that House-keepers may have an Opportunity of providing themselves in the Morning at the first Hand; upon Pain, that every such Retailer so offending, shall, every Time offending herein, forfeit the Sum of Forty Shillings, Proclamation Money; to be levied by Sale of his or her Goods, and applied for the Public Use and Benefit of the said Corporation.

And to the End that Forestalling, Regrating and Ingrossing of Provisions may be the better prevented, that no Persons or Persons, from and after the said Twenty Ninth Day of *September* Instant, shall buy, or cause to be bought, any Provisions or Victuals within the said Borough of *Newbern* coming to the said Market, or make any Bargain, Contract or Promise, for the same, or any Part thereof, so coming as aforesaid, upon Pain, that every such Forestaller, Regrator, or Ingrosser, shall forfeit the Sum of Forty Shillings, Proclamation Money; to be levied and applied as aforesaid.

> Municipal enactment in *North Carolina Universal Magazine*; or, *Universal Intelligencer*, September 14, 1764.

[Wilmington, June 24, 1783]. Early in the morning I went to the market, which is very good, relatively speaking, and among the fruits I noticed some peaches so large and beautiful that, without exaggeration, they were like oranges, their color mostly incarnate and on one side yellow.

> Miranda, *The New Democracy in America*, 15.

◈

Residents of Edenton and other towns kept livestock, though the animals quickly became nuisances or dangers. Townspeople in Hillsborough contended with hogs and geese, as did Wilmingtonians, who were also plagued by goats. In addition to the livestock, Bethania and Wilmington faced the threat of rabid dogs.

An Act to impower the Commissioners for the Town of Edenton to keep in Repair the town Fence and to erect and build a Pound, Bridges, Public Wharf and Market-house; as also to erect and build a School-house in the said Town and other Purposes therein mentioned. [...]

II. And be it further Enacted, by the Authority aforesaid, That no Person or Persons whosoever, except the Inhabitants of the said Town, shall keep, or cause to be kept any Horse, Cattle or Sheep, within the said Town, under the Penalty of Twenty Shillings, Proclamation Money, for each and every Offence; to be recovered and applied as in this Act is hereafter directed.

III. And be it further Enacted, by the Authority aforesaid, That none of the Inhabitants of the said Town shall keep, or cause to kept, running at large within the Bounds of the said Town more than Six Head of Sheep, one Cow and one Horse for one Lot, and so in Proportion for each and every Lot by him, her or them so possessed, under the Penalty of Twenty Shillings, Proclamation Money, for each and every Offence; to be recovered and applied as in this Act is hereafter directed.

Laws, 1745, in Clark, *State Records*, 23:232-233.

An Act to amend an Act, intitled, An Act for establishing a town on the land formerly granted to William Churton, gentleman, lying on the North side of the Eno river in the County of Orange. [...]

XII. And whereas, the allowing of hogs and geese to run at large in the said town, is found to be a great nuisance to the Inhabitants; be it Enacted by the Authority aforesaid, That none of the Inhabitants of the said town shall, on any pretence whatsoever, suffer any of their hogs or geese to run or be at large within the bounds of the said town; and any hog or hogs, goose or geese running at large in the said town, shall be forfeited to any person who shall seize or kill the same.

Laws, 1766, in Clark, *State Records*, 25:500-502.

[1765] WHEREAS the permitting Goats to run at large in the Borrough of Wilmington or the Liberties thereof is found by Experience to be very prejudicial to the Inhabitants thereof.

Be it Ordained by the Mayor, Recorder, Aldermen and Freeholders of the Borrough of Wilmington Convened in Common Council and it is hereby Ordained by the Authority of the same, That from and after the Twentieth day of March next no person or persons residing within the said Borrough or the Liberties thereof shall, on any pretence whatsoever keep any Goat or Goats runing at large within the said Borrough or the Liberties thereof, under the penalty of Twenty Shillings proclamation money each day for Every Goat he, she or they shall so suffer to run at large within the same, to be recovered by a Warrant from the Mayor, and to be applied to the Common Stock of the said Borrough.

And Be it further Ordained by the Authority aforesaid, That from and after the first day of February next untill the said Twentieth day of March every person or persons having a Goat or Goats runing at large in this Borrough or the Liberties thereof, shall keep such Goat or Goats Confined every night from Sunsett untill Sunrise the following day, under the like penalty of Twenty Shillings proclamation money for every Goat he, she or they shall suffer to run at large in the night as aforesaid to be recovered and applied as herein before is directed.

And that the Owners of Goats may be the more easily known, Be it further Ordained by the authority aforesaid That every person or persons owners of Goats, shall from and after the publication of this Ordinance, have the same branded or ear marked with his, her or their proper brand or mark, and such brand, or ear mark recorded with the Town Clerk. And every Goat or Goats that shall hereafter be found going at large in the said Borrough or the Liberties thereof, being unbranded or unmarked shall be seized and sold by order of the Mayor, Recorder, or any one of the Aldermen, and the money arising therefrom applied to the Common Stock of the Borrough, unless such Goat or Goats shall by the owner or owners thereof be proved to be his, her or their property, and the same be redeemed by such owner or owners paying the penalty or penalties herein before ordained.

> Lennon and Kellum, *Wilmington Town Book*, January 29, 1765, 161-162.

[1762] *May 9*. Today the evil one tried to disturb our minds, for our finest and best mare, which came in from the woods yesterday, went mad, bit at everything, and raged around until she died. Fourteen days ago there was a mad dog here, and we suppose it bit the mare. During the next days we had to kill several of our dogs also.

> Fries, *Records of the Moravians*, 1:246.

Whereas we are Informed that Sundry Dogs have been & are now infected with madness within the Bounds of this Town to the great hazard of the inhabitants. It is therefore order'd that every Owner of Dog or Dogs within said Town Shall imediately Order such to be chain'd or confin'd in a proper inclosure until the 5th May next to prevent any bad consequence that may ensue by sd. infection under the penalty of forty Shillings procl money besides the penalty Occurring from the Court of Assize, & we hereby give full Liberty to any Person or Persons whatsoever to kill & destroy any Dog or Dogs going [at] large within sd. Town after the 15th Instant till May afsd. Given under our hands at Wilmington this 14th, April 1752.

Lennon and Kellum, *Wilmington Town Book*, April 14, 1752, 56.

Urban residents also faced the threat of overbearing traffic.

An Act for the regulation of the Town of Salisbury, securing the Inhabitants in their Possessions, and to encourage the Settlement of the said Town. [...]

XI. And whereas the Too frequent Custom of immoderate riding Horses, and driving of empty wagons and Carts in and through the said Town, is found to have a very dangerous tendency: To prevent which, Be it Enacted by the Authority aforesaid, That no Person or Persons from and after the passing of this Act, on any Pretence whatever shall immoderately ride or strain any Horse or Mare, or drive any empty Waggon or Cart in or through the said Town or any of the Streets thereof; on Penalty of forfeiting and paying the Sum of Five Shillings Proclamation Money, for each and every Offence; to be recovered by Warrant, from under the Hand and Seal of any Justice of the Peace of the said County.

Laws, 1770, in Clark, *State Records*, 23:810-812.

At a Meeting of the Commissioners on Saturday August 22d 1772. Present: Archd. Maclaine, John Ancrum, Samuel Campbell, Commissioners. [...]

ORDERED, That the following persons shall pay the Fine inflicted for immoderate riding within the said Town, as it appears they have been guilty of that Offence, Vizt. James Nevin, John Ralph, John Walker, Senr., Erasmus Hanson, James Giekee, Francis Brice, James Weeks, and William Wilkinson.

Lennon and Kellum, *Wilmington Town Book*, 211-212.

Adult males were responsible for opening and maintaining streets and bridges, though in Wilmington, at least, many including town commissioners were oblivious to their responsibility, leading Janet Schaw to muddy her fine silk shoes as she walked the Wilmington streets to a ball.

At a meeting of the Commissioners-

August 8th. 1751 [1750?]

Present William Faris, John Sampson, Magnus Cowan

After receiving the several returns of the Overseers on Oath, We find the following persons deficient on Working on the Streets and Bridges,—Viz.

Hugh McBride 1 hand   4 day (workt)
John Gordon   1 hand   4 days
Thomas Cunningham   1 do.   4 do.
John Robinson 1—   4
William Mitchell   1 do.   4 do.
John Campbell 1   4
Francis Davies gave his note
Alexr McKeithen   2   4 workt
Samuel Theopt Steroom 2   4 each
Ralph Bugnion 2   1 each
James Coburn 1   4
Samuel Fels   1   4
Caleb Grainger 2   2 each wd ½ d each
John Walker   1   4
James Campbell   1   4 workt
Daniel McVicar   1   4
John Lyon (each 2½ d, not lyble)   3   4 each
Richard Richardson   1   4
Thomas Newton   1   4
William Birnie 1   4
William Wallace   1   4 run away
Ebenezar Bunting   1   3 workt
Richard Player 2   2 each
Ann Wright   2   3 ½ each, workt
John Rutherfurd & Co.   8
Caleb Mason   2 -   4 each
David Lindsay 2 -   2 each, not lyble
Patrick McVicar   1 -   4
Joseph Geery   1 -   4
Alexander McKay   1 -   4
Alice Marsden 1 -   4 workt

Put up at the Court House with the Following Advertisement—Viz. We are not Willing to Insist on Money from the above Defaulters (Which would lay them under some difficulties) We Give this Publick Notice that those who are willing to Work on the Streets appear at the Court House on Wednesday morning next at Six o'Clock to work their deficiencys, and those that doe not then Appear or Pay their fines shall have distress Immediately Levied on them without further Notice.

Lennon and Kellum, *Wilmington Town Book*, 36-38.

[...] [Wilmington, ca. March, 1775]. Let it suffice to say that a ball we had, where were dresses, dancing and ceremonies laughable enough, but there was no object on which my own ridicule fixed equal to myself and the figure I made, dressed out in all my British airs with a high head and a hoop and trudging thro' the unpaved streets in embroidered shoes [...] No chair, no carriage—good leather shoes need none. The ridicule was the silk shoes in such a place. [...]

Andrews, *Journal of a Lady of Quality*, 154.

Urban dwellers in crowded conditions found themselves more subject to the danger of disease, leading to the intervention of local authorities to attempt to protect the public health.

An Act for the better regulating the Town of Wilmington and for confirming and establishing the late Survey of the same, with the Plan annexed. [...]

XIII. And whereas many Lots are not yet cleared, nor proper Drains or Runs made, in many Places in the Parts of Town where there are most Inhabitants, to the Manifest Injury and Unhealthiness of the said Town, Be it therefore enacted, by the Authority aforesaid, That the Commissioners for the Time being, or the Majority of them, may and they are hereby impowered to Order the Proprietors of any Lot or Lots to clear all, or any Part of them, and to make proper Drains or Water-Courses through them, in Six Months after such Order, signed by the Commissioners for the Time being, or the Majority of them; and any Person refusing or neglecting to comply with the same, shall forfeit and pay Twenty Shillings, Proclamation Money.

Laws, 1745, in Clark, *State Records*, 23:234, 236.

[1772] ORDERED, That William Gabie, Rebecca Mortimer, John Green and the guardians or Trustees of William Green and Hannah Green, minors, Thomas Jones, Janet Cowan and the Attornies or Agents of Archibald and John Cotes, proprietors of the Lott occupied by James Blyth, do clear and drain their respective Lots within Six months after the date hereof, and keep the same so cleared and drained, under the Penalty inflicted by the said Acts. [...]

[1773] WHEREAS the necessary house belonging to John Burgwin, Esqr. erected upon his Lot where he now lives, and open to Market Street, is a nusance to the Inhabitants of this Town & the passengers that pass through the said Street. It is therefore Ordered that the said John Burgwin do remove the said necessary house or cause a vault to be sunk so as to remove the said nusance, within twenty days.

[1773] WHEREAS the necessary house erected on the Lot belonging to William Campbell, Esqr. & where Phillip Jones now dwells is a nusance to the neighbourhood adjoining to the said Lot, and the Inhabitants of this Town. ORDERED that the said Phillip Jones remove the said nusance within the Twenty days from this date upon the penalty of five shillings per day for every day he shall suffer the said nusance to remain afterwards. [...]

[1774] At this meeting it is agreed that Mr. Henry Toomer (being present & consenting) be appointed to undertake the Office of Scavenger of the Town for one year from the date, & that he immediately, or as soon as it can be done, cleanse the Streets effectually, and continue to keep the same Clean at least once every week if necessary, in consideration of which the Commissioners have agreed to pay him the sum of Twenty Pounds Proclamation money.

Lennon and Kellum, *Wilmington Town Book*, 199, 219, 223.

◦⟋⟍◦

Fire presented another hazard to which urban residents were more susceptible than those in the countryside. The threat of fire prompted towns to abandon wooden chimneys, hire chimney sweeps, and purchase fire engines and other firefighting apparatus. Such precautions apparently proved useless, at least in the instance of Wilmington, according to a traveler who visited the town in 1786.

An Act for enlarging the time for saving lots in the town of Hertford and other Purposes. [...]

III. And whereas, suffering wooden chimnies to be built in the said town may occasion accidents by fire, be it further Enacted, by the Authority aforesaid, that no person whatsoever shall hereafter erect any wooden chimney in the said town; and every person who hath already built any such wooden chimney therein, shall pull down the same within the term of five years next after the passing of this Act; and if any person or persons shall presume to act contrary thereto; in erecting any wooden chimney in the said town, or in failing to pull down or remove, within the time aforementioned, any such wooden chimney by him already erected therein, the directors mentioned in the before recited act, or any two of them, are hereby authorized, impowered and required, to pull down and destroy every such chimney, and shall not be liable to an action for damage for so doing; and if the directors of any of them shall be sued for the same, they may plead the general issue and give this act in evidence.

Laws, 1762, in Clark, *State Records*, 25:477-478.

[1775] *March 6.* (Helf. Con.) The chimney-sweeping has now been arranged, the boy Gottlob Krause will do it under the supervision of Matthes Oesterlein. Hereafter no chimneys shall be burned out; those that are used constantly shall be swept oftener than others; and all shall be swept at such times, and after making such arrangements, that no one is inconvenienced in kitchen work.

Fries, *Records of the Moravians*, 2:896.

At a Meeting of the Commissioners for the Town of Wilmington The 2d May 1755
Present Frederick Gregg, John Maultsby, John Walker, Arthur Mabson.
It was Ordered that all Owners of Houses Lately Taxed to Purchase a Watter Engine &c Was to pay the Said Sumes Into the Hands of Mr. Arthur Mabson before the 24th of last Month and as it appears Several persons have failed In So doing & Likewise In paying of the Town Tax So that Warrants of Distress was Issued.

> Fredk. Gregg
> John Maultsby Junr
> Arthur Mabson
> Jno. Walker

At a Meeting of the Commissioners the 17th May 1755—

Present Frederick Gregg John Maultsby John Walker—Ordered that John Maultsby the present Treasurer In the Room of Arthur Mabson, Pay to Capt. Benjn. Herron Sixty pounds Proclamation money which appears to be collected By Said Arthur Mabson & John Maultsby [...]

At a Meeting of the Commissioners the 2d Jany 1756 [1757].
    Present, Fredk. Gregg, Corns. Harnett, Daniel Dunbibin. [...]
Dr   Wilmington to Capt. Benjn. Heron for a Fire Engine
                                                                Sterling

	To a large Fire Engine Caseing &c	57	2		
	Freight from London to Portsmouth &c	2	1		
	Do. to South Carolina paid	2	15		
	Do. from Charles Town	1	15		
	Insurance on £61.18-@ 20 Per. Ct.	12	7	6	
	20 per. Ct. advance on £76- 6 Sterling	15	4	1	
	£	91	4	7	
	33 ⅓ Per Ct. Exchange	30	8	2	
	Reduced to Proclamation £	121	12	9	
21st May 1755	By cash paid you by John Maultsby			Cr	
	£60 Proc. £	60			
	By cash from D. Dunbibin £37. 3. 4	37	3	4	
	Proc.				
	By Ballce due Capt. B. Heron	24	9	5	
	£	121	12	9	

Lennon and Kellum, *Wilmington Town Book*, 80-81, 90.

Wilmington, to Wit:
    At a Meeting of the Commissioners the 25th January 1772. OR-DERED, That each and every Master and Mistress of a family in the said Town, shall, and they are hereby required within Six months after the date hereof, to provide him or herself with two good and sufficient Leather Bucketts with his or her name thereon, if there are not more than one Fire Place in his or her House; if two or three fire places, then such Master or Mistress, shall provide three such Bucketts, & if four or more Fire Places, then such Master or Mistress shall provide four such Bucketts to be kept hung up in some public place in their respective

Houses, to be ready in Case of Fire, under the penalty of Ten Shillings Procl Money per month for every Bucket such Master or Mistress shall neglect or refuse to provide as aforesaid, to be forfeited and paid upon inspection of the respective Houses in the said Town by the Commissioners or any of them, unless the several Bucketts required by this Order are provided: Note, Kitchen Chimnies, or other out Houses, are supposed to belong to each House.

Lennon and Kellum, *Wilmington Town Book*, 197.

TUESDAY, JUNE 20

My dear friend:
...The late fire has entirely destroyed the beauty of the town, if it ever possessed any. [...]
Wilmington without exception is the most disagreeable, sandy, barren town I have visited on the continent—consisting of a few scattered wood and brick houses, without any kind of order or regularity. I am extremely happy to think I shall leave it tomorrow. [...]

Wright and Tinling, *Quebec to Carolina in 1785-1786*, 286-287.

∽ఈ ♥ఎ

By clustering people together, towns offered opportunities for social interaction, contributed to such organizational efforts as the Masonic Order and dancing societies, and appealed to itinerant professionals. At the same time, more crowded conditions may have led to antisocial behavior, necessitating the purchase of ducking stools and admonitions against fighting.

Friday 11 [December, 1772] [...]
In the afternoon mostly loitering about—called at Geo. Grays & had my hair cut—Came home early & drank Tea. Walked with Mrs. Hurst home, & immediately returned, & was reading Lawsons' Oratory 'till I went to Bed- [...]

Saturday 12 Dec. [1772]
—Rose late—After Breakfast went up Town & wrote constantly in my Office till it was past one— passing by Horniblow's to go home M. Charlton, who was there, tapped to me at the Window, & very kindly

told me, when I went in, he only wanted to take me by the hand—These kind of attentions are pleasing, & make life pass more agreeably- [...]

Thursday 21 [January, 1773]
In the morning before Breakfast reading one of my new Magazines—Afterwards till Dinner very busy in my Office. In the afternoon, there for about half an hour, and then I gave myself a kind of holiday, playing a Game at Billiards with Buchanan (the first for many months)—walked with him and Worth, and on our return into Town, we met all the Ladies from Mr. Jones's whom we joined, and walked with round the Town to their house, where we spent the evening.

Higginbotham, *Papers of James Iredell*, 1:193-194, 210.

On *Thursday*, being the Feast of St. *John* the Baptist, the Members of the Ancient and Honourable Society of FREE and ACCEPTED MASONS, belonging to the LODGE in this Town, met at their Lodge-Room; and after going thro' the necessary Business of the Day, retired to the Long Room in the Courthouse, to dine, where was served up an elegant Dinner; the Lieutenant-Governor honoured them with his Company; where also dined many other Gentlemen: The usual and proper Healths were drank; and at drinking the KING and the CRAFT the Artillery fired.

North Carolina Magazine; or, Universal Intelligencer (New Bern), December 28, 1764.

New-Bern, Nov. the 2d 1785.
The gentlemen who have already subscribed, to the NEW-BERN DANCING-ASSEMBLY, are requested to meet at the Coffee-House, on Saturday next, at 12 o'clock.

The North Carolina Gazette or *New-Bern Advertiser*, November 3, 1785.

[1770] Upon my return, I understood, a Fellow was to exhibit Specimens of his Dexterity in Ballancing that Evening—I afterwards went there, with Miss Polly Jones—& really, he was surprisingly clever,—but the House was too confined for many of his Pranks, —he had a little recourse to slight of hand,—but here he performed miserably,—it was at Mr Jones's Warehouse,—the people who were there, were the dregs of the Town,-except a very few,—I came home about 8 o'Clock, [...]

Higginbotham, *Papers of James Iredell,* 1:176.

BOYLE ALDWORTH, *Limbner.*
JUST *arrived in this town, paints LIKENESSES on the following conditions, viz.*
Portraits for rings,   130
Do. for braceletts,   100 Dollars
Do. in crayons, as house ornaments from 1 *to* 2 *feet,*   75
       N. B. Enquire for Mr. Aldworth *at* Oliver's *tavern.*
Newbern, *Sept.* 29.

North-Carolina Gazette (New Bern), October 2, 1778.

An Act, for incorporating the Seaport of Beaufort, in Carteret Precinct, into a Township, by the Name of Beaufort. [...]
XII. And be it further Enacted, by the Authority aforesaid, That whosoever shall be found guilty of quarreling or fighting in the said Town or Township, or in any other Town or Township which now is, or hereafter shall be laid out within this Government, in the View of any Justice, or shall be thereof convicted, by the Oath of One creditable Witness, shall forfeit and pay, for every such Offence, the Sum of Ten shillings, and for Want of such Payment, shall Suffer Twenty Four Hours Imprisonment in the common Gaol, or else be set in the Stocks, for the space of Two Hours, at the Discretion of the Justice, provided that the Information be made within Twenty four Hours after such Offence shall be committed: [...]

Laws, 1723, in Clark, *State Records,* 25:206, 209.

Ordered that Mr. John Rombough do erect a public Ducking stool for the benefit of the Inhabitants of this County and that the said John Rombough do bring in an account of the Charges of the same in order that an allowance be made for the same out of the County Tax.

Minutes of the Chowan County Court of Pleas and Quarter Sessions, October 1767, State Archives.

At a meeting of the Commissioners of the Town of Wilmington on Tuesday the 14th June 1774. Present: John Burgwin, Archd. Maclaine, John Ancrum, Richard Player, Commissioners.

ORDERED that a Ducking Stool be provided for the use of the Town, and that the same be paid for out of the Town Tax.

Lennon and Kellum, *Wilmington Town Book*, 225.

Inventory of the Estate of John Ambrose Deceast April the 26 day 1784
One Hundred and Ninety five acres of land, one horse Saddle & Bridle
Ten head of Cattle that is to say five Cows four Earlings and one Calf
Two father Beds - One Rug and Two Blankets Two Shects & Two Bed Heads...
fifteen head of hogs and five pewter Basons & Two pewter Dishes and five pewter
plates and fourteen Spoons - - Two Iron pots & one pare of hooks one
Skillet and four Small Rack hooks: one Chest & Box and Six Chairs
One Woolling Wheel & Cards & one flax Wheel. one meal Bag and Sifter
One Barrell and meat Tub: One table. One washing Tub and one Water
pale & pigon and one looking Glass and four Books, one Razar = Three
Knives & five forks = One ax and one plow hoe. one horse Coller & hames
Two Weeding hoes - One pare of Cloth Shairs = Three Cow hides and one
Spike Gimblet - One hand Saw - one Stone Gug & Butter pot and Bottle
Three Jugs and Goards and one Basket and Two horse Bells & one Earthen
Pitcher and one hatchet and a Small quantity of Led -

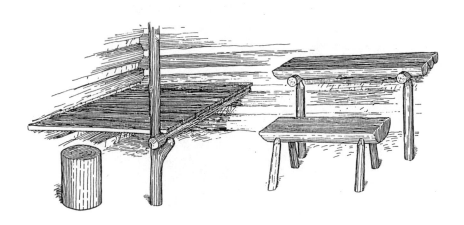

Upper. Inventories of decedents' estates usually included various implements needed to maintain the large degree of self-sufficiency of most North Carolinians. Illustration from Estate Inventory of John Ambrose, Onslow County Estate Records, 1762, Division of Archives and History. *Lower.* Although the homes of some North Carolinians boasted fine imported furnishings, the great majority did not. Most furniture would have been locally produced, sturdy, and crude. Illustration from Tunis, *Frontier Living*, 22.

Upper. North Carolina's large volume of exports of naval stores and pork meant that coopers were among the most valued craftsmen in the colony. *Lower.* The wolf pit mentioned on page 265 was probably similar to the one pictured here. Illustrations from Tunis, *Frontier Living,* 31, 55.

GEORGE WHITEFIELD, M.A.

Hone pinx.t   *V.M. Picot sculp.t*

The renowned Methodist preacher George Whitefield was well received during his several visits to the colony. See pages 267-270. Illustration from Ninde, *George Whitefield: Prophet, Preacher.*

A

COLLECTION

OF MANY

Chriftian Experiences, Sentences,

AND SEVERAL

Places of Scripture Improved:

ALSO,

Some fhort and plain DIRECTIONS and PRAYERS
for fiçk Perfons; with ferious ADVICE to Perfons
who have been fick, to be by them perufed and put
in Practice as foon as they are recovered; and a
THANKSGIVING for Recovery.

To which is added,
Morning and Evening Prayers for Families and Children, Directions for the LORD's-DAY, and fome Cautions
againft Indecencies in Time of Divine Service, &c.

Collected and Compofed for the Spiritual Good of his Parifh-
oners, and others.

By C. H. *Miffionary to the Honourable Society for the Propaga-*
tion of the Gofpel in Foreign Parts, and Rector of St. Paul's
Parifh, in North-Carolina.

O! how fweet are thy Words unto my Tafte, yea fweeter than
Honey to my Mouth, Pfal. cxix. 103.
I am well pleafed that the Lord hath heard the Voice of my
Prayer, that he hath inclined his Ear unto me; therefore
will I call upon him as long as I live, Pfal. cxvi. 12.

NEWBERN:
Printed by JAMES DAVIS, M,DCC,LIII.

North Carolina's first printing press was set up in 1749. Pictured here is the title page of
the first nongovernmental publication printed in the colony. See pages 235-236. Photograph from the files of the Division of Archives and History.

No⁼ 1450.

Lehrbücher
für die Jugend
in Nordcarolina,

entworfen

von

einer Gesellschaft
Helmstädtischer Professoren.

Erste Lieferung:

Katechismus

und

Fragebuch.

Leipzig,
bey Siegfried Lebrecht Crusius.
1787.

The German-language *Textbook for the Youth in North Carolina* was published in Germany in 1787 as a means of furthering the formal education of Lutheran students in western North Carolina. For documents relating to education, see pages 281-306. Illustration from *North Carolina Historical Review* 7 (January 1930): 83.

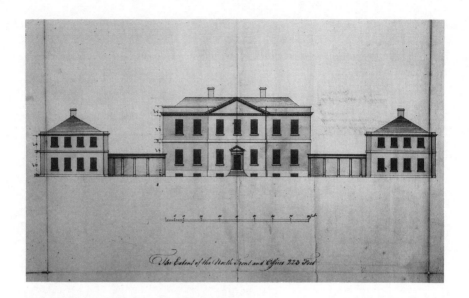

The Extent of the North Front and Offices 228 Feet

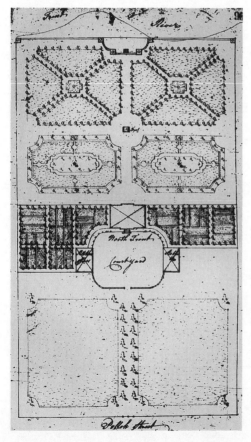

Completed in 1770, the governor's palace in New Bern, with its attendant formal garden, was the most impressive residence in the colony and the seat of the last two royal governors of North Carolina. See pages 128-129. Photographs from the files of the Division of Archives and History.

Travel and Transportation

Water travel offered a facility and cheapness that appealed to the early settlers along the coast. They used a variety of craft for their transportation. However, obstructions in the watercourses required constant efforts to render them navigable.

Nothing can be finer than the banks of this river [Cape Fear]; a thousand beauties both of the flowery and sylvan tribe hang over it and are reflected from it with additional lustre. [...]

This north west branch is said to be navigable for Ships of 400 tons burthen for above two hundred miles up, and the banks so constituted by nature that they seem formed for harbours, and what adds in a most particular manner to this convenience is, that quite across from one branch to the other, and indeed thro' the whole country are innumerable creeks that communicate with the main branches of the river and every tide receive a sufficient depth of water for boats of the largest size and even for small Vessels, so that every thing is water-borne at a small charge and with great safety and ease.

Andrews, *Journal of a Lady of Quality*, 158-159.

[...] They make very necessary Vessels for carriage of their Commodities by Water, which are called in these parts *Periaugers* and *Canoes*, which are the Boats made use of in this Country, and are generally made out of one peice of large Timber, and that most commonly of the *Cypress* kind, which they make hollow and shaped like a Boat, with Masts, Oars, and Padles, according to their size and bigness. Some of these *Periaugers*, are so large that they are capable of carrying forty or fifty Barrels of *Pitch* or *Tar*. In these Vessels likewise they carry Goods, Horses, and other Cattle from one Plantation to another over large and spacious Rivers; they frequently trade in them to *Virginia* and other places on this continent, no Vessel of the same Burthen made after the *European* manner is able to out Sail one of these *Periaugers*.

The *Canoes* are of less Burthen than the former, some will carry two or three Horses over these large Rivers, and others so small that they will carry only two or three Men. These are more ticklish than Boats, but no Boat in the World is capable to be rowed as fast as they are, and when they are full of Water they will not sink, and not only the *Indians* but even the *Christians* are very dexterous in managing of them.

Brickell, *Natural History*, 260-261.

[...] [May or June, 1775]. Mr Rutherfurd has a very fine boat with an awning to prevent the heat, and six stout Negroes in neat uniforms to row her down, which with the assistance of the tide was performed with ease in a very short time. [...]

Andrews, *Journal of a Lady of Quality*, 177.

The next Day about Noon, we embark'd in a Canoo to return to *Brunswick*, accompanied by Mr. Evans and two others, having about 80 miles to row on the River *Northeast*, which is deep enough for a Sloop of 60 Tons all the Way, and would be navigable for such quite up to Mr. Evans's, were it not for the Multitude of Logs that lie in it, part of them fast in the Sand, with great Snags or Limbs, and sometimes either End or the Middle quite above, or but little beneath the Surface: and in some Places we saw whole Heaps jambed together, almost from Side to Side, and so firm that they are immovable, being sound, heavy, fast and deep in the Sand, otherwise this would be a fine River, [...]

Meredith, *An Account of the Cape Fear Country, 1731*, 21-22.

Read the Petition of William Bryan praying leave to Clear and keep Open Core Creek from the River to his Mill, and it appearing to the Court that the same would be of Advantage to many of the Inhabitants of said Creek and parts Adjacent. Ordered he have leave Accordingly. And that he be Exempt from Working on the Public Roads as many Days as he Shall Employ his Hands in that Service.

Minutes of the Craven County Court of Pleas and Quarter Sessions, June 1774, State Archives.

∽⟨⟩⟩

As settlement moved to the interior, roads, approved by the county courts and constructed and maintained by the inhabitants, became increasingly numerous.

An Act to impower the Inferior Courts of the several Counties in this Province to order the laying out of Public Roads, and establish and settle Ferries; and to appoint where Bridges shall be built, for the Use and **Ease** of the **Inhabitants** of this Province; and to clear navigable Rivers and Creeks. [...]

I. Be it Enacted, by the Governor, Council, and Assembly, and by the Authority of the same, That all Roads and Ferries, in the several Counties of this Province, that have been laid out or appointed by Virtue of any Act of Assembly heretofore made, or by Virtue or any Order of Court, are hereby declared to be Public Roads and Ferries; and that from Time to Time, and at all Times hereafter, the Inferior Court of the several Counties in this Province, shall have full power and Authority to appoint and settle Ferries; and to order the laying out Public Roads, where necessary; and to appoint where Bridges shall be made, for the Use and Ease of the Inhabitants of each County; and to discontinue such Roads as are now, or shall hereafter be made, as shall be found useless; and to alter Roads, so as to make them more useful, as often as Occasion shall require.

II. And be it further Enacted, by the Authority aforesaid, That each Inferior Court within this Province is hereby authorized and impowered to call any Person or Persons in their respective Counties to Account, for any Monies such Person or Persons may have in his or their Hands, by Virtue of any Distress heretofore made for Default of Working on any Road in such County; and all such Monies to receive and apply towards keeping in Repair the Roads and Bridges on which such Default was made.

III. And be it further Enacted, That all Roads hereafter to be laid out shall be laid out by a Jury of Twelve Men, appointed by the said Inferior Courts respectively; Which Jury, being Freeholders, shall take an Oath to lay out the same to the Greatest Ease and Conveniency of the Inhabitants, and as little as may be to the Prejudice of any Private Person or Persons inclosed Ground; and the Damages which shall be sustained by any Private Person in laying out such Road, shall be ascertained by the same Jury, on Oath, who laid out such Road, to be equally assessed by the Inferior Court of Such County, and levied and Collected by the Overseer of such Road on the taxable Persons which ought to work on the same, and by him paid to the Party Injured.

Laws, 1764, in Clark, *State Records*, 23:607-608.

[...] The Court appoints Newel Bell Snr. Overseer of the Rode from the river side by his House to the marked tree appointed to be the Bounds between Craven County and Carteret County, and that all the said Male Taxables from above Black Creek to the Head of Newport

River Worke on the same and that they do as many Days work thereon as the said Taxables do on the South Side of said River. Executor of Thos. Lovick.

Minutes of the Carteret County Court of Pleas and Quarter Sessions, November 1763, State Archives.

Order'd that a Road be layd out from the Mouth of Richd. Horns path on the Tarr River Road, thence aCross Tosneot near Thoms. Horns junr., and a Strait Course to Turkey Creek near Margaret Taylors, and so to Mockasin near Jno. Clark's and that Richd. Barly Senr. Wm. Wilder Wm. Smelly Sen. Thomas Moneyham, Wm. Pugh Thoms. Horn jr. Henry Flowers, Thos. Horn senior Palgrion Williams Jno. Parker, Gabriel Parker, George Blackwell senr. Willa. Baily Jno. Baily Wm. Strickland and Jacob Strickland Or any 12 be a Jury to Lay off the Same, and that the hands of Thoms. Horn jr. Thoms. Eatman Mark Philips James Dean Wm. Smelly jr. Richd. Baily jr. Thoms. Moneyham Wm. Wilder Robert Culpeper, Benja. Culpeper, Nathan Horn, Jno. Clark, John Gent. Jacob Hardy, Jno. Kent Jams. Smellie Saml. Taylor Henry Moneyham and Job Wilder Work on the same, and that Richd. Baily senr. be Overseer thereof.

Minutes of the Edgecombe County Court of Pleas and Quarter Sessions, June 1759, State Archives.

V. Description of North Carolina by Alexander Schaw. [...]
"The roads on both sides of the river cross a few water runs, which in the country are called creeks; they are generally swampy along the sides, which are crowded with trees, bushes, vines, and brambles. Over all these creeks are wooden bridges. Wherever the land is dry, there is little or no brush. The woods in general are in the style of open groves in England, except in such places as have once been cleared and afterwards abandoned. These are always covered with brush. The roads upon the Northwest branch of the river grow more solid every mile above Wilmington, and long before they reach Cross Creek are very hard. The only making they bestow upon the roads in the flat part of the country is cutting out the trees to the necessary breadth, in as even a line as they can, and where the ground is wet, they make a small ditch on either side. The roads through swamp land are made by first laying logs in the direction of the road and covering them cross ways with small pine trees, layd regularly together over sod, with which the logs

210

are previously covered. The roads run constantly thro' woods, which tho' they are generally pretty open, yet objects at any considerable distance are intercepted from the eye, by the trees crowding into the line of direction as the distance increases.

Andrews, *Journal of a Lady of Quality*, 279-280.

A method prevails in this country of blazing the trees at certain distances, which furnishes a guide to the traveller, even in the ordinary obscurity of night. This is produced by simply slashing a strip of bark from two opposite sides of a tree. The white spots thus formed, may be seen for a great distance in an open forest. [...]

Watson, *Men and Times of the Revolution*, 59.

⋘⋙

Numerous streams and rivers required bridging, again the province of the county courts. The burden of construction first devolved upon those responsible for building roads, though eventually some of the bridges were funded by the taxes or erected privately for toll. Among the most impressive structures were the early drawbridges—Benjamin Heron's toll drawbridge in the vicinity of present Castle Hayne in New Hanover County, and the public drawbridge at Windsor in Bertie County.

Order'd that a Bridge be built a Cross Tosneot at or nigh Mr. Dews, and that Moses Coleman be Overseer for the Building thereof, and that he take the hands which workd under Lazarus Pope, Jeremiah Nicholas, and Martin Thorn, former Overseers, to Build the same.

Minutes of the Edgecombe County Court of Pleas and Quarter Sessions, June 1759, State Archives.

Read the Petition of Sundry Inhabitants etc. for a Bridge over Fishing Creek at or near Culpepers; Granted, Order'd that the same be Built that Wallace Jones, Nathan Whitehead and Thoms. Floyd, be Commissioners for Building the Same, and that the Expence thereof Except £20 Proclamation be paid by this County, and that £20, to be pd. by Mr. Osborn Jeffries who hath a Subscription for that purpose.

Minutes of the Edgecombe County Court of Pleas and Quarter Sessions, August 1757, State Archives.

North Carolina Bertie County ss. At a Court Holden for Bertie County on the XXIth Day of July Anno Domini 1757. Present His Majestys Justices.

The Court taking into Consideration the Act of Assembly of this Province Relating to Roads etc. And Thereupon doth appoint Thomas Whitmell and Henry Hunter Esquires and Mr. Joseph Hardy be and they are hereby appointed Commissioners to agree with some Person or Persons to Build a New Bridge Over Cashy River at the same Place where the Old Bridge now stands.

It is therefore Ordered that they or any two of them and they are hereby Impowered to agree with some one or more Persons to Build a New Bridge Over the said Cashy River at the Place aforesaid and make Report of their Proceedings to this Court at next Sitting to be Entered on the Records thereof.

Test. Benjn. Wynns
Clerk Court

Per Court Copy

Octr. 22d 1757. Pursuant to the within Order we the Subscribers have Agreed with Wm. King to build a New Bridg Over Cashy etc. to be finished on or before the Last day of March Next in a workman Like Manner he to have for said Work paid on the Tenth Day of June Next Twenty Eight Pounds Nine Shillings and Six Pence Proclamation Money So Says the Commissenoer.

Thos. Whitmell
H. Hunter
Jos. Hartdy

Bertie County ss. Octor. Court 1757.

Returned to Court as a Report from the Commissioners and ordered to be Entered and filed.

Test. Benjn. Wynns
Clerk Court

[*Addressed:*]
For Mr. Thos. Whitmell
Mr. Hen. Hunter
and Mr. Joss. Hardy

212

North Carolina Bertie County ss. At a Court Holden for Bertie County on the XXVth day of April MDCCLVIII. Present His Majestys Justices.

Thomas Whitmell and Henry Hunter Esqrs. Two of the Commissioners appointed by this Court to Contract and agree with a Person to Build Casia Bridge, appeared in Court and Reported that the said Bridge was Built agreeable to the Contract and order of this Court; And at the same time William King the Undertaker thereof Appear'd, and moved that the Court might Receive the same, Which was Accordingly done, And at the same time the said William King Moved the Court for an Order on the Sheriff for the Sum Contracted for, Which was Twenty Eight Pound Nine Shillings and Sixpence Proclamation money to be Paid on the Twenty Eighth day of June next.

Granted and Ordered that the sheriff Pay the same and Charge it in his Accounts with the County.

Benjn. Wynns Clerk
Court

Per Court Copy

Recd. June the 13th 1758 of John Baker the above Sum of Twenty Eight Pounds Nine Shillings and Six pence Proclamation Money I Say Recd. per

William King

> Proceedings of the Bertie County Court of Pleas and Quarter Sessions, July, October 1757; April 1758, Bertie County, Miscellaneous Records, Road, Bridge, and Ferry Records, 1734-1905, State Archives.

An Act to encourage Benjamin Heron, Esq., to build a bridge over the north-east branch of Cape Fear river at or near the place where the ferry is now kept by Edward Davis.

I. Whereas, a bridge over the north-east branch of Cape Fear river at or near the place where the ferry is now kept by Edward Davis would be much for the convenience of all travellers; and as the land on both sides the River belongs to Benjamin Heron, Esq., the said Benjamin

Heron is desirous of building a bridge there at this own expence, on condition that the benefit thereof be vested in him, his heirs and assigns forever:

II. Be it therefore enacted by the Governor, Council and Assembly, and by the authority of the same, That it shall and may be lawful for the said Benjamin Heron, his heirs, executors, administrators or assigns, to erect and build a good, strong and substantial bridge over the north-east branch of Cape Fear river, as near as he conveniently can to the place where the ferry is now kept by Edward Davis; which bridge shall have one wide arch of thirty feet for rafts and pettiauguas to pass through, and six feet high above high water mark, and be made to draw up occasionally for the navigation of vessels of large burthen; and after building and erecting the bridge as aforesaid, it shall and may be lawful for the said Benjamin Heron, his heirs, executors, administrators or assigns, to keep a sufficient gate thereon and take and receive from all persons that shall pass over the same at the following rates, that is to say: For every man and horse, six pence; for every four wheel carriage drawn by two horses or oxen, two shillings; and for every two wheel carriage drawn by one or two horses or oxen, one shilling; and for every horse or ox more, four pence each; and for every head of neat cattle, three half pence; and for every twenty hogs or sheep, eighteen pence, and so in proportion for a greater or lesser number of hogs or sheep; and for all travellers on foot, four pence.

III. And be it further enacted by the authority aforesaid, That after the said bridge is so built and completely erected as aforesaid (provided it shall be completed within four years after the passing of this act), it shall not be lawful for any person whatsoever to keep any ferry, build any bridge or set any person or persons, carriage or carriages, cattle, hogs or sheep, over the said river for fee or reward within six miles of the same, under the penalty of twenty shillings, proclamation money, for each and every offence, to be recovered by a warrant by the said Benjamin Heron, his heirs, executors, administrators or assigns, before any magistrate of the county of New Hanover, to be applied to the use of the proprietor of the said bridge at the time of the offence being committed.

Laws, 1766, in Clark, *State Records*, 25:506-507.

[...] [July, 1775]. This road begins at Wilmingtown and goes clear across the country to Virginia on one side and South Carolina on the other, and as its course lies across the river, it is crossed by a bridge, which tho' built of timber is truly a noble one, broader than that over the Tay at Perth. It opens at the middle to both sides and rises by pullies, so as to suffer Ships to pass under it. [...]

Andrews, *Journal of a Lady of Quality*, 202. The name of edifice was Heron's Bridge.

Know all men by these presents that we Thomas Shehon James Burn and Amos Turner are held and firmly bound unto Thomas Pugh Esqr. Chairman and the rest of the brethren Justices of the County Court of Bertie in the sum of six hundred and fifty [*illegible*] pounds currency, which payment to be made we bind ourselves our heirs Executors and Administrators jointly and severally firmly by these presents sealed with out Seals and dated this 18 day of December 1786.

The Condition of the above Obligation is such that the above bounden Thomas Shehan hath agreed with William Gray Jonathan Jacocks and George Ryan Commissioners for Building a Draw Bridge across cashy at Windsor for which the said Commissioners have agreed that the said Shehon shall be paid the sum of three hundred and twenty Eight pounds currency for finishing the said Bridge in the following manner (to wit). The Draw to be 26 feet in the Clear. The posts 10 Inches square 4 Large posts 12 Inches Square and braised up and down the other post to be braised down the River with good sufficient braises the bearer 10 by 12 Inches, the Heapers to be 5 by 8 and to be long enough to reach 2 or 3 pannels 4 Heapers in a pannel the Mud Sills sided 18 Inches 36 feet long the Bridge and be Covered with 2 Inch plank the miles to be 4 by 3 Inches and 2 to each side of each pannel each pannel knot to exceed 10 feet, the width of the bridge to be 10 feet in the Clear and covered with 12 feet plan 12 feet long the bridge to be 6 feet Higher than common tides in middle the ends 3 feet higher than the land on said Shehon's side of the river the draws to be Hung with 3 Large Iron hinges on each side of the bridge oposite each hinge a plate of Iron to be fixt about 8 Inches wide and an half of an Inch thick on each face of the sill that shuts together the draws to be opened with four Iron Chains and weights with Iron Sheaves and Rolers at the heads of the posts and fixt in such a manner as to answer the purpose intended the Timber and plank of the said bridge to be of the Hart of Good Cyprus and the plank to be 2 Inches thick and the Whole to be finished to the Satisfaction of the said Commissioners then the above Obligation to be void otherwise to be and remain in full force and Virtue.

Thos. Shehan (Seal)

Signed Sealed and delivered in the presence of

James Burn

The above Bridge to be Compleated By May Court Next.

Amos Turner (Seal)

Geor. West

John Pierse

[*Endorsed:*]

Thos. Shehon's Bond to the
Commissioners for Building the Bridge

> Contract for the construction of a drawbridge across Cashie River,
> December 18, 1786, Bertie County, Miscellaneous Records, Road,
> Bridge, and Ferry Records, State Archives.

❧❧

**Wider and deeper watercourses required ferriage. The county courts
appointed ferrykeepers, determined rates for passage, and sometimes
imposed additional requirements. Eventually the General Assembly
provided for free or public ferriage in select counties.**

[Fra]nces Lynangher Petition'd the Court to Grant him to keep the
Ferry from Wilmington to the Point Granted Rates Man and Horse 8d.
Single man, 4d. Single Horse 6d. a Carriage and one or two Horses or
Oxen 2s./ and for every Ox or Horse more 6d. for Swiming Cattle per
head 4d. for every 20 hoggs or sheep 3s./ less in proportion. [...]
Order'd that Frans. Lynangher Give Bond with two Sufficient
Security to keep the above ferry in manner following To provide One
Good Flat and two Canoes Imediately and Also to provide One other
Flat betwixt this and the Next Inferior Court and to keep one of the
Flats always at each Landing ready to take in Passengers etc.

> Minutes of the New Hanover County Court of Pleas and Quarter
> Sessions, June 1760, State Archives.

Ordered that all Ferry keepers within this County Imediately makeup
proper pens or pounds in Order to receive the Cattle to be ferried over
or to force them in the Water and a sufficient Number of Boats not less
then two to each Ferry.

Minutes of the New Hanover County Court of Pleas and Quarter Sessions, September 1760, State Archives.

<*August Term 1774.*> Rates of Licenced Ferry's in Rowan County
<*Saml. Bryan's Ferry.*> To bringing over Waggon and

Team with four or Six horses as the case may be	£ .5.
For a Cart with three or more horses	.3.
For every horse with a load thereon led	.6
For every man and horse, with Saddle Bags and other Travelling furniture	.6
For every single Horse, Cow or Stear	.4
For every Footman	.3
For every Sheep or Hogg	.2

<*Howard's Ferry.*> When Ferriages are cross the main River The Same Ferriage as above
When across the South fork only half the above rates
<*Trading ford Ferry.*> For bringing over a waggon and

Team with four or Six horses (as the Case may be) being the Number the Commonly have in the Geers	.6.
For every Cart with three or more horses meaning the Number in the Gears when Travelling in Common	.3.
For every led horse being loaded	.6
For every man and horse with Saddle Bags and other Travelling Furniture	.8
For every head of Black Cattle	.4
For every one of Horse kind Single	.4
For every Single man if brought in the boat	.4
If brought in the Canoe	.2

Minutes of the Rowan County Court of Pleas and Quarter Sessions, August 1774, State Archives.

An Act to impower the Justices in the several Counties therein Mentioned to establishing free Ferries and Bridges in their respective Counties; and lay a Tax for defraying the Charges thereof.

I. Whereas the Reason of the several Rivers running through the Counties of Hertford, Pasquotank, Rowan, Mecklenburg, Pitt, and Tyrrel, the Ferries and Bridges over which it is necessary for many of the Inhabitants to pass, to attend the Courts and other Public Meetings at the Court Houses in the said respective Counties, are expensive and Burthensome to such Inhabitants:

II. Be it therefore Enacted by the Governor, Council, and Assembly, and by the Authority of the same, That the Justices of the said respective

Counties or any seven or More of them, be and are hereby impowered to agree with the Owner or Owners, Keeper or Keepers of any Ferry or Ferries, Toll Bridge or Bridges, within their respective Counties, as they shall think necessary, for such Sum or Sums of Money as shall appear to them reasonable, to set over such Ferry or Ferries, or let pass over such Toll Bridge or Bridges any of the Inhabitants of the said respective Counties requiring the same, free from any Charge whatsoever, on any of the Days of the sitting of the Courts, Election of Members of Assembly, or Vestrymen, Meeting of the Vestry, or General Musters of the said Counties.

III. And be it further Enacted, by the Authority aforesaid, That the Justices of the said Counties are hereby authorized and required, Yearly, and every Year, at the same Time that they lay the County Levy, to lay a Tax not exceeding Six Pence, Proclamation Money, on each and every Taxable person in their respective Counties, to be collected and accounted for by the Sheriffs with the Justices of the respective Counties in the same manner as other County Taxes, and by them applied to the Discharge of the several Contracts to be made in Virtue of this Act; and the overplus (if any) to the Contingent Charges of the County.

Laws, 1769, in Clark, *State Records*, 23:785.

⋘⋙

When not on foot or on horseback, colonials used various fine wheeled conveyances such as gigs, sulkies, chairs, chaises, and phaetons, as well as work vehicles, including carts and wagons.

[...] *Friday, December 14* [1787]. This forenoon rode out on a visit to Colonel Kennedy's about two Miles from Washington he lives near the River side, a large Creek runs by his house, our party was Mrs. Thos. Blackledge in a Sulky, and Lucy Harvey, and myself on Horseback, we dined and drank Tea there, and spent a very agreeable day with Col. & Mrs. Kennedy, their Son John & daughter Miss Absoley, Miss Evans was there on a visit but scarcely spoke—Absoley is a pleasing Character, genteel in her person, mild and amiable in her manners, attentive to the Company; with graveness, a degree of Cheerfulness—She put me in mind of a lady I once loved—We return'd by Moonlight, & Mrs. Blackledge drove thro' the Woods with such Spirit all the way home, Lucy and myself rode full Gallop to keep up with her—

Rodman, *Journal of a Tour to North Carolina by William Attmore*, 1787, 27.

Sun: 3. [January 3, 1773]. As I longed much for an oppertunity of preaching I set off pretty early for Wilmington but was greatly distressed on the road. The excessive rain that fell the day before had raised the waters, and washed away a Bridge, so that I was at a loss what to do. At (length) I resolved to take the horse from the Chaise, put some planks for the wheels, and draw it over myself, which I did, and then got the horse over without any hurt, and proceeded on my journey to the Town. [...]

Maser and Maas, *The Journal of Joseph Pilmore, Methodist Itinerant, For the years August 1, 1769, to January 2, 1774*, 175.

[March, 1775]. We have been these three or four days here, but this is the first time it has been in my power to write, but I have now sat down to bring up my Journal from leaving Brunswick; which we did last Friday, under the care of Mr Eagle, a young Gentleman just returned from England and who owns a very considerable estate in this province. The two brothers were to follow and be up with us in a few miles, which however they did not. We were in a Phaeton and four belonging to my brother, and as the roads are entirely level, drove on at good speed, our guide keeping by us and several Negro servants attending on horse back. [...]

Andrews, *Journal of a Lady of Quality*, 146.

Those that drive and accompany waggons on a journey, sleep in the woods every night under a tree, upon dry leaves on the ground, with their feet towards a large fire, which they make by the road side, wherever night happens to overtake them, and are covered only with a blanket. Their horses are turned loose in the woods, only with leather spancills or fetters on two of their legs, and each with a bell fastened by a collar round his neck, by which they are readily found in the morning. Provisions and provender, both for men and horses, are carried along with them, in the waggon, sufficient for the whole journey.

Smyth, *A Tour of the United States*, 1:172-173.

Traveling through North Carolina, particularly the coastal plain, was often monotonous and lonely.

[January 17, 1774]. On the whole, the road from Charles Town to Wilmington is certainly the most tedious and disagreeable of any on the Continent of North America, it is through a poor, sandy, barren, gloomy country without accomodations for travellers. Death is painted in the countenances of those you meet, that indeed happens but seldom on the road. Neither man nor beast can stand a long journey thro' so bad a country where there's much fatigue and no refreshment; what must it be in their violent heats, when I found it so bad in the month of January!

Finlay, *Journal*, 67.

We arrived late in the day at Bath, after travelling over a most sterile and desolate sandy plain. The dreariness was scarcely relieved by the appearance of a house, except a few miserable tar burner's huts. We crossed Pamlico Sound in an open ferry-boat, a distance of five miles. After landing, we travelled the whole day amid a gloomy region of sands and pines. The road was spacious, and in a direct line. The majestic perpendicular pines, apparently towering to the clouds, imparted an imposing and solemn aspect to the scenery. The only relief from this monotony, and the cheerless and painful silence we found, was in noticing the watchful and timid deer grazing in the woods. The moment they perceived us approach, their long necks were arched, and their ears pricked up ready for a spring. Sometimes, however, they would gaze intently at us with a wild and anxious eye, and remain stationary until we passed. We gave chase to a wild Turkey who maintained his equal right to the road, like a true North Carolina republican, and in spite of our efforts he stretched away upon his long legs, far beyond our reach. [...]

Watson, *Men and Times of the Revolution*, 38.

As for variety in America, there is none. When you have traveled a hundred miles and been in a town or two, you have seen all that you can, as far as Virginia extends. It's the same thing, ditto, repeated— woods, rivers, swamps, etc., alternately afford you subject of reflection. But when you enter the charming and delightful state of North Carolina, which I have now had the pleasure of traveling through, then it becomes one same, dull, tiresome, and unvaried scene. You ride in stages (as they call them) without springs. The roads fortunately are not stony—otherwise the perpetual jolting this hot weather would be insupportable. All the livelong day you travel through pine woods of fifty and sixty miles without meeting a human being or passing a hut—I cannot call them houses. Now and then some oak trees relieve you a little from the innumerable pines. A few snakes twisting across the road and sometimes a wild deer are all the variety these disagreeable woods afford you. Think then, my dear father, what horrid traveling it is in North Carolina, where you have the same dull scene to repeat every day. [...]

Wright and Tinling, *Quebec to Carolina in 1785-1786*, 282.

⋘⋙

In addition to the wearisome surroundings, difficult roads, nonexistent bridges, and delays at ferries vexed the traveling public.

[...] [January 17, 1774]. From this Tavern we see the town of Wilmington at the end of an avenue cut through an island, two miles across; this island is in Cape Fear River, [...]

The island is a swamp, the road is laid with logs of trees, many of them are decay'd, so that the causeway is quite broken and full of large holes, in many places 'tis with difficulty that one can pass it on foot, with a horse 'tis just possible. This public avenue to the most flourishing town in the Province, will induce a stranger to believe, that the people in this country have no Laws, such is the report concerning North Carolina. [...]

Finlay, *Journal*, 66.

An Act to encourage and impower William Dry to make a Public Road through the great island opposite to the borough of Wilmington.

I. Whereas, a road through the great island opposite to the borough of Wilmington will be very beneficial to travellers going to and from South Carolina, and to others going to the town of Brunswick, and up the North-west river of Cape Fear, and the said William Dry, being desirous to make and finish the same:

II. Be it Enacted by the Governor, Council, and Assembly, and by the Authority of the same, That the said William Dry shall within six months after the passing of this Act, stake and lay off or cause to be staked and laid off, a road through the said island, beginning at his land on the said island opposite to market street in the said borough, and running westerly the nearest and most convenient way across to the north west river. [...]

Laws, 1764, in Clark, *State Records*, 25:487.

26th.—[January 26, 1774]. Learnt the story of the bad causeway leading to this place, and over which the Post passes in danger of life two miles. Publick report is, that the Governor and Province granted the ferry to Colonel William Dry for ever, on condition that he and his heirs should make and keep in good repair a high way thro' the Swampy Island before mention'd. The Colonel finds that he made a hard bargain, and he does not attempt to mend the road; he has been indicted more than once, yet the road is still bad. The King's attorney (his son in Law) has not yet prosecuted, tho' the world calls fye, and every person passing and repassing is in danger of breaking a leg or an arm, yet from year to year it is complain'd of and yearly grows worse. [...]

Finlay, *Journal*, 74.

[February 28, 1774]. Set out in the afternoon for New Bern in a very sultry day, 'tis reckoned 93 miles distant. From this day until the Tuesday following, on the road to Newbern. In the memory of the oldest man living there has not been such heavy rains nor of so long continuance. The whole country is overflow'd, all the bridges are carried away, every brook is swelled to a deep impassable river, in short we are here prisoners in a country Tavern. [...]

Finlay, *Journal*, 79-80.

When at last on the fourth day the expected boat for ferrying-over the horses arrived, the next morning was fixed for the passage, and everything arranged; but although we had now a right to hope for prompt service for once, we found ourselves deceived again when we came to the water-side at 8 o'clock. The gentleman who kept the ferry was still sleeping quietly in bed; we had to rouse him up, and then wait until he had called together a dozen negroes who were to look for two others whose business it was to tend the boat, which they only now began to make ready; more time lost. I mention this vexatious delay of purpose, and should not forget to add that we had other similar experiences. Travellers therefore must have a good supply of patience if they are not to be outdone at extreme carelessness which may often mean hindrance and loss to them, for there is no means of prevention or of compensation. To be sure, we were informed that we could bring action against the owner of the ferry for the loss of time and the expence involved, and might be certain of getting judgment; but we should have had to wait for a court-day, which was not worth the trouble.

Schoepf, *Travels in the Confederation*, 2:118-119.

⋖⋗

Although the General Assembly required that roads be posted and marked, many travelers encountered difficulty in finding their way.

XVI. And be it Enacted, by the Authority aforesaid, That all overseers of Roads shall cause to be set up, at the parting of all Roads within their several Districts, a Post or Posts, with Arms pointing the Way of each and every Road, with Directions to the most Public Places to which they lead with the Number of Miles from that Place, as near as can be computed; And every Overseer who shall refuse or neglect to do so, and keep the same in Repair, shall forfeit and pay, for every such Neglect, the Sum of Forty Shillings; to be recovered before any Justice of the Peace, and applied as other Fines in this Act directed.

XVII. And be it further Enacted, by the Authority aforesaid, That the several Overseers of the Roads, within Nine Months next after the passing of this Act, shall cause the Public Roads within their Districts respectively to be exactly Measured, where the same has not already been done; and shall at the End of each Mile, mark, in a Legible and durable Manner, the Number of such Miles, beginning, continueing, and making the Numbers in such Manner and Form, as the Inferior Courts of the Counties shall severally respectively direct; and every Overseer shall keep up and repair such Marks and Numbers within his District, And every Overseer refusing or neglecting to mile mark, or to repair the Mile Marks within his District, according to the Intent and Meaning of this Act, for the Space of Thirty Days after Notice of their being unmarked or out of Repair, shall forfeit and pay the sum of Twenty Shillings; to be recovered by a Warrant before any Justice of the Peace.

Laws, 1764, in Clark, *State Records*, 23:610-611.

April 11.—Tuesday. Set out fasting—rode 15 m. in the plainest right hand path according to direction, the last ten without a house; then at a very nasty hut was informed by an old sore eyed woman that my road was 10 m. to my right hand. Rather than go 10 m. back, I took direction to go the same distance thro' the woods. Pursuing my directions, was stopt by Creeks on both hands—attempting to pass them, mired my horse several times. Then as the last resource, determined to head the Creek to my right hand, which proved about 5 m. Then laying my course, no further difficulty intervened. [...]

"Biographical Sketch of Waightstill Avery," 4:251-252.

[...] I left Newbern soon after upon Harwood's track, and crossed the Trent by a rope ferry, seventy feet wide. I journeyed the entire day alone, through a wilderness of pines, over a flat, sandy country, with scarcely an inhabitant to be seen. Towards the close of the day I found myself entangled among swamps amid an utter wilderness, and my horse almost exhausted in my efforts to overtake Harwood. As night closed upon me, I was totally bewildered, and without a vestige of a road to guide me. Knowing the impossibility of retracing my steps in the dark, through the mazes I had traversed, I felt the absolute necessity of passing the night in this solitary desert. Feeling no apprehension that my horse would wander far from me, I turned him to shift for himself. I then placed my box under the sulky, and with my pistols fresh primed on one side, and my hanger on the other, I drew around me my grego, and, prostrated on the ground along with these, my only companions, half asleep and half awake, I passed the night in no trifling apprehension of falling a prey to wild beasts before morning.

At length, to my inexpressible satisfaction, the eastern horizon began to kindle up, and gradually to brighten more and more into the full blaze of day. I found my faithful horse true to his allegiance, and within reach. I harnessed up, and pressed with as much speed as possible out of this dreary retreat of solitude and desolation. My movements were some-what accelerated by observing a large bear stepping slowly along at a little distance from me. After several miles travelling I regained the road, and in the course of the forenoon overtook Harwood.

Watson, *Men and Times of the Revolution*, 40-41.

17th. Agreeable Weather early in the Morning, but rather cool; rode over a Causeway 3 Miles long:—it is in bad Order.— Took a "short Cut" to save 12 Miles Riding—Memorandum. Take no more short Cuts in North Carolina.—Had to cross two Mill Dams & met with great Difficulty. Rode through a very gloomy Cypress Swamp:—lost my

Way.—Saw Palmettos growing; they look like Fans.—Crossed Town Creek at Davis's Ferry;—very narrow.—Met with a Man at Davis's of the Name of Leonard;—a Relation of the Leonards at Princeton;—fortunately, for me, he was going to Lockwood's Folly: [...]

Johnston, "The Journal of Ebenezer Hazard in North Carolina, 1777, and 1778," 380.

⋖⋗

Lodging remained problematical, and when found, did not always prove desirable.

[...] [Lower Ferry, Wilmington, October 14, 1745]. One Jno. Malsby keeps this Ferry: he lived formerly at the Middle Ferry on Skuylkill, but left it & came to this Wilderness Country in hope of getting an Estate, by the purchase of Lands, but is much mistaken or I am. We were kindly entertained here but as the House is new, & no glass to be had for their Windows, & many air holes & the Wind very high at N. West, I slept miserably, the air coming on me almost from head to foot, but thro' Mercy got no Cold, tho' I was very apprehensive of it.

"William Logan's Journal of a Journey to Georgia, 1745," 14.

[...] To complete this pleasing scene, at night by way of easing myself of the fatigues of the day I was turned into an old barn that swarmed with rats and mosquitoes and, by way of a little variety, my bed (if you could call it one) was quite full of bugs and fleas. These, with the mosquitoes and the perpetual noise of millions of frogs, joined to the howling of the wild beasts in the woods, served at least to amuse me if I could not sleep. This is speaking rather ironically when I talk of any amusement, for I never remember to have spent so miserable a night. In the morning I was swelled all over with the bites of the bugs and mosquitoes.

Wright and Tinling, *Quebec to Carolina in 1785-1786*, 281. The writer's travail was suffered on the southwest shore of Albemarle Sound, some thirty-five miles northeast of the town of Washington.

[June, 1783]. At sunset I returned to Newbern with my friends Oram and Cook, who had given me the pleasure of joining me on this excursion. My plan had been to spend a few days there, but the happenstance of a swarm of bedbugs coming forth to greet me in bed when I lay down for a moment after dinner made me change my mind immediately. This insect is so abundant here that all the houses are generally contaminated, to which condition their wooden construction is no small contributor. Throughout the length of my stay I was obliged to sleep on the floor in the middle of a room, as there was no way of getting them out of bed. They are of such extraordinary size that a single one is the equivalent of three or four of those found in Europe. [...]

Miranda, *The New Democracy in America,* 8-9.

Feb. 22.—Wednesday, From Halifax 100 m. west of Edenton I set out for Hillsborough 100 still more west, rode 30 m., came late up with one Powels, and found him and one of his neighbors with two travellers at supper. I soon perceived the neighbor drunk; and there being but one room in the house, he reel'd and staggered from side to side thro' it, tumbling over, not chairs, for there were none in the House, but stools and Tables, &c. He was soon accompanied in the staggering scheme, by the Landlord and Travelers, first one and then both, who all blunder'd, bawl'd, spew'd and curs'd, broke one another's Head and their own shins, with stools, and bruised their Hips and Ribs with Sticks of the Couch Pens, pulled hair, lugg'd, hallo'd, swore, fought and kept up the Roar-Rororum till morning. Thus I watched carefully all night, to keep them from falling over and spewing upon me.

Feb. 23, 24 & 25.—Without shutting my Eyes to sleep, I set out at Day-break, and happy that I had escaped, continued my journey [...]

"Biographical Sketch of Waightstill Avery," 249.

[...] [Tar River, near Washington, December 18, 1787]. Mrs. Salter invited us to stay and take Coffee; and afterwards to lodge there, this seeming to be more pleasing to Mr. Jones, than to go on further, I readily agreed to it—And our Horses were put up. We spent the evening in conversation on different subjects, amongst the rest a good deal was said on Religion—At length Jones & I retired to go to rest, we found two Beds in our room, and proposed to ourselves each to take one to himself, but my fellow Traveller upon examining the one that by tacit consent had fallen to his lot, found it to be without Sheets, this circumstance rather disconcerted him, as I believe he had before heard me say, that I had as lieve sleep with a Snapping Turtle or a Two-Year-old Bull, as with *a Man,* However I soon relieved him by declaring that in present circumstances his Company would not be disagreeable, and we tumbled in and went to Sleep.

Rodman, *Journal of a Tour to North Carolina by William Attmore, 1787,* 30.

[June 19, 1786]. And what vexes me is the amazing expense, for your servant costs as much as yourself. I wished much to have left him in Canada with Mr. Blanchard, foreseeing the consequence of taking him; and yet scarcely anybody in America travels without. Gentlemen tell me I travel as cheap as most people and yet, upon an average, with stage hire, etc., it stands me in about a guinea a day. I am as great an economist as possible, but cannot for the life of me make it come lower. Mr. McCall said it always used to cost him more. I confess it's extremely provoking to pay so extravagantly and neither see or get anything satisfactory for your money. [...]

Wright and Tinling, *Quebec to Carolina in 1785-1786,* 282-283.

Religion

Opinions varied widely about the state of religion in North Carolina. Governor William Tryon, upon assuming the office of chief executive of North Carolina in 1765, offered his assessment of the religious scene in the colony. At approximately the same time zealous Anglican minister Charles Woodmason provided a different view from his perspective in the backcountry of North Carolina.

Every Sect of Religion abounds here, except the Roman Catholic, and by the best Information I can get, Presbytery, and a Sect who call themselves New Lights (not of the Flock of Mr Whitefield) but Superior Lights from New England, appear in the Front: These New Lights live chiefly in the Maritime Counties; the Presbyterians are settled mostly in the Back, or Westward Counties. The Church of England I reckon at present to have the Majority of all other Sects; and when a sufficient Number of Clergy as exemplary in their Lives, as orthodox in their Doctrine, can persuade themselves to come into This Country, I doubt not but the larger Number of every Sect would come over to the Established Religion. [...]

> William Tryon to the Society for the Propagation of the Gospel in Foreign Parts, July 31, 1765, Powell, *Correspondence of William Tryon*, 1:144.

[1765]. As to North Carolina, the State of Religion therein, is greatly to be lamented—If it can be said, That there is any Religion, or a Religious Person in it. A Church was founded at Wilmington in 1753. Another at Brunswick in 1756, the Walls of each are carried up about 10 or 12 feet and so remain. Governour Dobbs us'd Great Endeavours to get these Buildings finish'd, and to lay out Parishes—But lived not to effect it—But the present Governour has got an Act pass'd, for a Church to be built in each Parish or Distric, and Church Matters to be settled on the Plan of South Carolina. He has given Public Notice hereof to the Clergy—Inviting of them to come abroad Promising of them his Protection Encouragement and Support: At the same time mentioning what Numbers of Sectaries overspread the Country, and the Danger that not only the Church Established, but even Religion it Self will be totally lost and destroyed if not quickly attended too.

Here is an opening—A large Harvest for all that are sincerely dispos'd to act for the Glory of God and the Good of Souls—How many thousands who never saw, much less read, or ever heard a Chapter of the Bible! How many Ten thousands who never were baptized or heard a Sermon! And thrice Ten thousand, who never heard of the Name of Christ, save in Curses and Execrations! Lamentable! Lamentable is the Situation of these People, as to Spirituals, Even beyond the Power of Words to describe.

Woodmason, *Carolina Backcountry*, 76-77.

✧✧

From the beginning of the eighteenth century the Church of England was nominally the established or government-supported church in North Carolina. By law the General Assembly divided the colony into parishes and required the election of twelve vestrymen, who in turn selected two churchwardens to conduct the everyday affairs of the parish. According to provincial law, all eligible freeholders were required to vote for vestrymen. Legislation in 1765 mandated support for Anglican ministers.

An Act, for appointing Parishes and Vestries, for the Encouragement of an Orthodox Clergy, for the Advancement of the Protestant Religion, and for the Direction of the Settlement of Parish Accounts.

I. Whereas the present, as well as the future Happiness of Mankind, essentially depends on the Knowledge and Practice of true Religion; and a permanent and certain Provision for an Orthodox Clergy, may conduce to the Encouragement of pious and learned Ministers of the Gospel, to settle and reside in the several Parishes in this Province, to the Advancement of the Protestant Religion, and Encouragement of Vertue and Morality:

II. Be it Enacted, by the Governor, Council, and Assembly, and by the Authority of the same, That this Government be, and it is hereby divided into distinct Parishes, in the Manner following; That is to say, St. Paul's Parish, in Chowan County: Berkley Parish, in Perquimons County: St. John's Parish, on the South West Side of Pasquotank River, and St. Peter's Parish, on the North-East Side of Pasquotank River, in Pasquotank County: Currituck Parish, in Currituck County: Society Parish, in Bertie County; St. Andrew's Parish in Tyrell County: St. Thomas's Parish, in Beaufort County: St. George's Parish in Hyde County: North-West Parish, in Northampton County: St. John's Parish, in Granville County: St. Matthew's Parish, in Orange County: St. Luke's Parish, in Rowan County: St. David's Parish, in Cumberland County: St. Gabriel's Parish, in Duplin County: St. George's Parish, in Anson County; Edgecombe Parish, in Edgecombe County: St. Martin's Parish, in Bladen County:

St. James Parish, on the East Side of Cape-Fear River: And St. Philip's Parish, on the West Side of Cape Fear River, from the Mouth of the said River, running up the North-West River, to the Bounds of the County, inclusive, of the Island at the Mouth of the North-West and North-East Rivers, commonly called Eagle's Island, in New Hanover County: St. Patrick's Parish, in Johnston County: Christ-Church Parish, in Craven County: St. John's Parish, in Onslow County, and St. John's Parish, in Carteret County.

III. And be it further Enacted, by the Authority aforesaid, That the Freeholders of each respective Parish aforesaid, shall, and they are hereby impowered and directed to meet on the first Monday after the Tenth Day of June next after the Ratification of this Act, at the Court-house or Place where the County Court in each respective County aforesaid is or shall be held, or at the usual Place of electing Vestrymen, and on Easter-Monday every Third Year thereafter, then and there to choose and elect Twelve Freeholders to serve as Vestrymen for the Three Years next ensuing; which Vestrymen so chosen, shall, by the Sheriff or his Deputy, in each of the said Parishes respectively, be summoned to meet at the church, and where there is no Church, at the Court-house or Place where the County Court is or shall be held, within Forty Days next after such Choice, to qualify themselves according to the direction of this Act; [...]

VIII. And to enforce the Attendance of the Freeholders at all future Elections of Vestrymen; Be it further Enacted, That every Person qualified to Vote for Vestrymen in the several and respective Parishes, shall, and he is hereby required, duly to attend and give his Vote at all future Elections, at the Time, and in the Manner as is herein before directed, unless prevented by some bodily Infirmity, or legal disability; under the Penalty of Twenty Shillings Proclamation Money: To be recovered by Warrant from any Magistrate within the County. [...]

XI. And be it further Enacted, by the Authority aforesaid, That the Vestrymen of each and every Parish respectively, or a Majority of them, shall, and they are hereby directed, within Sixty Days after Easter-Monday, Yearly, to elect and choose out of the said Vestry, Two Persons to execute the Office of Churchwardens in each and every respective Parish; [...]

XIV. And be it further Enacted, by the Authority aforesaid, That the Vestry of each respective Parish, shall have full Power and Authority, and they are hereby directed and required, between Easter Monday, and the First Day of November, Yearly to lay such a Poll-Tax as they shall judge necessary, for purchasing Glebes, and satisfying the Expence of their respective Parishes.

Laws, 1754, in Clark, *State Records*, 25:298, 299, 300, 301.

Newbern, J*une* 13*th*, 1764.
NOTICE to the Freeholders of *Christ-Church* Parish, in *Craven* County, is hereby given, that on *Wednesday*, the 1st Day of *August* next, at the Court-House in *Newbern*, the Subscriber, or his Deputy, will attend; open the Poll for electing a Vestry for said Parish, and take the Suffrages of the Voters, as the Law Directs.

Richard Cogdell, Sheriff.
N. B. There is a Fine of *Twenty Shillings* on every Freeholder in the Parish who fails to attend, and give his Vote.

R. C.

North-Carolina Magazine; or, Universal Intelligencer (New Bern), July 27, 1764.

An Act for establishing an Orthodox Clergy.
I. Whereas making a reasonable and certain Provision for an Orthodox Clergy may tend to encourage Pious and learned Ministers of the Gospel to settle in the several Parishes in this Province:
II. Be it Enacted by the Lieutenant Governor, Council, and Assembly, and by the Authority of the same, That every Minister now or hereafter to be preferred to, or received, into any Parish within this Province, as incumbent thereof, shall have and receive a Salary of One Hundred and Thirty-three Pounds Six Shillings and Eight Pence, Proclamation Money; to be paid by the Church Wardens and Vestrymen, on or before the last Day of June, Annually: And every Minister may take and receive for the Services hereinafter mentioned, the following Fees, to-wit:
For Marrying, if by Licence, Twenty Shillings; if by Banns, Five Shillings.
For publishing Banns, and granting a Certificate thereof, One Shilling and Six Pence.
For preaching a Funeral Sermon, if required, Forty Shillings, Proclamation Money.
And may demand and receive the said Perquisites, if he shall not refuse or neglect to do the said Services although such services shall be performed by any other Person.

III. And be it further Enacted by the Authority aforesaid, That in every Parish of this Province, where a Glebe is not already purchased and appropriated; a Tract of good Land, to contain two Hundred Acres at least, shall be purchased by the Vestry, as a Glebe for the Use of the Incumbent of such Parish for the Time being, and his Successors forever; and until such Glebe shall be purchased, and buildings erected thereon, in Manner hereinafter mentioned, the Minister of such Parish shall have and receive the Sum of Twenty Pounds Proclamation Money, Annually. And where a Mansion House and convenient outhouses are not already erected, for the use of the Minister, It is hereby Enacted, That the Vestry of every such Parish, are hereby authorized, impowered and required, to cause to be erected and built on such Glebe, one convenient Mansion House, of thirty-eight Feet in Length, and Eighteen Feet in width, a Kitchen, Barn, Stable, Dairy and Meat House, with such other Conveniences as they shall think necessary. [...]

XI. And be it further Enacted, by the Authority aforesaid, That the Church Wardens and Vestry of each Parish, shall pay and satisfy to the Minister thereof, the Salary by this Act allowed him, on or before the First Day of August, in every Year: And in Case of Neglect or Refusal, the Minister shall and may, by Motion in the Superior Court have the like Remedy, Proceedings and Relief, against such Church Wardens and Vestry so neglecting or refusing, as is or may, by Virtue of this Act, be had against any Parish Collector, for Taxes by him to be collected and paid to the Church Wardens and Vestry.

XII. And be it further Enacted, by the Authority aforesaid, That the Minister of every Parish, shall preach at the Churches and Chapels which now are, or hereafter shall be erected in the Parish whereof he is Minister, and at such other suitable Places as the Vestry for the Time being shall Direct.

Laws, 1765, in Clark, *State Records*, 23:660, 662.

<&ð>

Parishes such as St. Paul's, which was one of the earliest parishes in the colony and coterminous with Chowan County, undertook to secure the services of lay readers and ministers. Some ministers reflected poorly on their church; others, like the Reverend Clement Hall, author of the first book published in North Carolina, proved tireless and selfless in their endeavors.

Ordered that the Rev Mr Clement Hall Clerk, be continued as a minister for the Parish of St. Paul's for the year 1746, at sixty Pounds proclamation money, he attending at Edenton to preach every other

Sunday & the same at the Chapels above—viz. Constant's and Knotty Pine Chapel.

Ordered that three Readers be appointed Viz One at Edenton, one at Constant's Chapel & one at Knotty Pine Chapel; & accordingly that Isaac Hunter be, & is hereby appointed Reader at Constant's Chapel & be allowed twenty Shillings proclamation money for the year; & that William Skinner be & is hereby appointed Reader at Knotty Pine Chapel & be allowed the same sum; & that Mr. Daniel Grandin be, & is hereby appointed Reader in Edenton & be allowed two Pounds proclamation money for his present year 1746, [...]

> Minutes of vestry, St. Paul's Parish, April 26, 1746, typescript, State Archives.

South Carolina, Charlestown, September 6, 1737

My Lord,

I have lately receiv'd a Letter from his Excellency the Governour of North Carolina, of which the following is a Paragraph, Concerning the ill Behaviour of Mr. Boyd, the Honourable Society's Missionary in that Colony:

After having expressed much Concern, that no farther assistance was to be expected from the Honourable Society, towards the Propagation of Religion in that Colony, than the one Missionary already there; His Excellency Subjoins concerning him & says: "But what makes the matter still worse is that this very Missionary is one of the Vilest & most Scandalous Persons in the Government. I gave you some Hints of his Idleness & Inclination to Drunkeness, when I had the pleasure of Seeing you at Edenton; But since that time, I have heard such accounts of his behaviour as are really Shocking. Particularly that on a Sunday, this Spring, at noon day, he was Seen by many Persons Lying dead Drunk & fast asleep, on the Great Road to Virginia, with his Horse's Bridle tyed to his Leg; this I have been assur'd of by Several Persons of the best Credit. As he is under your Inspection, I hope you will take some notice of such horrid practices." [...]

Boyd of North Carolina is dead; and as the Governor there writes me, *he died in the same Beastly Manner he lived.*[...]

> A. Garden to "My Lord," September 6, 1737; December 22, 1737, in "Letters to the Bishop of London from the Commissaries in South Carolina," 289-290, 295.

NORTH CAROLINA, Edenton May 19, 1752.

REVd SIR,

Since Easter I have (tho' in a bad state of bodily health) journey'd thro' my North Mission, rode about 174 miles in about 16 days, preached 13 Sermons most of the congregations being very large, some counted to be 4, 5, or 600 persons (insomuch that we were some times obliged to assemble under the Shady Trees because the houses would not contain them) baptized 336 white & 22 black children 5 white adults (brought up in anabaptism & quakerism) & 7 black adults after proper examination and left several others to be better instructed against the next opportunity & also perform'd several other ministerial duties among the sick &c—& dispersed part of the books for which they were thankful, & hope to disperse them all before long (God willing) among such people as most want & will make the best use of them & lend them to others &c. I have now thro' God's gracious assistance & blessing in about 7 or 8 years, tho' frequently visited with Sickness, been enabled to perform (for aught I know) as great ministerial duties as any minister in N. America, viz to journey about 14000 miles. Preach about 675 Sermons. Baptize about 5783 white children 243 black children, 57 white adults & 112 Black adults in all 6195 persons & sometimes administered the Holy sacrament of the Lords Supper to 2 or 300 communicants in one journey besides churching of women, visiting the sick &c.

Rev. Clement Hall to the Secretary, May 19, 1752, Saunders, *Colonial Records*, 4:1314-1315.

A COLLECTION OF MANY Christian Experiences, Sentences, AND SEVERAL Places of Scripture Improved:
ALSO,
Some short and plain DIRECTIONS and PRAYERS for sick Persons; with serious ADVICE to Persons who have been sick, to be by them perused and put in Practice as soon as they are recovered; and a THANKSGIVING for Recovery.
To which is added, Morning and Evening Prayers for Families and Children, Directions for the LORD'S—DAY, and some Cautions against Indecencies in Time of Divine Services, &c.
Collected and Composed for the Spiritual Good of his Parishoners, and others.
By C. H. *Missionary to the Honourable Society for the Propagation of the Gospel in Foreign Parts, and Rector of St. Paul's Parish, in* North-Carolina.

O! how sweet are they Words unto my Taste, yea sweeter than Honey to my Mouth, Psal. cxix. 103.

I am well pleased that the Lord hath heard the Voice of my Prayer, that he hath inclined his Ear unto me; therefore, will I call upon him as long as I live, Psal. cxvi. 12.

NEWBERN:
Printed by JAMES DAVIS, M, DCC, LIII.

Hall, *A Collection of Many Christian Experiences*, title page.

❧❧

The Anglican parishes undertook a number of civil as well as religious functions. Most were assumed by the county courts by the end of the colonial era. Among parish responsibilities was the purchase of weights and measures to serve as the county standard, payment of bounties on wild animals (vermin), and processioning land.

[...] In obedience to a late Act of Assembly made in March last impowering the Vestry of each precinct to provide a Standard for Weights and Measures. And it being debated how the said Weights and Measures are to be procured.

Agreed that the Church Wardens shall Use their Utmost Endeavor by the first Convenience to send for Weights and Measures as the <*Anno Domini 1702.*> Law directs and agree with some person for that purpose at as Cheap a rate as possible, [...]

Minutes of vestry, St. Paul's Parish, June 30, 1702. Cain, *Records of the Church of England*, 433.

Pursuant to the Direction of a late act of Assembly Relating to killing Vermin The following Persons produced Certificates which was allowed of by this Vestry and the Certificates Destroyed.

Ordered that the Said persons be allowed as follows (Viz.).

Mr. John Lewiss for One woolf Sculp		£4. 0. 0
Mr. Henry Bonner One woolf Sculp	£4. 0. 0	
Do. Two Wild Catts at 20s. Each	2. 0. 0	6.15. 0
Do. Thirty Squirrel at 6d. Each	0.15.0	
<(105)> <1743.> Mr. John Benbury Ninety		
Six Squirrels Scalps at 6d. Each		2. 8. 0
Mr. John Luten One woolf scalp		4. 0. 0
Mr. John Halsey One wild catt	£1.0.0	
Do. fifty Squirrels at 6d. Each.	1.5.0	2. 5. 0
Mr. William Benbury One hundred and Eighty		

one Squirrels at 6d.		£4.10. 6
Mr. Orlando Champion five woolfs scalps at 80s.	£20.0.0	
Do. Six Wild Cats Do. at 20s. Each	6.0.0	26. 0.0
Mr. John Blount Two Wolfs at 80s. Each		8. 0.
Mr. Joseph Ming Two Wolves at 80s.	£8. 0.0	
Do. Twenty Six Squirrels at 6d.	0.13.0	8.13.
Mr. Thomas Hoskins Two wolves' Scalps at 80s.		8. 0. 0
Mr. Jacob Butler Eight Wolves Do. at 80s.	£32. 0.0	
Do. Two Wild Cats Do. at 20s.	2. 0.0	45. 9. 6
Do. Four hundred and fifty nine Squirrels at 6d.	11. 9.6	
		£120. 1.[...]

Minutes of vestry, St. Paul's Parish, April 4, 1743, typescript, State Archives.

The Vestry Taking into Consideration the Law for Settleing the Title and Bounds of Peoples Lands By Freeholders appointed to procession the same on oath &c. accordingly proceed to Divide the Parish into Convenient Cantons, and to appoint Two freeholders in Each Canton processioners to procession the same according to Law as follows.

Minutes of vestry, St. Paul's Parish, October 23, 1764, typescript, State Archives.

∾⥾⥿∾

Care of the poor constituted one of the most important functions of the parishes, and remained a responsibility of the Anglican church throughout the colonial era.

Ordered that William Flury be allowed at the rate twenty Shillings pr. Month from the 8th day of May last for keeping Gideon Brice. [...]

Ordered that John Gregory be allowed at the rate of Three pounds ten shillings pr. year for keeping Elizabeth Hoskins orphan of Thomas Hoskins from the first of May last.

Ordered that William Hinton be allowed at the rate of Three pounds ten shillings pr. year for keeping Elizabeth Parker the year to begin the twentieth of May last.

<Issued for 20 Shillings> Ordered that Katherine Hays be allowed at the rate of eight pounds pr. year for keeping two of her orphan children

Mary, and Elizabeth, <*Issued for All 1771.*> and that she be now paid twenty shillings of the Same.

<(252)> <*St. Pauls Parish 1770.*> <*Issued To T. Hodson Esqr.*> Ordered that William Parker be paid Three pounds ten Shillings provided he procure Sarah Hoskins orphan of Thomas Hoskins deceast to be bound an apprentice to him at this present Inferior Court and Endemnifie the Parish from any further Charge on acct. of said orphan.

Ordered that Henry Moor be allowed at the rate of five pounds pr., year for keeping Edward Streator an orphan of Thomas Streator deceast from the first of February Last. [...]

The Parish of St. Paul in Acct. with William Walton C. W.			Cr.		
	£	S. D.	£	S.	D.
To sundry articles bought for the use of persons maintained by the Parish			2.10.	0	
To making 2 Coats and 4 Shirts				6.	
To 2 pr. Shoes				4.	
To keeping John Goodin three months and nine days			1.	5.	
To attending at Farlees Chapel two days				10.	
To keeping Moses Wellwood 53 Days			1.	3.	6
			5.19.	4	
			2.10		
			3. 9.	4	

June 20th 1770 proved before Richard Brownrigg

£ S. D

June 18th 1769

By fines recd. from Major Walton for the use of the Parish   2.10

Minues of vestry, St. Paul's Parish, June 20, 1770, typescript, State Archives.

[...] <*Issued*> Ordered that Robert Mure be allowed Three pounds ten Shillings for boarding Joseph Simpson ten weeks.

<*Issued.*> Ordered that Mr. Thomas Hoskins pay Katherine Hays Six pounds and Six pence for keeping her two Children &. to this Day and that her allowace be discontinued.

<*Issued.*> Ordered that Docter Dickenson be allowed his acct. of Thirteen pounds two shillings for sundry services by him done to the poor of this Parish.

Ordered that Elizabeth Knight be allowed at the rate twenty five shillings per month for keeping her daughter Kiziah and her Child from the 9th of may Last till Some other person will Keep them for Less.
<(260)> <*St. Pauls Parish 1772*> <*Issued*> Orderd that Joshua Mewborn Be allowed nine pounds four Shillings and nine pence for keeping Jacob Privit 13[½] months till this Day and finding him one Shirt.

Order'd that William Lister his allowance be Continued for keeping Mary Johnston till further orders.

<*Issued.*> Ordered that the Church wardens Pay Jacob Privit Two pounds Seven Shillings and Six pence Every Three months to Enable him to Support him Self he being a poor old man.

<*Issued to J. G.*> Ordered that Samuel Green be paid Eight Pounds fifteen Shillings for keeping Moses Welwood fourteen month Last Past.[...]

> Minutes of vestry, St. Paul's Parish, June 17, 1772, typescript, State Archives.

AN ACT AND FURTHER CONTINUE AN ACT ENTITLED AN ACT CONCERNING VESTRIES

"Whereas an Act concerning Vestries" made in the Year One thousand seven hundred and Sixty four and further continued by an Act made in the year One thousand seven hundred and Sixty eight, will expire with the end of this Session of Assembly, and it being necessary that the said Act should be amended and further Continued

Be it therefore Enacted by this Governor Council and Assembly, and by the authority of the same, That the said recited Act, and every clause and article therein, be and Continue in force for the Term and Space of Ten Years from and after the passing hereof, and from thence to the end of the next Session of Assembly and no longer.

And Whereas the Number of poor people hath of late years much increased throughout this Province, and it will be the most proper method for their Maintenance, and for the prevention of Great mischief arising from such numbers of unemployed poor to provide houses for their Reception and employment.

Be it therefore Enacted by the Governor Council and Assembly and by the authority of the same That it may be lawful for the Vestry of every parish in this Colony where they find it necessary and Convenient to order and cause to be erected Purchased or hired one or more House or Houses within their Parish for the Lodging, maintaining, and employing of all such Poor people as shall be upon the Parish or who shall desire relief from the Vestry or Church Wardens and to employ all such poor persons in such Works as shall be directed by the said Vestry or Churchwardens and to take and apply the benefit of their labour for and towards their maintenance and support and to provide Cotton, Hemp Flax or any other necessary materials, implements or things for setting the said Poor to Work, And, where any parish shall be too small to purchase erect or hire such House or Houses, it shall and may be lawful for the Vestries of any two or more of such Parishes lying adjoining or convenient [blank] having such House or Houses for the reception [blank] of the poor of their Respective parishes and the said Vestry or Vestries shall have power to purchase or rent a Tract of Land on one or more Lot or Lots in any Town whereon the said House or Houses shall stand or be erected or convenient thereto not exceeding one Hundred Acres for the use of the said Poor and to levy a reasonable allowance in their Parish Levies for the Education of such poor Children as shall be placed in the said House or Houses until they shall be bound out according to Law.[...]

And be it further Enacted by the authority aforesaid that the Vestry of every Parish wherein any House or Houses for the reception of the Poor shall be, shall have full power and do authority to make and ordain proper rules and orders for and concerning the work employment and Correction of such Poor Persons as shall be placed and sent there pursuant to this Act and to contract with and appoint one or more fit person or persons to [blank] the said House or Houses and to oversee the Poor belonging or sent to such House or Houses which person or persons so to be appointed shall have full power to set all such poor persons as shall be placed [blank] there to work and labor according to these several [blank] and the rules and orders of the vestry and Church-warden and to [blank] inflick Corporal punishment on such persons under [blank] care and management who will not conform themselves to the [blank] Rules and Orders or who shall behave refractorialy not exceeding Ten Lashes at one time or for one Offence and the person or persons so to be appointed shall annually at the laying of the parish Levy or when thereto require under a true account to the Vestry of the Poor under his or their Care and of the profits arising from their Labours and how the same have been disposed of and moreoever shall be liable to be displaced by the Vestry when they shall see fit.

And be it further Enacted by the Authority aforesaid That if any poor person shall refuse to be placed or to continue at any House or Houses to be appointed for the reception of the Poor in pursuance of this Act, he or she so refusing shall in no wise be intitled to ask dun and or receive any relief or Sum or Sums of Money from the Vestry or Churchwardens of his or her Parish except the Vestry or Churchwardens by reason of his or her sickness or Old age shall adjudge them incapable of labour and order otherwise.

And be it further enacted by the authority aforesaid that the Churchwardens of every parish shall keep a book wherein the names of all person who receive relief from the parish shall be Registered with the time they were admitted on the parish and the Occasion of such admittance which Book shall be by them produced to the Vestry at the laying of the parish Levy or as often as the said Vestry shall think convenient and the name of such poor persons shall be called over and the reasons of their receiving relief, examined and such of the said poor shall then be continued on the Parish or discharged therefrom as the said Vestry shall direct and that the Poor of every Parish may be better known.

Be it further Enacted by the authority aforesaid That every Person who shall receive relief from the parish and be sent to the said House or Houses shall upon the Shoulder of the right sleeve of his or her uppermost Garment in an open and visible manner, wear a Badge with the name of the Parish to which he or she belongs cut either in Blue or red or green Cloth as the Vestry or ChurchWardens shall direct and if any poor person shall neglect or refuse to wear such Badge the Vestry or Churchwardens of such Parish may punish such Offence either by ordering his or her allowance to be abridged suspended or withdrawn or the offender to be whipped not exceeding five lashes for one offence or at one time And if any person not intitled to relief as aforesaid shall presume to wear such Badge he or she so offending shall in like manner be whipped for every such Offence by order of any Justice of the peace until he or she shall immediately paydown the sum of ten Shillings to the Churchwardens for the use of the poor of that Parish where the offence shall be committed.

Act of Assembly, 1774, in CO 5/341. British Records, State Archives.

❧☙

Parishes obtained funds to meet their expenses by means of fines collected by the churchwardens and by annual taxes imposed on the inhabitants of the parishes.

At a Vestry begun and Held at Constants Chappel August the 9th 1755.
    According to Adjournment.[...]
The Parish of St. Pauls in Account with John Halsey

	£. S. D.
1754 Octobr. 15 By a Fine from Hannah Clay for a Bastard Child	1. 5. 0
By a Fine from William Wilkins for Profane Swearing	1. 5. 0
By a Fine from Elizabeth Ford for a Bastard Child	1. 5. 0
By a Fine from Sarah Hunter	1. 5. 0
By a Fine from Francis Robins for Swearing	0. 3. 9
By a Fine from Mary Jones for a Bastard-Child	1. 5. 0
	£ 6. 8. 9

The Parish of St. Pauls [...]

Ordered That a Tax or Levey of Two shillings and Eight Pence Proclamation Money be Leveyed on Each and Every Taxable Person in This Parish for This Present year to Defray the Contingent Charges, Thereof, and That The Same be Collected by some person To be Appointed by The Vestry [...]

> Minutes of vestry, St. Paul's Parish, August 9, 1755, typescript, State Archives.

⊷⊶

Anglican churches were few, and required extensive effort and time to construct. Among them were St. James Church in Wilmington and St. Philip's Church in Brunswick Town.

An Act for the better Regulation of the Town called Wilmington, in New Hanover County; and to establish the Church of the Parish of St. James, to be built in the said Town. [...]

XII. And be it further Enacted, by the Authority aforesaid, That the Church of the Parish of St. James, in New Hanover County, shall be built in the said Town of Wilmington; and all Sums of Money already raised, or which shall be hereafter raised, by Levies, on the Inhabitants of the said Parish, for building a Parish Church, shall be employed to build a Parish Church in the said Town.

> Laws, 1740, in Clark, *State Records*, 23:146, 148.

An Act for building a church in Wilmington, in St. James Parish, in New Hanover county.[...]

I. Whereas the church of St. James's Parish, in New Hanover county, is by law appointed to be built in the town of Wilmington; and whereas many well disposed persons have subscribed liberally thereto, and a further sum is yet necessary to carry on and compleat the same:

II. Wherefore we pray it may be Enacted, And be it Enacted by his Excelly Gabriel Johnston, Esqr., Governor by and with the advice and Consent of his Majesty's Council and the General Assembly of this Province, And by the Authority of the same, That a Tax of one shilling and four pence Proclamation Money be laid on all the Taxables of the said Parish of Saint James's for the space of three years from the ratification hereof to be collected yearly and every year as all other Taxes usually are by the Sheriff of New Hanover County and to be by him accounted for and paid yearly to the Commissrs in this Act hereafter appointed or the Majority of them.

III. And to encourage a further and larger subscription, for compleating the said church in a decent manner, be it enacted by the authority aforesaid, that every subscriber shall have a proper place in the said church, to build a seat or pew upon in proportion to his subscription, as the commissioners or the majority of them, may determine; which piece or parcel of ground so adjusted and set off, shall be an estate of inheritance to such person or persons his or their heirs or assigns, forever such person or persons building, or causing to be built, such seat or pew as the commissioners may judge proper and regular, so as the same be set up and finished within six months after compleating the said church.

Laws, 1751, in Clark, *State Records*, 25:243.

An Act to appoint commissioners to receive, collect and apply, subscriptions towards building of a church in the town of Brunswick, in St. Philip's Parish, and for other uses therein mentioned.

I. Whereas several well disposed persons are inclined to subscribe and contribute several sums of money towards building a church in the town of Brunswick, in the parish of St. Philip, and county of New Hanover for the more effectual collecting and applying the said subscriptions.

II. We pray it may be enacted, and be it enacted, by his excellency Gabriel Johnston, Esq; Governor, by and with the advice and consent of his Majesty's Council, and the General Assembly of this Province, and it is hereby enacted by the authority of the same, that the honourable Matthew Rowan, and James Hasell, Esqrs. John Russel, and William Dry, Esqrs. Richard Quince and John Davis, gentlemen, be and are hereby appointed commissioners, with full power and authority, to collect and receive of and from all and every person and persons, contributing to the building of the said church, the several sum or sums of money, or other donations whatsoever, which shall at any time hereafter, be by such person or persons severally subscribed and contributed.

Laws, 1751, in Clark, *State Records*, 25:244-245.

An Act for raising Money by a Lottery, towards finishing the Churches at Wilmington and Brunswick; and for applying the Produce of the Slaves, and other Effects taken from the Spaniards at Cape Fear, in the Year of our Lord One Thousand Seven Hundred and Forty Eight, to the same Purposes.

I. Whereas by an Act intituled, an Act for raising Money for finishing the Churches in the Parishes of St. James's and St. Philip's, in New Hanover County, by a Lottery, several Persons were appointed Managers for undertaking, carrying on, and drawing a Lottery as therein mentioned; but the greatest part of the Tickets therein remaining unsold, and the Time for Drawing the same being now expired, the Method for raising Money for the Purposes aforesaid is now become ineffectual: And whereas it is imagined, that the Scarcity of Proclamation Money in this part of the Province, had prevented many Persons from purchasing Tickets, who might have inclined to have become Adventurers therein, if the Money had not been immediately payable on the Purchase of the Tickets; and the Method of selling them as hereafter mentioned, being rendered more easy to the Purchasers a Sufficient Number might be sold to enable the Managers to have the same drawn in a short Time. [...]

VII. And whereas the finishing the building of the said Two Churches will be greatly expedited, provided the Money arising by the Sale of the Slaves, and other Effects saved out of the Wreck of the Spanish Privateer that blew up before Brunswick, in the Year One Thousand Seven Hundred and Forty Eight, and is now in Private Hands, unapplied to any Public use, might be appropriated to the compleating the said Two Churches: Be it Enacted by the Authority aforesaid, That the Slaves and other Effects, saved out of the Spanish Wreck as aforesaid, or taken from the Spaniards at the Time of their Invasion, not already sold; as also the Money arising by the Sale of those which have been sold, after deducting the Expences of such Sales, shall be applied towards the compleating the building the said Two Churches, in Manner following; that is to say, Two Third Parts of the Net Proceeds towards finishing the Church at Brunswick; and the other Third Part towards finishing the Church at Wilmington, and to no other use or purpose whatsoever.

Laws, 1760, in Clark, *State Records*, 23:535, 537.

ᡪᠥᡄᠥ

Although the Anglican Church was the established church, the earliest organized sect in North Carolina was the Society of Friends or Quakers. George Fox, founder of the Society of Friends in England, briefly visited the Albemarle region in 1672, deviating from his tour of Virginia. In addition to itinerants from England, North Carolina Quakers produced their own traveling ministers, among whom was Thomas Nicholson, who visited the Cape Fear area in 1746. Well organized, Quakers convened yearly, quarterly, and monthly meetings within the colony.

[...] The next day, the 21st of the Ninth Month, having travelled hard through the woods and over many bogs and swamps, we reached Bonner's Creek; and there we lay that night by the fireside, the woman lending us a mat to lie on.

This was the first house we came to in Carolina; here we left our horses, over-wearied with travel. From hence we went down the creek in a canoe to Macocomocock River; and came to Hugh Smith's house, where people of the world came to see us (for there were no Friends in that part of the country), and many of them received us gladly. Amongst others came Nathaniel Batts, who had been governor of Roanoke; he went by the name of Captain Batts, and had been a rude, desperate man. He asked me about a woman in Cumberland, who, he said, he was told, had been healed by our prayers and laying on of our hands, after she had been long sick and given over by the physicians; and he desired to know the certainty of it. I told him we did not glory in such things, but many such things had been done by the power of Christ.

Not far from hence we had a meeting among the people, and they were taken with the truth: blessed be the Lord! Then passing down the river Maratick in a canoe, we went down the bay Coney-oak, and came to a captain's house, who was very loving, and lent us his boat, for we were much wetted in the canoe, the water flashing in upon us. With this boat we went to the governor's house; but the water in some places was so shallow that the boat, being laden, could not swim; so that we were fain to put off our shoes and stockings, and wade through the water some distance. The governor, with his wife, received us lovingly; but there was at his house a doctor who would needs dispute with us. And truly his opposing us was of good service, giving occasion for the opening of many things to the people concerning the light and spirit of God, which he denied to be in every one, and affirmed that it was not in the Indians. Whereupon I called an Indian to us, and asked him whether or no, when he did lie or do wrong to any one, there was not something in him that reproved him for it. He said there was such a thing in him that did so reprove him; and he was ashamed when he had done wrong, or spoken wrong. So we shamed the doctor before the governor and the people; insomuch that the poor man ran out so far that at length he would not own the Scriptures. We tarried at the governor's that night; and next morning he very courteously walked with us himself about two miles through the woods to a place whither he had sent our boat about to meet us. Taking leave of him, we entered our boat, and went that day about thirty miles to one Joseph Scott's, one of the representatives of the country. There we had a sound, precious meeting; the people were tender, and much desired after meetings. Wherefore at a house about four miles further, we had another meeting, to which the governor's secretary came, who was chief secretary of the Province, and had been formerly convinced.

I went from this place among the Indians, and spake unto them by an interpreter; shewing them that God made all things in six days, and made but one woman for one man; and that God did drown the old world, because of their wickedness. Afterwards I spake to them concerning Christ, shewing them that He did die for all men for their sins, as well as for others; and had enlightned them as well as others; and that if they did that which was evil He would burn them, but if they did well they should not be burned. There was among them their young king, and others of their chief men, who seemed to receive kindly what I said to them.

Having visited the north part of Carolina, and made a little entrance for Truth upon the people there, we began to return towards Virginia, having several meetings in our way, wherein we had very good service for the Lord, the people being generally tender and open; blessed be the Lord! [...]

Journal of George Fox, 299-300.

I. On the first of the 4th mo., 1746, I set out on a journey, towards Capefare, being accompanied with my wife and others, to the Quarterly Meeting which was a comfortable Meeting; having to my companion in the ministry my well esteemed friend Stephen Scott, and also accompanied by our friends Phinehas and Zachariah Nixon, who were chosen by the Yearly Meeting, to accompany us in a friendly visit, to friends at

Capefare, and to settle matters amongst them in relation to Church Discipline, we had a near and affectionate parting, with friends after the said Meeting, and went that evening to the house of Caleb Elliott, the next day rode to the house of Robert Peel and the 3rd day had a Meeting at his house, and went that evening to the house of Thomas Knox, and the 4th day over Roanoak, and Tar river, at the falls to the house of Isaas Ricks, the next day had a Meeting there with the people, who appeared tender and hopeful, a preceius Meeting it was, and ended with praises to the Lord, the Father of all our mercies, and from thence on our way, that evening, but not having convenient opportunity of lodging in any house, we rode on till some time in the night, and lay in the woods, the next morning got early on our way and travailed hard all day, the way being rough and unpleasant, we were very weary, but got over Nuce River, and to the inhabitants of Capefare, to the house of one Henry Bradley, where the people were civil to us, the next day being the 7th of the month we got to the house of Jonathan Evans, and had a meeting, the day following, (being first day, of the week) at his house, to which came several people that seemed very raw, but after some time grew more solid, so that I believe truth was over them, from thence the next day to the house of Michael Blocker, which seemed to be to good satisfaction and went that evening over Capefare River, to the house of Richard Dunn, at Dunn's Creek, and tarried with friends there one day, the day following had a Meeting at their Meeting house, it being the 11th of the sd. mo. where truth went over opposition, altho we met with deep exercise with one John Crews, who had come from Pennsylvania, out of the unity of friends, but seeked to introduce himself as an Member and Minister, in them parts, we went that evening to the House of John Locks and had a Meeting there, the next day which was attended with a degree of Divine favor; from thence to the House of Edward Jones, and the next day had a Meeting at the house of John Upton, where truth was plentifully declared, and the people seemed to be well affected therewith, [...]

"The Journal of Thomas Nicholson," 174-175.

[...] <*1760.*><*5th mo.*>From [*illegible*] Quartly Meeting held in the Old Neck in the County of Perquimons it and 1st days of 5th and 6th months 1760.

It appears to this meeting by the petition of friends of Northampton Edge Comb and Hertford Counties. they the Inhabitance of Said Counties Called Quakers, Requested to have a Monthly Meeting Settled amongst them at their meeting at Rich Square in said County the first seventh day in each month and also a general first days meeting the day following which Said request of theirs is approved by this Meeting and accordingly granted and friends appoints Joseph Robinson Benjamin Wilson John Nixon Francis Toms to visit said friends upon the Setting Said meeting and make report to next Quartly Meeting.

Francis Nixon Clk.
of the Quartly Meeting

<6th mo.> <1760.> North Carolina.

At a Womens Monthly Meeting held at Rich Square Meeting house the 7th day of the 6th mo. 1760. After some time spent in Solemn worship the meeting proceeds to the proper Service thereof and in the first place appoints Mary Holowell clerk of Said Meeting and furthermore appoints Mary Knox and Elisabeth Hall of the above Said Meeting Overseers their being nothing further offered necessary to be minuted This Meeting concludes and adjourns till next in course.

<7th mo.><1760.> North Carolina.

At a Monthly Meeting held at Rich Square meeting house in Northampton County 5th day of 7th mo. 1760. This meeting appoints Mary Copeland wife of John and Rachel Copeland Overseers of the first day meeting Settled at John Copelands in Hertford County nothing further offered necessary to be minuted The meeting concludes and adjourns till the next in course.

<8th mo.><1760.> North Carolina.

At a Monthly Meeting held at Rich Square Meeting house in northampton County 2nd day of 8th mo. 1760. The Querys being read in this Meeting and was answered to pretty good Satisfaction friends appoints Eisabeth Hall Charity Peelle to attend the Quartly Meeting and represent the state of this meeting there being nothing further offered nesessary to be mintted this meeting concludes and adjourns till next in course.

<9th mo.><1760.> North Carolina.

At a Monthly Meeting held at Rich Square Meeting house in Northampton County 6th day of 9th mo. 1760. Ede Richardson requested to be taken under the care and notice of friends Mary Knox and Elisabeth Hall is appointed to visit the young woman and make report to the next

Monthly Meeting there being nothing further offered nesessary to be minuted this meeting conclude and adjourns till next in course.

<10 mo.><1760.> North Carolina.

At a Monthly Meeting held at Rich Square meeting house in Northampton County the 4th day of 10 mo. 1760. Ede Richardson requested last month by Meeting to be taken under friends care Mary Knox and Elisabeth Hall being appointed to visit her and make Report to the next Monthly Meeting found good Satisfaction nothing further offered needful to be recorded this meeting concludes and adjourns till next in course.

<11 mo.><1760.> North Carolina.

At a Monthly Meeting held at Rich Square Meeting house in Northampton County 1st day of 11 mo. 1760. Thomas Holowell and Mary Peelle published their intentions of taking each other in marriage the first time This meeting appoints Elisabeth Hall and Rachel Daughtry to inspect into the young woman's clearness and make report to nex meeting. The Querys was read in this meeting and answered to pretty good satisfaction friends appoints. Elisabeth Hall and Mary Knox to attend the Quartly Meeting nothing further offered needful to be recorded this meeting concludes and adjourns till next in course.

<12 mo.><1760.> At a Monthly Meeting held at Rich Square meeting house in Northampton County 4th day of 12 mo. 1760.

Elisabeth Hall and Mary Daughtry being appointed by last Monthly Meeting to enquire into Mary Peelles clearness in relation to marriage we finding her clear have had satisfaction therein Thomas Holowell and Mary Peelle appeared at this meeting and Desired an answer to their proposals last Monthly Meeting matters appearing clear they are left at liberty. This meeting appoints Rachel Daughtry and Rachel Copeland to attend the marriage of Mary Peell Thomas Holowell and make report to next meeting nothing further offering needful to be recorded this meeting concludes and adjourns untill the next in course.

<3rd mo.><1761.> North Carolina.

At a Monthly Meeting held at Rich Square meeting house in Northampton County 3rd day of 1st mo. 1761. Rachel Daughtry Rachel Copeland was appointed by last Monthly Meeting to attend the marriage of Thomas Holowell for good orders sake and make report to this meeting things was carried on decently and in good order nothing further offering needful to record this meeting concludes and adjourns un till next in course.

<2ond mo.><1761.> North Carolina.

At a Monthly Meeting held at Rich Square meeting house in Northampton County 7th day of 2ond mo. 1761. The querys were read in this meeting and answered to in some measure to pretty good Satisfaction this meeting appoints Elisabeth Hall and Mary Knox to attend the Quartly meeting and Represent the state of this meeting nothing further offered need ful to be recorded this meeting concludes and adjourns till the next in course.

Two months last we suppose by ansient Friends.

<11th mo.><1761.> North Carolina.

At a Monthly Meeting held at Rich Square meeting house in Northampton County 4th day of 4th mo. 1761. nothing offered needful to be recorded this meeting concludes and adjourns un till the next in Course.

<5th mo.><1761.>

At a Monthly Meeting held at Rich Square meeting house in Northampton County 2nd day of 5th month 1761.

It is the mind of this Meeting that Ede Richardson is in unity amongst friends Isaack Horn and Ede Richardson has published their intentions of takeing Each other in marriage first time this meeting appoints. Esther Ross and Mary Ross to inspect into the young womans clearness and make Report to next monthly meeting. This meeting appoints Ann Horn and Ester Ross Overseers of the first day meeting held at Tar River in Edge Comb County. Querys was read in this meeting and answered to pretty good Satisfaction this meeting appoints Mary Knox and Rachel Copeland to attend the Quartly meeting and represent the state of this meeting nothing further offered needful to record this meeting Concludes and adjourns till next in Course [...]

this meeting concludes and adjourns till next in course.

<6th mo.><1763.> At a Monthly Meeting held at Rich Square meeting house in Northampton County 4th day of 6th mo. 1763.

Nothing offered needful to be recorded this meeting concludes and adjourns till next in course.

<7th mo.><1763.> At our Monthly Meeting held at the Rich Square meeting house in Northampton County 2nd day of 7th mo. 1763.

It appeared in this meeting that Mary Copeland has acted in a Disagreeable maner Contrary to truth and friends appoints Narak Duke and Sarah Hall to heal with Mary Copeland and make their Report to next monthly meeting. Nothing offered needful to be recorded this meeting concludes and adjourn till next in course.

<8th mo.><1763.> At our Monthly Meeting held at the Rich Square meeting house in Northampton County the 7th day of 7 mo. 1763.

John Knox and Phariba Mathews appeared at this meeting and Declared their intentions of takeing Each other in marriaage and friends appoins Mary Knox and Sarah Hall to Inquire into Pharibas Mathews clearness in relation to marriage and make their report to next Monthly meeting the friends appointed by last Monthly Meeting to treat with Mary Copeland Report they had no full Satisfaction thererefore this meeting thinks it proper their care should be continued towards the said Mary Copeland the Querys wer called over to and answered to to Satisfaction this meeting appoint Sarah Duke and Elysabeth Bryant to attend the Quartly Meeting to Represent the State of this meeting nothing further offered needful to record this meeting Concludes and adjourns till next in course.

<9th mo.><1763.> At a Monthly Meeting held at the Rich Square meeting house in Northampton County 3rd day of 9th mo. 1763.

John Knox and Pharaba Mathews appeared at this meeting and Desired an answer to their former proposals matters appearing clear they are left at their Liberty to consumate their marriage. This meeting appoints Elizabeth Hall and Mary Peelle to attend the marriage and make their report to next Monthly meeting Josiah Brown son of Walter and Mary Brown Sarah Hall Daughter of Moris Hall both of this county both appeared at this meeting and Declared their intentions of takeing each other in marriage. This Meeting appoints Sarah Hall, and Christian Duke to enquire into Sarah Halls clearness in Relation to Marriage and make their report to next Monthly Meeting nothing further offered needful to record this Meeting concludes and adjourns till next in course.

<10th mo.> At our Monthly Meeting held at the Rich Square meeting house in Northampton County the 1st day of 10th mo. 1763.

The friends appointed last Monthly meeting to attend the marriage of John Knox Returned a satisfactory account to this meeting also Josiah Brown and Sarah Hall both appeared at this meeting desireing an answer to their proposals matters appearing clear they are left at their Liberty to consumate their marriage friends appoints Rachel Daughtry and Charity Peelle to attend the marriage of Josiah Brown and make their report to next Monthly Meeting nothing further offered needful to record this meeting concludes and adjourns till next in course.

<11th mo.><1763.> At our Monthly Meeting held at the Rich Square meeting house in Northampton County the 1st day of 11th mo. 1763 the friends appointed last Monthly Meeting to attend the marriage of Josiah Brown returned a satisfactory account to this meeting Sarah Hall and Rhoda Draper Produced Certificates from the monthly meeting held in the Isle of White County in Virginia Dated 25th day of the 9th mo. 1763. Signifying their being members in unity which certificates were read and approved by this meeting the Querys were called over and answered to tolerable Satisfaction [...]

> Minutes of the Women's Monthly Meeting, Rich Square, Northampton County, 1-4, 10-11, microfilm.

⋘⋙

Also numerous were the Baptists, who appeared early and in their various manifestations spread throughout the colony. Jonathan Thomas and others in Edgecombe sought a license for a meeting-house in 1759, and two years later Thomas obtained a license to preach. In 1760 John Winfield secured the right to preach in Hyde County. In 1772, the Reverend Morgan Edwards, one of the outstanding Baptist preachers in early America, compiled data to write the history of the Baptists in North Carolina. Included was a list of Baptist churches and ministers at the time.

On the Petition of Jno. Thomas and others, of the Profession of Anabaptist for Lycencing the Meeting House built by that Society on the Said Thomas's Land near Jonathan Thomas's, according to the Act of the Parliament of Great Brittain. It is Orderd, that the Same be Lycenced according to Law and the prayer of said Petition. [...]

Johnathan Thomas a Nonconformist Preacher produced an Ordination in Writing signed by George Graham and John Moore the Pastures of the Baptists ordaining and appointing him to forth and

Preach the Gospell according to the Tenet of that Church and he thereupon took the Oaths of Allegiance and Subscribed the Tests appointed for that Purpose.

> Minutes of Edgecombe County Court of Pleas and Quarter Sessions, September 1759; September 1761, State Archives.

John Winfield a Decenting Preacher appeared in Court and Subscribed the profession of his Christian faith in these, Words, I, John Winfield profess faith in god the father, and in Jesus Christ his Eternal son, the true god, and the holy Spirit of god Blessed for ever more, and I, acknowledge the holy Scripture of the Old and new Testament to be given by Divine Inspiration and took the Oaths, and Subscribed the Declaration and Declared his Approbation, and Subscribed the Articles of Religion in according to the Statute in that Case made and provided (Except the Several Articles in the said Statute Excepted).

Permission is hereby granted by the Court to John Winfield to preach the Gospel in a house belonging to the Anabaptists, Standing upon the Land of Robert Winfield on Jones's Creek, which is set apart to him for that purpose, [...]

> Minutes of the Hyde County Court of Pleas and Quarter Sessions, September 1760, State Archives.

APPENDIX I

Hitherto we have treated the norcarolina-baptists under several distinctions. In the following table the distinctions are dropped, and their present state exhibited in one point of view. The churches and ordained ministers in roman characters; the branch[46]es and unordained ministers in italic; the letters r, s, a, t, denote regular, arminian, separate, tunkers

Churches & branches	Ministers & assistants	When Constituted	From Newburn	Mem Fam
Hitchcock (r)	Henry Easterling	Mar. 28, 1772	200 WbS	14 28
Quehuky (r)	William Burgess	Dec. 11, 1755	120 NW	115 150
Tar-river-falls (r)	John Moore	Dec. 3, 1757	110 NW	64 100
Swifts-creek	*John Tanner*			
Fishing-creek (r)	William Walker	Dec. 6, 1755	150 NW	250 500
Benefields-creek				
Sandy-creek				
Gile's-creek				
Lower-fishing-creek (r)	Charles Daniel	Oct. 13, 1756	120 NW	74 350
Swifts-creek	*William Powell*			
Rocky-swamp				
Pasquotank (r)	Henry Abbot			172 300
	James Gamel			
Bartee (r)	James Abbington			
Tosneot (r)	Jonathan Thomas			
Tar-river (r)	Henry Ledbetter	Apr. 3, 1761		42 56
Flatriver				
Redbanks	Jeremy Ream			
Great-cohara (r)	Edward Brown			
Three-creeks (r)				
Bladen-county (r)	Steph. Hollingsworth			
Bear Creek (r)	George Graham			
Swifts-creek (r)	Joseph Willis			
Sa[p.47]ndy-creek (s)		Nov. 22, 1755	250 NW	14 40
	Tiden Lane			
	James Billingsley			
Little-river (s)		Sep. 9, 1760	270 SW	48 60
Rocky-river	*John Bullin*			
Jone's-creek	*Edmund Lilly*			
Mountain-run				
Shallowfords (s)	Joseph Morphy	1769	300 W	185 350
Forks of the Atkin	*David Allen*			
Mulberry-fields	John Cates			
	David Chapman			

New river (s)	Elnathan Davis	Oct. 1764	190	198
			WbS	310
Collins-mount	*Thomas Brown*			
Deepriver	*Nathaniel Powell*			
Tick-creek	*James Steward*			
Caraway-creek	*John Robins*			
Rocky-river	*Drury Sims*			
	George Williams			
Newriver (s)	Ezekiel Hunter			
Southwest (s)	Charles Markland			
Grassy-creek (s)	James Reed			
Lockwoods folly (s)	_____ Guess			
Trent (s)	James McDonald			
Catawba (t)	Sam. Saunders	1742		30 40
Atkin (t)	Conrad Kearn			29 40
Ewarrry (t)	Jacob Studeman			30 19
Contantony (a)	Joseph Parker			
Matchipungo (a)	Wm Fulsher			
Meherin (a)	Wm Parker			
Be[p.48]ar-river (a)	Wingfield			
Newse	Joshuah Herron			

Churches, 32. Ordained ministers, 30. Members, 3591. Families, 7950. Souls, (allowing 5 to a family) 39, 750.

G. W. Paschal, "Morgan Edwards's Materials," 394-395.

❦

The Scots and Scot-Irish brought the Presbyterian Church to North Carolina. So numerous and so adamant were Presbyterians in the backcountry that they proved too daunting for Anglican minister Andrew Morton.

The presbiterian Congregation of Catheys Settlement by their Elders and others have Signified and in open Court certified to the Justices thereof that they have built a Meeting-house in the Settlement aforesaid, called and Known by the name of the presbyterian Frame meeting house for the public Worship of God, according to the decsipline of the Church of Scotland, tis therefore Ordered by the Court,

That the said presbyterian Meeting House be deemd and held a public Licencesed Meeting-House; and that all those who shall hereafter meet therein shall be intituled to all the Immunities and privilidges, granted by the Several acts of Parliament in such Case made and Provided: and also that the above Certificate and this Order be Registered.

Minutes of the Rowan County Court of Pleas and Quarter Sessions, August 1770, State Archives.

Letter from Mr Andrew Morton to the Secretary.

NORTHAMPTON NORTH CAROLINA
August 25: 1766

REVEREND DOCTOR,

I wrote to you in June last informing you of my Journey to my new mission in Mecklenburgh County—From Newbern I pursued my Journey to Cape Fear where I received such Intelligence as discouraged me from proceeding any further—There I was well informed that the Inhabitants of Mecklenburg are entire dissenters of the most rigid kind—That they had a solemn leage and covenant teacher settled among them That they were in general greatly averse to the Church of England—and that they looked upon a law lately enacted in this province for the better establishment of the Church as oppressive as the Stamp Act and were determined to prevent its taking place there, by opposing the settlement of any Minister of the Church of England that might be sent amongst them—In short it was very evident that in Mecklenburg County I could be of little use to the honorable Society and I thought it but prudent to decline embroiling myself with an infatuated people to no purpose and trusting that the Venerable Society, upon a just representation of the matter would not be dissatisfied with my conduct.

Saunders, *Colonial Records,* 7:252-253.

Methodism appeared in North Carolina in the eve of the Revolution. The Reverend Joseph Pilmore, one of the first Methodist ministers to visit North Carolina, found a sympathetic audience in New Bern in 1772. Founder of the Methodist Church in the United States and famed circuit rider Francis Asbury first visited North Carolina in 1780, where he met an ambivalent reception.

Sat: 26. I had the honour of dining with Mr. Edwards, Secretary to the Governor, where I was treated with the highest respect; & in the evening, most of the genteel people in the Town attended the preaching, and all behaved as if they had long professed the Gospel! How different this, from the behaviour of the people in many parts of England: *there,* many of the genteel people dispise all *serious* religion—*here*, they honour and esteem it.

Sun: 27. Breakfasted with Coll. Cogdel, where everything was conducted in a truely genteel and Xtian manner; dined with Mrs. Smith, a Gentlewoman who is a friend to religion, and in the afternoon, had a very large congregation in the Court-house, and God gave me great freedom of mind to declare His whole consel, and preach the Gospel to all without respect of persons. Afterwards two gentlemen waited on me at my lodgings, and we spent the evening togither in the greatest harmony and delight.

Mon: 28. Breakfasted with Mr. Ellis, a merchant, in Newburn where I had much agreable conversation, and was exceedingly happy. At night we had the house crouded indeed, and the people were all attention while I explained and inforced the words of our Lord, "Be ye therefore ready", and the word had free course, and wrought effectually upon the minds of the people. Spent the rest of the evening with a Baptist Preacher, and concluded the day in praise and prayer.

Tues: 29. I wrote Letters to my dear friends in Philadelphia and N. York, with whom my heart is as closely united as ever, and I hope we shall never be divided in time or eternity. At night, I had the Court-house full again, and it was one of the stilest and most solemn congregations I ever preached to in Europe or America! Thus far the Lord has helped me, and I'll steadfastly trust him for all thats to come.

Wed: 30. Dined with Mr. Cornell, where I met with the greatest hosilitality and respects; at six in the evening, a great multitude attended to hear my last sermon for the present, and it was a time that will not soon be forgotten. My mind was quite at liberty, my heart was happy, and preaching was a delightful task, therefore I enlarged more than usual, and though we had most of the genteel people of the Town, I did not behold one trifler among them! In all my travels through the world, I have met with none like the people of Newburn! Instead of going to Balls and Assemblies as people of fashion in general do, especially at this season of the year, they came driving in their Coaches to hear the word of the Lord, and wait upon God in his ordinances! And their behaviour to me at the last was such as I cannot pass over in silence without the greatest ingratitutde. The morning I was to leave the Town two Gentlemen waited on me, and delivered me a Letter, in which several small Bills of North Carolina money were inclosed, which the Gentlemen had subscribed among themselves, and sent me as a token of their love and respect. Thus the Lord prepares my way before me, and all my wants are well supplied. I set off on this journey trusting in

Providence alone, and hitherto I have wanted nothing. O may I ever trust in God, and steadily follow the great Captain of my Salvation till my weary pilgrimage is past, and then praise him in the heaven of heavens for evermore.

Maser and Maas, *The Journal of Joseph Pilmore, Methodist Itinerant, For the Years August 1, 1769 to January 2, 1774*, 172-173.

Friday, 16. I crossed Roanoke (North Carolina), felt a little better, though weak. We rode near thirty miles, was like to faint in the carriage; but at brother Edward's felt refreshed, and ease from pain; slept well; blessed be God!

Saturday, 17. I am in peace, and much blest always when travelling. Preached at Jones's barn to about one hundred people; spoke on Heb. iv, 11-15; was weak, but spoke long. A few felt and understood. The unawakened appeared unmoved; my discourse was not for them. I think my immediate call is to the people of God: others seem in a hardened state; they have heard much, obeyed little. Went to Mrs. Yancy's an afflicted, distressed woman, sunk into rigid mortification, thinking she ought to fast excessively.

Sunday, 18. I rode fifteen miles to brother Bustion's, and preached to about five hundred people; was much led out on Isaiah lv, 6, 7. The people were solemnly attentive: I was tempted to think I had done well; but I opposed the devil and overcame him. Brother Dickins spoke on charity very sensibly, but his voice is gone; he reasons too much; is a man of great piety, great skill in learning, drinks in Greek and Latin swiftly; yet prays much, and walks close with God. He is a gloomy countryman of mine, and very diffident of himself. My health is recovered; thank the Lord. Thus he makes my strength sufficient for my day; glory to God!

Monday, 19. Rose about five o'clock, was a little disturbed in my rest with company. Brother Dickins drew the subscription for a Kingswood school in America; this was what came out a college in the subscription printed by Dr. Coke. Gabriel Long and brother Bustion were the first subscribers, which I hope will be for the glory of God and good of thousands. We set off in the rain, rode over Fishing Creek to Davis's, ten miles; I spoke on 1 Thess. i, 8, 9, had some light, but the people were very little moved; rode twelve miles to Gabriel Long's, through the woods. I hope John Dickins will ever after this be a friend to me and Methodism. My health is greatly restored; am blest among my friends.

Tuesday, 20. After an hour spent in prayer, private and in the family, I read a few chapters in the Bible; began reading Watt's first volume of Sermons; was pleased and profited. Preached at noon to fifty people, on Titus ii, 11-14, had some liberty among the people; they were very little affected—but the faithful, for whom I principally spoke, were tender; then rode over to Joseph John Williams's, a rich man of this world, and I hope sincere. I am kept through mercy.

Wednesday, 21. I had to ride alone better than twelve miles to Mr. Duke's; when I came there, found about thirty people, and they quite ignorant. After preaching I took dinner, and in talking found three or four of them tenderly serious; gave them advice: the man and his wife have had conviction, and have sinned it away. They say it was the disputes of the Baptists that turned them aside. I then rode home with Mr. Green, a Presbyterian; and was much blest in reading Watt's first volume of Sermons.

Thursday, 22. I rode to Jenkins's and spoke plainly to about eighty people, and found the word was fitted to their cases; met class; it was a day of peace to me; the Lord was with me at this poor, but good man's house. I was kept by the power of God; my soul is breathing after the Lord at all times. There is a hardness over the people here: they have had the Gospel preached by Presbyterians, Baptists, and Methodists; the two former appear to be too much in the spirit of the world; there is life amongst some of the Methodists, and they will grow because they preach growing doctrines. I heard of Mr. Hart, from Charleston, passing north, and one of the Countess of Huntingdon's men turning Baptist. They have soon turned about; but they may follow Mr. Whitefield in Calvinism.

Friday, 23. I have peace, the Lord is my portion; this was a day of fasting; I rode fifteen miles, preached, prayed, and sung near two hours; ate a little about four o'clock, and preached at Nutbush Creek chapel, (a little log-house, about twenty-five feet long and twenty wide,) to about one hundred and fifty people; here I found a broken society. Rode home with Dr. King; his wife was in society. I slept in peace, and rose about five o'clock: my heart is with God! Glory be to thee, O Lord! I had too mean an opinion of Carolina; it is a much better country, and the people live much better than I expected from the information given me.

Clark, *Journal and Letters of Francis Asbury*, 1:357-360.

The German migration to North Carolina brought Lutherans to the backcountry of the colony, some of whom appealed to Governor Tryon and the Anglican Church for assistance in securing a minister.

WHEREAS in the counties of Rowan, Orange, Mecklenburg and Tryon, situated in the province of North Carolina in America, are already settled near three thousand German protestant families, and being very fruitful in that healthy climate, are beside, vastly increasing by numbers of German protestants almost weekly arriving from Pennsylvania and other provinces of America; and having been hitherto without the means of grace, and being unable to maintain a learned and orthodox minister of their language and persuasion, whereby a great ignorance in the word of God and a melancholy dissoluteness of living has already prevailed , & will doubtless still more prevail,

In order that such an evil, which must provoke the Almighty God to anger and vengeance, may be effectually removed, near sixty German Lutheran protestant families have united themselves humbly to implore His Excellency TRYON, then Governor of the said province graciously to countenance, under the great seal of the province, that two of their members namely Christopher Layrle and Christopher Reintelmann are deputed by them humbly to beg of the protestant brethren and other friends to the Kingdom of Christ in England Holland Germany their benevolence and charity to enable them in supporting a learned and orthodox protestant minister, in order that the means of grace may be duly administered and the Kingdom of our blessed Lord Jesus Christ be likewise established and propagated among them.

His Excellency Governor Tryon has according to his known humanity countenanced their petition under the great seal of the province and referred the case to the Honorable Society for the propagation of the gospel in foreign parts, established in London; which society has likewise piously countenanced under their seal this undertaking as appears by the following copies.

A copy of his Excellency's recommendation.
NORTH CAROLINA.
BY HIS EXCELLENCY WILLIAM TRYON ESQUIRE HIS MAJESTY'S CAPTAIN GENERAL AND GOVERNOR IN CHIEF IN AND OVER THE SAID PROVINCE.
To all persons whom it may concern.

Whereas sixty German families of the Lutheran Church forming a settlement on the second bank [creek?] in Rowan County in this Province request of me to countenance their procuring a Minister and Schoolmaster in their own Language in the manner expressed in their memorial annexed, and such their intention and proposal being certified as laudable by the Revd. Mr. Drage Rector of St. Luke's Parish in the said County, as well as in Consideration of the loyal and prudent behavior of the Inhabitants of the settlement, I do by these Presents refer to the Bishop of London and to the Society for the propagation of the Gospel in foreign Parts the Consideration of the annexed Memorial, and recommend such charitable support as by them shall be thought necessary for carrying the said laudable purposes into Execution.

Given under my hand and the great seal of the said Province at Newbern the first day of February in the year of our Lord one thousand seven hundred and seventy one, and in the eleventh Year of his Majesty's reign.

Wm. TRYON (*Seal*)

By his Excellency's Command
  I. EDWARDS Priv. Sec.

Copy of the pious countenance of the Honorable Society for the propagation of the gospel in foreign parts.

At a General Meeting of the Society for Propagation of the Gospel in Foreign Parts held in Dean's Yard Westminster on Friday July 19th 1771, A Petition with a Testimonial thereunto annexed by his Excellency Governor Tryon From the German Settlers on Second Creek in Rowan County North Carolina having been laid before the Board

The Society did approve the pious & useful design therein contained, and declared that in case the proposed Subscription shall meet with success and such a sum shall be raised as shall afford a reasonable prospect of establishing a fund adequate to the permanent support of a Minister and Schoolmaster in the said settlement, They will contribute to such fund and give such encouragement thereto as corresponds with their ability and the Nature of their Institution.

D. BURTON (*Seal*)

By order of the Society
ABINGDON STREET, WESTR. July 19th, 1771.

Saunders, *Colonial Records*, 8:630-631.

[...] "The church service I try to make as solemn and as suitable to the occasion, but with all as simple, as possible. I can however not restrict my discourse to three quarters of an hour; for there are members of my congregations who often ride as far as 3 German miles (18 miles) to church, and furthermore there is only one service every four weeks in each church. Christenings take place after the sermon in presence of the entire congregation. When the Lords Supper is held on Sundays, the preparations for it occur on the preceding Fridays. Private confessions are unknown here. Public penance imposed by the church I have abolished. [...]

Report of Rev. Mr. Roschen, 1789, in Boyd and Krummel, "German Tracts," 247.

∞⟨⟩∞

Highly unusual among North Carolina sectaries was the Unitas Fratrum or Moravians, who established a communal society in the colony in the 1750s. Their industriousness and thrift as well as their piety impressed Carolinians and visitors alike, including Elkanah Watson. Also distinguishing the Moravians was their penchant for detailed record keeping, represented by this excerpt from the diary kept for the town of Bethabara in 1754.

[1786]. The moment I touched the boundary of the Moravians, I noticed a marked and most favorable change in the appearance of buildings and farms, and even the cattle seemed larger, and in better condition. Here in combined and well directed effort, all put shoulders to the wheel, which apparently moves on oily springs. We passed in our ride, New Garden, a settlement of Quakers from Nantucket: they too were exemplary and industrious. The generality of the planters in this State depend upon negro labor, and live scantily in a region of affluence. In the possessions of the Moravians and Quakers, all labor is performed by whites. Every farm looks neat and cheerful; the dwellings are tidy and well furnished, abounding in plenty.

In the evening I attended service in the Moravian chapel. This was a spacious room in a large edifice, adorned with that neat and simple elegance, which was a peculiar trait of these brethren and their Quaker neighbors. On our first entrance, only two or three persons were visible; but the moment the organ sounded, several doors were simultaneously opened. The men were ushered in on one side, and the women upon the other, and in one minute the seats were filled and the devotees arranged for worship. The devotions on that occasion, consisted merely in their chanting a melodious German anthem, accompanied by the organ.

In the morning, I was introduced to Mr. Bargee, their principal. He conducted me through all their manufactories, and communicated to me, with much intelligence, many facts in relation to the tenets and habits of this devout and laborious sect. Salem comprehended about forty dwellings, and occupies a pleasant situation. The founders of the establishment had emigrated from Bethlehem thirty years before. They purchased a tract of about 90,000 acres of excellent land, agreeably intersected by the head-waters of the Yadkin. The society embraced about 1,000 persons, occupying several villages, and scattered over their territory on good farms. Every house in Salem was supplied with water brought in conduits one mile and a half. In all respects, social, moral, and religious, they were identical with the brethren at Bethlehem, whom I have already described.

Watson, *Men and Times of the Revolution*, 255-256.

Jan. 1st. We arose with contentment. The strangers soon went on their way. This morning our cabin took fire, but it was discovered in time and extinguished. Had it started during the night it would probably have destroyed our house. Br. Kalberlahn scalded his foot with hot water. At noon we had a short service, and Br. Grube notified us that the Holy Communion would be celebrated this evening if nothing interfered. During the afternoon he spoke with each of the Brethren who were all found to be in an humble and contrite frame of mind. Toward evening Mr. Hampton and his son arrived, so we were again prevented from holding the Communion Service; we were very sorry, but could not help ourselves, as we have only the one small cabin, and cannot lodge anyone elsewhere. In the evening service we read the account of the Circumcision of Jesus; then commended our cabin once more to His protection, and laid ourselves down in trustful sleep.

Jan. 2. After morning prayers Mr. Hampton went home. The weather is again mild after several very cold days. The other strangers also left, and in the evening we had Lovefeast, followed by the Communion; the Lamb of God, slain for our sakes, seemed very near, and again laid His blessing upon His humble followers in North Carolina. Then once more we sought our resting places.

Jan. 3. On rising we sang a hymn that touched our hearts; then each went to his work. Several Brethren built a stable, others rived clapboards, others prepared for drawing maple sap, etc. In the evening we began to read the small Hymn Book, and will continue it each evening. Br. Grube held the singstunde and evening prayers; then we lay down to rest.

Jan. 4. Br. Loesch held morning prayers. Two Brethren continued preparations for tapping the maple trees, so that we may make vinegar and some molasses for use in Lovefeast. At noon a man came wishing to sell us corn, but as we are out of money we can buy nothing more. At night we had singstunde and evening prayers.

Jan. 5. We arose well and in good spirits. It began to rain heavily. Two of the Brethren went a mile away to dig a wolf-pit. Today we boiled some maple sugar. In the evening we had a Lovefeast, which we enjoyed, and began to read the report of the Single Brothers Synod. Then we had singstunde and evening prayers.

Jan. 6. Sunday. In the morning we prayed the Church Litany. It rained hard all night, and our cabin leaked. At noon we read one of Count Zinzendorf's sermons. During the afternoon our Bands met in sweet companionship. In the evening we read more about the Single Brothers Synod; then commended ourselves for this night to Jesus, and lay down to rest.

Jan. 7. After morning prayers the Brethren began again to clear ground. The creek that runs by our house is so high that most of the bottom is under water. Br. Kalberlahn had to stay in bed on account of his foot, which he recently scalded. In the afternoon a place for a small dwelling house was staked off near the spring. In the evening we again read from the record of the Single Brethren's Synod, then had singstunde and evening prayers. Br. Feldhausen shot a deer by moon-light near our house.

Jan. 8. Br. Loesch conducted morning prayers. The Brethren began to fell trees for logs for our new house. Br. Petersen was badly hurt as he and Br. Beroth cut down a tree. As the tree fell a branch caught in another tree, then stuck Br. Petersen on the head, making an ugly wound and throwing him to the ground. The Brethren ran to his assistance but found him senseless and they feared he was dead. One ran to the cabin with the news, and everybody, including Br. Kalberlahn, hurried thither. Br. Kalberlahn bled him, and he soon recovered his senses, then we carried him home and Br. Kalberlahn bound up the wound. We all pitied Br. Petersen, and Br. Kalberlahn again suffered great pain in his foot, and so there were two patients in our little cabin. In the evening we had a short singstunde, then lay down to rest.

Jan. 9. After morning prayers Br. Kalberlahn dressed Br. Petersen's injured head, which pains him greatly. The skull does not appear to be fractured, and we hope he will soon recover. At noon we sang a short liturgy. During the afternoon two Englishmen appeared and asked to spend the night with us. It is very inconvenient for us to entertain strangers for our space is small, and we have nothing for them to sleep on. Otherwise we were all in good spirits today.

Jan. 10. After morning prayers two of the Brethren went to the bottom a mile away to clear a place for a meadow. In the afternoon an Englishman from the Etkin came, bringing several skins from which he wished to have two pairs of breeches made. Br. Petersen is still very weak, but accepted the job in the hope that the Saviour would soon restore his health. In the evening we had singstunde, then lay down to our rest.

Jan. 11. After morning prayers John Williams returned to his home seven miles away. In the afternoon it rained. Evening we read from the Single Brothers Synod record, then had singstunde and evening prayers.

Jan. 12. It has been unusually warm recently. Br. Lung was sick. Br. Petersen's head and Br. Kalberlahn's foot are improving. In the morning it rained; the Brethren fenced in our new garden. It was a real spring day. In the evening we had Lovefeast, and read from the new Hymn Book, and refreshed our souls. We also conferred together and decided not to build the new house just yet, as there was so much work to be done in preparing land for corn. Meanwhile we will content ourselves in the little cabin. After Lovefeast we had evening prayers, then lay down to rest.

Jan. 13, Sunday. We had morning prayers as usual. Br. Lung was quite ill last night, and several others are complaining. After the noon liturgy Br. Loesch went to Mr. Haltem's to see about various things. In the afternoon Br. Grube conducted the Band meetings; we thought much of our dear Bethlehem, and especially of the Brn. Gottlob and Nathanael, who should have reached home by this time. It was a very warm day, almost like summer time. Br. Grube held the evening services, and commended us to the Saviour's care.

Jan. 14. Several Brethren are not well. Two went half a mile from here to dig a wolf pit; there are many wolves about and our cattle are in danger. Br. Loesch returned at noon.

Jan. 15. The Brethren cut wood for a new fence.

Jan. 16. The same.

Jan. 17. After morning prayers Herman and Merkli went to Mr. Haltem's to buy meal and corn and

Jan. 18. they came back. Mr. Haltem's son came with them on a visit.

Jan. 19. All are well and happy today. After morning prayers most of the Brethren went to cut wood and split rails. Mr. Haltem's son went home. In the evening Mr. Jung and the younger Guest from Dan River arrived, and spent the night with us.

Jan. 20. Sunday. In the early morning we prayed the Church litany. After breakfast the two strangers went their way toward the Etkin. Evening we had Lovefeast, and read a good deal from the new Hymn Book; then had our Choir liturgy, and closing the day peacefully went to rest.

Jan. 21. After morning prayers the Brethren continued cutting wood and splitting rails. The two strangers who were here yesterday returned, and Mr. Haltem with them, and all three stayed over night. Our sleeping quarters are so small that there was not place enough for everybody. In the evening we had a English song service.

Jan. 22. After breakfast the Brethren continued their work. At noon Mr. Haltem and the two other men went home.

Jan. 23. Br. Loesch held morning prayers. After breakfast most of the Brethren went to clear the meadow; and in the afternoon some split rails and others felled trees for the mill. In the evening we read again from the record of the Single Brothers Synod, then had singstunde.

Jan. 24. After morning prayers the Brethren went contentedly to their work. After the noon liturgy Br. Herman went eight miles to order certain things from David Stuart. Two men from Dan River arrived and spent the night. The one came to have the doctor cure his leg.

Jan. 25. All are well and happy today. After morning prayers the two Englishmen left. At noon we sang a liturgy. Afternoon Br. Herman returned; Br. Loesch ran the line for the fence. Br. Loesch held the singstunde and evening prayers.

Jan. 26. At the close of the morning service Br. Grube announced Communion for this evening. In the afternoon he spoke with the Brethren who all expressed a longing to partake of the Lord's Supper. In the evening we had Lovefeast, and an unusually blessed Communion.

Jan. 27. Sunday. Our Saviour was near us in our morning prayers. The rest of the day we spent quietly together. It was like a beautiful summer day. In the evening we read some of Christel's hymns, sang the "Te Pleuram," and so closed the day in peace.

Jan. 28. After morning prayers the Brethren went to work; some split rails, others built the new fence. At noon was the usual liturgy.

Jan. 29. During the morning two men from the Meho River came to consult the doctor about a patient. One of them so urgently begged Br. Kalberlahn to go with them that we decided to send him, but the horses could not be found, so he could not go. In the evening two Englishmen came from Deep River, five miles south-east of our line, and spent the night.

Jan. 30. Several Brethren went out very early to search for the horses. After morning prayers the two strangers went on toward the Pilot Mountain. About nine o'clock the Brethren brought in the horses; Br. Kalberlahn prepared for his journey and set out to see the patient on the Meho, accompanied by Br. Herman. It was unusually beautiful, summerlike weather. In the afternoon Isaac Ferry came with two men from the Etkin, to take the doctor to see his sick wife; one of the others brought work to our tailor. They remained over night.

Jan. 31. After breakfast the strangers returned home. The Brethren were busy cutting wood and splitting rails. Evening we had singstunde.

Fries, *Records of the Moravians,* 1:89-93.

Roman Catholics were few in North Carolina, and their number was reduced by one in 1752, when Daniel Johnston was executed for counterfeiting.

NEWBERN, October 20.

On Monday last were executed at the Gallows near this Town, pursuant to their Sentence, Daniel Johnston, alias Dixon, William Jillet, and David Smith, alias Griffith (see *Gaz.* No. 92.) They were attended to the Gallows by the Rev. Mr. Lapierre, who also attended them while in Goal. They all appeared very penitent, and express'd much Sorrow and Condition for their Crimes, which they confess'd ; and Jillett and Johnston declar'd Patrick Moor to have been the sole Constriver and Promoter of the wretched Scheme, for which they suffer'd, and which would have been so destructive to the Community, had it succeeded. Johnston died a stanch Roman Catholick, and was very earnest and pathetic in his Prayers for the Friends and Followers of the Lords Lovat, Kilmarnock, Balmerino, and all the Rebels that suffer'd in the late Rebellion, and heartily pray'd for a Continuance of that noble Spirit, which he hop'd was yet alive in Scotland among the Well-wishers of the Pretender.

Virginia Gazette (Williamsburg), November 10, 1752.

Itinerant ministers often visited North Carolina. Among them was George Whitefield, famed evangelist whose preaching sparked the Great Awakening. Whitefield passed through the colony in 1740 on his first tour of America, dining with James Murray in the Lower Cape Fear. Returning to North Carolina in 1764 and 1765 on his sixth and last visit to America, Whitefield as always was well received.

NORTH CAROLINA.

Wednesday, Dec. 19. Finding myself somewhat stronger, and the horse also being in better order, we took a short day's journey of about twenty-six miles, and were most affectionately received by Colonel O____n, in North Carolina. A little while after our coming in, I begged leave to lie down to rest my weary limbs. In some way or other, in my absence, my friends acquainted our host who I was; upon which he was so rejoiced that he could not tell how to express his satisfaction. His wife also seemed most anxious to oblige, and they were only concerned that they could do no more for us. The honest old man told us, that his son-in-law, who lived about three miles off, ever since he heard of me in the *News*, wished that I would come thither. This is not the first time, by many, that I have found the advantage of things my adversaries have inserted in the public papers: they do but excite people's curiosity, and serve to raise their attention, while men of seriousness and candour naturally infer that some good must be doing where such stories and falsities are invented. It often gives me unspeakable comfort, to see how wisely God overrules everything for the good of His Church. [...]

Saturday, Dec. 29. Thought proper to rest to-day for the ease of our beasts. Had another opportunity of writing some letters to England. Dined with Mr. Murray, the naval officer, who gave us an invitation last night to his house, and spent the remainder of the day in writing down some things that lay upon my heart. Sanctify them, O Lord, to the promoting Thy glory, and the good of mankind.

Sunday, Dec. 30. Wrote more letters to my friends in England. Read prayers, and preached, both morning and evening, in the Court House, to as many as could be expected at so short a warning. There being many of the Scotch among the congregation, who lately came over to settle in North Carolina, I was led in the afternoon to make a particular application to them, and to remind them of the necessity of living holy lives, that so they might prove a blessing to the province, and giving proof of their zeal for those truths which they had heard preached to them, with great purity and clearness, in their native country. [...]

George Whitefield's Journals (1737-1741), 370-371, 377-378.

JAMES MURRAY TO THE REV. GEORGE WHITEFIELD.

WILMINGTON, CAPE FEAR, JUNE 24th, 1740.

DR. SIR...I heartily thank you for the two barrels flower that you were so kind to Send Me, & the sermons &c with the good advice you give me along with them is very Obliging, & Confirms Me in the Opinion I have always had of you Since I had the hapiness of you acquaintance that you are Sincere disinterested & indefatigable in promoting true Religion, —Christianity. Your Sermons here had (as we have reason to believe) a good Effect on Several of your hearers, & the accot of them made many others sorry they were absent.

As the great aim of your life is to do good by propagating the Gospel, it is the opinion of many People of good sence that there is Not a Province in America where your preaching is So Much wanted as in this.

May therefore hope you'll persist in your first resolution of Staying Sometime among us in your way from the nor'ward.

Tiffany, *Letters of James Murray*, 66.

NEWBERN, *November* 23.

On Friday last, the Revd. Mr. *Whitefield* arrived here, from the Northward, in his Way to *Georgia*. At the Request of the Gentlemen of this Town, he stayed here till Sunday last, and preached a most excellent Sermon in our Church, to a very numerous and crouded Audience; Persons of all Ranks who had Notice of his preaching, flocking to hear him. In the Afternoon he left us, and set out on his Journey to *Georgia*.

North-Carolina Magazine; or, *Universal Intelligencer*, November 23, 1764.

We have been favored with another Sermon from the Reverend Mr Whitefield since my last. He arrived here on his return from the Southern Provinces on Thursday evening in Passion Week and as I was very sensible that the People were very desirous to hear him I waited upon him and offered him the reading desk and Pulpit on Good Friday which he thought proper to refuse on account of his Asthma but accepted of the pulpit on Easter Sunday—Several that had been tinctured with the principles of Methodism came a great many miles to hear him, but had the mortification to hear both their principles and practice in general condemned. For his Sermon, the very digressive was clear of enthusiastic Rant and really a good one the substance of it contradictory to some of their principal Tenets and particularly severe against a vile prejudice to which they were very much addicted vizt of making their religion a mere Cloak as pretext for their indolence and sloth. As his name had been frequently made use of here to countenance the principle and practice of an Idle dissolute and disorderly Sect, against which some part of his discourse was particularly levelled—I must say his preaching had been of infinite service and I should be glad

269

to see him more frequently provided he would always preach in the same strain.

> Rev. James Reed to the Secretary, July 10, 1765, Saunders, *Colonial Records*, 7:97-98.

∽⟨ఋ⟩⤳

Legislation attempted to reinforce the influence of Whitefield and combat immorality in the colony, and governors sought to add their influence, but many remained unmoved.

An Act for the better Observation and keeping of the Lord's Day, commonly called Sunday; and for the more effectual Suppression of Vice and Immorality.

I. Whereas in well regulated Governments, effectual Care is always taken that the Day set apart for Publick Worship, be observed and kept holy, and to suppress Vice and Immorality: Wherefore,

II. We pray that it may be Enacted, And be it Enacted, by his Excellency Gabriel Johnston, Esq., Governor, by and with the Advice and Consent of his Majesty's Council, and General Assembly of this Province, and it is hereby Enacted, by the Authority of the same, That all and every Person and Persons whatsoever shall, on the Lord's Day, commonly Called Sunday, carefully apply themselves to the Duties of Religion and Piety and that no Tradesman, Artificer, Planter, Labourer, or other Person whatsoever, shall, upon the Land or Water, do or exercise any Labour, Business or Work, of their ordinary Callings (Works of Necessity and Charity only excepted), nor employ themselves either in hunting, fishing, or fowling, or Use any Game, Sport, or Play on the Lord's Day aforesaid, or any Part thereof, upon Pain that every Person so Offending, being of the Age of Fourteen Years and upwards, shall forfeit and pay the Sum of Ten Shillings, Proclamation Money.

III. And be it further Enacted, by the Authority aforesaid, That if any Person or Persons shall prophanely swear or Curse, in the Hearing of any Justice of the Peace, or shall be convicted of prophanely swearing and cursing, by the Oath of one or more Witness or Witnesses, or confession of the Party before any Justice or Justices of the Peace, every such Offender shall forfeit and pay the sum of Two Shillings and Six Pence, of the like Money, for every oath or curse. And if any Person, executing any Public Office, shall prophanely swear or curse, being first convicted, as aforesaid, such Person shall forfeit and pay the Sum of Five Shillings, of the like Money, for each and every Oath or Curse.

IV. And be it further Enacted, That if any Person or Persons shall prophanely swear or curse, in the Presence of any Court of Record in this

Government, such Offender or Offenders shall immediately pay the Sum of Ten Shillings, of the like Money, for each and every Oath or Curse; to be deposited in the Hands of the Chairman of the said Court, and by him accounted for and paid, as hereinafter is directed; or to sit in the Stocks, not exceeding three Hours, by order of such Court.

V. And be it further Enacted, by the Authority aforesaid, That every Person convicted of Drunkenness, by View of any Justice of the Peace, Confession of the Party, or Oath of one or more Witness or Witnesses, such Person so convicted shall, if such Offence was committed on the Lord's Day, forfeit and pay the Sum of Five Shillings, of the like Money; but if on any other Day, the Sum of Two Shillings and Six Pence, for each and every such Offence.

VI. And for the better Execution of all and every of the foregoing Orders, Be it further Enacted, That all and every Justice and Justices of the Peace, within his or their respective County, shall have full Power and Authority to convene before him or them, any Person or Persons who shall Offend in any of the Particulars before mentioned, in his or their Hearing, or on other legal conviction of any such Offence, and to impose the said Fine or Penalty for the same, and to restrain or commit the offender until it is satisfied, or to cause the same to be levied by Distress and Sale of the Offender's Goods, returning the Overplus, if any, to the Owner: And in Case such Offender be unable to satisfy such Fine, to cause him to be put in the Stocks, not exceeding Three Hours.

VII. Provided always, That all Information against the aforesaid Offences shall be made within Ten Days after such Offence or Offences committed, and not after.

VIII. And be it further Enacted, by the Authority aforesaid, That all Fines accruing and becoming due by Virtue of this Act, shall be levied as soon as may be after Conviction, One Half to the Informer, the other Half to the Use of the Parish where such Offence shall be committed; and the Chairman and Justices of the several Courts of the several Counties of this Province, are hereby directed to account for, upon Oath, and pay such Fine or Fines as shall or may by them or any of them, be received, by Virtue of this Act, to the Church Wardens of the respective Parishes of this Governmend, at least once a Year, when they same shall be demanded by the Church Wardens; under the Penalty of paying the Sum of Twenty Pounds, Proclamation Money, for every Refusal, to be levied and applied as aforesaid.

IX. And be it further Enacted, by the Authority aforesaid, That if any Persons commit Fornication, upon due conviction, each of them shall forfeit and pay Twenty Five Shillings, Proclamation Money, for each and every such Offence; to be recovered and applied to the same Use as the other Fines in this Act.

X. And be it further Enacted, That any two Justices of the Peace, upon their own knowledge, or Information made to them, that any single Woman within this County is big with Child, or delivered of a Child or Children, may cause such Woman to be brought before them, and examine her, upon Oath, concerning the Father; and if she shall refuse to declare the Father, she shall pay the Fines in this Act before mentioned, and give sufficient Security to keep such Child or Children from being chargeable to the Parish, or shall be committed to Prison, until she shall declare the same, or pay the Fine aforesaid, and give Security as aforesaid. But in Case such Woman shall, upon Oath, before the said Justices, accuse any Man of being the Father of a Bastard Child or Children, begotten of her Body, such Person so accused shall be adjudged the reputed Father of such Child or Children, and stand Charged with the Maintenance of the same, as the County Court shall Order, and give Security to the Justices of the said Court to perform the said Order, and to indemnify the Parish where such Child or Children shall be born, free from Charges for his, or her, or their Maintenance, and may be committed to Prison until he find Securities for the same, if such Security is not by the Woman before given.

XI. And be it further Enacted, That the Two said Justices of the Peace, at their Discretion, may bind, to the next County Court, him that is charged on Oath, as aforesaid, to have begotten a Bastard Child, which shall not be then born, and the County Court May continue such Person upon Security until the Woman shall be delivered, that he may be forthcoming when the Child is born.

XII. And be it further Enacted, by the Authority aforesaid, That this Act shall be Publicly read, Two several Times in the Year, in all Parish Churches and Chappels, or for want of such, in the Place where Divine Service is performed in every Parish within this Government, by the Minister, Clerk or Reader of each Parish, immediately after Divine Service; that is to say, on the First or Second Sunday in April, and on the First or Second Sunday in September, under the Penalty of Twenty Shillings, Proclamation Money, for every such Omission or neglect; to be levied by a Warrant from a Justice, and applied to the Use of the Parish where the Offence shall be committed; and the Church Wardens of every parish are hereby required to provide a Copy of this Act, at the Charge of the Parish.

XIII. Provided always, That nothing herein contained shall be construed to exempt any Clergyman within this Government, who shall be guilty of any of the Crimes hereinbefore mentioned, from such further Punishment as might have been inflicted on him for the same, before the making of this Act; any Thing herein contained to the contrary notwithstanding.

Laws, 1741, in Clark, *State Records*, 23:173-175.

PROCLAMATION AGAINST DRUNKENNESS, SWEARING AND CURSING

North Carolina Ss   Govr Martin
      By his Excelly Josiah Martin Esq &ca—
           A Proclamation
     Whereas it is an indispensible duty above all Beings to promote the Honor and service of Almighty God; and to discourage and suppress all Vice profaneness Debauchery & immorality, which are a reproach to religion & Government, and have a fatal Tendency to the Corruption of mankind. And whereas nothing can so effectually engage the Divine Blessing as a strict Observance of the Duties enjoined by religion, in which our most Gracious Sovereign is an illustrious Example to all his people. And that it is most truly pleasing to his Royal Mind to see religion Piety & Good manners flourish and extend over all His Dominions; I have in Consideration thereof, and by and with the advice & Consent of His Majesty's Council thought fit to issue this my Proclamation hereby enjoining all Persons in authority to give all possible encouragement to religion and Virtue, as well by their own Examples as by their Countenance to all orderly and Well disposed persons, and their utmost discouragement & restraint of the profane disorderly and Licentious of all denominations. And I do hereby strictly Charge and Command, All his Majesty's Judges, Sheriffs, Justices of the Peace, and all others whom it may Concern within this Province to be Vigilant & strict in the Discovery and the effectual prosecution and Punishment of all persons who shall be guilty of Drunkenness Blasphemy, profane Swearing & Cursing, Lewdness Profanation of the Lords Day or other Dissolute immoral or disorderly Practices. And that they take Care to put in Execution all Laws now in force in this Province for the Punishing and Suppressing Vice and Irreligion.
     Given under my hand &c at Newbern, Augt 30, 1771
                JOSIAH MARTIN
God save the King

Corbitt, "Historical Notes," 314.

ORDERED, That the Constables of the said Town, do in Turn, walk the Streets on Sundays, near the place of Worship, during the time of Divine service, and take up or disperse all such persons who are Noisy, Riotous, or whose conduct may tend to disturb those assembled on that Solemn Occasion.

> Lennon and Kellum, *Wilmington Town Book*, January 22, 1772, 200.

However, in one respect I find a pretty near resemblance between the two Colonies: I mean the state of religion. At a low ebb indeed in both provinces. 'T is certainly high time to repeal the laws relative to religion and the observation of the Sabbath, or to see them better executed. 'T is certainly to the last degree false politicks to have laws in force, which the legislators, judges, and executive officers not only break themselves, but practically and too often openly and avowedly deride. Avowed impunity all offenders is one sign at least that the law wants amendment or abrogation.

> Howe, "The Southern Journal of Josiah Quincy, Junior, 1773," 462-463. The "two colonies" referred to by the author are North and South Carolina.

⋞⋟

Adultery, fornication, and worse were too prevalent.

Information being formerly made by Joseph Wickar Esqr. against Jackub Johnston for Liveing in adultry with Ann Johnston which information appearing to be true it's ordered that they no more Cohabit or live together under the penalty of fifty pounds to be levied on the Estates of the Said Jackub and Ann on breach of the aforesaid Order.

> Minutes of the Carteret County Court of Pleas and Quarter Sessions, March 1727/28, State Archives.

Mr. Justice Harrell Returned to this Court Timothy Ryalls Bond for bringing before this Court Mary Musick who lives with the said Timothy and is Bigg with Child and the said Mary appearing Confest <*she was with Child but Designd to father to Discover the father It is thereupon Considered and Ordered that the said Mary Musick Do stand Committed*> that she was Bigg with Child and That Timothy Ryall begott of her Body the said Child whereof she is now Pregnant. It is thereupon Considered and Ordered that the said Timothy Do give Bond in the Sum of £25 Ster. to [*illegible*] the Church warden [*illegible*] of Society Parish from maintaining the said Child And that he pay the Fine of Five Pounds (he being a Marryed Man) for Adultery and that the said Mary Do pay the Sum of fifty shillings for Fornication or stand Comitted and pay Costs and accordingly the said Timothy and Mary in Open Court paid their fines which was Delivered to Mr. Harrell one of the Churchwardens of Society Parish. And accordingly the said Timo. became bound of the Sum of £25 etc.

Minutes of the Bertie County Court of Pleas and Quarter Sessions, November 1731, State Archives.

July 12 [1783]. At ten o'clock in the morning I parted from all my friends in Newbern and, crossing the river Trent on the ferry, took the road to Beaufort. At two o'clock in the afternoon I arrived at the Allways Inn, twenty-three miles from Newbern. The road is quite good, as they generally are in this region, the ground being hard, gravelly, and level everywhere, but the happenstance of much rain in the previous days resulted in all the wooden bridges being destroyed and it was with much effort that I continued the trip, for I had to do without the horses and sulky. This was just a little bit tiring, but a moderate and clean meal and the company of Comfort and Constance, daughters of the innkeeper, fifteen to eighteen years old and very good looking, soon made me forget the excursion. That evening there was a good supper and better conversation with the girls; after all had retired for the night, one had no embarrassment in coming at my request to continue the conversation in my bed.

Miranda, *The New Democracy in America*, 10-11.

North Carolina Bertie County. ss. George the Third by the Grace of God King of Great Britain etc.
(Seal) To the Sheriff of our said County Greeting
We Command you (as before to take the Body of Margaret Asbell)...(if to be found in your Bailiwick) And her safely keep so that you have her before our Justices at our next Inferior Court of Pleas and Quarter Session to be holden for said County at the Court House thereof on the Second Tuesday in October next then and there to Answer unto us by our Attorney General on a Certain Presentment made by the Grand Inquest for the Body of our said County for Repeated Bastard Getting Herein fail not And have there this Writ.

Witness Benjamin Wynns Clark of our said Court at Bertie the xvith day of July Anno Domini. MDCCLXI in the 1st year of our Reign.

Benjn. Wynns

Clerk Court

Bertie County, Criminal Papers, 1734-1780, State Archives.

Iyaquin March 3d 1773.

Dr. Sir,

I am sorry to address You on the present Occasion but Justice and my regard to You and all my Friends in and near Halifax make it appear indispensable lest You should continue your hospitable Attention to a Villain, whom I unfortunately introduced to Your Acquaintance. Without farther preface I proceed to inform You that while I was absent at Newburn my Brother (sorry I am to call him such) laid Schemes for seducing Mrs. Burke. I am sure this astonishes You—how much will You be effected when I tell You he came into her Bed Chamber in the dead of Night stript to his Shirt and endeavoured to get to Bed to Her, fortunately he was discovered by a young Girl who slept with Mrs. Burke time enough to alarm her and by this means alone, I suppose, escaped forcible Violation.

He began his villainous Enterprises by endeavouring to persuade Mrs. Burke that I was jealous of her, treasured up several little Incidents which were the result merely of good humoured chat between her and me, and endeavoured to pervert them into Symptoms of the strongest Suspicion finding these not strong enough he added many from Invention but still without Success. Mrs. Burke had too strong a Conviction of the contrary. She well knew my Opinion of her Honor and delicacy as well as of her affection for Me, would not admit of the slightest Suspicions to her Prejudice, finding this ineffectual he endeavoured to debauch her principles and recommended to her the example of Persons of Rank in England and flatly proposed what he called an Amour, this Insolence was warmly resented, and he was strictly commanded to avoid all such Liberties and Mrs. Burke used every means to avoid him that her Situation would allow, his Instrusions however gave her [vilest] pain, and in this distressed Situation She remained without A Friend to counsel or assist her, and impatiently waiting my Return At length he proceeded to the Act of Rudeness which I first mentioned, which You will easily believe threw her into Agonies.

She now resolved on quitting her own house, and taking shelter with You, and sent for Mr. Johnston that he might lend her his

Assistance and advise, he persuaded her to wait a few days and probably I should return. I came Sir and relieved her from her distress, had I longer remained at Newbern You would probably have been troubled with a more early Visit than we at parting expected. When he found his Devilish purposes every way frustrated, and that it became too probable I should hear of his baseness, he took the vilest methods to frighten her into a concealment such as, alledging several things he had heard her say, that he had it in his Power to ruin her Reputation, and that he would be credited in whatever he should alledge against Her together with much unmanly Artifice of the same Kind. But this Behaviour was far from succeeding. Mrs. Burke with the boldness and Wisdom of Innocence (for surely Innocence is always wise) Immediately made Mr. Saunders Copy the part of his Letter to her containing these Calumnies and question him particularly with regard to them, to this he returned a Letter Recanting and expressing Penitence, still begging her to conceal the Affair from Me and requesting her rather to take her Revenge into her own hands and to dispatch him with a loaded Pistol. But I have troubled You too long on this disagreable Subject. My Intention was to prevent Your entertaining him as You allways did, like the Brother of Me which You regarded As I flatter myself you do Me. This Sir is dictated by a principle of Justice independent of Revenge, tho' I cannot think even the latter could be blamed. The Offence would be heinous in an Acquaintance to whose care I had entrusted my house and Family in my Absence, it becomes doubly so in so near a relation, but surely Sir the Guilt is beyond measure when it is considered he owed Me every kind of Obligation. That I reliesed him from the lowest distress and placed him in the Rank and Condition of a Gentleman, Opened my House and my Bosom to him without Reserve shared with him whatever followed from my Industry with no sparing hand, used all the little Credit and Interest I possessed entirely for his Advantage And at the very Time when he was endeavouring to do me an Irreperable Injury, I had even been successfully employed in laying the foundation of his future Fortune. Yet Sir, I do not publish his Villainy through Revenge but I cannot bear that my Friends through Regard for Me should be betrayed into Acts of Kindness to such a Man. When I listen to Revenge I am tempted to take one of a different Kind but after I withdrew my Protection and Countenance from him he becomes very contemptible.

Mrs. Burke prays the Ladies of Your good Family will accept of her best Compliments Give Me leave to join Mine. And to Subscribe Myself with all possible Respect Your etc.

Colonel Alexr. McCulloch

[Thomas Burke] to Alexander McCulloch, March 3, 1773, Thomas
Burke Papers, Letterbook, State Archives.

&⫞&

**Interracial relations, though legally prohibited, surfaced both in the
form of marriage and in longstanding, nonmarital relationships. At the
same time, white slaveowners took advantage of their female bondser-
vants.**

An Act for an additional Tax on all free Negroes, Mulattoes,
Mustees, and such Persons, Male and Female, as now are, or hereafter
shall be, intermarried with any such Persons, resident in this Government.

I. Whereas Complaints have been made by divers Freeholders and
other Inhabitants of this Government, of great Numbers of Free
Negroes, Mulattoes, and other Persons of mixt Blood, that have lately
removed themselves into this Government, and that several of them
have intermarried with the white Inhabitants of this Province; in
Contempt of the Acts and Laws in those Cases made and provided: [...]

III. And be it further Enacted, by the Authority aforesaid, That from
and after the Ratification of this Act, any White Person or Persons
whatsoever, Male or Female, Inhabitant of this Government, or that
may or shall remove themselves hither from other Parts, that now is,
or hereafter shall be, married with any Negro, Mulatto, Mustee, or other
Person being of mixed Blood, as aforesaid, shall be, and are hereby made
liable to the same Levies and Taxes, as the Negroes, Mulattoes, or other
mixed Blood, as herein above is expresed; [...]

Laws, 1723, in Clark, *State Records*, 23:106.

[...] George Cummins Came into Open Court and made Information that a Servant Woman Named Christian Finney was on the 5th day
of November 1735 last past was brought to Bed of a Mulatto [...]

Ordered that Cary Godbe be Sommoned to Appear to the Next
Court to make Answer to such things as Shall be part to him by this
Court Concerning Xtian. Finny Cohabitenc with a Negro belonging
unto the said Godbe. [...]

This Court Mett According to Adjournment Capt. Cary Godbe hath
produced a Mulatto Boy born of Christian Finny and it appears that
said Child was born the 15th July 1739 and this Court hath ordered that
said Boy Serve the said Godbe until he Arrive to the Age of Thirty one
years pursuant to An Act of Assembly. [...]

This Court Met According to Adjournment Whereas it Appears to this Court that Christian Finny hath [*illegible*] for a Mulato Man Child on the 20th day of October 1743 this Court hath ordered and bound the said Mulato Man Child unto Daniel Rees until he Arrive to the Age of Thirty one years Pursuant to an Act of Assembly.

Minutes of the Carteret County Court of Pleas and Quarter Sessions, December 1736; June, September, December 1743, State Archives.

A mischief incident to both these provinces is very observable, and very natural to be expected—the intercourse between the whites and blacks. The enjoyment of a negro or mulatto woman is spoken of as quite a common thing: no reluctance, delicacy or shame is made about the matter. It is far from being uncommon to see a gentleman at dinner, and his reputed offspring a slave to the master of the table. I myself saw two instances of this, and the company very facetiously would trace the lines, lineaments and features of the father and mother in the child, and very accurately point out the more characteristick resemblance. The fathers neither of them blushed or seem[ed] disconcerted. They were called men of worth, politeness and humanity. Strange perversion of terms and language! [...]

Howe, "Southern Journal of Josiah Quincy, Junior," 1773, 463. "Both these provinces" refers to North and South Carolina.

I am sorry to say, however, that I have met with few of the men who are natives of the country, who rise much above my former description, and as their natural ferocity is now inflamed by the fury of an ignorant zeal, they are of that sort of figure, that I cannot look at them without connecting the idea of tar and feather. Tho' they have fine women and such as might inspire any man with sentiments that do honour to humanity, yet they know no such nice distinctions, and in this at least are real patriots. As the population of the country is all the view they have in what they call love, and tho' they often honour their black wenches with their attention, I sincerely believe they are excited to that crime by no other desire or motive but that of adding to the number of their slaves.

Andrews, *Journal of a Lady of Quality*, 154.

For NORTH-CAROLINA in America,
THE SHIP DOBBS GALLEY,
Capt. James Leslie, Burthen 200 Tons,
a prime Sailor, being well mann'd and
Victalled, and properly fitted with
every Thing commodious for Passengers of every Degree, and will be ready
to sail from CARRICKFERGUS about the
First Day July next at farthest.
    Whoever has a Mind to go as Paf-
senger, Redemptioner, or Servant, may
apply to Samuel Smith Merchant in Belfast, Robert Willson
Merchant in Larne, or to the Captain on board his Ship at
Carrickfergus, where they will know the Terms, and meet
with good Encouragement.

Advertisement for emigrant passengers to North Carolina, 1753. The vessel was touted as having superior qualities as a passenger vessel, and the notice went on to proclaim that it would welcome anyone as "Passenger, Redemptioner, or Servant." *Belfast Newsletter*, May 26, 1753.

For Cape Fair, North Carolina, to touch at New York,

THE good Brigantine HARRIOT, burden 180 tons, double decked, a prime failer, one year old, with good accommodotions, will be ready to fail with paffengers from LEITH in July next, or fooner if required, as feveral paffengers have already engaged. Any number of perfons that the veffel can conveniently carry, may have their paffage to either of the above places, on very moderate terms. The fhip will be well victualled and manned; and as great inconveniencies have arifen from want of frefh air in bad weather, the veffel will be fitted up with air-ports and grating-hatches. A furgeon alfo goes paffenger, to fettle in North America, who will be ready to give his affiftance to any one whofe fituation may require it.—For particulars, enquire of Capt. Thomas Smith, at Mr James Young's, brewer, Leith, or of Mr George Parker, Burntifland.———N. B. Good encouragement will be given to a few Coopers, Houfe-carpenters, and other tradefmen, who are wanting to go to N. America.

The owners of the *Harriot*, sailing from Leith, Scotland, to North Carolina and New York, claimed such amenities for emigrants as inlets for fresh air and medical attention, if required. From *Caledonian Mercury* (Edinburgh), May 28, 1774.

Education

Indicative of the importance that North Carolinians attached to education, in their wills many deceased provided funds for the instruction of their children, other relatives, and occasionally the poor.

JOHN BAPTISTA ASHE'S WILL, 1731

Item. I will that my Slaves be kept to work on my lands, and that my Estate may be managed to the best advantage, so as my sons may have as liberal an Education as the profits thereof will afford; and in their Education I pray my Exers. to observe this method: Let them be taught to read and write, and be introduced into the practical part of Arithmetick, not too hastily hurrying them to Latin or Grammar, but after they are pretty well versed in these let them be taught Latin & Greek. I propose this may be done in Virginia; After which let them learn French, perhaps Some French man at Santee wile undertake this; when they are arrived to years of discretion Let them Study the Mathematicks. To my Sons when they arrive at age I recommend the pursuit & Study of Some profession or business (I could wish one to ye law, the other to Merchandize), in which Let them follow their own inclinations.

Item. I will that my daughter be taught to write and read & some femanine accomplishments which may render her agreable; And that she be not kept ignorant as to what appertains to a good house wife in the management of household affairs.

JOHN BENNET'S WILL, 1710

[...] my further will is that forty Shillings be taken of my whole Estate before any devesion be made to pay for ye Schooling of two poor Children for one whole year.

MARY CONWAY'S WILL, 1774

[...] And I do earnestly intreat my Executors to pay a strict regard to the Educating of my said Son in such manner as shall be necessary to qualify him for such Business or profession as his Genius shall most incline to.

EDWARD MOSELEY'S WILL, 1745

Item, When it shall be necessary to give all or any of my sons Other Education than is to be had from the Common Masters in this Province; for I would have my Children well Educated, it is then my Will that

Such expence be Defrayed Out of the profits of Such Childs Estate & not Otherwise.

JOHN PFIFER'S WILL, 1775 [...]

It is also my Will, & I do humbly Request my Executors to take all Reasonable pains to have my before mentioned Children instructed in the Christian Faith, & to have a reasonable Education, & in perticular my sd. son, Paul to be put through a liberal Education & Colleged, if there should be any sufficiency of my personal Estate left to his Share. [...]

CULLEN POLLOCK'S WILL, 1749 [...]

Item, It is my Will & desire that my thre Daughters have as good Education as can be had in this Province, & that my two Sons when they have got what learning they can have in this Province, that they be sent to Boston for farther Education, & their to remain untill they be eighteen Years of Age in ye care of some discrete Person to direct what Education will be most usefull for them; [...]

Grimes, *Wills and Inventories*, 16-17, 41, 128, 317, 329-330, 339.

∽⊙⊙∾

Opportunities for education were few, for schools were scarce and appeared long after the permanent settlement of North Carolina. Often they were associated with religious bodies such as the Anglicans, Presbyterians, and Moravians. Some offered instruction in practical as well as academic subjects. In some secular schools, at least, custom demanded that teacher and students negotiate for Christmas holidays.

The next Precinct is Pasquotank, where as yet there is no Church built; the Quakers are Here very numerous. The Roades are I think the worst in the Countrey; but it's closser Seated then the Others and better Peopled in Proportion to it's Bigness. In their way of Liveing they have much the Advantage of the rest, being more Industrious carefull and Cleanly; but above all I was Surpris'd to See with what Order, Decency, and Seriousness they Perform'd the Public Worship considering how ignorant People are in the Other Parishes. This they Ow to the Care of one Mr. Griffin who came there from Some Part Of the West Indies and has for three yeares past lived amongst them, being Appointed Reader by their Vestry; whose diligent Instructions and Devout Example has Improved them So far beyond their Neighbours and by his descreet

Behaviour has gaind Such a general Good Caractor and Esteem; That the Quakers themselves Send their Children to his School, tho' he has Prayers twice a Day at Least, and Oblig'd them to their Responses, and all the Decencies of Behaviour as well as Others. [...]

> Mr. Gordon to the Secretary, May 13, 1709, Cain, *Records of the Church of England 1699-1741*, 85-86.

[...] Theres one Mr. Mashburn who keeps a School at Sarum on the frontiers of Virginia, between the two Governments and Neighbouring upon 2 Indian Towns, who I find by him, highly deserve encouragement and could heartily wish, the Society would take it into consideration and be pleased to Allow him a Sallary for the good services he has done and may do for the future. What children he has under his care can both write and read very distinctly, and gave before me such an acct. of the Grounds and Principles of the Christian Religion that Strangely Surprized me to hear it. [...]

> Mr. Rainsford's Letter to Jno Chamberlaine Esq, July 25, 1712, Cain, *Records of the Church of England, 1699-1741*, 143.

My Letters of April and October have informed the venerable Society how I [have] agreed with this Vestry to continue their Minister another Year, upon their consents to find me a House: They imagine their Promise is made good by giving me Leave <*turn over*> to lodge in the Garrett of a little House. Below it serves for a Chapel of a Sunday and a School thro' the Week Days. [...]

> James Moir to Revd Sir, March 26, 1745, Cain, *Records of the Church of England, 1742-1763*, 39, forthcoming. Moir is writing from Brunswick.

Nov. 23. (Aelt. Conf.) School charges for those living outside Bethania will be 4d per week; in Bethabara it will have to be 6d, as there are so few children. In Friedberg the Stewards can charge those outside the Society 4d.

> Extracts from the Minutes of the Aeltesten Conferenz, Aufseher Collegium, and Gross Helfer Conferenz, 1773. Fries, *Records of the Moravians*, 2:774.

Thursday, December 20 [1787]. We were alarmed in our Quarters before day, by the firing of Muskets at some little distance from the house in which we lay—We found that the firing was at a school House in the neighborhood, of our Quarters, with powder only; tis the custom here for School Boys upon the approach of Christmas, Easter and Whitsuntide, to rebel against their Schoolmaster, in order to force him to grant them a holiday; the boys rise early in the Morning and go to the School House, which is considered as their Fort, they barricade the Door and Windows, carry into the house with them victuals and blankets, with water and wood, sufficient to sustain the Siege that they expect from the Master; Upon his approach at the usual School hours, he finds himself shut out, he demands the cause, the Garrison acquaints him that they are determined to have a holiday, this is frequently denied, and now commences the Siege, the Master tries to force his way into the house, they resist him by every means in their power, and sometimes give him some very serious hard knocks, throw Stones &c. It is generally looked upon as a piece of fun; the Master pretends to be solicitous to subdue them, and if he catches any Stragler from the Fort, he will flog him heartily & it is understood on these occasions that the boys are to be peaceable, except during the actual storm of the enemy, when they are at liberty to maul him to their hearts content—This Scene is sometimes continued many days, at last the Master proposes terms, that he grants them so many days holiday; which if satisfactory being accepted by the Garrison, peace is again established in the little community. Sometimes however the Master not being a good humour'd Man & not entering into their views, finds means to subdue the Garrison, and threshes the Ringleaders heartily—[...]

Rodman, *Journal of a Tour to North Carolina by William Atmore, 1787,* 17, 33-34.

❦

At least two individuals left bequests for the establishment of free schools for the benefit of the children of the less affluent.

JAMES WINRIGHT'S WILL, 1744 [...]

Item, I Will and Appoint that the Yearly Rents & Profitts of all The Town land and Houses in Beaufort Town, Belonging unto me, with the other Land Adjoining thereto (Which I purchased of John Pindar), after the Decease of my wife Ann, to be Applyed to the Uses hereinafter Mentioned for Ever, (to Wit) for the encouragement of a Sober, discreet, Quallifyed Man to teach a School at Least Reading, Writing, Vulgar & Decimal Arithmetick, in the aforesd. Town of Beaufort, wch. said Man Shall be Choosen and Appointed by the Chair Man (& the Next in Commission) of Carteret County Court, and one of the Church Wardens of St. John parish in the aforesd. County and Their Successors for Ever. Also, I Give and Bequeath the Summ of Fifty pounds Sterling (provided that my estate Shall be Worth so much after my Just Debts and other Legacys are paid and Discharged) to be Applyed for the Building and finishing of a Creditable House for a school & Dwelling house for the said Master to be Erected and Built on Some part of my Land Near the White house Which I bought of the aforesaid Pindar, and my True Intent and Meaning is, that all the Yearly profitts & advantages Arising by the aforesd. Town Lotts and Lands thereunto adjoining as aforesd., with the Use of the sd. Land for Making & Improving a plantation for the planting & Raising of Corn &c. (if the aforesd. Master or teacher of sd. School shall think proper to plant & Improve the Same) be entirely for the use & Benefitt of ye sd. Master and his Successors During his and their Good Behaviour. Also, that the sd. Master shall not be obliged to teach or take under his Care any Scholar or Scholars Imposed on him by the Trustees herein Mentioned, or their Successors, or by any other person, But shall have free Liberty to teach & take under his Care, Such, and so many Scholars, as he shall think Convenient and to Receive his Reward for the Teaching of them as he and the persons tendering them Shall agree. [...]

Will of James Winright, Grimes, *Wills and Inventories*, 456-457.

JAMES INNES' WILL, 1754 [...]

I also give & bequeath, att the Death of my Loving Wife, Jean Innes, my Plantation Called Point Pleasant, & the Opposite mash Land over the River, for which there is a Separate Patent, Two Negro young Women, One Negro young Man, and there Increase; all the Stock of Cattle and Hogs, halfe the Stock of Horses belonging att the time to that Plantation With all my Books, and one hundred Pounds Sterling, or the Equivalent thereunto in the currency of the Country, For the Use of a Free School for the Benefite of the Youth of North Carolina. [...]

Will of James Innes, Grimes, *Wills and Inventories*, 265.

When schools were unavailable, parents and tutors offered instruction. Widow Penelope Dawson taught her son. Those who lacked such attention later regretted the omission.

[... Billy] is very much improvd in his reading since for notwithstanding I have so much company I have made it a rule never to neglect Attending his reading four times a day and writing twice and I believe he has never kept half so strict with any of his masters, [...]

> Penelope Dawson to "My Dear Cousin" [Samuel Johnston], March 9, 1774, Hayes Papers.

CAPE FEAR Janry. 27th 1770.
As I know you can't say your catechism, I will just inform you, that in the second Commandment it is laid down as a certain Truth, that the sins of *Fathers* are visited on their Children for three or four Generations: Among the omissive sins of mine; that of having neglected to provide for me in my youth, a competent writing master, is one, the consequence of which is, writing, is the most painful Exercise to me in the world; you are therefore to consider this Letter (Business being the object of it) as a strong mark of my Esteem for you.—Mr Bodley (who is now waiting for this Epistle) has been so obliging as to spend some Days with me, he is, I think, a very respectable Gent and highly merits the friendly regard of every good man. Does it not lie in your way to lend him an assisting hand in his Difficulties? if it does, to do so, would be to act a part worthy of yr self.—I shall conclude with requesting the Favor of you to Dress yourself in the best manner your want of Taste in that science, will permit, and after scraping your Politest Bow, present by best respects to the good Ladies & Gents of Edenton.
I am Dr Sir with Truth Your most obt hum Servt,
M. MOORE.

> M. Moore to ?, January 27, 1770, Saunders, *Colonial Records*, 8:173.

Academies, forerunners of high schools, appeared just before the Revolution, combining elementary instruction with advanced learning. That in New Bern, apparently quite successful, closed upon the firing of its teacher, but reopened later according to advertisements in a New Bern newspaper.

An Act for the building of a House for a School and the Residence of a School Master in the Town of New Bern.

I. Whereas, the Inhabitants of the Town of New Bern, and Craven County, for the encouraging and promoting of Learning, are willing and desirous of building a House for a School, with proper Conveniences for the Residence of a School-Master, in the said town, by Subscription; and Part of the Four Lots formerly appropriated for the building of a Church on, and other Purposes, by an Act of Assembly passed the Twenty First Day of August, One Thousand Seven Hundred and Forty, being deemed the most proper and convenient Part of the said Town for the same:

II. Be it therefore Enacted, by the Governor, Council, and Assembly, and by the Authority of the same, That Half of Two of the said Lots, known in the Plan of the said Town by the Numbers of 59, and 60, beginning at the Corner of Craven and Pollock Streets, and running along Pollock Street Six Poles and a half; then across the said Two Lots, Number 59 and 60, in a parallel Line with Craven Street, Thirteen Poles to the North Side of Lot Number 60; then along the said lot in a parallel Line with Pollock Street to Craven Street then along Craven Street Thirteen Poles to the Beginning; shall, and is hereby vested in the Reverend Mr. James Reed, Mr. John Williams, Mr. Joseph Leech, Mr. Thomas Clifford Howe, Mr. Thomas Hasten, Mr. Richard Cogdell, and Mr. Richard Fenner, and their Successors, as Trustees, for the Uses and Purposes aforesaid, for ever, and for no other Use or Purpose whatsoever; and they the said Trustees, and their successors, or the Majority of them, are hereby invested with full Power and Authority to make such Rules and Orders from Time to Time as to them shall seem most proper, for the building, encouraging, and regulating the same; and shall and may, from Time to Time, appoint such Person or Persons as they shall judge most fit and proper to keep the said School; and on the Misbehaviour of any Schoolmaster, to appoint such other Person as they shall judge more proper, in the Room and Stead of such misbehaving Schoolmaster.

III. And in Order that the Number of the said Trustees may be kept up; Be it further Enacted , by the Authority aforesaid, That on the Death or Removal out of the Province of any of them, it shall and may be lawful for the Majority of the remaining Part of them, together with a Majority of the surviving Persons who shall subscribe and pay to the Amount of Five Pounds towards building and promoting the said School, who shall be present at any Election herein after directed, from Time to Time, as often as Occasion shall require, to choose at the said

School-house, some other Person in the Room and Stead of every such Trustee, they the said surviving Trustees first giving due Notice to the said Subscribers, of the Time such Choice is to be made, by giving at least Ten Days Notice thereof, by putting up Advertisements at the Church and said School-House Doors.

Read three times and ratified in open Assembly, 9 March, 1764.

Laws, 1764, in Clark, *State Records*, 25: 484-485.

Newbern, June 13*th*, 1764.

NOTICE to the Freeholders of *Christ-Church* Parish, in *Craven* County, is hereby given, that on *Wednesday*, the 1st Day of *August* next, at the Court-House in *Newbern*, the Subscriber, or his Deputy, will attend; open the Poll for electing a Vestry for said Parish, and take the Suffrages of the Voters, as the Law Directs.

Richard Cogdell, Sheriff.[...]

AT which Time and Place, the several Subscribers to the *School-House*, in *Newbern*, are desired to give their Attendance, and elect *Two Commissioners*, and *One Treasurer*, to direct, and superintend, the Building of the said *School-House*.

North Carolina Magazine; or, Universal Intelligencer (New Bern), July 13, 1764.

[...] There is also in this town, built by subscription, a very large and handsome school house, endow'd with charter privileges by the legislative body of the province, under the directions of 11 Trustees, chosen by the subscribers and from among themselves; tis perhaps now one of the best regulated schools of the kind in America, there is a master and one usher all ages and both sexes are admitted, the present master's name is Tomlinson from London, a very sober religious man as well as good schollar; and an excellent penman. There is now about 70 fine Little boys and girls, and daily increasing from remote parts of the province; that they begin to talk of a second usher. [...]

John Whiting to "Revnd Sir," April 8, 1767, Frederick Nash Collection.

Reverend Sir

My last was on the 2d of July 1771, since which there has been great Contention about our little Academy. I shou'd have sent you a more early Account of it, cou'd I have done it with any Satisfaction; but I found it difficult to find out the whole truth, and the real Causes of discontent. The most material Intelligence I have been able to receive, even after the most diligent Search, has been only from Mr. Tomlinson himself, Mr. Parrot, Mr. Tomlinson's late Assistant, and one dissenting Trustee. The rest of the Trustees, whether from a Consciousness of having acted wrong, or some worse Motive, intirely decline all Conversation with me about it.

When Mr. Tomlinson opened his School, he was apprised of the excessive Indulgence of American parents, and the great difficulty of keeping up a proper discipline; more especially as his School consisted of Numbers of both Sexes. He was therefore very cautious, and used every little Artifice to avoid Severity as much as possible. But when the Children grew excessive headstrong, stubborn and unruly, and likely to endanger the Welfare of his School, he used to correct and turn them out of School, and make some little difficulties about their Readmission. Unfortunately for Mr. Tomlinson, this piece of policy gave very great Umbrage to two of the Trustees, who ever since their Children were corrected and turned out of School, have been his most implacable Enemies. One of them has acquired a very considerable fortune by trade, and has four or five of the trustees intirely at his Devotion. The Circumstances and Influence of the other, are inconsiderable.

You may see by the Act of Assembly for establishing the School, which I sent you the 23d of January 1767, that one penny per Gallon, for a limited time is laid upon all spirituous Liquors imported into Neuse River, for the Benefit of the School; out of which Twenty pounds per Annum is to be paid to the Schoolmaster to enable him to keep an Assistant, and the rest is to be applied to the Education of poor Children, not exceeding Ten. Mr. Tomlinson presuming that this Duty upon spirituous Liquors wou'd be honestly applied, by the Encouragement of the trustees, wrote to his Correspondent in London, who procured him an Assistant, Mr. Parrot, properly qualified in every Respect, and entered into Bonds with him for a Term of Years in behalf of Mr. Tomlinson. About twelve Months after the Arrival of Mr. Parrot, great Umbrage was given to the potent trustee by Mr. Tomlinson's correcting and turning one of his Children out of the School, for very disobedient and stubborn behaviour; and a dissenting minister about the same time opened a School at Wilmington, which is near one hundred Miles distant, when Six Boys, which Mr. Tomlinson had under his Care from that place, were taken away, for the Conveniency of being nearer home, which reduced his Scholars to about forty four. The trustees had never sent more than five poor Children to School. And as Mr. Tomlinson found his School reduced, he petitioned the trustees to send him five more, the better to enable him to continue Mr. Parrot. But behold the Consequence! A Meeting of the trustees was appointed, (not a general one, for I had no Notice of it, but of such as cou'd be depended upon to answer particular purposes) and an Order made a Copy of which you have inclosed, that he shou'd dismiss the five poor Children, which were then at School, under a Pretext of Want of Money to repair the Schoolhouse. I call it a pretext, because their own Accounts will shew, that they had Money enough then due, and in their treasurer's hands, not only to have made all necessary Repairs, and continued the five poor Children, but likewise to have educated five more according to Mr. Tomlinson's Request. And tho some repairs were really wanting, yet they have not laid out a single Shilling in any repairs from that day to this. And the dissenting trustee, who was at that Meeting, lately informed me, that the five poor Children were taken away, not for Want of Money, but with a design to distress Mr. Tomlinson.

When Mr. Tomlinson found his School still more reduced by the dismission of the five poor Children, he represented to Mr. Parrot; the hardship of continuing him as Assistant, who generously consented to cancel the Bonds, and provide for himself. The greatest difficulty seemed then to be removed. Mr. Tomlinson had sufficient Employment for himself in the School, and Mr. Parrot, who is a good Mathematician and Penman, supported himself by Hackney writing.

But tho' Mr. Tomlinson was now perfectly easy, yet resentment cou'd not sleep. The Correcting and turning the Children of two of the trustees out of the School, was, like the Sin against the Holy Ghost, never to be forgiven. Mr. Tomlinson's destruction was determined upon, but how to accomplish it was the difficulty. Mr. Parrot was therefore tampered with to open a School in opposition to him. But Mr. Parrot saw thro' their design of making a Tool of him, and tho he detested their proposal, yet he gave soft Answers, implying, that if the School shou'd at any time be vacant, he wou'd accept it; provided he had no better employment. Mr. Tomlinson therefore was to be turned out to make room for him; but Governor Tryon was in the Way, who had been an Eye Witness of Mr. Tomlinson's Conduct and had a particular Value and Esteem for him. But at length Governor Tryon was removed to New York, and a new Governor succeeded him, who was a Stranger to Mr. Tomlinson, and then was the Time to strike the fatal Blow. Accordingly on the 14th of last September, there was a Meeting of the trustees, (not a general one, for tho' a trustee, I had no

Notice of it, not being a proper person for such business as they were then about) when they did their utmost to turn Mr. Tomlinson out of the School. A Copy of their proceedings on that day, you have inclosed, and upon which I wou'd beg Leave to remark; That when they took the poor Children away, there were no Complaints of Neglect, but only of Want of Money. But now Mr. Tomlinson is accused of neglecting his School by the Trustees, and what seems very surprising, by no body else. They were the only Accusers, and the only Judges.

Mr. Tomlinson has taught School here upwards of Eight Years, and I never heard him accused of neglecting his School, till after the 14th of last September; and since that time only by one person, who is greatly in his debt, besides the Trustees that endeavoured to displace him. And I verily believe, they might with as much Justice have accused him of robbery, or wilful Murder.

Two or three days after, Mr. Tomlinson informed me, how the trustees had used him, and was very desirous of a public hearing before the Governor. And, tho' I was at that time very sick, yet I waited upon the Governor along with him, who received us very graciously. But his Excellency being a Stranger, and not knowing how far he was legally authorised to interfere, prudently declined granting him a public Hearing, till he had the Attorney General's Opinion, a Copy of which I have sent you inclosed, and by which you will perceive that he cou'd not legally interfere at all. Mr. Tomlinson's Case therefore seem'd to be desperate and Nothing was to be done, but turn out immediately.

The full Number of trustees is Eleven. At that time there were two Vacancies, and I had no Notice of their Meeting. Eight Met, and one dissented; therefore Mr. Tomlinson was dismissed by the Voice of Seven. But to give this Dismission the Appearance of a more general Voice, they proceeded immediately to fill up the Vacancies, and elected two new Trustees, sent for them and swore them in, and then signed a Nomination for Mr. Parrot. I have sent you Copies both of the Dismission and Nomination, which you will find of the same Date, and the Nomination signed by Ten, to induce the Governor to believe that Mr. Tomlinson was dismissed by the Voice of Ten, tho' he was dismissed by the Voice of Seven only; for they got the two new elected Trustees, as well as the trustee that dissented, to sign the Nomination for Mr. Parrot.

But here the Trustees met with a difficulty, they were not aware of. They knew Mr. Parrot's distressed Circumstances, and never doubted but he wou'd readily accept the School. But when the time of trial came, he let them see, that he had too much Sense to be made a Fool of, and too much honour to supplant a worthy honest Man. In short, he refused to accept the School, when offered in such a base and dishonourable Manner; which redounded so much to his Credit, that he has lately got into decent employment in the Secretary's Office, which, I hope will give him a comfortable Subsistance at present, and be a Step towards his future Advancement.

And now for the last Effort of disappointed Resentment. After the Trustees had sent for Mr. Tomlinson with an Intention to dismiss him, (tho he had not the least Notice or Suspicion of it, having never heard of any Accusation) they settled Accounts with him, and gave him an order upon their treasurer for his Money, a Copy of which you have inclosed, and then the president in the name of the Society in a very abrupt manner dismissed him. But a few days after, finding Mr. Tomlinson not very willing to turn out, and Mr. Parrot unwilling to accept the School, the potent trustee went to the treasurer, and by his own Authority forbad the payment of Mr. Tomlinson's Order. The treasurer acccordingly refused payment, and Mr. Tomlinson is obliged to sue for his Money, tho the treasuer has due and in his hands above Two hundred Pounds.

I never dispaired of bringing about a reconciliation till this last affair happened. It shewed such a depravity of mind, that I thought it dangerous to continue any longer a Member of the incorporated Society, and therefore resigned. And I believe the venerable Society will never blame me for resigning in such a Situation. I saw I cou'd do no Good, and therefore wou'd not suffer my Name to give a santion to others to do Mischief. Besides I was obliged to resign for my own preservation, and to keep out of the way of Strife and Contention.

The Majority of the trustees are wealthy men, but I cannot learn, that any of them ever passed thro' a reputable School, or have the least knowledge of any of the learned Languages, or liberal Sciences, or of the difficulty of governing a School. And I shall leave you to judge of the Honour and Integrity of some of them from the inclosed List of Debts due to Mr. Tomlinson, which he gave me last Christmas. The want of such considerable Sums must greatly distress any man in his Station. He therefore grew urgent in his Demands, which united his Debtors more firmly in their opposition, and caused them to speak very disrespectfully of him before their Children. For such as will not pay their honest Debts, seldom fail to abuse their injured Creditors.

You see it was not either for Want of Inclination or power, that they did not turn Mr. Tomlinson out of the School, but only for Want of a proper Person to succeed him. He is therefore determined to resign the School next April and follow some other Employment.

I have been the more particular in the above Relation, from the Duty I owe to the venerable Society, and the great Regard I have for Mr. Tomlinson, who I verily believe is a sincere Christian, and has been very basely treated. He is certainly one of the most peaceable and inoffensive men living, enters into no parties, meddles with no body's business but his own, and not addicted to any one visible Vice. And if the Trustees did really think him guilty either of too much Severity, or Negligence, or any other Indiscretion or Misdemeanor, why did they not admonish or reprimand him? But that wou'd neither have paid their Debts, nor sufficiently gratified their Malice and Resentment.

I sincerely wish the Act for establishing the School was repealed. I am sure, it never will answer any good Intention, while such an unlimited power is intrusted in the hands of the Trustees. They shou'd be obliged to lay their Accounts annually before the Commander in Chief for his Inspection, who shou'd have a Check upon them both in the Admission and Dismission of the Master. Tis true, the Governor has a Power of licensing the Master, which I thought wou'd have been a sufficient Restraint, but you may see by the Honourable Marmaduke Jones's Opinion inclosed, which is fuller than the Attorney General's, the Governor's Licence is a mere trifling, if any Restraint at all. And if the Bishop of London wou'd point out the defects of the present Act and get it repealed, I believe it wou'd not be difficult to get a much better passed at the Next Session of the Assembly. Or if that cou'd not be done, the Schoolhouse had better revert to the Subscribers in general, than remain the Property of a few, who so shamefully abuse their Trust. [...]

Rev. James Reed to the Secretary, February 15, 1772, Cain, *Records of the Church of England, 1764-1789*, vol. XII, forthcoming.

[...] BY Permission and Encouragement of the Trustees the Public School House of this Town is again opened, where Youth may be taught the *English*, *Latin*, or *French* Tongue; as also Writing, Arithmetic, Algebra, Trigonometry plain and spherical, Astronomy, Navigation, Surveying, Geography, the Use of the Globes, or any other Part of the Mathematics, the *Italian* Method of Bookkeeping, at the established Price of the said School, which may be known by enquiring of Mr. *Davis*, Printer of this Paper, and one of the Trustees.

New Bern, June 30, 1775.

North-Carolina Gazette (New Bern), June 30, 1775.

⊰๏⊱

The General Assembly contemplated a college for North Carolina in the 1750s, and in 1770 acceded to the request of Presbyterian residents by chartering Queen's College in Charlotte, for which a lottery was instituted to raise money. The legislation was disallowed by English authorities.

An Act for founding establishing and endowing of Queen's College in the Town of Charlotte in Mecklenburg County.

Whereas the proper education of Youth has always been considered as the most certain source of tranquility, happiness and improvement both of private families and of States and Empires and there being no Institution or Seminary of Learning established in this Province, whither the rising generation may repair, after having acquired at a Grammar School a competent knowledge of the Greek, Hebrew and Latin Languages to imbibe the principles of Science and virtue and to obtain under learned, pious and exemplary teachers in a collegiate or academic mode of instruction a regular and finished education in order to qualify them for the service of their friends and Country, and whereas several Grammar schools have been long taught in the western parts of this Government, in which many students have made very considerable progress in the languages and other literary attainments, and it being thought by many pious, learned and public-spirited persons that great and singular benefits & advantages would be derived to the Publick, could some one of them receive the encouragement and sanction of a Law, for the establishment thereof on a lasting & permanent basis, wherefore Be it enacted by the Governor, Council and Assembly and by the authority of the same that Messrs. Edmund Fanning, Thomas Polk, Robert Harris, Junior, Abraham Alexander, Hezekiah Alexander, John McNitt Alexander, Ezekiel Polk, Thomas Neal, Wm. Richardson, Hezekiah T. Balch, Joseph Alexander, Waitstell Avery, Henry Patillo and Abner Nash, be and they are hereby formed and incorporated into a Body Politic or Corporate, by the name of the Fellows and Trustees of the incorporated Society, for founding, establishing and endowing Queens College in Charlotte Town and by that name to have perpetual succession and a Common Seal, and that they and their Successors by the Name aforesaid shall be able and capable in Law to purchase, have receive enjoy possess and retain to them and their Successors for ever, in special trust and confidence to and for the uses and purposes of founding establishing & endowing the said College, and supporting a President of the same and the number of three or less tutors, any Lands, Rents, Tenements and Hereditaments of what kind nature or quality whatsoever and also to sell, grant, demise, alien or dispose of the same, and also receive and take any charity, gift or donation, whatsoever to the said College and by the same name to sue implead be sued and impleaded, answer and be answered in all Courts of Record whatsoever.

Laws, 1770, in Clark, *State Records*, 25:519d-519e.

SCHEME OF A LOTTERY FOR RAISING THE SUM OF FOURTEEN HUNDRED AND FORTY POUNDS FOR BUILDING A COLLEGE IN *Mecklenburg* County, in *North Carolina.*

1	Prize of £1000	is	£1000	
1	500		500	
1	300		300	
2	200		400	
3	100		300	
5	50		250	
10	25		250	
20	10		200	
40	5		200	
1931	3 4		6179	5
First drawn,	10 8		10	8
last drawn,	10 8		10	8
			£9600	

2016 Prizes.
3984 Blanks.
6000 Tickets, at 32s. Proclamation or four Dollars   £9600
Fifteen per Cent to be deducted from the Prizes.

The said Lottery to be drawn on the 22d Day of *August* next, at the Courthouse in *Mecklenburg*, under the Inspection of Messieurs *Morris Moore, Richard Henderson, Richard Caswell, Hugh Waddell, Alexander Martin, Thomas Neal, John McKnight Alexander,* and *Hugh Montgomery*, or any three of them, who are to be on Oath to see the same done faithfully.—TICKETS to be had at the Post Office in *Williamsburg, Virginia.*

Virginia Gazette, Purdie and Dixon (Williamsburg), June 4, 1772.

Education embraced more than academic instruction, as seen in the wills of Wyriot Ormond and Governor Gabriel Johnston. The governor's executors complied with his wishes, and Penelope, who married John Dawson, fulfilled his aspirations, according to James Iredell, who appreciated well educated women.

WYRIOTT ORMOND'S WILL, 1773 [...]

My principle desire is that of the Education of my two Daughters, which I strongly Rely on the Care of my Executors and each of them, Begging in my Last Moments that they will Continue their Love and Friendship to those little Orphans; And I die Satisfyed, that this request will be put in Execution, and that no Expense be thaught too Great provided it doth not effect the principal of their Estates; I not only mean that part of their Education which Respects their Schooling, but Every Other that Can be had for their Advantage.[...]

Will of Wyriot Ormond, Grimes, *Wills and Inventories*, 324.

GABRIEL JOHNSTON'S WILL, 1751

[...] And I Earnestly Request my Dearest Wife to be a kind tender Mother to my Dear little Girl, and to bring her up in the Fear of God and under a deep Sense of her being always in his Presence, and in Sobriety and Moderation Confining her Desires to things Plain, neat and Elegant, and not aspiring after the Gayety, Splendor and Extravagances; and Especially, to take Care to keep within the Bounds of her Incomes, and by no Means to Run in Debt.

Will of Governor Gabriel Johnston, Grimes, *Wills and Inventories*, 269.

Sir

I desire that youll take Ms. Penelope Johnston under your Care and if possible place har at Mr. Dunwidies in Williamsburg and if you can not place her at the Governor desire that youll place her at in Some Family of Good Regulation where She may have the advantage of receiving an education Suitable to her Birth and Fortune. I Should not chuse to have her at any other Place than Williamsburgs as I appreciate She will have the advantage of the best company and Education there, you are Likewise desired to Supply her with all necessaries Suitable to her rank in a plain but neat and fashonable manner.

I am Sir your very Humble and most Obedient Servant.

Willr: Cathcart

Novembr. the 22 1755

[*Addressed:*]
To The Honourable John Rutherfurd Esquire
att Mount Galland

> Will Cathcart to John Rutherfurd, [November 22, 1755], Hayes Papers.

Mrs. Dawson lives over the Sound, which is just before us, and is the Daughter of Governor Johnston. She has been a Widow upwards of two years, and has three charming Children, two Girls and a Boy. This lady is about 28, and in point of excellence of understanding, Goodness of heart, and a most polite, attractive behaviour, she is generally allowed to be above all kind of competition. [...]

> James Iredell to Francis Iredell, Sr., July 20, 1772, Higginbotham, *Papers of James Iredell,* 1:107.

What a dignified Readiness of Mind do you not show in your choice of Books, many of which you select for useful Instruction, instead of constantly reading those of frothy Entertainment. What a Happiness to have a Mind capable of even exalted Studies! What Goodness, and Command of Attention, to apply to them! Indeed, my dear Hannah, you cannot conceive the Joy I felt when your Sister told me you was reading Burnet's Theory. What Brutes are those who would deny your Sex any degree of literary attainment! For my own Part, I know of no Character more pleasing than a sensible Woman who has read elegantly and judiciously, who is fond of this honorable Exercise of her mental Powers, [...]

> James Iredell to Hannah Johnston, c. April 1773, Higginbotham, *Papers of James Iredell,* 1:149.

ക്ക

The joy of reading, exemplified by young William Few, who lived in the vicinity of Hillsborough, and private libraries, including that of Dr. John Eustace, reflected the educational attainments of North Carolinians.

In that country at that time there was great scarcity of books. My father's whole library consisted of a folio bible, Tillotson's Sermons,

Barclays' Apology, and a few other religious books which I read over and over, for I was fond of every book I could get.

About this time my father purchased Dyche's Dictionary and a set of the Spectators, with which I was greatly delighted, although I found the Spectators were wrote in a style different from those books I had been accustomed to, and contained many words I did not perfectly understand, which often made it necessary to apply to the dictionary for a definition. In this way I soon acquired the knowledge of those books and read them with additional pleasure and much improvement. The principles of moral rectitude they contained were then so deeply impressed on my mind that I shall never cease to feel their influence. About the year 1767 my father bought a farm seven miles distant, which was placed under my care, and it required my whole attention.

It became my duty every Monday morning to go to the farm and remain until Saturday, and I was employed at the plow. It was my practice every Monday to take with me a book which I read at leisure hours, and took it with me to the fields, and when fatigued I retired to a shade and read. By those means labor became pleasant and agreeable, while the mind was amused and the understanding improved. Here I enjoyed the greatest part of one year in uninterrupted peace and tranquility. I had only two objects in view; reading to acquire knowledge, and the cultivation of the soil which alternately exercised my corporal and mental faculties. I now experienced that the proper and equal exercise of body and mind insures the greatest portion of human happiness. I was successful in my labor; the season was favorable and I raised a good crop.

"Autobiography of Col. William Few of Georgia," 345.

AN INVENTORY of the personal Estate of Doctor John Eustace deceased which hath come to the knowledge or possession of Margt. Eustace his Addministratrix, that is to say.

Books, & first Folios
Universal dictionary of Arts & Sciences 2 Vol
Independant reflection

Quarto
Brayer's French & English Dictionary, Historia Universalis, Jeffrey's Voyages Stich'd, Ainsworth Latin & English Dictionary, Laws of North Carolina, South Carolina Justice (missing)

Octavo

Johnson's English Dictionary Abridged, Bellamy's English Dictionary, Foster's discourses, Sharp's Intriduction to Un: History, Brook's Garettur, Schrivelle's greek & latin lexicon, Salmon's grammar, present state of Europe, Puttendorff de Officio &c. Walshe's theory of the Earth, Oeconomy of Love a Poem, Jolliamed; or discourse between an Indian Philosopher & French missionary, Jermippers redivivus; or the Sages? triumph &—Salmon's Chronology, Baker on learning, Smith's moral Sentiments, War of the Beasts, Thompson's Seasons, Philosophy of revelation, Derham's Phisiotheology, Complete angler, Holmes's latin grammer, Poisies diverses, American Magazine for 1745, London Magazine for 1757 & 1761, Universal Magazine 3d & 5th Vols, Smollet's Continuation 2d & 4 Vols, Howels state of England, Compleate Housewife, Nelson's Justice, Antidote against popery, Guliver's Travels 1s Vol, Joubert's french & latin dictionary, Christian faith asserted &c.

Duodecimo &c

Synonymorum Sylva, Salmon's Garetteer, Last Will of Basil Valentine, 9 Vols Voltaire's works in blue Paper, Cleora; or the fair inconstant, Young's Night Thoughts, Fisher's Young man's best Companion, Gordon on the Rebellion, Montesquieu's lettres persanes, Brightlands English Grammar, Memoirs of Brandenburgh, Gentleman instructed 2 Vol, Swift's Works 2d Vol, Six Voyages de Cyrus, Theobalds Shakespear 8th Vol, Passion of the Soul bt DesCartes, Latin Bible, Memoirs sur les Artis &c, Familiar Coloquies greek & Latin, Manyngham's discourses, New treatise of Natural Philosophy, Human Prudence, Bayse's Pantheon, Sherlock's discourses 4 Vol, Relation de la Cour de Rome, Garth's dispensary, Traders sure guide, Spectacle de la nature 7 Vol, Rudiments of ancient History, Pope's Homers Iliad, Hume's Essays-4 Vol, Brown's estimate of manners &c, British Apollo 2 & 3d Vol, Manners, Gray's poems, Table of the Beers-? 2 Vol, Lives & Characters of Classical authors 2 Vol, Steel's Christian Hero, Pope's Epistles, origin of Evil, School of Man, Existence of God demonstrated, Paradise Lost, Smart's Horace-2 Vol, News readers pocket Book, D'Argens's philosophy-2 Vol, Literaires Nouvelles &C, Tristram Shandy, a full Set, Groece Gramatics, Select Scotch & English poems, Court Register 581-63 inclusive 6 Vol, Companion to the Almanack 1768, Minute Philosopher, Ramsay's Poems, The Woman-hater, a Novel 2 Vol, Musicale Miscelany, Piregrim Pickle-4 Vol, Coloquies french & Latin, Tom Jones-3 Vol, Old Woman's Magazine 2nd. Vol, Farquhar's Works-2 Vol, 3 Vol

Plays, Sir Launclot Greaves, Bische's art of poetry 1st 2d & 4th Vol, Londin in miniature, Joseph Andrews-2 vol Spectator 2d Vol, Female Spectator 4th Vol, Roderick Random 2 Vol, catesbys letters, Letters of Abilard & Heloise, Universal passion, stiched Otways Works 1st Vol, Man of Taste & Court of Lilliput, Martin's Introduction to English, Compendious History of England, Boyer's compleate french master, Steele's plays, a new set of pocket maps, 2 prayer books, Littleton's dialogues of the dead (missing), original poems, British antidote to Scotch poison; or caracaturas of the times 4 Vol stiched.

Books on Physick Surgery & Anatomy &c
Folio
Anatomical Tables
Quarto

Renodoeus's dispensatory, Shaw's Boer haave 2 Vol, Lewis's Materia medica, Heister's Surgery, Disertatio medica by Weshart & others, Le Febure's chemistry, Meade's medicinal works.

Octavo

Medical observations, Effects of air on human bodies, Huxham on fevers, Van Swieton's Commentaries, Mihles aliments of Surgery, Astruc's pathology, Sharp's critical inquiry

Langrishe's theory & practice of Physic, Brown's institutions in Physick, Burton's midwifery, Strother on Sickness & Health, Fullers Pharmacopoeia, Lee on botany, Hillary on Air, Petit on the bones, Turner on the Venereal disease, Lobb on painfull distempers, Groinvelt's rudiments of physic, Quinton's observations, Preternatural state of the animal humors, Gaubi's pathology, Flemyng's Phisiology, James's Dispensatory, Celsus de medicina, Thompson's Anatomy, Surgical Pharmacy, Morgan's philosophical principles of medicine, Paxton's Phisics-medical dictionary, Le Dran's cases in Surgery—Observations in Surgery, Chine's theory of fevers, Elabaratory laid open, Lind on the Scurvy, Arbuthnot on Aliments, White on the nerves, Quincy's Lexicon, Pringle on the diseases of the army, Gooche's cases in Surgery, Brooke's introduction, Barry on digestion &c Home's principia medicenoea, Chiselden's anatomy, Life of a Boerhaave, Aprorismi practici, Sharp's Surgery, Gaubi's medicinal forms, Sprengells' Hippocrates, Morgan's practice of physic, Van Sweiton's Commentaries abridged, Brooks's practice of physic, De Moneky on diseases in W. India Voyages, Hatter's phisiology, Quincey's dispensatory, Swan's Syednham, Hillary's inquiry,

300

Account of inoculation, Smelly's midwifery, The Ladies pysical directory, Le Clerc on bandiges and dressings dissertated medica by Gowdie, The way to health, long life &c.

Duodecimo &c.

Councill's Midwifry, Essay on the Government of Children, Theobald's dispensatory, Boerhaave's materia medica, Lommius's medicinal observation, latin same in English Demettrodo discendiartum medicam, Friends' chemistry, London dispensatory, Boerhaave's aphorisms, Russel on Sea water, Culpepper's dispensatory, Basil Valentine's Triumphal chariot of Antimony, Boyle's Chemistry, Hipporeatis's aphorisms, *** contractus Lasher's dispensatory, Keill's Anatomy, Best method of preserving health, Boerhaave's praxis medica 3 Vol, *** Historia plantarum, Hattur's physiology, Chirac's Surgery, Monro on the bones, rational reconomy of human bodies, Strother's Pharmacopoeia, Barthalon's Lexicon, Boerhaave's consultations of medicine,

Pamphlets

Dominicetti's appology, Thompson's discourse on the small pox, Friends prelutiones chymica, Essay on wamr bathing, Stork's essay on hemlock, Ludwig on Vegetables, Tennent's epistle to Dr. Mead, Dissertation on Inocluation, Chandler's treatise on the disease called a Cold, method of treating gun shott wounds, Treatise on the virulent gonnorrhea, Cowper on Peyser's medicine for the Veneral disease, Huxham on Antimony, method of curing fevers, Essay on circulation of the blood, *** on dry zripes?, Abstract of Berkley on Tar-water, Dissertatis medica de incubo, *** de pluonalbo, De anima medica protectio, Aphorismi botanici, Quiotionum et responsionum chirurzicarum &c. Dissertatio medica by Gowdie, observations on Night shade

Inventory of Dr. John Eustace, 1769. Grimes, *Wills and Inventories*, 490-492.

◈

Among printed materials, newspapers broadened the perspective of colonials and exerted a great influence on their thinking. Four appeared in North Carolina before the Revolution, including the *Cape Fear Mercury* in Wilmington. In addition, Carolinians subscribed to sheets from Virginia.

NEWBERN, *March* 2.

Mr. DAVIS,

AN unexpected accident brought me to town from my lonely retreat, where I am more happy in general, than those who make hasty strides to be rich. The labourious, but innocent toils of the day, and the clear water of my running spring, prepare me for a quiet repose at night.

As a subscriber, I peruse your papers when they come to hand, and think you take a great deal of pains to entertain your readers with all good news the times afford. In publishing what is disagreeable to the friends of independency and just rights of human beings, you are sparing and cautious, which I think is necessary and prudent in the present exigency of the times. As we planters in general are wanting in *education* and judgment, therefore the printers have a great share in forming our common ideas. In your last weeks gazette, you entertained us with an account of the memorable battle of the kegs on the river Delaware, which gives offence to some and makes others laugh at the fiction, but as we are not always capable of judging for ourselves, you ought, when you publish such facetious tales, to add at the bottom by way of a large P. S. that it is only a joke.

North-Carolina Gazette (New Bern), March 13, 1778.

THE SUBSCRIBERS to this PAPER and to the SALSBURY-RIDER, are requested to Pay their Subscriptions; in *Anson County* to Mr. *Kershaw* or his Agent;—at the Court-House in *Mecklenburg* to Mr. *William Patterson*; or Mr. *Jeremiah McCafferty*; —in *Charlotte* to Mr. *John McKnit Alexander*;—in *Rowan* to Mr. *Maxwell Chambers*, or Mr. *William Steel* in *Salisbury*;—in *Surry* to Mr. *Lanier*, or *Col. Armstrong*;—in the upper part of *Guilford*, to Major *John Campbell*, or the *Revd David Caldwell*;—in the lower part of *Guilford*, to *Col. John MGee*.

It is expected this NOTICE will be duly attended to, and in October next a person will be at these *different Places* to Receive the Money.

N.B. Scarce any thing hath yet been Paid for the *Rider*, except in *Surry*, where every Subscriber paid *one year's Subscription* when they Signed the Agreement.

Cape Fear Mercury (Wilmington), September 22, 1773.

THE Subscribers for the *Virginia* Gazette of Mess. *Dixon* & *Hunters*, and Mr. *Alexander Purdie*, by Means of Applications to the Subscriber for that purpose, are hereby requested to pay up the Balance for the

Years expired, and also that 12 s. 6d. *Virginia* Money, be paid down by those who choose to continue the same another Year; and it is expected that those Subscribers who decline taking them a second Year, will pay in the same Proportion for the Time past, since the Year expired, to the Time of Payment. I am advised by the Printers, that the Scarcity and Dearness of Paper is such, that unless the Money is punctually paid at the Time of subscribing, and old Arrears paid up, it will not be in their Power to serve their Customers. The Subscriber thinks that (from the Recommendation which he has given of those Subscribers who only paid a Dollar at Entrance) he is in some measure bound to request the speedy Payment of the Sums due. [...]

North-Carolina Gazette (New Bern), August 8, 1777.

∞🙂∞

The institution of a postal system also contributed to the enlightenment of North Carolinians. The General Assembly early provided for the transmission of official dispatches. Private correspondence was conveyed by rider or friends. Not until 1770 was a permanent post established, largely through the efforts of Governor William Tryon. It connected North Carolina to lines already established in Virginia and South Carolina, but the route consisted of a single highway along the coast which often proved difficult to traverse.

II. And It Is Hereby Enacted that all Letters superscribed for his Majestie's service directed to or Subsigned by the Governor or other Publick Officer or by some Field Officer in the Militia at such time when the Government is Actually Engaged in War against the Indyan Enemie shall be Immediately Conveyed from Plantation to plantation to the place & persons to whom they are directed under the Penalty of Five pounds for each default one halfe to the Government and the other half to him or them which shall Sue for the same to be recovered in any Court of Record within this Government wherein no Essoign, Protections, Injunction or Wager of Law shall be allowed or Admitted of. [...]

Laws, 1715, in Clark, *State Records*, 23:81.

Williamsburg, May 25. We hear for certain, that there is now a Post settled from *Charles-Town* to *Edenton*, which return'd last *Monday* was Se'ennight to *Charles-Town*; and that the Postage of Letters from thence to *Cape Fear*, and *Edenton*, amounted to £80 *North-Carolina* Money:

By which it may be reasonably expected, that in a short Time, the Number of Letters will greatly increase from the Northward.

Virginia Gazette (Williamsburg), May 25, 1739.

South Carolina, Charlestown, April 24, 1739.
AS the Assembly of this Province have allowed *Two Hundred Pounds* a Year, for the carrying on a Post from this to the Northern Colonies; and whereas several Gentlemen of this Place have generously agreed to support the remaining Expence as far as *Cape Fear;* we are desired to give Notice that the said Post will proceed for *George-Town, Cape-Fear, Edenton* and so through the Northern Colonies on the *Twentieth* Day of every Month, and endeavour to return to *Charlestown* as expeditiously it may be, or on the *Nineteenth* of the following Month at farthest.

South-Carolina Gazette (Charleston), April 26, 1739.

AN ACT to encourage and support the Establishment of a Post office in this Province.

Whereas the Postmasters General hath lately established a Post Office in this Province and employed Riders or Mail bearers at an Expence much exceeding the Amount of the Postage received for the Conceyance of letters and Packets through this Province, for the encouragement of so usefull an Establishment and that mail be not delayed

Be it Enacted by the Governor, Council and Assembly, and by the Authority of the same, That every Owner or Keeper of a public Ferry in this Province shall on the arrival of any post Rider or bearer of a Mail from any Post Office in this Province, immediately and with the utmost dispatch transport the said Post Rider or Mail bearer with his Mail across the Ferry in preference to any other Passenger who may be there and about to cross the said ferry without asking or receiving any gratuity fee or Reward from the said Post Rider or mail Bearer whatsoever. And for the encouragement of the said Ferry men and that they may be the more readily induced to Expedite the Mail

Be it Enacted by the Authority aforesaid That every such Ferry man shall, for every time he shall transport any post Rider or Mail Bearer across his Ferry, be allowed double the same allowed by Law for the like service in other instances on producing his Account sworn to before a Justice of the Peace in the County where he resides to the Treasurer of the District, who is hereby required to pay the same, and such

Account with a Receipt from the Ferry man, shall be deemed a sufficient Voucher for the Treasurer on his Settlement with the Publick.

And that the Mail be not delayed by reason of any Accident that may befall the said Postrider or Mail Bearer

Be it Enacted by the Authority aforesaid, That if any Accident shall at any time happen to a Post Rider or Mail bearer on the Road either by sickness of himself, failure of the Horse or otherwise, it shall and may be lawful for him to apply to such Person as may be nearest resident to the place where such Accident may happen, which Person is hereby required to convey the Mail to the next Stage for which he shall be intituled to receive from the Acting Postmaster General of the Province or his depity at the Stage where the Mail shall be delivered, One shilling per mile for every Mile he may have carried the said Mail on the Delivery thereof.

And be it further Enacted by the Authority aforesaid, That this Act shall continue and be in force for Two years and from thence to the end of the next Session of Assembly.

Act of 1770, CO 5/340, fs. 222-223, 226.

William Tryon to the Assembly

[New Bern]

[January 16, 1771]

Mr. Speaker and Gentlemen of the House of Assembly.

His Majestys Post Master General having for some Months past opened a Communication by Post between the Southern and Northern Provinces on this Continent by establishing a regular intercourse between Charles Town, and Suffolk in Virginia, which has been so long solicited especially by the Commercial Interest of this Province and it being since found from experience, that the Riders, or Mail Bearers, meet with great difficulties and Delays at the many Ferries in this province, I would recommend it to You to make Provision, Authorizing all such Riders to pass the Ferries free of any Charges, and the respective Owners of the Ferries allowed to bring in a Claim on the public for the Same; and also in Cases of Sickness or the Riders horses failing them, to impower them to require from any Persons living nearest on the Road, to carry the said Mail to the next Stage, and the person so carrying the Mail, to be paid by the acting post Master General of the Province so much per Mile for such Service.

Wm Tryon

Newbern 16th January 1771.

William Tryon to the Assembly, [January 16, 1771], Powell, *Correspondence of William Tryon*, 2:569.

A *View* of the progress of His Majestys mails from the time that the Post leaves Charles Town in South Carolina until his arrival at Suffolk in Virginia.

The Post leaves Charles Town of a Wednesday and arrives at	number of miles rode	Day of the arrival of the mails at the different stages.	number of days on road	days the mails are at rest	By this it appears that the mails are 27 days on the road between Charles Town and Suffolk in which time they travel 433 mile which is but 16 miles per day. It is here shewn that the letters lie bye 16 days at different offices.
George Town	60	Friday	3		
Brunswick	115	Sunday	5		
Wilmington	15	Monday	6		
New Bern	93	Thursday	9	9	
Bath	43	Sunday	19	4	
Edenton	52	Friday	24	3	
Suffolk	55	Monday	27		
	433		27	16	

The Tardiness of the post discourages correspondence by his Majesty's mails to and from the Southern district.

From what I have heard said in the Carolinas on the subject of the Posts, it is my opinion that if there were a regular weekly post establish'd from Town to Town in the Southern district, correspondence wou'd encrease much; and to avoid delays, the route shou'd be changed and the Mails for Petersburgh, Halifax, Tarborough, Newbern, Wilmington, Brunswick, Geo. Town and Charles Town, be sent the upper road, from New Castle or Williamsburg.

Finlay, *Journal*, entry for May 17, 1774.

Recreation and Entertainment

Recreational pursuits varied greatly as shown by activities in Charlotte and Edenton.

An Act for establishing the Court House in the Town of Charlotte, in Mecklenburg County, and for regulating the said Town.

[...] II. And whereas the frequent firing of Guns, Running Horse Races and playing at Long Bullets in the said Town is found to have a dangerous Tendency to prevent which,

III. Be it Enacted by the Authority aforesaid, that from and after the passing hereof no Person whatsoever shall shoot with a Gun except it be to kill Cattle or Hogs, or immoderately ride or strain any horse or horses, or play at Long Bullet within the Limits of the said Town under the Penalty of paying the Sum of Twenty Shillings for each Offence, to be recovered by a Warrant before any Justice of the Peace of the said County, by one of the Trustees.

> Laws, 1774, in Clark, *State Records of North Carolina*, 23:966.

Ordered, that the Sheriff of this County prevent, so far as it may be in his Power any Person or Persons from playing at the Game of Fives and every other Game within the Court-House, and from daubing the Walls thereof. [...]

> Minutes of the Chowan County Court of Pleas and Quarter Sessions, June 1774. State Archives.

⧳⧳⧳

Among the lower orders of society men engaged in running and wrestling matches to demonstrate their physical prowess, but such activities gave way to the infamous wrestling contests characterized by biting and gouging and to boxing.

We arrived in the heighth of a quarrel there between two Men; the Landlady applied to me to part 'em, I told her "No, let them settle their own differences." They were going to fight out in the Road, when one of the company declared he wou'd massacre the Man who should attempt to Gouge, (that is, endeavors to run his thumbs into the eyes of the other, scoop out his eye balls) Womble, one of the disputants declared "I cannot fight without a Gouge" [...]

Rodman, *Journal of a Tour to North Carolina by William Attmore, 1787*,
43. The venue of the contest was Jones's Tavern, between Tarboro
and Washington.

An Act to Prevent Malicious Maiming and Wounding.

I. Whereas many mischievous and ill-disposed Persons have of late,
in a malicious and barbarous Manner, maimed, wounded and defaced,
many of his Majesty's Subjects: For the Prevention of which inhuman
Practices,

II. Be it Enacted, by the Governor, Council, and Assembly and by
the Authority of the same, That if any Person or Persons, from and
after the ratification of this Act on Purpose, shall unlawfully cut out,
or disable the Tongue, put out an Eye, slit the Nose, bite or cut off a
Nose or Lip, bite or cut off or disable, any Limb or Member of any
Subject of his Majesty in so doing to maim or disfigure in any of the
Manners before mentioned, such his Majesty's Subjects; that then and
in every such case, the Person or Persons so offending, their Counsel-
lors, Abettors and Aiders, knowing of, and privy to the offense as
aforesaid, shall be, and are hereby declared to be felons, and shall
suffer as in case of Felony; provided that no Attainder of such Felony
shall extend to corrupt the Blood, or forfeit the Dower of the Wife, or
the Lands, Goods, or Chattels, of the Offender.

Laws, 1754, in Clark, *State Records*, 23:420.

[...] I desire of you in a Special manner, to take into your consideration the barbarous and inhuman manner of boxing which so much
prevails among the lower sort of people This practice is attended with
circumstances of cruelty as is really shocking to human nature; and I
have been informed of no less, than four person, who within these Two
years, have come to a violent death by This atrocious Custom. I am
afraid the laws now in being are defective in this Affair, and as you are
The Guardians of duty by a particular law, to put a Stop to such bloody
horrid quarrels.

Governor Gabriel Johnston to the Upper House, June 12, 1752,
Saunders, *Colonial Records*, 4:1318.

The delicate and entertaining diversion, with propriety call GOUG-
ING, is thus performed: —When two boxers are wearied out with
fighting and bruising each other, they come, as it is called, to close
quarters, and each endeavours to twist his fore-fingers in the ear-locks

of his antagonist. When these are fast clenched, the thumbs are extended each way to the nose, and the eyes *gently* turned out of the sockets. The victor, for his expertness, receives shouts of applause from the sportive throng, while his poor eyeless antagonist is laughed at for his misfortune." Such are the very words of Morse, in his American Geography, under the head of North Carolina.

That the European reader may give immediate credit to the existence of this most horrible practice called *gouging*, I have quoted the words of a native author. It is in vain for later writers to gloss over the subject; to pretend that this custom was *once* practised in America; or that such was the revenge which *once* prevailed in the breast of civilised man. It is my avowed purpose to paint "the manners living as the rise;" and upon this point, with pain am I compelled to declare, that this more than savage custom is daily practised among the lower classes in the southern states. [...]

The eye is not the only feature which suffers on these occasions. Like dogs and bears, they use their teeth and feet, with the most savage ferocity, upon each other.

A brute, in human form, named John Stanley, of Bertie county, North Carolina, sharpens his teeth with a file, and boasts of his dependence upon them in fight. This monster will also exult in relating the account of the noses and ears he has bitten off, and the cheeks he has torn.

A man of the name of Thomas Penrise, then living in Edenton, in the same state, attempting at cards to cheat some half-drunken sailors, was detected. A scuffle ensued; Penrise knocked out the candle, then gouged out three eyes, bit off an ear, tore a few cheeks, and made good his retreat.

Near the same place, a schoolmaster, named Jarvis Lucas, was beset by three men, one Horton, his son, and son-in-law. These ruffians beat the unfortunate man till his life was despaired of, having bitten, gouged, and kicked him unmercifully. On the trial of an indictment for this outrageous assault, a Carolina court of justice amerced them in a small fine only.

In the county of Pitt, upon Tar river, in North Carolina, lived a family, by name Dupray; of such extraordinary propensity for mischief, that it could not be determined whether the father or his sons were most wicked. These ruffians long lived upon plunder, and the principal object in committing their depredations appeared to be amusement. Falling into company one evening with an Irish taylor, at a small public-house, they insisted on his joining them at a game at cards. On his refusal, they began to quarrel; when, dreading the consequences, the

Hibernian adroitly put out the candle, and crept under the table. The young ruffians seized their father, whom they mistook for the taylor, and, from the severity of beating, gouging, biting, butting, and kicking, actually killed their parent. This horrid outrage, connected with the mischief and depredations committed by this family, drove the parricides out of the state, to the great joy of the more peaceable inhabitants.

Another bestial mode of assault used by men in North Carolina, is properly called butting. This attack is also copied from the brute creation, and is executed nearly in the same manner as practised in battle between bulls, rams, and goats. A traveller has endeavored to confine butting to the negroes, but he must excuse my implicating the white man in this brutal act. [...]

An American pugilist is equally dexterous with his feet, which are used, not only against his antagonist's shins, but are applied, with the utmost violence, against those parts which the contending beasts of the field never assail. Hence ruptures, loss of eyes, mutilated noses, and indented cheeks so frequently surprise and shock the traveller. A fellow named *Michie*, in my presence, boasted "that he could kick any man, six feet high, under the chin, and break his jaws."

Janson, *The Stranger in America*, 307-310. The author made these observations between 1793 and 1806.

⊷⊷

The more genteel enjoyed tea and conversation, though at the time of the Revolution Elizabeth Catherine DeRosset in Edenton diplomatically sought the permission of the local committee of safety to satisfy her tastes.

[Edenton, August 22, 1770.] Just stept over to Mr Jones's piazza-chatted a little with Mrs. Jones & Mrs. Hall, & then went up to Town—met with Mr Skinner at Smith's—received from him a packet for Mr. Johnston—was desired to inform him, there would be an Opportunity for Philadelphia in 8 or 10 days—shut the Windows of Mr Johnston's & our office—afterwards drank Tea at Mrs Barker's with her & Miss Elbeck [...]

Higginbotham, *The Papers of James Iredell*, 1:173.

[March, 1775]. The carriage soon came up, and we again got into it. I now observed that the road was inclosed on both sides, and on the first turning the carriage made, we found ourselves in front of a large house from the windows of which beamed many cheerful tapers, and no sooner were we come up to the gate than a number of black servants came out with lights. Mr Eagle dismounted, and was ready to assist us, and now welcomed us to his house and owned that the whole was a plan only to get us to it, as he feared we might have made some objections; he having no Lady to receive us. I had a great mind to have been angry, but was too happy to find myself safe, and every thing comfortable. We found the Tea-table set forth, and for the first time since our arrival in America had a dish of Tea. [...]

Andrews, *Journal of a Lady of Quality*, 147.

[...] Tho' I don't break your family rules, I drink a dish of tea in my own chamber every morning. Tea! say you! I do have tea! Yes truly, I do! You must know Sir—whether from the sympathies of the times or not? I can't say—but, certainly, on the 10th of Sept. I was taken very sick; indeed, not only looked so but, was very ill. I thought if I could drink tea, I should recover much sooner; but, as I did not choose to do this in private, I asked leave of the Committee, and they gave me a very gracious permission in the consideration of my age and infirmities. [...]

E. C. DeRosset to John Burgwyn, n.d. [c. 1775], in Battle, *Letters and Documents, Relating to the Early History of the Lower Cape Fear*, 28.

৵৵৵

The Christmas holiday was widely observed in North Carolina.

Dec. 24 [1770]. In the evening the congregation, including the children, rejoiced over the Incarnation of our God. In the first service, at six o'clock, Christmas hymns were sung, and the Christmas Story was told to the children. After half an hour's intermission there was Lovefeast, the story of the Birth of the Saviour was read from the Bible, and hymns were sung to Br. Volk's violin accompaniment. Then honey-cakes and verses were distributed, and the service closed with earnest prayer. The children were full of wonder and joy, it being the first time they attended such a service.

Fries, *Records of the Moravians*, 1:409.

Friday Dec. 25 [1772].

Serenaded before I got up with a Band of Musick, the sound of which soon raised me. Tom gave me an Invitation from his Master which I was obliged to decline, being before engaged to Horniblow. Went up Town, returned and drest myself. Having just done Breakfast I repaired to my Journal—.

Let me for a moment address myself to my great Creator with humble adoration and gratitude for the Blessings communicated to Mankind on that heavenly day (such it most assuredly was) which this is Designed to commemorate. May my Mind ever be impressed with feelings suited to the grand and happy Occasion.—and may it be my constant Endeavor so to discharge my duty as hereafter to be intitled (by the Mercy of God and my great Redeemer) to the Rewards, which are promised to every one who, with sincerity and truth, shall to the best of his understanding and ability, practise the duties of Morality— those laws of virtuous, or at least of innocent, Conduct which all ought to conform to, and which all who do conform to will certainly meet with the approbation of the Divine Being— [...]

Higginbotham, *Papers of James Iredell*, 1:200.

25th. Xmass. [1777]. Heard Mr. Earl preach in the Church. The Clarke, previous to singing an Hymn to, the Tune of "God save the King" said "Let us sing upon this solemn & rejoicing Occasion, a few Lines composed by Dr. Whitefield." The Parson's Notes were very yellow & the last Leaf loose, from which I conjecture they were rather ancient & had been much used. Our Landlord, Geo. Gray, entertained his Lodgers today gratis & genteely. We had, inter Dia, Arrack Punch and Venison.—Spent the Evening with Chas. Bondfield Esqr.—Had a Frolic afterwards. Guns were fired at noon by Way of rejoicing, & all the Negroes had a Holiday. [...]

Johnston, "The Journal of Ebenezer Hazard in North Carolina, 1777 and 1778," 367-368.

❧❧

Public celebrations—the King's birthday, the Fourth of July, and the recognition of the Treaty of Paris that ended the American Revolution—merited joyous festivities.

"To His Excellency William Tryon Esqur. Captain General and Governor in Chief and over the Province of North Carolina.

The humble Address of the Ministers and Congregations of the United Brethren in Wachovia.

May it please your Excellency

Upon this solemn Occasion the Celebration of the Birthday of our most gracious King the United Brethren in Wachovia inviolably attached to His Majesty's Government, esteem themselves particularly favored by the presence of this Representative to this province in the person of your Excellency. [...]

Moravian Camp

Bethabara June 6th 1771." [...]

The rest of the day was spent brightly and happily, and when it was quite dark His Excellency set off rockets in front of his tent. The windows looking on the Square were illuminated.

Fries, *Records of the Moravians*, 1:464-465.

In celebration of this day great numbers of Guns have been fired at Stanly Wharf and Mr. Ellis' ship three Different firings from each from early in the morning, mid day & evening and Liquor given to the populace. Stanly and Ellis seemed to vie with each other in a contest who should do the most honor to the day, but Mr. Ellis had the most artillery.

R. Cogdell to Gov. Caswell, July 4, 1778, in Clark, *State Records*, 22:758.

NEWBERN, *July* 10, 1778.

ON Saturday last, the ever memorable FOURTH of July, the RISING STATES of America entered the THIRD year of their INDE-PENDENCE, in spite of numerous fleets and armies; in spite of tomahawk and scalping knife; in spite of the numberless wicked and diabolical engines of cruelty and revenge, played off against us by the magnanimous and heroic, humane and merciful George the Third, the father of his people, and his wicked and abandoned soldiery. On this day, the bright morning star of this western world arose in the east, and warned us to immerge from the slavish tyranny and servile dependence on a venal and corrupt court, and assume to ourselves a name among nations; a name terrible to tyrants, and wrote in indelible characters by the Almighty as a refuge from persecution. This day was observed here with every possible mark and demonstration of joy and reverence; tripple salutes were fired from the batteries in town, and on board the ship Cornell, and the privateer brig BELLONA, belonging to this port, the gentlemen of the town met, where many toasts suitable to the importance of the day were drank, and the evening happily concluded.

North-Carolina Gazette (New Bern), July 10, 1778.

[New Bern]. *June 17*. Today, to the sound of drums and a volley from four small campaign pieces brought up beforehand for this purpose, with a company of militia under arms (each soldier and officer with uniform and musket of different type), the cessation of hostilities and the preliminary treaties with England were announced in the field. By way of celebration for this event, starting at one o'clock there was a barbecue (a roast pig) and a barrel of rum, from which the leading officials and citizens of the region promiscuously ate and drank with the meanest and lowest kind of people, holding hands and drinking from the same cup. It is impossible to imagine, without seeing it, a more purely democratic gathering, and it confirms what the Greek poets and historians tell us of similar concourses among those free peoples of Greece. There were some drunks, some friendly fisticuffs, and one man was injured. With that and the burning of some empty barrels as a *feu de joie* at nightfall, the party ended and everyone retired to sleep.

Miranda, *The New Democracy in America: Travels of Francisco de Miranda in the United States, 1783-1784*, 7-8.

[...] On Monday last was celebrated in this town, the anniversary of St. Andrew's Day. — An elegant dinner was provided at Mr. Dorsey's, and after partaking thereof, the following toasts were drank: —
1. Memory of St. Andrew.
2. King, Queen, and Royal Family.
3. Old Rickey.
4. Kirk of Scotland.
5. Success to the British navy.
6. Riches to the generous, and power to the merciful.
7. United States of America.
8. General WASHINGTON.
9. Governor and State of North-Carolina.

10. Navigation and trade.

11. Success to our hopes, and enjoyment to our wishes.

12. Constancy in love, and sincerity in friendship.

13. Happy we have met - happy may we be - happy may we part - happy may we meet again.

The Wilmington Centinel, and General Advertiser, December 3, 1788.

✥

Dancing appealed to all classes, and formal dances graced many occasions, including the arrival of Lieutenant Governor William Tryon in New Bern in 1764, the presence of Chief Justice Martin Howard in New Bern in 1767, and the election of James Milner as legislative representative of the town of Tarboro in 1772.

Dancing they are all fond of, especially when they can get a Fiddle, or Bag-pipe; at this they will continue Hours together, nay, so attach'd are they to this darling Amusement, that if they can't procure Musick, they will sing for themselves. Musick, and Musical Instruments being very scarce in *Carolina*.

Brickell, *Natural History*, 40.

In the Evening, there was a very elegant BALL, in the Great Ball-Room in the Court house, where were present his Honour the Governor, and his Lady, the Mayor, Mr. Recorder, and near 100 Gentlemen and Ladies.—About Ten in the Evening the Company withdrew to the Long Room over the Ball-Room, where was spread a very elegant Collation: After Supper, the Gentlemen and Ladies returned to the Ball-Room, and concluded the Evening with all imaginable Agreeableness and Satisfaction. The Courthouse was beautifully illuminated the whole Evening.

North Carolina Magazine; or, Universal Intelligencer (New Bern), December 28, 1764.

I have had the honour of dining & drinking tea, with my lord chief justice Howard, sundry times; he is very alert, in high spirits, and extreemly complaisant, & polite & greatly improv'd & refin'd, whether it is to be ascribed to the European air, or American fire, I dont pretend to Determine; but think it is allowed that the latter is the greatest refiner; and perhaps the sons of liberty may claim some acknowledgement for his present honorary & lucrative scituation, into which theyhaveriggled him: He is very much caress'd by the Carolineans, they are much pleased with his free, facetious & polite behaviour, for he is really a man of sense, and a gentleman he says many complaisant things in praise of the province, & the people, with which he seems to be greatly pleas'd & indeed who would not be charm'd with a Country, which affords the delightful prospect of £1200 p. annum currency, which they tell me is at least the chief justice's income. The Gentlemen of Newbern, complimented him with an elegant ball, at which I had the honour of being present, & the ladies made a very Brilliant appearance, his lordship opened the ball, & Danced Till 12. in a very sprightly manner, to the great satisfaction of the Ladies.

John Whiting To Revnd Sir, April 8, 1767, Frederick Nash Collection, State Archives.

TARBOROUGH, *in* EDGCUMBE *County,* NORTH CAROLINA, *September* 19, 1772. LAST Tuesday, agreeable to our Charter, came on the Election of a Representative for this Borough, when JAMES MILNER, Esquire, of Halifax, was unanimously elected to represent us in the next General Assembly of this Province. A considerable Number of the most respectable Inhabitants of the Borough and County assembled here that Day, where there was a very genteel Entertainment provided them at Mr. Hill's, by Order of our worthy new Representative. In the Evening there was an elegant Supper, and a Ball, which was greatly embellished by a very numerous and brilliant Appearance of most charming Ladies, and the Whole conducted with a Decorum and Festivity which sufficiently denoted the real Satisfaction of the Company. Indeed, from Mr. Milner's excellent Character, and distinguished Abilities, we justly entertain the most sanguine Hopes of his invariably promoting, to the utmost of his Power, the Welfare of the Province in general, and of this Borough and County in particular.

May Milner's Name in future Annals shine,
And Edgcumbe's grateful Sons approve each Line;
May future Patriots aim, like him, to be
Renown'd for Honour and Integrity;
And may the Nine, in their harmonious Lays,
Attest his Merit and record his Praise.

316

Virginia Gazette, Purdie & Dixon (Williamsburg), October 22, 1772.

Horse racing, whether quarter horse sprints or dashes around oval tracks that accompanied many towns, including Hillsborough, proved a popular diversion, though it might have had untoward consequences. In addition to importing horses from England, colonials bred their animals.

Horse-Racing they are fond of, for which they have Race-Paths, near each Town, and in many parts of the Country. Those Paths, seldom exceed a Quarter of a Mile in length, and only two Horses start at a time, each Horse has his peculiar Path, which if he quits, and runs into the other, looses the Race. This is agreed on to avoid Jockying. These Courses being so very short, they use no manner of Art, but push on with all the speed imaginable; many of these Horses are very fleet.

Brickell, *Natural History*, 39.

HYDER ALI

IS now in high order, and will ſtand as formerly at MILTON, the plantation of the ſubſcriber at Batchelor's creek, ſix miles from this place, being on the maid road to Weſt's ferry, en Neuſe river, in order to cover mares, for ſix pounds the ſeaſon, or fifty ſhillings the leap. In caſes of mares coming for the leap, it is expected that the money will be ſent with them as otherwiſe the charge will be made for the whole ſeaſon.

HYDER ALI is a beautiful dark bay, upwards of fifteen hands high. He was got by Old Mark Anthony, his dam by the imported horſe Bajazet, his grand dam by Crawford.

The mares that are put to this horſe will have the advantage of one hundred acres of good paſturage gratis; but the ſubſcriber will by no means be anſwerable for any accident er eſcape.

WILSON BLOUNT.

Good racing horses were highly prized. Hyder Ali was one of the most famous ones in the history of the sport in the colony. From the *North Carolina Gazette* (New Bern), June 4, 1791.

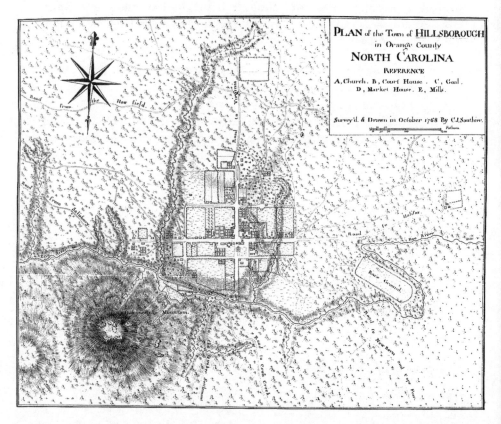

Hillsborough, incorporated by act of assembly in 1759 under the name "Childsburgh," was renamed in 1766 to honor the earl of Hillsborough. This plan was drawn in 1768 by Claude Joseph Sauthier, who did the same for other towns in the colony. The plans were later published. Photograph from the files of the Division of Archives and History.

Saturday, November 24 [1787, New Bern]. Races again today, four Horses started; a mistake happen'd, the Horses being nearly abreast some of the people halloed, "set off," "go," &c. which the riders supposed to be Orders from the proper judges; they set off, and run the course with great eagerness, the blunder created some anger and a good deal of Mirth. The Riders were young Negroes of 13 or 14 years old who generally rode bareback.—

I have attended the Races yesterday and today rather from motives of curiosity than any love to this Amusement, and think I shall hardly be prevailed on to go ten Steps in future to see any Horse Race—The objections and inconveniences attending this kind of Amusement, obvious to me, are,

1st. Large numbers of people are drawn from their business, occupations and labour, which is a real loss to their families and the State.

2d. By wagering and betting; much quarreling wrangling, Anger, Swearing & drinking is created and takes place, I saw it on the present occasion prevalent from the highest to the lowest—I saw white Boys, and Negroes eagerly betting 1/ 2/ a quart of Rum, a drink of Grog &c, as well as Gentlemen betting high—

3d. Many accidents happen on these occasions—

One of the Riders a Negroe boy, who rid one of the Horses yesterday, was, while at full speed thrown from his Horse, by a Cow being in the Road and the Horse driving against her in the hurry of the Race—The poor Lad was badly hurt in the Head and bled much—

The second day, one of the Horses at starting, run violently amongst the people that sat in a place of apparent security, it was precisely the spot where I thought there was the greatest safety, for foot people— More might be added.

Rodman, *Journal of a Tour to North Carolina by William Attmore, 1787,* 17-18.

Here Mr. Robert Howe commanded; a man of no small consequence in his own estimation, who has since arrived at the rank of major general in the American army.

Mr. Howe, otherwise not an unworthy man, was always so very fond of ostentation, that he almost starved his poor wife and family at home, in order that he himself might be able to cut a figure every year at the races in Virginia and Maryland.

Smyth, *A Tour of the United States of America*, 2:88.

[...] How is Miss Sukey Cornell? I saw Mrs. T. Gilchrist when in Liverpool, who told me that her brother, Wiley Jones, had paid his addresses to her, but that her father had said he would never consent to his daughter's marriage with any person who would risk a fortune on a horse race—upon which he very properly and spiritedly declined any further solicitation, saying, that as it was his favorite amusement he would not be under any engagement to release it before marriage; but that if it had afterwards happened that his wife should solicit it as a favor, he would submit to any thing for her satisfaction. [...]

Nathaniel Dukinfield to James Iredell, February 23, 1774, in Higginbotham, *Papers of James Iredell*, 1:223-224.

The noted Horse BAJAZETT

STANDS at *Ellis's* Square in *Newbern*, and will cover the ensuing Season at FIVE POUNDS the Season, or FORTY SHILLINGS the Leap, and 23. and 6d. to the Groom and the Mares (if required) will be pastured, and good Care taken of them, tho' at the Owner's Risk. He was got by the famous *Bajazett*, best Son of the *Godolphin Arabian*, his Dam by *Sweap Stakes*, Grandam by *Bay Bolten*, great Grandam by *Brimmer*, great great Grandam by *Dodsworth*, out of the *Layton Barb* Mare. He is reputed a very sure Horse, and is as handsome and high-blooded as any that has ever been imported into *America*.

RICHARD ELLIS.

Newbern, March 3, 1775.

The Subscriber's Horse
TELEMACHUS
WILL stand the ensuing Season at *Pembroke*, four Mile above *Newbern*, on *Trent* River, and will cover at the low Rate of Three Pounds the Season, payable if the Party chooses it in Corn, at 15 s. a Barrel. He puts up with this easy Mode of Payment with a View to encourage the Gentlemen Farmers of this Part of the Province the more readily to enter spiritedly on this very profitable and public spirited Business of breeding good Horses; as their Neighbours of *Halifax, Virginia*, and other Places, have done before them. *Telemachus* is of a most beautiful Colour, 15 Hands high, finely formed, and rising five Years old. He was got by the celebrated Horse *Jolly Roger*, whose Sire was an *Arabian* of the highest Character in *England*; his Dam was the famous *Bonny Jane*, an

imported Mare of the *Godolphin* Family, whose Performances on the Turf are well known in *Virginia*: So that tho' this Horse cannot boast of having drawn his first Breath in the much favoured Island of *Great Britain*, yet it is hoped his Pretensions (next to *Bajazett*, who he does not pretend to rival) will be thought to stand very fair in the Calendar of Fame. An excellent Pasture for Mares, and good Care will be taken of them, though at the Owner's Risk.

A. NASH.

March 14, 1775.

North-Carolina Gazette (New Bern), April 7, 1775.

Cock fighting, in addition to horse racing, was also a popular public diversion.

Cock-fighting they greatly admire, which Birds they endeavor to procure from *England* and *Ireland*, and to that intent, employ Masters of Ships, and other Trading Persons to supply them.

Brickell, *Natural History*, 40.

COCK-FIGHT.

The sportsmen of the neighbouring counties are informed, that on Monday next, the 8th instant, a main of 21 cocks will be sought in this town, at which much sport is expected.

North-Carolina Journal (Halifax), May 1, 1797.

Hunting, particularly deer hunting, attracted many, though its abuses evoked legislation from the General Assembly.

[Wilmington, June 24, 1783]. Deer are plentiful, and deer hunting is the favorite sport of the gentlemen and country folk. I went on some of these excursions and assure you that at every moment I expected one of the participants to have a leg, arm, or head broken. The fashion is to dash forth on horseback behind the discovered buck through a forest covered with branches, the horse sometimes barely having room. The horse is already accustomed to this and, happen what may, charges after the game and acts as the guide; the rider bends down, grasping the neck of the horse. There is no lack of mournful reminders of this sport in the region.

Miranda, *New Democracy in America*, 15.

[December 8, 1787]. About 9 O'Clock, a party of us, embark'd to cross Tar River to go on a Deer Hunt, the Company were, Capt. Dill, Messrs. Thos. Blackledge; Nuttle; Whipple, Bonner, Capt. John Wallace; and myself, we row'd in Dill's boat by two Sailors; John Blount Esqr. was to cross over in a Canoe and meet us, over the River at his Farm near which we were to hunt this Morning—The method of hunting is generally as follows,

One part of the Company go into the Wood with the Hounds and usually carry their Guns along, here they begin to trail for the Deer Tracks, and put the Dogs on the Scent, the other part of the Company are station'd in different places where it is known that the Deer usually cross the Forest towards the River, for a hunted Deer when hard push'd by the Dogs and Hunters generally makes for the Water where they can swim with great strength and swiftness,—A party is station'd in a Canoe or Boat to pursue him, if he takes the Water,—If he takes the River They must seize him by the Tail and lift him by it and drown him.—All this we tried but without getting a Deer—I was station'd at a Neck of Land that joins a small peninsula to the Main and was known to be a good place for the reception of a herd running down I stood at my Post for about two hours with the vigilance of a Sentinel looking for an enemy with 7 small bullets in my Gun, to pepper him well, but no Buck came near me; one of our party shot at a Doe a considerable distance from him, but without effect, she got away—While I stood at my Post five Hounds pass'd me within 30 Yards, and shortly open'd their Music, soon after, I heard a most dreadful squealing of Pigs, I was afterwards told that a party of the Neighbors were out hunting Wild Hogs; when the dogs seize them, the Men come up, tie the feet of the Hog taken, and leave him on the spot for the present, then halloe the dogs after the rest of the herd. [...]

Rodman, *Journal of a Tour to North Carolina by William Attmore, 1787*, 24-25.

An Act to prevent hunting for, and killing Deer in the Manner therein mentioned.

I. Whereas many Persons do, under a Pretence of hunting for Deer in the Night-time, by firelight, kill and Destroy Horses and Cattle, to the great Prejudice of the Owners: To prevent Which for the Future,

II. Be it Enacted, by the Governor, Council, and Assembly, and by the Authority of the same, That if any Person shall be discovered Hunting, with a Gun in the Night Time by Fire Light, such Person shall forfeit and pay, for every Offence, Forty Shillings, Proclamation Money, to be recovered, by any Person who shall sue for the same, before any Jurisdiction having Cognizance thereof, with Costs.

Laws, 1764, in Clark, *State Records*, 23:656.

❧❧

Gaming or gambling possessed a powerful appeal according to a sojourner in Wilmington as well as colonial statutes.

I Live Very much Retired for want of a Social Set, The Gentlemen of this Town might be so if they pleas'd, but an Intollerable Itch for Gaming Prevails in all Companies, This I Conceive is the Bane of Society and therefore Shun the Devotees to Cards And pass my hours Chiefly at Home with my Pipe and some agreeable author. [...]

Peter DuBois to Dear Sir [Samuel Johnston, Jr.], March 5, 1757, Hayes Papers.

An Act to suppress excessive and deceitful Gaming.

I. Whereas excessive and deceitful Gaming hath been found Injurious to the Inhabitants of this Province, and tend greatly to the Discouragement of Industry, Corruption of Youth, and Destruction of Families; For Remedy whereof,

II. Be it Enacted, by the Governor, Council, and Assembly and by the Authority of the same, That from and after the passing of this Act, any Tavern-keeper who shall permit or suffer any Gaming within his House, Stall, Booth Harbour, or other Place, (Back gammon only excepted) shall, for such Offence, upon Conviction thereof, before the Court of the County wherein the same shall be committed, forfeit his License, and be further Liable to Indictment, and Fine, at the Discretion of the said Court; And any Person or Persons who shall hereafter win at any Game or Games, or by betting or Wagering, in any Manner whatsoever, (Horse racing only excepted) more than Five Shillings in Twenty Four Hours, or the Value thereof in any Goods, Commodities, or other Article or Articles, shall, upon Conviction of the Same before any Court or Magistrate, having Cognizance thereof, forfeit all such Monies, Goods, Commodities, or other Article or Articles, or the full Value thereof; one half to the Informer, and the other Half to be applied to the Use of the Parish wherein such Offence shall be committed.

Laws, 1764, in Clark, *State Records*, 23:611.

An Act to prevent Card Playing, and other deceitful Gaming.

I. Whereas Card playing and other deceitful Gaming, hath been found injurious to the Inhabitants of this Province, and tend greatly to the discouragement of Industry, Corruption of Youth, and destruction of Families: For Remedy whereof,

II. Be it Enacted by the Governor, Council, and Assembly, and by the Authority of the same, That from and after the passing of this Act, any Tavern Keeper who shall permit or suffer any Gaming within his House, Booth, Stall, Arbour, or other Place (Whist, Quadrille, Picquet, Backgammon, and Billiards only excepted) shall for such Offence, upon conviction thereof before the Court of the County wherein the same shall be committed, forfeit his License, and be further liable to Indictment and Fine, at the Discretion of the said Court; and any Person or Persons, who shall hereafter win at any Game or Games, or by betting or Wagering in any Manner whatsoever (Horse Racing only Excepted) more than Five Shillings in Twenty Four Hours, or the Value thereof in any Goods, Commodities, or other Article or Articles, shall, upon Conviction of the same, before any Court or Magistrate having Cognizance thereof, forfeit all such Monies, Goods, Commodities, or other Article or Articles, or the Full Value thereof; one Half to the Informer, and the other Half to be applied to the Use of the Parish wherein such Offence was committed: [...]

Laws, 1770, in Clark, *State Records*, 23:838.

∞

Among the games of chance, billiards was the first to be restricted by law, but to no avail, and subsequently colonials enjoyed the game, as attested by James Iredell in Edenton and visitor Francisco de Miranda in New Bern.

IX. And be it further Enacted by the Authority aforesaid, That every Person that hath erected a Billiard Table or Billiard Tables, or shall hereafter erect or keep a Billiard Table, after the Ratification of this Act shall at the next Court of the respective Counties where such Billiard Table or Billiard Tables is or are erected or Kept, apply to the Justices of the said Court, and Annually take out, for each and every Billiard Table, a Licence, in the usual Manner as Ordinary-Keepers obtain their Licence, under the Penalty of forfeiting Fifty Pounds Proclamation Money, for suffering any Person to play at Billiards, before such License first had and obtained, [...]

Laws, 1753, in Clark, *State Records*, 25:252.

[Edenton, August 25, 1770]. 6 o'Clock
Most of this afternoon at the Billiard Table,—I played a good deal, but came off clear—which is more than I usually do—tho' I know very well, I frequently lose thro' Carelessness—I will go & see how Mr Jones does—

Higginbotham, *Papers of James Iredell*, 1:176.

[Wilmington, June 24, 1783]. Major Walker, for whom I brought a letter of recommendation, and Mr. Blount, a businessman—both were men of respect in the town—showed me the interior. Afterwards we went to the billiard house, where we played a few games until noontime. This game has taken such strong roots in the country that none of the towns I passed through lacked two or three billiard tables. The wives complain that their husbands spend too much time at this French custom, introduced during the war.

Miranda, *New Democracy in America*, 14-15.

❦

At the outbreak of the American Revolution the Continental Congress in 1774 forbade "extravagance and dissipation" as unbecoming to patriots, and local committees of safety enforced the proscription.

8. We will, in our several stations, encourage frugality, economy, and industry, and promote agriculture, arts and the manufactures of this country, especially that of wool; and will discountenance and discourage every species of extravagance and dissipation, especially all horse-racing, and all kinds of gaming, cock fighting, exhibitions of shews, plays, and other expensive diversions and entertainments; [...]

Commager, *Documents of American History,* 1:86.

WILMINGTON, 26 NOVEMBER 1774.
The Committee met according to adjournment. Present: Francis Clayton, John Ancrum, James Walker, Robert Hogg, John Quince, Archibald Maclaine.

The committee finding that several gentlemen intended to start horses, which they have had some time in keeping, for the Wilmington subscription-purse, on Monday the 28th instant, and the General Congress having particularly condemned horse-racing as an expensive diversion, the Committee thought proper to send the following admonitory circular letter to the several gentlemen who had kept horses for the race, to wit-

Wilmington, 26th November, 1774.
Sir-
The Continental Congress lately held at Philadelphia representing the several American colonies from Nova Scotia to Georgia, associated and agreed among other things, for themselves and their contituents, to "Discountenance and Discourage every species of extravagance and dissipation, especially all horse-racing and all kinds of gaming, cock-fighting, exhibitions of shows and plays and other expensive diversions and entertainments"; and we being a majority of the Committee chosen by the freeholders of Wilmington to observe the conduct of all persons touching the association of the said Congress, think it our indispensible duty to inform you that in our opinion, the avowed intention of running horses for the subscription purse near this town on the 28th instant, if carried into execution, will be subversive of the said association and a breach of the resolves of the General Congress; and that if the gentlemen who intended to enter horses for the said purse (of whom we understand you are one) persist in running the race, we shall be under the disagreeable necessity of bearing public testimony against a proceeding which immediately strikes at the ground of the association and resolves by disuniting the people.
You must be sensible, Sir, that the Americans have not the most distant prospect of being restored to their former rights or of succeeding in their attempts to defeat a venal and corrupt ministry and parliament but by an unanimous adherence to the resolutions and advice of their representatives in the late General Congress; and, as a friend to your country, we have no doubt but you will readily relinquish an amusement

that however laudable in other respects, is certainly attended with considerable expense and even distruction to many individuals; and may very justly be condemned at a time when frugality should be one of our leading virtues. [...]

Resolved That the permission of Billiard Tables in this Town is repugnant to the Resolves of the General Congress & that the proprietors of them have notice thereof. They were accordingly Served with Such Notice and appeared at the Committee & declared their acquiescence in the Resolves. [...]

Resolved That Balls & dancing at Public Houses is Contrary to the Resolves of the General Congress. It is the Opinion of this Committee that every Tavern keeper in this Town have Notice given them not to suffer any Balls or Public Dancing at their Houses, as they wish to avoid the Censure of the people. [...]

The Committee being informed of a Public Ball to be given by Sundry persons under the Denomination of The Gentlemen of Wilmington at the House of Mrs. Austin this Evening, & as all public Balls & Dances are Contrary to the Resolves of the General Continental Congress, & a Particular Resolve of this Committee, Ordered that the following Letter be sent to Mrs. Austin to forewarn her from Suffering such Public Ball & Dancing at her House—

Madam—

The Committee appointed to see the Resolves of the Continental Congress put in Execution in this Town, Acquaint you that the Ball intended to be given at your House this Evening is Contrary to the Said Resolves, we therefore warn you to decline it & Acquaint the parties concerned that your house cannot be at their Service consistent with the good of your Country.

By order of the Committee.

(Signed) Tho. Craike.

McEachern and Williams, *Wilmington-New Hanover Safety Committee Minutes, 1774-1776*, 3, 13, 14, 18.

SOURCES CITED

A New Voyage to Georgia. By a Young Gentleman . . . (London, 1737).

Americanus, Scotus, "Informations Concerning the Province of North Carolina," (1773), edited by William K. Boyd, *North Carolina Historical Review*, 3 (October 1926).

"Autobiography of Col. William Few of Georgia," *Magazine of American History*, 7 (November 1881).

Bartram, William, *Travels Through North and South Carolina, Georgia, East and West Florida...* (Charlottesville: University Press of Virginia, 1980).

Battle, Kemp P., ed., *Letters and Documents Relating to the Early History of the Lower Cape Fear* (Chapel Hill: The University, 1903).

Belfast Newsletter (Belfast, Ireland).

Bertie County Court Minutes, State Archives, Raleigh.

Bertie County Criminal Papers, State Archives, Raleigh.

Bertie County Miscellaneous Records, State Archives, Raleigh.

"Biographical Sketch of Waightstill Avery," *North Carolina University Magazine*, 2d ser., 4 (August 1855).

Boyd, William K., and Charles A. Krummel, "German Tracts Concerning the Lutheran Church in North Carolina during the Eighteenth Century, " *North Carolina Historical Review*, 7 (1930).

Brickell, John, *The Natural History of North Carolina* (1737) (Raleigh: State Library, 1911).

Brunswick County Tax List, State Archives, Raleigh.

Burke, Thomas, Papers, State Archives, Raleigh.

Bute County Court Minutes, State Archives, Raleigh.

Byrd, William, *Histories of the Dividing Line Betwixt Virginia and North Carolina*, edited by William K. Boyd (Raleigh: North Carolina Historical Commission, 1929).

Cain, Robert J., ed., *Records of the Church of England, 1699-1741*, vol. 10 of *The Colonial Records of North Carolina [Second Series]* (Raleigh: Department of Cultural Resources, 1999).

——, *Records of the Executive Council, 1755-1775,* vol. 9 of *The Colonial Records of North Carolina [Second Series]* (Raleigh: Department of Cultural Resources, 1994).

Cape Fear Mercury (Wilmington).

Carteret County Court Minutes, State Archives, Raleigh.

Chowan County Court Minutes, State Archives, Raleigh.

Chowan County Personal Accounts, State Archives, Raleigh.

Chowan County Miscellaneous Records, State Archives, Raleigh.

Clark, Elmer T., ed., *The Journal and Letters of Francis Asbury*, 3 vols. (Nashville: Abingdon Press, 1958).

Clark, Walter, ed., *The State Records of North Carolina*, 20 vols. (Raleigh: State of North Carolina, 1895-1911).

CO 5/340-341, Colonial Office Records, Public Record Office, Kew, England. Photocopies in British Records Collection, State Archives, Raleigh.

Commanger, Henry Steele, ed., *Documents of American History*, 2 vols. (New York: Appleton-Century-Crofts, 1963).

Corbitt, D. L., ed., *Explorations, Descriptions, and Attempted Settlements of Carolina, 1584-1590* (Raleigh: Department of Archives and History, 1953).

————, "Historical Notes," *North Carolina Historical Review*, 3-5 (April 1926, July 1927, January 1928).

Craven County Court Minutes, State Archives, Raleigh.

Craven County Miscellaneous Records, State Archives, Raleigh.

Edgecombe County Guardians' Accounts, State Archives, Raleigh.

Edgecombe County Inventories and Accounts, State Archives, Raleigh.

Finlay, Hugh, *Journal Kept by Hugh Finlay, Surveyor of the Post Roads on the Continent of North America* (Brooklyn: Frank H. Norton, 1867).

Ford, Worthington Chauncey, ed., "Letter of Rev. James Maury to Philip Ludwell on the Defence of the Frontiers of Virginia, 1756," *Virginia Magazine of History and Biography*, 19 (July 1911).

Fries, Adelaide, et al., eds., *Records of the Moravians in North Carolina*, 11 vols. (Raleigh: 1922-1969).

George Whitefield's Journals (1737-1741) (Gainesville, Fla.: Scholars' Facsimiles and Reprints, 1969).

Granville County Bastardy Bonds and Papers, State Archives, Raleigh.

Granville County Coroners' Inquests, State Archives, Raleigh.

Granville County Miscellaneous Records, State Archives, Raleigh.

Grimes, Bryan, comp., *North Carolina Wills and Inventories* (Raleigh: Trustees of the Public Libraries, 1912).

Hall, Clement, *A Collection of Many Christian Experiences, Sentences, and Several Places of Scripture Improved* (1753; reprint, Raleigh: State Department of Archives and History, 1961).

Hayes Papers, Southern Historical Collection, University of North Carolina at Chapel Hill.

Higginbotham, Don, ed., *The Papers of James Iredell*, 2 vols. (Raleigh: Department of Cultural Resources, 1976).

Hooker, Richard J., ed., *The Carolina Backcountry on the Eve of the Revolution. The Journal and Other Writings of Charles Woodmason, Anglican Itinerant* (Chapel Hill: University of North Carolina Press, 1953).

Howe, Mark A. Dewolfe, ed., "The Southern Journal of Josiah Quincy, Junior, 1773," *Massachusetts Historical Society Proceedings*, 49 (June 1916).

Hyde County Miscellaneous Records, State Archives, Raleigh.

Jackson, Donald, and Dorothy Twohig, eds., *The Diaries of George Washington*, 6 vols. (Charlottesville: University Press of Virginia, 1976-1979).

Johnston County Court Minutes, State Archives, Raleigh.

Johnston, Hugh Buckner, ed., "The Journal of Ebenezer Hazard in North Carolina, 1777 and 1778," *North Carolina Historical Review*, 36 (July 1959).

Jones, Rufus, ed., *The Journal of George Fox.* (New York: Dutton, 1969).

"Journal of a French Traveler," *American Historical Review*, 26 (July 1921).

Lawson, John, *A New Voyage to Carolina*, edited by Hugh Talmadge Lefler (Chapel Hill: University of North Carolina Press, 1967).

Lennon, Donald R. and Ida B. Kellum, eds., *The Wilmington Town Book, 1743-1778* (Raleigh: State Department of Archives and History, 1973).

"Letters to the Bishop of London from the Commissaries in South Carolina; Letters from Alexander Garden, Commissary, 1729-49," *South Carolina Historical Magazine*, 78 (October 1977).

Maser, Frederick E., and Howard T. Maas, eds., *The Journal of Joseph Pilmore, Methodist Itinerant, For the Years August 1, 1769 to January 2, 1774* (Philadelphia: Message Publishing Company, 1969).

McEachern, Leora H. and Isabel M. Williams, eds., *Wilmington-New Hanover Safety Committee Minutes, 1774-1776* (Wilmington, N.C.: New Hanover County American Revolution Bicentennial Association, 1974).

Mecklenburg County Court Minutes, State Archives, Raleigh.

Minutes of the Women's Monthly Meeting, Rich Square, Northampton County, (microfilm), State Archives, Raleigh.

Miranda, Francisco de, *The New Democracy in America: Travels of Francisco de Miranda in the United States, 1783-1784*, edited by John S. Ezell (Norman: University of Oklahoma Press, 1963).

Nash, Frederick, Collection, State Archives, Raleigh.

New Hanover County Court Minutes, State Archives, Raleigh.

New Hanover County Deeds, State Archives, Raleigh.

New Hanover County Will Books, New Hanover County Courthouse.

Newsome, Albert Ray, ed., "Records of Emigrants from England and Scotland to North Carolina, 1774-1775," *North Carolina Historical Review*, 11 (April 1934).

——, "Twelve North Carolina Counties in 1810-1811," *North Carolina Historical Review*, 6 (January 1929).

North Carolina Gazette (New Bern).

North-Carolina Journal (Halifax).

North-Carolina Magazine (New Bern).

Onslow County Estates Records, State Archives, Raleigh.

Orange County Court Minutes, State Archives, Raleigh.

Parker, Mattie Erma Edwards, *North Carolina Higher-Court Records, 1670-1696*, vol. [2] of *The Colonial Records of North Carolina [Second Series]* (Raleigh: Department of Cultural Resources, 1968).

Paschal, George W., ed., "Morgan Edwards' Materials Toward a History of the Baptists in the Province of North Carolina," *North Carolina Historical Review*, 7 (July 1930).

Pennsylvania Gazette (Philadelphia).

Perquimans County Court Minutes, State Archives, Raleigh.

Powell, William S., ed., *The Correspondence of William Tryon and Other Selected Papers*, 2 vols. (Raleigh: Department of Cultural Resources, 1980-1981).

——, *The Countie of Albemarle in Carolina* (Raleigh: State Department of Archives and History, 1958).

Powell, William S., James K. Huhta, and Thomas J. Farnham, eds., *The Regulators of North Carolina: A Documentary History, 1759-1776* (Raleigh: State Department of Archives and History, 1971).

Price, William S., Jr., *North Carolina Higher-Court Records, 1702-1708*, vol. 4 of *The Colonial Records of North Carolina [Second Series]* (Raleigh: Department of Cultural Resources, 1971).

——, *North Carolina Higher-Court Minutes, 1708-1723*, vol. 5 of *The Colonial Records of North Carolina [Second Series]* (Raleigh: Department of Cultural Resources, 1977).

Quinn, David Beers, ed., *The Roanoke Voyages, 1584-1590*, 2 vols. (London: The Hakluyt Society, 1955).

Rodman, Lida Tunstall, ed., *Journal of a Tour to North Carolina by William Attmore* (Chapel Hill: James Sprunt Historical Publications, 1922).

Rowan County Court Minutes, State Archives, Raleigh.

Saunders, William L., ed., *The Colonial Records of North Carolina*, 10 vols. (Raleigh: State of North Carolina, 1886-1890).

Schaw, Janet, *Journal of a Lady of Quality; Being the Narrative of a Journey from Scotland to the West Indies, North Carolina, and Portugal, in the years 1774 and 1775*, edited by Evangeline W. Andrews and Charles M. Andrews (New Haven: Yale University Press, 1921).

Smyth, John F. D., *A Tour of the United States of America*, 2 vols. (New York: Arno Press, 1968).

South-Carolina Gazette (Charleston).

St. Paul's Parish, Minutes of Vestry (typescript), State Archives, Raleigh.

State Gazette of North Carolina (Edenton).

Swem, Earl Gregg, ed., *An Account of the Cape Fear Country* [by Hugh Meredith] (Perth Amboy, N.J.: Charles F. Heartman, 1922).

"The Journal of Thomas Nicholson," Publications of the Southern History Association, vol. 4 (Washington: The Association, 1900).

"The Journal of William Moultrie While a Commissioner on the North and South Carolina Boundary Survey of 1772," *Journal of Southern History*, 8 (November 1942).

Tiffany, Nina Moore, ed., *Letters of James Murray, Loyalist* (Boston: privately printed, 1901).

Todd, Vincent H., ed., *Christoph von Graffenried's Account of the Founding of New Bern* (Raleigh: Historical Commission, 1920).

Tyrrell County Court Minutes, State Archives, Raleigh.

Virginia Gazette (Williamsburg).

Wake County Court Minutes, State Archives, Raleigh.

Watson, Winslow C., ed., *Men and Times of the Revolution; or, Memoirs of Elkanah Watson* (New York: Dana and Company, 1856).

"William Logan's Journal of a Journey to Georgia, 1745," *Pennsylvania Magazine of History and Biography*, 36 (1912).

Williams, John, Papers, State Archives, Raleigh.

Wilmington Centinel, and General Advertiser (Wilmington).

Wright, Louis B., and Marion Tinling, eds., *Quebec to Carolina in 1785-1786. Being the Travel Diary and Observations of Robert Hunter, Jr., a Young Merchant of London* (San Marino, California: Huntington Library, 1943).

Index

Index

Butler, J., 99
Butler, Jacob, 237
Butler, Robert, 49
Byrd, William, 127n

Caesar, Mr., 66
Cahoone, Macajiah, 15
Cain (slave), 133
Cains, Christopher, 15
Cains, John, 15
Cains, Richard, 15
Cains, William, 15
Caithness, County of, Scotland, 72-74
Caldwell, David, 302
Calloway, John, 134
Cambel, _____, 188
Campbell, Alexr., 75
Campbell, Hector, 75
Campbell, James, 167-168, 186, 198
Campbell, John, 108, 134, 186, 198, 302
Campbell, Joshua, 116
Campbell, Samuel, 197
Campbell, William, 200
Canada, 227
Cannady, Wagstaff, 125
Cape Fear, 44-45, 68, 78, 92, 128, 244-247, 256, 267-268, 286, 303-304
Cape Fear River, 40, 68, 174, 180, 182, 184, 187, 207, 213-214, 221-222, 231, 247
Cape Lookout Bay, 114
Caraway Creek Church, 255
Carrickfergus, Ireland, 34, 70
Carteret County, 92, 179, 205, 209, 231, 285
Carteret, George, Sir, 85
Cary, Molly, 56
Cary, Thomas, 181
Casewell, Mathew, 121
Cashy Bridge, 213
Cashie River, 212, 215
Castle Hayne, 211
Caswell, Richard, 295
Catanoch, John, 73-74
Catawba Church, 255

Cates, John, 254
Cathcart, Dr., 32
Cathcart, Willr., 296
Catheys Settlement, 255
Cattle, fowl, hog, game, 3, 35, 64, 72-75, 85-87, 124, 134-136, 174, 193-195, 207, 214, 216-217, 262, 265, 285, 307, 323
Catto (slave), 133
Caudle, Sam., 173
Caulkins, Elias, 15
Caulkins, William, 15
Celia (slave), 39-40
Chabster, Scotland, 73
Chambers, Maxwell, 302
Champion, John, 123
Champion, Orlando, 237
Chapman, David, 254
Charleston, South Carolina, 25, 187, 202, 220, 234, 259, 303-306
Charlotte, 191-192, 294, 302, 307
Charlton, John, 120
Charlton, M., 203
Charlton, Mr., 42-43
Charlton, William, 121
Charlton, William, Junior, 121, 123
Chattoka, 67
Cheers, John, 15
Cheeseborough, John, 15
Chowan County, 4, 10, 50, 80, 102-104, 109, 182-183, 230, 233
Chowan River, 67, 142n
Christ Church Parish, 231-232, 288
Churton, William, 190, 195
Clark, _____, 97
Clark, Barbara, 45
Clark, James, 46
Clark, Jno., 210
Clark, Thomas (Tommy), 45
Clay, Hannah, 242
Clayton, Francis, 326
Clayton, Henry, 50
Cletherell, John, 9
Clifton, John, 15

Dukinfield, [Nathaniel], 160
Dunbibin, Daniel, 186, 202
Duncan, Alexander, 112
Duncan, James, 73
Dunn's Creek, 247
Dunn, John, 79-80
Dunn, Richard, 247
Dunning, John, 123
Duplin County, 230
Dupray, _____, 309
Durton, D., 261

Eagan, Elizabeth, 16
Eagle's Island, 231
Eagle, Mr., 219, 311
Eagles, Richd., 15
Eagleson, John, 16
Earl, Mr., 312
Earle, Joseph, 16
Earley, John, 123
Easterling, Henry, 254
Easton, John, 179
Eatman, Thos., 210
Eden House, 159
Edenton, 4, 10, 24-25, 31, 43, 83, 87,
    103-104, 109, 120-122, 127*n*, 141,
    146, 168, 170, 182-184, 194, 226,
    233-235, 303-304, 306-307, 309-
    310, 324-325
Edgecombe County, 55, 59, 62, 135,
    188-189, 230, 247, 250, 252, 316
Edgecombe Parish, 230
Education, apprenticeship, schools, 1,
    3, 21, 30, 35, 45-47, 52-53, 60-61,
    100, 102, 132-133, 172, 194, 238,
    240, 258, 260, 281-306, 309
Edward, _____, 258
Edward, Jno., 5
Edwards, I[saac], 256-261
Edwards, John, 115
Edwards, Morgan, 252
Elbeck, Miss, 310
Elliott, Caleb, 247
Ellis's Square, 320
Ellis, Mr., 25, 84, 257, 313

Ellis, Richard, 320
Ellis, Robert, 16
England, 65, 68, 88, 129, 174, 179, 210,
    219, 229-230, 245, 256, 260, 268,
    276, 299, 314, 317, 320-321
Eno River, 190, 195
Espay, James, 119
Etheridge, John, 16
Etheridge, Samuel, 16
Etkin, 264-265, 267
Europe, 11, 64, 69, 140, 157-158, 179,
    226, 257, 299
Eustace, John, 297-298
Eustace, Margt., 298
Evans, Jonathan, 247
Evans, Miss, 218
Evans, Mr., 208
Evans, Robert, 62
Evans, Susannah, 106
Event, James, 134
Ewarrry Church, 255
Ewell, Lydia, 42
Ewell, Solomon, 42

Falconar, John, 51, 121
Fanning, Edmund, 42, 150-151, 294
Faris, William, 185, 198
Farlees Chapel, 238
Farr Parish, Sutherland, Scotland, 72-73
Faulkner, William, 16
Fayetteville, 187-188
Feldhausen, Br., 264
Fels, Samuel, 198
Fendell, Robt., 124
Fenner, Richard, 287
Fergus, John, 16
Few, William, 297
Finney, Thomas, 185
Finny, Christian, 278-279
Fisher, _____, 142
Fishing Creek, 211, 258
Fishing Creek Church, 254
Fitzpatrick, Brian, 124
Flatriver Church, 254
Florra (slave), 133

343